DOLLARS AND SENSE

Third Edition

DOLLARS AND SENSE

An Introduction to Economics

Third Edition

Marilu Hurt McCarty
Georgia Institute of Technology

Scott, Foresman and Company

Glenview, Illinois

Dallas, Tex.
Oakland, N.J.
Palo Alto, Cal.
Tucker, Ga.
London, England

In Memory of John Ottley McCarty

Photo Credits: Chapter 1: © Doug Wilson/Black Star; Chapter 2: © Ed Grazda/Magnum; Chapter 3: © Janice Rubin/Uniphoto; Chapter 4: © Courtesy Commonwealth Edison; Chapter 5: © Wide World; Chapter 6: © Scott, Foresman; Chapter 7: © Ray Fisher; Chapter 8: © Scott, Foresman; Chapter 9: © Bruce L. Wolfe/Uniphoto; Chapter 10: © Wide World; Chapter 11: © Alex Webb/Magnum; Chapter 12: © *Insight* from University of Notre Dame; Chapter 13: © USDA; Chapter 14: © Suzanne J. Engelmann/Shostal.

Library of Congress Cataloging in Publication Data

McCarty, Marilu Hurt.
 Dollars and sense.

 Includes bibliographies and index.
 1. Economics. I. Title.
HB171.5.M137 1982   330   82-681
ISBN 0-673-15603-6   AACR2

Preface

An important goal of *Dollars and Sense* is to help students develop the kind of economic reasoning necessary to analyze and understand the issues they will confront in a rapidly changing world. To this end, the text emphasizes a set of basic economic tools and shows how these tools can be applied to such topics of current debate as minimum-wage legislation, the environment, inflation and unemployment, poverty and public assistance, fiscal policy and taxation, and the energy crisis. The continuing goal of this Third Edition is to make the subject matter and methods of economics more meaningful and comprehensible to today's college students.

Dollars and Sense is written for use in one-term economics courses for students with little or no background in economics. The treatment of current issues should help students from other disciplines acquire habits of systematic thought that they can carry with them to their own fields of study. At the same time, the text provides the kind of analytical foundation that will enable interested students to proceed to more advanced study with greater understanding of the scope and methods of economics.

The Third Edition of *Dollars and Sense* incorporates some worthwhile changes suggested by users of earlier editions. The chapter on "Supply and Demand" has been divided into two chapters: one more sharply focused on demand and current issues involving demand, and the other including derivation of supply through analysis of production costs. We feel the expanded treatment more fully prepares students for issues discussed in later chapters. The chapter on "Labor Resources and the Labor Movement" has been moved from the second half of the book to the first, augmenting the microeconomic emphasis in the first part and tying in more explicitly with the discussion of product and resource markets in the chapter on "Measuring Economic Activity."

The Third Edition also includes a new introductory section and a number of new topics—Gibson's paradox and real interest rates, nonbank financial intermediaries, supply-side economics, aggregate supply and productivity, the theory of rational expectations, and others. There is also expanded treatment of recent economic conditions and the economic policy of the Reagan administration. Whenever possible, the text takes an interdisciplinary approach to these topics, in the hope of integrating economics into a more comprehensive view of human problems. This book should thus serve as a bridge between the social sciences and the world of business for the liberal arts student, the technical student, the commercial student, and the interested citizen.

ORGANIZATION AND COVERAGE

Each chapter is divided into two main parts. The first, "Tools for Study," presents both verbally and graphically the basic analytical tools of economics. Economic behavior is described and analyzed, and the results of behavior appraised within the full context of actual social, political, technical, and environmental conditions. The second part of each chapter, "Theory in Practice," includes practical applications of the topics discussed in the first part, examining recent events, debates over current policy, and business practices.

Chapter 1 introduces the student to the economic problem and the function of an economic system as a means of allocating resources. The concepts of scarcity, opportunity costs, and marginal reasoning are discussed and applied. Problem-solving through marginal analysis is introduced at the level of the family unit and local government.

Chapters 2, 3, and 4 provide the core of microeconomic analysis: how price and output decisions respond to supply and demand in the free market, and how imperfectly competitive markets fail to respond optimally to supply and demand. Chapter 5 deals with supply and demand of productive resources, with emphasis on labor resources and the labor movement. Chapters 6–9 provide the core of macroeconomic analysis: the definition and measurement of gross national product, the equilibrium level of GNP, and the use of fiscal and monetary policy to affect equilibrium.

Chapters 10–12 present current domestic problems and issues: inflation, unemployment, and poverty. Recent policy applications include wage and price controls, collective bargaining procedures, and the crisis in social security. Chapters 13 and 14 consider the broader long-range problems of economic growth and international economic relations. Current applications include population growth and the food crisis, exchange instability, and multinational firms.

SPECIAL FEATURES

This text incorporates a number of special features to make it more attractive and useful to instructors and students alike:

Level and method of presentation. A determined effort has been made to use familiar language and to enliven explanations with humor, personal experiences and observations, and invitations for the student to relate topics to his or her own life. Simple equations and graphs are used only occasionally as reinforcement of verbal descriptions and for further development of basic principles in applied situations.

Tools for independent study. Two features of the text encourage independent, self-paced instruction by the student. The *Learning Objectives* at the start of each chapter give the student a set of goals to accomplish and questions to answer (or analyze intelligently) while reading. The *Self-Check,* a set of multiple-choice questions separating the two parts of each chapter, allows the student to test his or her mastery of the concepts presented in *Tools for Study*. Answers and explanations for the self-checks are listed at the back of the text.

Terms to remember. Important terms and concepts in each chapter are set off in boldface type and are formally defined at the end of the chapter.

Problem-solving tools. The *Theory in Practice* section of Chapter 1 presents a six-step model for analyzing and solving economic problems that can be used throughout the book as well as independently outside the book or course.

Viewpoints. Short *Viewpoint* essays throughout the text discuss topics of special interest and show how economics operates within a historical, social, and political framework.

Topics for discussion. Discussion questions at the end of each chapter include review questions requiring definitions or factual information as well as "brain teasers" which ask the student to apply the tools studied to current issues.

Supplementary materials. Although the text itself includes many features of a workbook, a **Study Guide** which reinforces and expands the material covered in each chapter is also available to students. In addition, an **Instructor's Manual** is available.

Reading lists. Each chapter includes a brief list of recent articles in news magazines and professional journals, selected for their clear, straightforward language and relevance to fundamental economic principles.

ACKNOWLEDGMENTS

I am especially indebted to my good friends and colleagues who reviewed portions of the original manuscript and offered worthwhile suggestions and comments: Carl Biven, Jack Blicksilver, Sherman Dallas, Eva Galambos, Virlyn Moore, Beverly Shaffer, and my father, A. Raymond Hurt. I also appreciate the help and advice of a number of reviewers of the Second Edition of this text and of the current version:

Roger H. Goldberg, Ohio Northern University
Richard B. Hansen, University of Northern Iowa
Ken Hise, Valencia Community College
George E. Hoffer, Virginia Commonwealth University
Donald J. Isbell, J. Sargeant Reynolds Community College
Nicholas Karatjas, Indiana University of Pennsylvania
Jerry Knarr, Hillsborough Community College
William Little, Lake Land Community College
Kenneth D. Patterson, Oregon State University
Ted Scheinman, Mt. Hood Community College
Richard W. Stratton, University of Akron

Errors and omissions are, of course, entirely my own.

Marilu Hurt McCarty
Georgia Institute of Technology

Overview

Contents

DOLLARS AND SENSE

Third Edition

CHAPTER 1

Scarcity and Choice

or Nothin' Ain't Worth Nothin'— But It's Free

Tools for Study

Learning Objectives

After reading this chapter, you will be able to:

1. explain the economic problem facing all societies.
2. list the three questions every economic system must answer.
3. explain the concept of opportunity cost and how opportunity costs affect choice.
4. construct and apply a model of production possibilities.
5. construct and interpret a graph.
6. use a method of problem solving.

Issues Covered

How do production possibilities change over time?
How does a family budget its income efficiently?
How can a government plan its expenditures efficiently?

We Americans love a challenge. Our ancestors readily took up the challenge of settling a wild and remote continent. They cleared the land, suffered the winters, and raised the cities. They fought for the right of self-government, and took responsibility for using our national resources to satisfy national goals.

The tradition of pursuing noble goals has continued with each new generation of Americans, and our efforts have succeeded beyond our forefathers' grandest dreams. We have prospered greatly, and we have extended our prosperity to more and more segments of our own population, as well as to populations abroad. Material prosperity has brought improved health and living conditions, better education and job opportunities, and—most important—the potential for fullest personal development to us all.

Challenges did not end with the pioneer era. In fact, the problems faced by today's generation have more insidious implications than any we have faced before. More of the world's people want more things. At the same time, many of the world's resources are becoming depleted or are concentrated in the hands of those whose views on resource use are different from ours. Conflicts arise for access to the "good life," and alas, our capacity to inflict damage on each other has grown along with our capacity to do good. Today's Americans will be forced to make difficult choices, to decide complex issues which may impose pain now for the sake of benefits far in the future.

Many of our new problems involve economics. Economics is both the basis for our prosperity and the reason for our struggle. Through understanding economics, we—as individuals and as a nation—may make the decisions, shoulder the responsibilities, and find the solutions to the problems that divide us.

That is our challenge!

ECONOMICS AS A SCIENCE

As human beings, we try to make sense of our environment. We do not like to think of ourselves as mere combinations of cells with specialized functions enabling us to consume food, grow hair (some in greater abundance than others!), and so forth. We grow uneasy at the thought that we are, after all, only engaged in some collective "milling around" here on our planet during our life spans. We seek some order in our surroundings and some place for ourselves in the universe.

This drive to understand and explain our environment has existed throughout recorded history, but it began to thrive during the period of European history known as the Renaissance, beginning around the fourteenth century. More plentiful food supplies and gradual improvement in standards of life made it possible for some workers to use their time for tasks other than the production of necessary food and shelter. Instead, they could devote their energies to investigating the mysteries of the world environment.

In the beginning, the emphasis was on the natural and physical sciences. Investigations into astronomy led to the rather satisfying conclusion that heavenly bodies are subject to laws governing their orderly movement through space. Investigation of the human body led to discovery of the circulation of the blood, showing that we ourselves are orderly systems controlled by understandable biological laws. *Natural laws* became the basis of our knowlege about the physical world.

Eventually scholars turned to the social world to look for the natural laws that controlled people's relationships with each other. The year 1776 marked an important year in the parallel development of two social sciences: political science and economics. It was the beginning of the American nation as an experiment in political democracy, and it was the year when Adam Smith published *An Inquiry into the Nature and Causes of the Wealth of Nations,* the first full explanation of how an economic system works.

THE PROBLEM OF SCARCITY

Why is an economic system necessary? Throughout the history of life on this planet, we have faced the problem of *scarcity:* limited amounts of material, labor, and equipment to fill our ever expanding and unlimited wants. Scarcity of resources means that obtaining some of the things we want requires us to give up other things. If all goods were *free,* that is, if all of us could have as much as we wanted of everything, we wouldn't need an economic system.

There are, in fact, some goods that we may consider **free goods**. Fresh air and sunshine may be free on a tropical island. Each person can have as much as he or she wants and there will still be enough for everyone else. In a crowded city, on the other hand, fresh air may be very much an *economic* good—we must pay a price (such as the cost of pollution control) in order to obtain it. And unfortunately, as we soon discover, most goods are **economic** goods.

Because resources are scarce, they must be used wisely. Every community, whether of cave dwellers or high-rise apartment renters, must establish a system for allocating its scarce resources. Resources must be channeled into production of goods and services the community wants most. How much of the limited land should be used to produce wheat and how much to produce strawberries? How much of the limited metal resources should be used for autos and how much for air-

Viewpoint

ECONOMICS AND THE HISTORY OF IDEAS

The study of economics developed along with the natural sciences. But as a *social science,* economics suffered from a distinct disadvantage. Investigation of the social world could not be as systematic nor as unbiased as investigation of the physical world; social scientists brought to their explorations their own prejudices and political self-interests. Another difficulty was that the social world itself was constantly changing, providing a moving target for the social scientists.

A changing world environment has made for changes in economic theory. Modern economic theory originated during the Industrial Revolution, when competition was vigorous and served to check excessive market power. This environment produced an economic theory known as *laissez-faire,* emphasizing freedom of individual enterprise without government interference. According to theory, an economic system would function best if individuals were free to pursue their own self-interest.

The sharpest change in this theory followed the worldwide depression of the 1930s. With a government "hands off" policy, production in the United States fell by almost half. John Maynard Keynes, a noted economist of the time, suggested that government intervention might occasionally be necessary to correct some of the tendencies of the economic system. Acceptance of an active government role in economics was formalized in the Employment Act of 1946, making the federal government responsible for regulating economic activity. Government's role was more precisely defined in the Humphrey-Hawkins Act of 1980.

In recent years, debate has centered on whether the concentration of power in business and government has grown too great. Some economists favor a return to reliance on laissez-faire; others feel that there is a need for greater national economic planning. (Some might even suggest that we start all over from scratch!)

Economic issues change. Analysis and policy evolve in response to changing social, political, and economic conditions. (Then there's the tale of the old economics professor who asks the same examination questions year after year but keeps changing the answers . . . .) Economics is a developing course of study. Economics must always question the theories and policies of the past and look to the changing needs and opportunities of the future.

planes? How much of the limited labor power should be used to build dams and how much to teach college students?

We can't have all we want of every good or service. So we must choose what we want most!

The Economic Problem

The problem of scarce resources and unlimited wants is often referred to as the **economic problem**. Every society faces limitations on its ability to provide for its ever expanding wants. With existing technology there are limits to the quantities of goods and services that can be produced from available resources. This means that a society must use its stock of resources carefully so as to achieve a combination of goods and services that most nearly fits the needs and desires of its people.

Scarce Resources

A society uses four types of resources in the production of goods and services: land, labor, capital, and management or entrepreneurial ability. These resources are also called "factors of production."

Land
Land may be thought of as "natural resources." It includes all the original and nonreproducible gifts of nature: fertile soil, minerals, fossil fuels, and water. All are fixed in amount but, when combined with human ingenuity, may be induced to yield goods and services.

In years past, the vastness of the earth's resources tempted us to regard them as inexhaustible and, therefore, free. Recent threats of specific shortages, however, remind us that we still must avoid wasteful exploitation.

Labor
Labor may be thought of as "human resources." It is the purposeful activity of human beings: teachers, psychiatrists, lathe operators, roustabouts, statisticians. Failure to use productively a single willing hour of labor results in a *permanent* sacrifice of the good or service it might have produced.

Capital
Capital may be thought of as "manufactured resources." Capital includes the tools and equipment that strengthen, extend, or replace human hands in the production of goods and services: hammers, sewing machines, turbines, bookkeeping machines, components of finished goods, specialized skills. Capital is sometimes said to permit "roundabout" production: goods are produced indirectly through a manufactured instrument rather than directly through physical labor. To construct capital requires that we postpone consumption of goods today so that we may produce more goods in the future. (Economists do not think of money as capital, since money by itself cannot produce other goods.)

Management or Entrepreneurial Ability
Management or **entrepreneurial ability** may be thought of as the "creative resource." It provides the spark that combines other resources toward some desired goal. Entrepreneurial ability is provided by the owner or developer, creator, or administrator of a productive enterprise.

The first three resources are certainly important. But the fourth may be even more critical for producing the maximum quantity and quality of desired goods and services.

THE THREE QUESTIONS: WHAT? HOW? FOR WHOM?

Resources available for use in production can be combined in a variety of ways. To decide how to make use of its resources, a society must answer three basic questions.

1. The society must first decide *What?* to emphasize in production. "How much military equipment?" and "How much food?" might be the options facing a nation preparing for war; "How many consumer goods?" and "How

many machines?'' the critical choice for a newly developing economy; "How many agricultural products?" and "How many manufactured goods?" the choice for a nation dependent on international trade.

Whatever goods and services the society chooses to produce, it must at the same time sacrifice other goods and services it might have chosen.

2. Second, a society must decide *How?* resources should be combined to produce the desired output. If the society is rich in land, it may choose to emphasize the use of land in production. This was true in our own country in the nineteenth century and is true in Argentina and Australia today. If workers are plentiful, the society may emphasize the use of labor as in populous Japan. If the society is rich in capital resources, it may emphasize the use of machinery as in the United States today. A country with infertile land and few other resources may choose to develop and encourage entrepreneurial ability through training in business management.

Whatever resources the society chooses to use in production, it must at the same time sacrifice other goods and services the resources could have produced.

3. Finally, any economic society must decide *For Whom?* output is to be produced. Who is to be rewarded at the time goods and services are distributed? Brain surgeons or industrial designers? Poets or ballet dancers? Teachers or economists? Normally, a person's reward will reflect the relative value the society places on the goods or services that person produced. A generous reward will encourage greater production of a good or service that is in demand.

Needless to say, whatever groups the society chooses to reward generously, it must at the same time reward other groups less well.

ORGANIZING PRODUCTION

How have societies organized themselves to answer the three questions discussed above? There have been three major types of organization, as well as many variations and combinations of the three.

The Traditional Economy

Very primitive communities generally organize for production by *traditional* means—repeating within the family generation after generation the familiar patterns of production and distribution. Farming families continue to till the land. Cobblers, carpenters, and tailors pass on their skills within the family.

A traditional economic system is necessary where resources are few and the margin between life and death is very narrow. The community may barely be able to feed itself, with little surplus available for building capital equipment. Because of the hazards of life, the people must avoid any change from tried-and-true methods. As a result, there is little opportunity for technological advance.

Traditional economies continue to exist today in remote parts of Africa, Asia, and Latin America. You may know of particular families and communities in the United States which still continue old patterns of production in traditional ways.

The Command Economy

In some communities new resources are gradually discovered and better production techniques developed. In time it becomes possible to produce more goods than the minimum necessary for life. When there is a potential surplus of output, societies must decide how to use the surplus.

For a growing economy the three questions may be answered by a system of *command*. In command economies a central authority decides what the desired priority of needs is, makes plans accordingly, and then sees that they are carried out. Often the particular plan focuses on some national goal such as military power or economic growth. A central authority can ensure that the sacrifices necessary for building capital equipment are made. The USSR used command to build industrial capacity after the Communist revolution. Even the United States uses command by levying taxes to be used for building public projects.

You can imagine how difficult total national planning would be in a complex modern economy. It would be particularly difficult without computers and without rapid transportation and communication facilities.

The Market System

In *Wealth of Nations,* Adam Smith described a third method of organizing scarce resources for production. It was the *market system* that developed in the newly industrialized countries of Western Europe. The market system was different from production planning under either the traditional or the command system. Under a free market system production and distribution were planned by the people of the community themselves. *What?, How?,* and *For Whom?* were decided by the people who actually produced and used the goods and services.

Just as in political democracy, the people would vote—with their dollars!—for the goods they wanted most. The expectation of profit would encourage business firms to produce the goods and services the public wanted. Then the receipt of profit would provide successful producers the funds for investment in new machinery, factories, and transportation facilities, and for research into new products. According to Adam Smith, all of this would enrich the lives of citizens and move the nation into ever rising levels of material wealth.

ECONOMIC EFFICIENCY

This, then, is our challenge—to use our resources carefully for producing the goods and services we want most. In fact, the fundamental goal of economics can be expressed in a single word: *efficiency*. Efficiency refers to the quantity of output

obtained from a single unit of input: output/input. *An economic system is efficient if it produces the* **maximum** *quantity of goods and services with the* **minimum** *quantity of productive resources.*

The United States has chosen the free market system as the basis for its economic system* because we believe it is most efficient. The market system includes the means for achieving two kinds of efficiency: technical efficiency and allocative efficiency. **Technical efficiency** refers to the total quantity of goods and services which may be produced with existing resources and available technology. Our free market system provides incentives to encourage business firms to produce the largest possible quantity of goods and services with the smallest use of scarce land, labor, capital, and entrepreneurial ability. **Allocative efficiency** refers to the kinds of goods and services the people want. Our free society guarantees each individual the right to choose the way in which he or she wants to live, including how we work and how we spend our incomes. Choosing freely enables us to allocate our nation's resources toward producing the things we want.

Because resources are scarce, production is limited. Deciding to use resources in one way will mean the sacrifice of other things we might have had. We want our system to be efficient: to produce the most of what we want with the least sacrifice of what we might have had. Understanding economics helps us make these choices efficiently.

OPPORTUNITY COSTS

Choosing is the subject matter of economics. Regrettably, every choice involves a trade-off, or cost. The cost to society of the use of a resource in the production of one good or service is the loss of the next most desired good or service it *could have produced.* Economists refer to such alternative uses as the **opportunity costs** of using productive resources in a particular way.

* although we have elements of tradition and command

The cost to an athlete of a tennis match is the golf game he or she might have played (or the nap in the shade). The cost to a homemaker of a loaf of homemade bread is the book he or she might have read (in addition to the flour, eggs, and so forth). The cost to a college student of intensive study for one course is the ''A'' he or she might have earned in another.

A consumer must also make decisions based on opportunity cost. With limited financial resources, a consumer's decision to spend a dollar for one item means the sacrifice of another item he or she might have bought instead. The purchase of a sweater for $15 may require the sacrifice of a pair of concert tickets.

The same reasoning applies to a producer's use of limited productive resources. When a firm employs an acre of land, an hour of labor, or a piece of machinery, it must consider alternative uses of these resources. Tools and materials can be used to build schools or bridges, ice rinks or pizza parlors, airplanes or trains. The cost of each choice is the other good or service we must give up. An acre of land used for tennis courts is not available as a parking lot!

Choosing efficiently means that opportunity costs are held to a minimum. It means that society has allocated its limited resources to achieve the *most* desired goods and services with the *least* sacrifice of other goods and services we might have had. Choosing efficiently is difficult in a complex economy like ours. Economists demonstrate the problem of choosing through an **economic model.** A model is a simplified view of reality, which includes the fundamental characteristics of the economic environment but omits nonessential details. An economic model helps us focus on the major problem and shows the effects of alternative solutions.

PRODUCTION POSSIBILITIES

The problem of opportunity costs can be seen by studying a model of production possibilities.

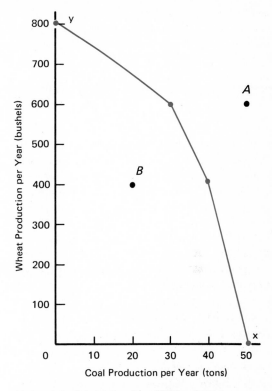

Figure 1.1 Production Possibilities Curve.
Given its limited resources and state of technology, a society can produce any combination of goods up to its production possibilities frontier. Point *A* is beyond this society's present capabilities; point *B* underutilizes the society's resources.

Given its resources and level of technology, any society faces a range of combinations of goods and services which it can produce. It may choose to allocate all resources toward one major objective—food production, for example, or industrial development, or military power. A wealth of resources and a small population may allow a society to produce more frivolous goods—sports cars, electric can openers, and whirlpool baths.

It is helpful to illustrate the model of production possibilities with a graph such as the one in Figure 1.1. Suppose a society can produce two

Table 1.1   Production Possibilities Curve.

Wheat (bushels per year)	0	400	600	750	800
Coal (tons per year)	50	40	30	10	0

goods, coal and wheat. The two axes on Figure 1.1 represent quantities of each. The horizontal axis represents quantities of coal, measured in tons on a scale from 0 to 50. The vertical axis represents wheat, measured in bushels on a scale from 0 to 800.

Table 1.1 shows the possible combinations of wheat and coal that can be produced.

If all resources are devoted to coal production, the maximum output per year is 50 tons. Follow the horizontal axis to 50 tons in Figure 1.1 and notice the point x which represents the maximum quantity of coal this society can produce. If 50 tons of coal are produced, the economy will produce no wheat. The *opportunity cost* of 50 tons of coal is the amount of wheat which could have been produced instead. (As we will see, the opportunity cost of 50 tons of coal is 800 bushels of wheat.)

If all resources are devoted to the production of wheat, the maximum output is 800 bushels. Follow the vertical axis to 800 bushels and notice the point y which represents the maximum production of wheat. If 800 bushels of wheat are produced, the economy will produce no coal. The *opportunity cost* of 800 bushels of wheat is 50 tons of coal.

If the society wants some of both goods (without heat, it's difficult to make bread), maximum possible combinations of output are as follows: 40 tons of coal and 400 bushels of wheat; 30 tons and 600 bushels; or 10 tons and 750 bushels. Locate these points by moving along the horizontal scale the appropriate distance and then moving up the vertical scale.

A line connecting the points of production possibilities has been called just that—the **production possibilities curve**—the frontier beyond which the society cannot produce. Point A on Fig-

ure 1.1, for example, represents quantities of coal and wheat (50 tons and 600 bushels) that are impossible to produce with existing resources and technology. Point B is a combination of output which underutilizes the society's resources. At point B, some miners and farmers are unemployed, causing a *permanent* loss of the output they could have produced. (How much coal and how much wheat would be produced at B? How much more coal could be produced? How much more wheat?*)

When the United States entered World War II, observers in this country and abroad were amazed at the speed with which our economy was able to begin producing tanks, planes, guns, and ammunition. We were able to move quickly into war production because during the Great Depression of the 1930s we had been experiencing severe unemployment. In 1933, 12 million workers, or one quarter of the work force, were unemployed. (Many others were underemployed: working at jobs beneath their full capacity.) We were at a point *inside* our production possibilities curve (say, at point B in Fig. 1.1). The wartime emergency shifted unemployed workers, idle machines, and empty factories into useful work.

Conditions were different in the 1960s. Except for a relatively small number of workers who would normally be changing jobs, the nation was operating at full employment. Then problems began to develop in South Vietnam, and the worsening military situation seemed to call for increased production of the tools of war.

President Johnson hoped that more military goods could be produced without reducing civilian production. Economists remembered the model of production possibilities. They pointed out that to produce more of one type of output would involve opportunity costs. Civilian production would have to be cut. The economy could move *along* its production possibilities curve, but not *beyond it!*

In a command economy, civilian production can be reduced by executive order. Then the re-

---

* 20 tons and 400 bushels; any combination on the production possibilities curve.

quired resources can be moved into military production. Even our free market economy has means of forcing consumers to reduce their spending so that resources can be moved into purposes desired by government. In fact, a tax increase was proposed to do just that.

It was several years before the tax proposal was finally enacted, however. In the meantime, consumers continued a high level of consumer purchases while government increased purchases of military goods. The economy was spending beyond its production possibilities.

When there is greater spending than goods being produced, the ultimate result is rising prices. Consumer and government buyers bid against each other for the limited quantities of goods, and prices are forced up. A general increase in prices is called **price inflation.**

Inflation prevented consumers from buying all the civilian goods they wanted, so the economy did remain on its production possibilities curve after all. In fact, price inflation acted as a kind of tax. While consumers continued to spend more dollars, each dollar would buy less. The result was a decline in the production of consumer goods, releasing scarce resources for military purposes.

Have you noticed that the production possibilities curve in Figure 1.1 is bowed out in the middle? The largest combinations of total output are near the center where some resources are used to produce wheat and some to produce coal. Why is this? All resources are not equally suited to the production of coal or wheat. When workers can choose among two or more types of jobs, they will generally choose to work where they are more productive, and they will become more skillful as they work. Furthermore, if too much labor is employed in wheat production, each worker will have less of other fixed resources—land and machinery—with which to work. Total wheat production may not grow very much as more workers are added. To use all resources in one industry or the other would pull the curve down at the edges, causing a bulge in the center.

It is not practical to draw a model of production possibilities with more than two axes, but we might imagine a multidimensional figure in which the possible combinations of *all* goods are shown. Then any society must choose the appropriate combination for which its resources will be used. Producing on its production possibilities curve will mean **technical efficiency. Allocative efficiency** depends on choosing the most desired point on the production possibilities curve. Thus, allocative efficiency depends on producing what people want.

MAKING CHOICES

Choosing is the subject matter of economics. Economics includes habits of thinking that help people choose better—to weigh the benefits of every choice against the costs and to arrive at efficient decisions. The economic way of thinking is important to us in our roles as producers as well as in our roles as consumers.

As producers we weigh the benefits of every production decision against the costs of resources to be employed. Scarcity forces us to arrange our wants according to priorities and our resources according to their relative scarcity and alternative uses. This helps us produce the goods we want *most* with the resources we have in greatest abundance: boats from fiberglass, wheat from Western plains, and clothing from cotton.

As consumers we weigh the benefits of every spending decision against the costs. We compare the benefits of a new car with a family trip to Europe, a night on the town with a new sport jacket, or a motorcycle with a year's membership in a health club. We want to get the most benefit out of each dollar of our limited budgets.

CHOOSING AT THE MARGIN

Many of our decisions are based on comparisons at the margin. The *margin* is the edge or border where we must decide whether to take one more step, whether to use one more unit of resource or purchase one more unit of consumer goods. **Marginal analysis** is used unconsciously in many everyday decisions, but it is especially useful in economic decisions.

We even make marginal decisions when we allocate our time. We continue one activity until the benefits gained from spending one more minute are less than the benefits from spending that minute in some other activity. In this way a student allocates study time, or a worker allocates work time among a number of tasks. (Even a hedonist allocates pleasure time by comparing the benefits gained from spending one more minute in recreation with the benefits of spending that minute resting!)

We also make marginal decisions when we allocate our money. We spend for one item until the benefits gained from spending one more dollar are less than the benefits of spending that dollar on something else. A student spends money on concert tickets up to the point where he or she believes a football game would be more enjoyable.

Business firms behave similarly when deciding on levels of production. Autos are produced until production of one more auto would bring in less revenue than it costs to produce. A barber keeps his shop open until one more hour brings in less revenue than the cost of operation.

Business firms also use marginal analysis to decide how many resources to use in production. Salespeople are hired until hiring one more worker adds less to sales revenues than the worker's wage. Land is bought for shopping centers until one more acre of space adds less to revenue than it costs.

In effect, our entire economic system makes decisions at the margin. We increase total production until one more unit will be worth less than the resources required to produce it.

Economics is the study of choices in the market system. In the second half of this chapter you will see how economic decisions are made by a hypothetical family and by a government, both of which have to choose among several alternatives. In the following chapters you will learn how markets work in theory, and how they often work in the "real world."

Self-Check

1. The economic problem is concerned primarily with:
a. relieving poverty.
b. redistributing wealth.
c. motivating people to work harder.
d. choosing how to use society's scarce resources.
e. gathering data for economic analysis.

2. Whenever society chooses to produce one type of output:
a. it must sacrifice some other type of output.
b. resources will be fully employed.
c. it avoids opportunity costs.
d. it may also increase all other types of output.
e. it avoids the problem of decision making.

3. Which of the following is *not* an example of a scarce resource?
a. trained brain surgeons
b. fresh air in a large city
c. coal
d. screwdrivers
e. All are scarce, although supplies of some are greater than others.

4. Which of the following is *not* a true description of a capital resource?
a. Construction of capital allows us to produce more goods in the future.
b. Capital is money.
c. Capital allows roundabout production.
d. Production of autos requires more capital than production of hamburgers.
e. Nations differ in the quantities of capital owned.

5. Which of the following correctly describes a free market economy?
a. It is not necessary to make sacrifices in a free market economy.
b. Under the market system a central authority plans economic growth.
c. A market economy provides little opportunity for technological advance and growth.
d. A market economy responds to dollar "votes" of consumers.
e. The market system is based on preserving past methods of production.

6. Which of the following statements is false?
a. Even simple day-to-day decisions involve opportunity costs.
b. If there were no scarcity, there would be no opportunity costs.
c. Opportunity costs are foregone alternatives.
d. Opportunity costs are always measured in dollars.
e. The production possibilities curve illustrates the problem of opportunity costs.

Theory in Practice

HOW TO CONSTRUCT AND INTERPRET A GRAPH

Economists use graphs to illustrate important relationships. Graphs are like road maps. They help
express ideas quickly with few words. There are
many symbols which we recognize instantly without explanation. How would you interpret these
symbols?

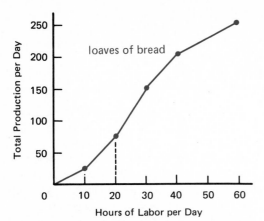

Figure 1.2 Daily Bread Production at Country Kitchen Bakery.
The graph illustrates a direct relationship between the two values. As hours of labor increase, bread production also increases.

A graph is like a symbol.

With a little practice, you can learn to construct and interpret graphs. You will find them useful in your study of economics and in your work after you leave school. In economics we will be interested in graphs measuring such things as income, employment, total production, and price. A graph is drawn on two axes or perpendicular lines. The horizontal axis may express time or numbers of items. The vertical axis shows a value associated with each time period or item.

We have already seen how a graph is used to show a society's production possibilities. Now we will look at another example. Figure 1.2 is a graph of quantity of production associated with various amounts of labor.

The horizontal axis on Figure 1.2 shows hours of labor employed per day at Country Kitchen Bakery. The vertical axis shows daily production of bread. For example, if 10 hours of labor are employed, only 25 loaves will be produced. Follow the dotted line from 10 hours up to 25 loaves. If 20 hours are employed, 75 loaves will be produced. Again follow the dotted line from 20 hours to 75 loaves. Points for each combination of labor and production are plotted on the graph. Then lines are drawn connecting all the points.

Since some bread will be produced even with .5, 23.75, or 51.33 hours of labor, the line has been drawn as a continuous curve.

The zero point (0) on the graph is called the *origin*. The graph of bread production begins at the origin because when 0 hours of labor are employed, no bread is produced.

Over the range of employment shown, in Figure 1.2 there is a **direct relationship** between hours of labor and bread production. What happens to one value happens to the other: as labor increases, bread production also increases. Likewise, as labor decreases, bread production decreases. In other graphs the relationship between two values might be *inverse*. Opposite things would happen to the values: as one value increases, the other would decrease; as one value decreases, the other would increase. We have already seen an example of an **inverse relationship** in the production possibilities curve in Figure 1.1.

The data in the table below Figure 1.3 describe grain production from one acre of land

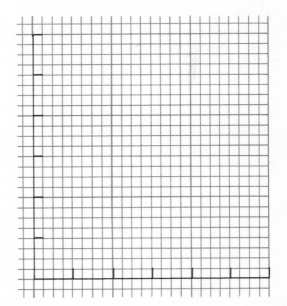

Figure 1.3 Construction of a Graph.

Pounds of Fertilizer	0	10	20	30	40	50
Bushels of Grain	100	150	175	200	200	175

when various amounts of fertilizer are applied during a growing season. Use the information to construct a graph on the figure. Label the horizontal axis *pounds of fertilizer per season*. Label the vertical axis *bushels of grain per season*. On the horizontal axis mark off spaces representing 10, 20, 30, 40, and 50 pounds of fertilizer. On the vertical axis mark off spaces representing 50, 100, 150, 200, 250, and 300 bushels of grain. Plot the points shown in the table.

Even if no fertilizer is used, the field will produce 100 bushels of grain during the growing season. Your first point should lie on the vertical axis at 100 bushels. Follow a line up from 10 pounds of fertilizer to 150 bushels for your second point. Plot all the points and connect them with a continuous line.

What can you learn from this graph? Describe its shape. Why do you think it has this shape? Based on your graph, what would you estimate output to be if 25 pounds of fertilizer is applied during the growing season? Is there a direct relationship between use of fertilizer and grain production? Over what range? A portion of your graph illustrates an inverse relationship between use of fertilizer and output. When fertilizer is increased from 40 to 50 pounds, grain production falls. Can you explain this result?

CHANGES IN PRODUCTION POSSIBILITIES

We have used the model of production possibilities to illustrate a nation's maximum output of goods and services. Production possibilities may change over time. As new resources are discovered, production possibilities will increase, moving the production possibilities curve out to the right.

Advances in technology also expand production possibilities. The shape of the new curve will depend on whether research and development are directed more toward one type of production or the other. The production possibilities curve in Figure 1.4a shows a nation with increased capacity for producing wheat. Figure 1.4b shows increased capacity for producing coal.

On the other hand, depletion of resources or failure to develop new resources could reduce production possibilities in the future, moving the curve back to the left. Figure 1.4c shows a backward shift in production possibilities. In this case, the nation can produce less of both goods.

Changes in technology and resources will affect the shape of the production possibilities curve. The shape of the curve shows relative costs of production and the opportunity cost of each production decision. For example, technological advance

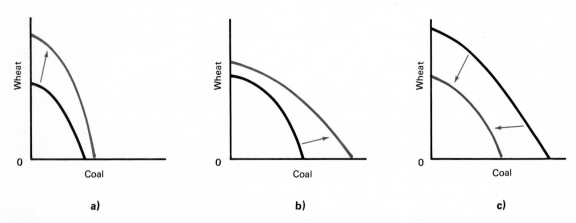

a)   b)   c)

Figure 1.4   Changes in Production Possibilities.
Increased capacity for producing wheat (a), or for producing coal (b), is shown by a shift of the production possibilities curve to the right. Reduced capacity for producing both goods (c) is shown by a shift of the curve to the left.

favoring wheat production will reduce relative costs and opportunity costs. Fewer other goods must be sacrificed for each additional unit of wheat produced.

America's progress as an industrial nation was largely a result of advances in the technology of agriculture. As fewer workers and machines were needed to produce food, more could be used to build factories and capital equipment.

America has prospered also because of our large, integrated national market. Our rich and varied resources have enabled regions to specialize in many different types of production. There are no barriers to free trade among regions: no customs duties, no currency exchanges, no restrictions which might slow the free movement of goods. When regions specialize for selling to a wide consumer market, it is possible to develop advanced technology for improving efficiency. The result has been a continued shift to the right of production possibilities, with rising material standards of living for our people.

How will each of the following affect the position and shape of a nation's production possibilities?*

1. a war which devastates much of the farmland and kills many young workers
2. the "Green Revolution" which increases the use of chemical fertilizers, disease-resistant seeds, pesticides, and herbicides in agriculture

---

*1. a backward shift of production possibilities.

2. increased production possibilities for food and other agricultural products

3. increased production possibilities for goods and services using relatively large amounts of labor

4. whether production possibilities decrease or increase depends on whether rebellious attitudes result in lower or higher worker productivity

5. increased production possibilities

6. incentives to expand production and satisfy the larger market

7. reduced production possibilities for goods requiring relatively large inputs of restricted resources

8. reduced production possibilities for goods and services using that resource

---

3. state-supported vocational schools to provide low-cost training to disadvantaged groups
4. widespread emphasis on "doing one's own thing," rejecting society's standards, and refusing to conform to accepted behavior (a number of possibilities are debatable here)
5. the "Puritan ethic" with its condemnation of conspicuous wealth and its emphasis on hard work and thrift
6. the formation of a "Common Market" of Western European nations, within which barriers to free trade are gradually removed
7. legislation forbidding certain uses of a region's air, water, and landscape
8. a trade embargo which reduces imports of a commodity necessary in all production

PROBLEM SOLVING

We make choices every day that involve economics. Should we buy a second pair of shoes or a pair of slacks or, perhaps, save the money? Should we buy a car or rely on public transportation? Should we take a new job that offers a higher salary or stay at our old job within walking distance of our home? Should we do our own repairs around the house or hire a professional?

These simple examples illustrate a number of economic concepts you have already learned: scarcity, opportunity cost, production possibilities, marginal analysis. In fact, we are making a marginal decision when we decide to buy a second pair of shoes rather than a pair of slacks. The opportunity cost of the shoes is the slacks we could have bought instead, or the interest we could have earned by saving the money. Since we do not have enough money to buy both goods, we must choose one or the other (the economic problem). Making choices is not always easy, but a knowledge of economics can help ensure the maximum benefit from each decision.

How can we learn to think "economically"? We may learn to use economic reasoning *automatically* only after we are well acquainted with economics. (It is hard to think in a foreign language until you have mastered the language!) However, through conscious effort, we can begin to apply economic concepts and principles to our daily lives. Through use of the following six-step problem-solving method, we can start on our way to independent economic thinking:*

1. Define the problem.
2. Specify the goals or objectives.
3. Identify the economic concepts involved.
4. List the alternative choices available.
5. Evaluate each alternative.
6. Decide which alternative is best in light of the evaluation and goals.

Now let us take a look at two specific problems to see how this method can help use economics for solving problems.

Family Budgeting

The Wilcoxes live in a one-bedroom apartment for which they pay $335 a month, including utilities. Both the Wilcoxes work and together earn a yearly income of $15,000 after taxes. (This is the amount available to them for spending.) Lately they have been complaining of not knowing where the money is going. For the past year, it seems, they have been unable to save any of their income, even though they feel that a certain portion should be saved for emergencies or future needs. They also know that certain expenditures are necessary and cannot be eliminated. These include housing costs (rent and utilities), purchases of food and other household needs, and transportation to and from work (they do not own a car and must use public transportation).

According to their calculations, the minimum they feel they can spend on these three things is as follows: $4,000 a year for housing, $2,000 a year

* For more information on problem-solving methods, see Fels and Uhler, *Casebook of Economic Problems and Policies* (West Publishing Co., 1974), and Elbing, *Behavioral Decisions in Organizations,* 2nd Edition (Scott, Foresman and Co., 1978).

for food, and $1,000 a year for transportation. Other purchases they may wish to make include additional units of housing (in the form of home furnishings, new electrical appliances, etc.), food, and transportation. They may also wish to use some of their income for recreation, health care (including insurance), and clothing. However, the necessary payments for housing, food, and transportation come first—that is, they will allocate a portion of their income ($7,000) to cover these expenses before deciding on other uses of their income.

To summarize, the Wilcoxes feel that they are not spending their income wisely. They decide to plan a family budget for using their income more *efficiently:* to obtain the greatest possible benefits within their limited income. The benefits they hope to achieve include housing, food, transportation, recreation, health care, clothing, and savings.

How will they allocate their income among these categories? How will they evaluate their choices among the alternative ways of using their income? Let us see how the problem-solving method can help:

1. *Define the problem.* The problem, as the Wilcoxes put it, is that they do not know "where the money is going." There are too many unnecessary or improper expenditures and too little saving (in this case, zero saving). The Wilcoxes are not getting the maximum possible benefits out of their income.
2. *Specify the goals or objectives.* The Wilcoxes' goal is similar to that of the economic system as a whole: to use their available resources *efficiently.*
3. *Identify the economic concepts involved.* The concepts include: rationing (the family must decide how to allocate their limited income); opportunity cost (money spent is not available for saving, money saved is not available for spending, and money spent on one good is not available for spending on another good); and marginal analysis (the family must decide how to make use of each additional unit of income).
4. *List the alternative choices available.* The Wil-

coxes must spend a portion of their income on housing, food, and transportation ($7,000 out of $15,000). However, there are a number of ways to use the remaining $8,000. The family can: (1) spend the money on additional units of housing, food, or transportation; (2) spend the money on other things such as health, recreation, and clothing; (3) save the money; or (4) a combination of these.

5. *Evaluate each alternative*. To simplify their decision-making, the Wilcoxes break down their income into units of $1,000. They now have 15 units of income each year which they must decide to allocate among the benefits available to them.

In order to evaluate their choices, the Wilcoxes must have some way of measuring the value of the different choices. After some thought, they come up with a measure they decide to call *utility points* or *utils*. They must buy 4 units, or $4,000, worth of housing, 2 units or $2,000 worth of food; and 1 unit, or $1,000, worth of transportation. Because these are their most important expenditures, the Wilcoxes assign a value of 100 utils to each unit of spending on these items. Less important expenditures are assigned values of fewer than 100 utility points.

The first four units of spending on housing are worth 100 utils to them, or a total of 400 utils; the first two units of food are worth a total of 200 utils; the first unit of transportation is

worth a total of 100 utils. The Wilcoxes assign utils to additional units of these three items, as well as to units of recreation, health needs, clothing, and saving, according to the importance they attach to each. Table 1.2 shows the different values assigned by the Wilcoxes.

Thus far, the Wilcoxes have allocated 7 units, or $7,000, of their income. This has given them a total of 700 utility points or utils. How will they use their next unit of income? As shown in Table 1.2, a fifth unit of housing or a third unit of food would not be a wise choice. The next unit of housing gives them 85 utils; the next unit of food gives them 70 utils. They will obtain the most total benefit by using the next unit of income to purchase one unit of health care. A unit of health care will provide 95 utils, the largest amount available among the remaining choices. The value of 95 means that, after their most important expenditures are taken care of, they will want to spend their next $1,000 on health care before using the money for anything else.

The Wilcoxes will save the next unit, since the first unit of saving provides 90 utils. (The high value reflects the importance of saving to the Wilcox family.) The next choice could be a first unit of clothing or a fifth unit of housing, since both give them 85 utils. The following choice will then be the 85-util item they did not choose.

6. *Decide which alternative is best in light of the*

Table 1.2 Utility Points from the Use of Each Unit of Money (measured in utils).

	Housing	Food	Transportation	Recreation	Health Care	Clothing	Saving
1st unit	100	100	100	80	95	85	90
2nd unit	100	100	80	75	60	70	80
3rd unit	100	70	40	60	25	55	70
4th unit	100	50	0	60	0	30	40
5th unit	85	25		45		0	0
6th unit	70	0		35			
7th unit	40			20			
8th unit	20			0			
9th unit	0						

evaluation and goals. The Wilcoxes will repeat step 5 until they have allocated all their income (fifteen units). For each successive unit of income they will consider alternative uses and choose the alternative which gives them the most utility points. Their final budget is shown in Table 1.3. The Wilcoxes will use their $15,000 income in such a way that they obtain 1,370 utility points, the maximum amount possible.

Could the Wilcoxes have made other choices which would have produced the same 1,370-point total? If family income falls by $4,000, how will the Wilcoxes use the additional income?

Most families do not go through such detailed steps when planning a budget. However, the process is quite similar in principle to the Wilcoxes' plan. A family planning a budget will consider alternative uses of their income and allocate each unit according to the benefits they expect to receive from its use. They will not choose, for example, to use $1,000 for recreation if they need that money to pay the rent!

The Wilcox family budget provides a good example of marginal decision-making. The Wilcoxes planned their budget in steps: How many more units should they spend on housing? What is the value of an additional expenditure on recreation compared with an additional expenditure on transportation? By comparing benefits at the margin, the Wilcoxes are able to use their resources more efficiently.

Of course, if the Wilcoxes understand economics, they realize the importance of opportunity costs in their decision. The opportunity cost of the first unit of recreation is the lost opportunity for a unit of saving. Every time they make a decision to allocate one unit of their income, they are giving up all the other possible uses of that income.

Government Expenditures

Governments, like families, allocate their budgets among public projects according to priorities. They compare benefits and costs for each additional unit of expenditure. However, unlike families, their primary concern is *social* rather than *private* benefits. They select projects which provide the greatest benefits per dollar for the community as a whole.

Major expenditures by government are not typical marginal decisions. Public projects involve large lump sums. A road must go *from* somewhere *to* somewhere. A swimming pool must be of a certain minimum size. You can't build three fourths of a gymnasium! Many public projects are not divisible into small units.

Table 1.3   Wilcox Family Budget.

Good or Service	No. of Units Used	Total Income Used for Each Good or Service	Total Utility Points from Each
Housing	5	$ 5,000	485
Food	2	2,000	200
Transportation	2	2,000	180
Recreation	2	2,000	155
Health Care	1	1,000	95
Clothing	1	1,000	85
Saving	2	2,000	170
Total Income		$15,000	
Total Utility Points			1,370

Benefits of public projects are difficult to measure. The value of a public service is the amount its users would pay for it if it were provided by private business. How much would you pay for the use of public roads, public education, community protection against smallpox, or a swimming pool in the city park? Your willingness to pay depends on your own expected benefits which *you* may not be able to measure!

Total costs are also difficult to measure. The cost of land, labor, and materials is easy to calculate. (These costs measure the opportunity costs of using resources in certain ways.) However, there are other long-range costs which should also be considered. The disruption and dislocation of homes and businesses during construction imposes costs on the community that may be impossible to measure.

Table 1.4 gives hypothetical benefit and cost data for three groups of public projects. Benefits and costs are expressed in terms of thousands of dollars. For example, a new school costs $6,500,000 to build, but will provide benefits to the community worth $19,500,000.

See if you can go through the six problem-solving steps for this example. (Your goal is to obtain the maximum social benefit for each dollar spent.) First calculate the *expected benefit-cost ratio,* or the benefits per dollar of each project, by dividing costs into benefits. Assume the community is limited to a budget of $10 million. What projects would you select? What is the total cost of the projects?

A ratio greater than 1 means that benefits outweigh costs; a ratio less than 1 means that costs outweigh benefits. What would a ratio of 1 mean? Which projects are definitely not desirable? Are there other worthwhile projects which must be postponed? (Answers can be found at the end of Topics for Discussion.)

SUMMARY

1. Scholars in earlier centuries sought to understand the natural laws that govern physical and social environments. The economic theory of the free-market system and the political theory of democracy developed together. Both processes depended

Table 1.4 Benefit and Cost Data for Public Projects.
(Figures are in thousands of dollars.)

	Benefits	Costs	$\dfrac{\text{Benefits}}{\text{Costs}}$ = Benefit-Cost Ratio
Education			
New School	$19,500	$6,500	_____
Gymnasium	1,000	800	_____
Driver-Training			
Course	750	500	_____
Transportation			
Highway	$ 4,000	$2,000	_____
Rapid-Transit			
Service	6,000	8,000	_____
Bus Service	1,750	500	_____
Recreation			
Stadium	$ 1,200	$ 900	_____
Golf Course	1,000	2,000	_____
Pool	1,200	500	_____

on the free exercise of individual rights and responsibilities.

2. Economics deals with the problem of scarce resources and unlimited wants: the economic problem. Land, labor, capital, and management or entrepreneurial ability are scarce resources.

3. An economic system is necessary for organizing scarce resources for producing the goods and services the community wants. An economic system helps answer the questions *What?* to produce, *How?* to produce it, and *For Whom?* to produce it.

4. A community answers the three questions through its economic system. The system may be based on tradition, command, or free markets. Adam Smith's *Wealth of Nations* described the operation of a free market system.

5. The United States economy is based primarily on free market principles. We believe a free market economy is most efficient: both in terms of technical efficiency and allocative efficiency.

6. However a community chooses to answer the three economic questions, it will suffer opportunity costs. Opportunity costs are the sacrifice of other choices that might have been selected. Economics helps us compare the benefits of each choice with its costs.

7. Graphs are useful in economics. The graph of production possibilities illustrates both opportunity costs and the problem of scarce resources.

TERMS TO REMEMBER

free goods: goods in such abundance that they have no price.

economic problem: the problem of scarce resources and unlimited wants; it is faced by every society.

land: the original and nonreproducible gifts of nature.

labor: the purposeful activity of human beings.

capital: produced means of production; tools and machines are examples.

management or **entrepreneurial ability:** the creative combination of other resources toward some desired goal.

technical efficiency: using resources to produce maximum possible output with existing technology.

allocative efficiency: using resources to produce

goods and services the people want.

opportunity costs: the goods and services we give up when we choose to use resources in one way rather than another.

economic model: a simplified view of reality for explaining an economic problem.

production possibilities curve: a graph showing the maximum quantities of output a society can produce, given its limited resources and level of technology.

price inflation: a general increase in prices; a rise in some prices that is not offset by a fall in other prices.

marginal analysis: a way of making decisions based on comparing the costs and benefits of producing or acquiring one more unit of something.

direct relationship: for two values, when one increases, the other increases; when one decreases, the other decreases.

inverse relationship: for two values, when one increases, the other decreases.

TOPICS FOR DISCUSSION

1. The following terms were used frequently in this chapter. They are not strictly economic terms but are used in everyday conversation. Explain how they are involved in the study of economics.

   law or principle
   priorities and rationing
   costs and benefits
   efficiency and model

2. Make sure you understand the three questions that any economic society must decide.

3. A famous soprano can earn $100 an hour recording operatic arias. However, she has a taste for home-grown tomatoes and spends many hours cultivating her own garden when she could be performing. How would you determine the cost of her tomatoes?

4. Use a production possibilities curve to illustrate limited time for study. Suppose you must prepare lessons in mathematics and Spanish, and you have only ten hours to work. If you devote the entire time to mathematics, you can work 50 problems. If you devote the entire time to Spanish, you can translate 25 pages. Other possibilities are:

Spanish (in pages)	0	8	15	20	25
Mathematics (problems)	50	45	40	25	0

Construct a production possibilities curve using these quantities. Label the horizontal axis *Spanish* and the vertical axis *Mathematics,* and graph the appropriate quantities. (Remember to move along the horizontal axis first, then up the vertical axis.)

Is your curve bowed out in the center? What is the opportunity cost of the first 8 pages of translation? the first 25 problems? What is the maximum total work you could accomplish in the limited time? Based on your experience, can you make a reasonable decision how to allocate your time? If you need a good grade in Spanish to pass the course, will this influence your decision?

Suppose you receive a gift of an electronic calculator. Your production possibilities will increase as shown below:

Spanish	0	8	15	20	25
Mathematics	75	70	65	40	0

Show your new production possibilities curve on the same graph. You have experienced technological progress!

5. Many women are taking jobs outside the home. Their choices involve marginal decisions. They must compare the benefits with the costs of their new jobs. Some benefits and costs are listed below. Can you add others?

Benefits	Costs
salary	income taxes
opportunities for advancement	transportation costs
intellectual stimulation	home-cleaning costs
new social contacts	loss of social contacts
	loss of time for cultural or physical development

What social and technological changes in recent years have changed the nature of benefits and costs? What personal changes may have changed the relationships between benefits and costs for particular individuals?

6. *(Answers to Government Expenditures)* Ratios are as follows: Education—3, 1.25, 1.5; Transportation—2, .75, 3.5; Recreation—1.33, .5, 2.4. The community should choose the school, the driver-

training course, the highway, the bus service, and the pool. The gymnasium and the stadium are also worthwhile. The rapid-transit service and the golf course are definitely not recommended.

SUGGESTED READINGS

"Americans Change: How Demographic Shifts Affect the Economy," *Business Week,* February 20, 1978, p. 64.

Cameron, Juan and Kirkland, Richard I., Jr., "Five Burdens that Make a Rich U.S. Feel Poor," *Fortune,* January 14, 1980, p. 72.

"Earth's Creeping Deserts," *Time,* September 2, 1977, p. 58.

Feldstein, Martin, "Transition to——?" *Across the Board,* March 1981, p. 62.

"A Fillibuster Ends but Not the Gar War," *Time,* October 17, 1977, p. 10.

Friedman, Milton, and Friedman, Rose, "The Tide is Turning," in *The United States in the 1980s,* Peter Duignan and Alvin Rabushka, eds., Stanford University: Hoover Institution, 1980, p. 3.

Guzzardi, Walter, Jr., "Judges Discover the World of Economics," *Fortune,* May 21, 1979, p. 58.

"Is America Running Out of Water?" *Newsweek,* February 23, 1981, p. 26.

Johnson, Paul, "Has Capitalism a Future?" *Across the Board,* February 1980, pp. 27–33.

Madden, Carl, "2008," *Across the Board,* October 1976, p. 15.

"Mining the Wealth of the Ocean Deep," *New York Times Magazine,* July 17, 1977, p. 14.

Nickel, Herman, "The Corporation Haters," *Fortune,* June 16, 1980, p. 126

Okun, Arthur M., "Our Blend of Democracy and Capitalism," *Across the Board,* March 1979, pp. 69–76.

Rogers, James T., "Vacuuming the Sea Bottom," *Across the Board,* December 1980, p. 38.

"Russia: Special Section," *U.S. News and World Report,* October 24, 1977, p. 42.

"The Shrinking Standard of Living," *Business Week,* January 28, 1980, p. 72.

Stein, Herbert, "The Never-Never Land of Pain-Free Solutions," *Fortune,* December 31, 1979, p. 72.

Thurow, Lester, *The Zero-Sum Society,* New York: Basic Books, 1980, Chapters 1 and 8.

or The Customer
Is Always Right

Demand

Tools for Study

Learning Objectives

After reading this chapter, you will be able to:

1. list the characteristics of competition.
2. explain and illustrate the law of demand.
3. list factors affecting demand and illustrate their effects.
4. explain why consumers respond differently to price changes for different goods.

Issues Covered

How does price elasticity of demand affect a firm's revenue from sales?

How do firms use price elasticity to set price?

Why is there a tax on cigarettes?

People "in the ordinary business of life" were the subject of early investigations into the economic environment. Production of goods for exchange, motivation of suppliers, and business adjustments to changing market conditions became the subject matter of economics as a *social science*.

THE INVISIBLE HAND

The economist Adam Smith had great respect for the market system. He saw how free markets could quickly answer the question *What?* based on the wants of consumers. According to Smith, the free market would work to enhance the "sacred rights" of all people. He was sure that, if left to itself to work according to its natural laws, the market system would ensure these rights. An important right was the right to enjoy the highest level of life possible within the capacity of the community's productive resources and technology.

Smith based his beliefs on a process he called the "invisible hand." His reasoning was as follows: Each individual should be left to pursue his or her own self-interest in the marketplace without government interference. The pursuit of self-interest would yield the greatest possible wealth for both the individual and society as a whole. The individual would be led, as if by an "invisible hand," to decisions which would yield the maximum benefit to all.

For example, suppose Consumer A wants something that Consumer B produces. In exchange for Consumer B's product, Consumer A must produce something Consumer B wants. Both individuals benefit from the exchange because they are giving up something of less value to themselves than what they receive in return. By pursuing their own self-interest, they have increased their total welfare. Neither loses; both gain.

Indeed, Smith had a certain reverence for the system that he believed would promote the essential dignity of all people!

COMPETITION IN THE MARKET

If Adam Smith's ideal market is to work, there must be *competition* in the marketplace. Four conditions must be met if there is to be perfect competition:

1. There must first be many buyers and sellers, all seeking their own advantage. Buyers and sellers must be small in relation to the size of the market, so that no one can affect price by buying more or less or by offering more or less for sale. Each must be a *price taker*.
2. There must be perfect knowledge of selling conditions throughout the market.
3. There must be ease of mobility to the most favorable market for buying or selling. Buyers must be able to seek the lowest prices and sellers the highest prices for their goods.
4. Finally, the products of one manufacturer must be just like those of all others in the industry. Products must be identical so that buyers will refuse to pay a premium price for the output of a particular seller. Autos, soft drinks, and cigarettes, for example, must have no real or apparent differences making one seller's output more desirable than another's.

It is a little like the gentleman who decided to play a joke on the pet-shop operator. He asked to purchase a canary, and while the salesclerk was ringing up the sale, he chatted about what a nice pet the bird would be. The customer smiled and explained that he really didn't need a pet, already owning a nice cat. But occasionally the cat liked to have a little fun and exercise and so . . . . The clerk drew back in indignation, ordering the customer from the premises. Chuckling inwardly at the success of his joke, the customer headed for the door where an elderly lady had been listening to the entire conversation. She tugged at his sleeve to get his attention and whispered, ''They're fifty cents cheaper down the street.'' (Test yourself: Explain how this story illustrates the four characteristics of a competitive market.)*

BUILDING A MARKET MODEL

The study of how individual markets work is called **microeconomics.** Consumers enter a market to purchase goods and services. Business firms respond by producing the goods and services consumers want. Microeconomics, therefore, is the study of the relationship between consumer wants and producer response. The amount consumers would be willing and able to buy at various prices is called *demand*. The amount business firms would be willing and able to sell at various prices is called *supply*. Combining demand and supply yields a *model* of the market for a particular good or service. In this chapter we will focus on the elements significant to consumer demand. In the next we will focus on supply and show how a market model may be used to determine the actual price and quantity sold of a good or service.

Market Demand

The basis for consumer demand is *tastes* or preferences and *income* or ability to buy. An individual

---

* other sellers, information about prices, buyer's ability to walk down the street, and identical canaries

Table 2.1 Hypothetical Demand Schedules for Tape Cassettes (per month).

Price	Consumer A's Demand	Consumer B's Demand	Sum of Consumer Demands = A + B + . . . + n = Market Demand
$8	3	6	13,000
7	4	7	17,000
6	5	8	21,000
5	6	9	25,000
4	8	10	29,000
3	10	12	33,000

consumer's own choices are shown in his or her **demand schedule** for a particular good or service. The choices of all consumers together combine to form market demand schedules.

Table 2.1 gives demand schedules for two hypothetical consumers and for all consumers taken together in the market for tape cassettes. The market demand schedule shows the total quantity which all consumers would purchase at any given price over a certain period of time. The schedules indicate that at lower prices the quantity demanded by Consumers A and B and by all consumers taken together would be greater.

Figure 2.1a (see page 28) is a graph of Consumer A's demand schedule. It shows that Consumer A would buy 3 tape cassettes for a price of $8. A tenth cassette would be worth only $3 to Consumer A. He or she would buy a total of 10 cassettes only if the price is $3. Figure 2.1b is a graph of Consumer B's demand schedule. Consumer B's tastes or income would permit him or her to purchase more tapes at every price.

Figure 2.1c is a graph of market demand. The market demand curve shows the amounts that all consumers in the market would be willing and able to purchase at various prices. Consumers would purchase a total of 13,000 tape cassettes per month if the price were to be $8, but would buy a total of 33,000 at a price of $3. (Interestingly, it is possible to show on Figure 2.1c the total expenditure or total revenue from the sale of tapes at any price by

forming a rectangle whose northeast corner touches the demand curve. Can you explain why?)*

The Law of Demand

Consumer demand helps answer the question *What?*. An individual consumer demand curve shows the quantity of a good or service the consumer would buy at various prices. A consumer would normally be willing to pay a high price to acquire one unit, and perhaps even the first few units, of a good or service. Eventually, however, more units will not be as useful as the first. This means that a consumer would buy more units only if price is lower.

A consumer's demand for tape cassettes and pizzas and all other goods and services can be shown to be *inversely related* to price. At high prices fewer units would be purchased. At low prices more units would be bought. The inverse relationship between price and quantity demanded is known as the **law of demand.**

* Total revenue is price times quantity. The area of a rectangle is height times base. A rectangle formed under the demand curve has price for its height and quantity for its base. Therefore, the area of the rectangle = height × base = price × quantity = total revenue.

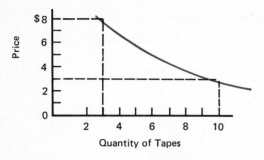

a) Consumer A's Demand

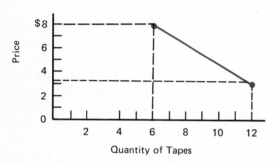

b) Consumer B's Demand

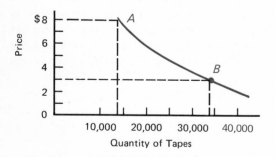

c) Market Demand

Figure 2.1   The Demand for Tape Cassettes.

ELASTICITY OF DEMAND

Because the usefulness of some goods diminishes quickly, their demand curves slope downward rather sharply as we acquire more units during a particular period of time. Salt is an example of a good of which the first unit bought is useful, even essential. But further purchases in any one time period could become a nuisance! Consumers would not buy much more salt even if price falls drastically, and they would not buy much less if price rises.

Economists describe demand for such goods as *price inelastic:* quantity demanded is not very responsive to price changes. Necessities with few substitutes generally have relatively inelastic demand. These are items that we must buy in some certain quantity, but we find little use for more than that quantity.

Demand for many other goods is *price elastic:* quantity demanded is quite responsive to price changes. Luxuries and goods with many substitutes often have relatively elastic demand. We will decide to buy or not depending on their prices. Can you think of examples of goods or services with inelastic and elastic demand? For instance, how would you respond to changes in the price of dental services, meat, doughnuts, airline tickets, wallpaper, and gasoline?

Elasticity of demand will affect total expenditure for a good. If market demand is relatively elastic, consumers will respond significantly to price changes. A price rise will cause a substantial drop in sales, and revenue from sales will fall. On the other hand, a price reduction will cause a substantial increase in sales, and revenue from sales will increase. Henry Ford discovered this result in the early days of the automobile industry. Ford found he could increase total revenue from sales by *reducing* auto prices. (Can you explain this result in terms of elasticity?)

If market demand is inelastic, consumers will not respond very much to price changes. They will buy roughly the same amount regardless of price, so that a price increase will increase sales revenues and a price reduction will reduce sales revenues. Arab oil-producing nations understand this result well. During the 1970s, they discovered they could increase total revenue from sales by *increasing* oil prices. (Explain this result in terms of elasticity.)

DETERMINANTS OF ELASTICITY

Price elasticity of demand differs among types of goods and services. Analysts have concluded that elasticity of demand for a particular good depends on: *(1) the availability of substitutes; (2) the importance of the item in the consumer's budget; and (3) the time it takes to develop a substitute.*

When there are many substitutes, a consumer can change spending plans freely. A small increase in the price of a good will cause a sharp drop in sales, as consumers substitute similar but lower-priced goods. A small decrease in price will cause a large increase in sales, as consumers purchase the cheaper good rather than its higher-priced substitutes. Goods with many substitutes generally have elastic demand.

When purchasing the good requires a large portion of a consumer's budget, purchases will respond readily to changes in price. If the good is a small item in a consumer's budget or if its price is very low, consumers will not change their spending plans very much. Hence, a large item will generally have elastic demand; a small item, inelastic demand.

Finally, demand is generally more elastic over long periods of time. Over time, consumers can find substitutes to replace goods whose prices have risen, and consumers can find new ways to use goods whose prices have fallen. After years of struggling to adjust to higher gasoline prices during the 1970s, quantity demanded finally began to drop in 1979–80. (In 1981 consumers faced a different sort of budget crisis when a bad crop year pushed up the price of peanut butter. For peanut butter lovers who will accept no substitute, the time required for responding to the higher price may be long indeed!)

Of course, different consumers may have different elasticities of demand for the same good. A consumer's elasticity of demand depends on whether he or she considers the good a necessity (few substitutes) and how important the good is in the consumer's own budget.

Demand Versus Quantity Demanded

A demand curve shows the quantities consumers would be willing and able to purchase at various prices. A change in the price of a good would result in a change in the **quantity demanded.** A change in quantity demanded is reflected on the graph as a movement along the demand curve. In Figure 2.1c, a change in price from $8 to $3 would result in a movement along the demand curve from point *A* to point *B*. The change in quantity demanded is from 13,000 units to 33,000 units.

However, factors other than price affect consumers' decisions to buy. Other factors affecting consumer choices must be held constant while drawing a single demand curve. *Changing the other factors that affect consumer purchases will cause changes in demand and shifts in* **market demand** *curves.*

Determinants of Demand

Some other factors that affect demand are: (1) income of buyers; (2) number of buyers in the market; (3) consumer tastes; (4) prices of related goods; and (5) expected future price changes. How do these other factors affect a market demand curve?

Suppose that Consumer A's income doubles. He or she might now be willing to buy twice as many tape cassettes at every price level as before. The old and new demand schedules are shown in Table 2.2. If we graph both schedules on Figure 2.2, we see that the new demand curve lies to the right of the old one. There has been a *change in demand.* In this case, there has been an *increase in demand,* as shown by a shift of the demand curve to the right. At each and every price, Consumer A would buy more than before. A decrease in demand (if Consumer A's income had been cut in half, for instance) might mean that, at each and every price, Consumer A would buy less than before. A *decrease in demand* would be shown by a shift of the demand curve to the left. (Pencil in a decrease in demand on Figure 2.2.)

We have seen that a change in quantity demanded refers to a movement along the demand curve. It is brought about by a change in the price of the good. A change in demand refers to a shift of the entire demand curve to a new position. It is brought about by a change in a factor other than the price of the good. An increase in demand shifts the curve to the right, a decrease to the left. (Test yourself: In 1981 certain auto manufacturers offered rebates in the hope of increasing car sales. Would rebates cause a change in quantity demanded or a change in demand?*)

The other factors which affect demand have similar results. If the number of buyers in the mar-

Table 2.2   Consumer A's Demand Schedule for Tape Cassettes (per month).

Price	Old Demand Schedule	New Demand Schedule
$8	3	6
7	4	8
6	5	10
5	6	12
4	8	16
3	10	20

ket should increase, for example, we can expect the demand for the good to increase. Merchants in a small town are generally pleased when a new highway is built, bringing more tourists and travelers into their shops and shifting demand curves to the right.

A change in consumer tastes also affects demand. Suppose that consumers decide that reading or going to the movies is a better way to spend their leisure time than listening to tape cassettes.

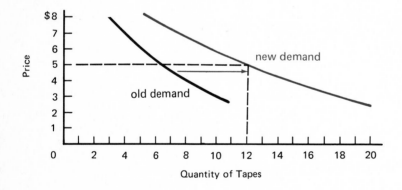

Figure 2.2   Change in Demand.
An increase in income causes an increase in Consumer A's demand for tape cassettes. An increase in demand is shown by a shift of the entire demand curve to the right. At a price of $5 the consumer will now be willing to purchase 12 tape cassettes.

* a change in quantity demanded

Demand for tape cassettes would decrease. (On the other hand, the demand for books or movie tickets would increase.)

The fourth factor affecting demand is prices of related goods. Some goods are **substitutes** in consumption. Substitutes are goods which are similar to or can be used in place of one another—pizza and hamburgers, cars and mass transportation, rock concerts and sporting events. An increase in the price of one good would reduce *quantity demanded*. Purchasing less of this good would cause an *increase in demand* for its substitute. What would you expect to happen to the demand for butter if the price of margarine should increase?

Some goods are complementary in consumption. **Complementary goods** are goods that "go together"—cars and gasoline, tape recorders and cassettes, beer and pretzels. If the price of tape recorders should rise, we might expect the demand for tape cassettes to fall (shift to the left).

Finally, expected future price changes affect demand. Expected price increases encourage consumers to "buy now and beat the price rise." Expected price reductions discourage current purchases. Lately, U.S. consumers have grown painfully familiar with the former kind of expectations, and many market demand curves have shifted to the right. (Test yourself: What would you expect to happen to the market demand curve for air travel during the week before announced rate reductions are scheduled to take effect?*)

* shift to the left

Self-Check

1. **Perfect competition does *not* depend on:**
   a. a large number of buyers and sellers.
   b. information about market conditions.
   c. distinguishing characteristics of the product.
   d. ease of movement among markets.
   e. small size of firms relative to size of the market.

2. **For most goods and services:**
   a. quantity demanded is low at low prices.
   b. quantity demanded is high at high prices.
   c. demand is based on costs of production.
   d. quantity demanded is inversely related to price.
   e. quantity demanded is directly related to price.

3. **Consumer A's demand for pizza is price inelastic. This means that A:**
   a. would prefer hamburger to pizza.
   b. would buy all the pizza she or he can afford.
   c. would not buy pizza if its price increases.
   d. would buy roughly the same amount regardless of price.
   e. would respond significantly to price changes for pizza.

4. **Which of the following is an example of a change in quantity demanded?**
   a. Consumer tastes shift away from Kentucky Fried Chicken and toward Mexican dinners.
   b. All consumers who want CB radios already have them.
   c. A major discount firm conducts a "One-Third Off Sale."
   d. High gasoline prices reduce automobile sales.
   e. Unemployed auto workers must reduce their own living standards.

5. **Most consumers probably have inelastic demand for:**
   a. oranges
   b. gasoline
   c. college textbooks
   d. filet mignon
   e. magazines

6. **Which of the following pairs does not belong with the others?**
   a. paper and pen
   b. turkey and liverwurst
   c. hammer and nails
   d. bread and jam
   e. shoes and stockings

Theory in Practice

Industrial corporations in the United States devote much effort to estimating elasticity of demand for their products. A firm's revenue from sales depends on its pricing policy and on the consumers' responsiveness to price.

Elasticity of demand is defined as percent change in quantity demanded relative to percent change in price. If $\%\Delta Q_d$ is greater than $\%\Delta P$, we say that demand is elastic; consumers respond significantly to price change. If $\%\Delta Q_d$ is less than $\%\Delta P$, we say demand is inelastic; consumers respond only slightly to price change. If $\%\Delta Q_d$ is

equal to $\%\Delta P$, we say that elasticity of demand is unity.

Differences in elasticity may be reflected by differences in the shapes of demand curves. Look at Figure 2.3a. On Figure 2.3a a small percentage increase in price (from $1.00 to $1.10) causes quantity demanded to fall by one-half. Demand is highly elastic over this range of the demand curve. Now look at Figure 2.3b. On Figure 2.3b a large percentage increase in price (from $1.00 to $10.00) causes quantity demanded to fall only slightly. Demand is highly inelastic over this

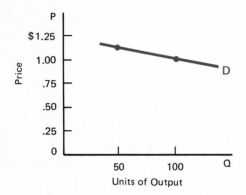

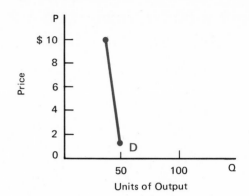

Figure 2.3a   An Elastic Demand Curve.

Figure 2.3b   An Inelastic Demand Curve.

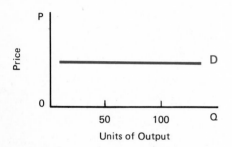

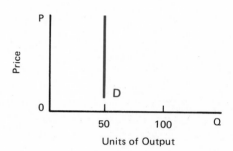

Figure 2.4a   Infinitely Elastic Demand.

Figure 2.4b   Perfectly Inelastic Demand.

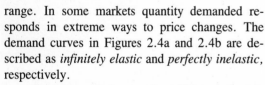

range. In some markets quantity demanded responds in extreme ways to price changes. The demand curves in Figures 2.4a and 2.4b are described as *infinitely elastic* and *perfectly inelastic,* respectively.

Most demand curves reflect different elasticities at different price levels. The demand curve in Figure 2.5 is called a linear demand curve because its slope is constant over its entire length. Price elasticity is computed according to the following fraction: e_d = percentage change in quantity demanded/percentage change in price =

$$\%\Delta Q_d / \%\Delta P$$

Both numerator and denominator are in terms of percentage change.

To calculate a percentage change it is necessary to measure the actual change and compare it

with a total, or base, value. Since the total value changes, it is appropriate to use as base the average of the two values before and after the change. Thus, a price reduction from \$500 to \$400 represents an actual change of $P_1 - P_2 = \$500 - 400 = \$100$; in percentage terms a \$100 price reduction is $\%\Delta P = (P_1 - P_2)/1/2(P_1 + P_2) = 500 - 400/1/2(500 + 400) = 100/450 = .22 = 22$ percent. According to Figure 2.5 a price reduction of \$100 causes quantity demanded to increase from zero to 100 units. In percentage terms the change in quantity is $\%\Delta Q_d = (Q_1 - Q_2)/1/2(Q_1 + Q_2) = 0 - 100/1/2(0 + 100) = -100/50 = -2.00 = -200$ percent. This means that elasticity of demand is

$$e_d = \%\Delta Q_d / \%\Delta P = -200/22 = -9.09$$

along this segment of the demand curve. This

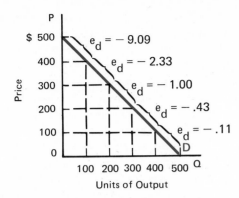

Figure 2.5 Computing Elasticity of Demand.

$$e_d = \frac{\%\Delta Q}{\%\Delta P} = \frac{Q_1 - Q_2/\frac{1}{2}(Q_1 + Q_2)}{P_1 - P_2/\frac{1}{2}(P_1 + P_2)}$$

value has been written alongside the linear demand curve in Figure 2.5.

Other elasticity computations have been performed similarly and the results added to the figure. We have performed the computations as if price is to be reduced and quantity increased, but the results would be identical if we reversed the direction of price and quantity.

Notice that all the elasticity values have a negative sign. Demand elasticity is almost always negative since price reductions generally cause quantity demanded to increase. The result is opposite signs for the numerator and denominator of the elasticity fraction. Likewise, a price increase generally causes quantity demand to fall, and the fraction is negative. However, the magnitude of elasticity is more significant to business planners than the sign, so we will generally omit the minus sign and just remember that demand elasticity is negative.

Notice also that price elasticity varies along the demand curve from a high (negative) value at high prices to a low (negative) value at low prices. Along one very small segment of the demand curve, price elasticity is precisely equal to one; that is, percentage change in quantity is precisely equal to percentage change in price.

Variations in elasticity affect the level of total revenue from sales. Figure 2.5 has been reproduced as Figure 2.6a to illustrate the effect of price changes on total revenue under different elasticity conditions. Figure 2.6b shows total revenue at various price and quantity levels. The horizontal axis of Figure 2.6b corresponds to that of Figure 2.6a and represents quantity sold at various price levels. The vertical axis represents total revenue, calculated by multiplying price times quantity at various points on the demand curve:

$$\text{Total Revenue} = TR = P \times Q.$$

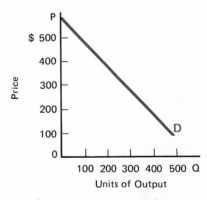

Figure 2.6a   A Linear Demand Curve.

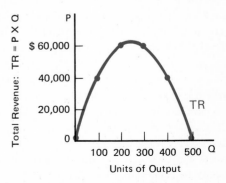

Figure 2.6b   Total Revenue Associated with Various Points on a Linear Demand Curve.

Look first at the demand curve and a price of $500 where zero units are sold; then look at a price of $0 where 500 units are sold. Total revenue associated with both points is zero, plotted accordingly on Figure 2.6b. Now select other points on the demand curve, calculate total revenue, and plot the point: at P = $400, Q = 100, and TR = $400 × 100 = $40,000; at P = $300, Q = 200, and TR = $60,000; at P = $200, Q = 300, and TR = $60,000; at P = $100, Q = 400, and TR = $40,000.

The total revenue curve in Figure 2.6b is typical of TR curves associated with linear demand curves. All such TR curves would have maximum total revenue associated with price and quantity combinations in the midrange, with total revenue declining toward zero outside that range. Compare the TR curve with elasticity data calculated previously and note that maximum total revenue is associated with price elasticity equal to one: $e_d = 1$. Along a very small segment of the demand curve, percentage changes in price cause equal percentage changes in quantity demanded, so that total revenue neither rises nor falls.

The result is different along other segments of the demand curve. To see why, begin high on the demand curve where we found price elasticity to be $e_d = 9.09$. Percentage price reductions cause substantially greater gains in quantity demanded, and total revenue increases. Similarly, price increases would cause substantially greater decreases in sales with the opposite result. The behavior of total revenue along this segment of demand reflects the relatively greater responsiveness of quantity demanded to price changes.

Now look at the lower segment of demand where $e_d = .11$. Percentage price reductions cause only slight gains in quantity demanded, and total revenue falls. Price increases would cause only slight losses in sales so that total revenue increases. This time, the behavior of total revenue reflects the relatively smaller responsiveness of quantity demanded to price changes.

These results suggest certain conclusions. If a firm has the power to set its own price (as in some monopolies), it might seek a revenue-maximizing price and quantity combination at the point on its demand curve where $e_d = 1$. Reducing price to that level would cause greater percentage changes in quantity demanded and increase TR; or raising price to that level would cause smaller losses in sales. Most firms do not have the power to set price, of course. In fact, we have asssumed in this chapter that competition exists in the market so that no firm can affect price. (We will relax that assumption in Chapter 4.) Moreover, for many firms maximum revenue is not itself an appropriate goal. Firms must consider production costs)the subject of Chapter 3) and the profit remaining after all costs are paid. This makes maximum profit the more appropriate goal. We will have more to say about this concept later.

USING ELASTICITY TO SET PRICES

Whereas competitive firms normally lack the power to set price, there are certain circumstances where a firm can separate its markets and vary price according to elasticity in the separate markets. Imagine a typical clothing retailer who sells in consumer markets in different parts of town. Two hundred units are sold a day at a unit price of $25 for total revenue of TR = P × Q = $25 × 200 = $5000. The retailer suspects that consumers differ in the different neighborhoods with respect to tastes, incomes, portion of income spent for clothing, and willingness to accept substitutes for the product. In fact, consumer demand in one neighborhood might be described as highly inelastic: consumers will continue to buy substantially the same quantities regardless of price so that elasticity at a price of $25 is only $e_d = .5$. Consumer demand in the other neighborhood is more elastic: consumers respond significantly to price change so that elasticity at a price of $25 is 1.5.

Demand curves representing the two neigh-

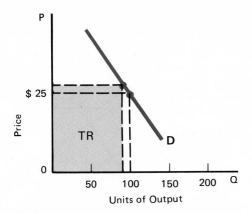

Figure 2.7a Price Discrimination; Market for Clothing (1).

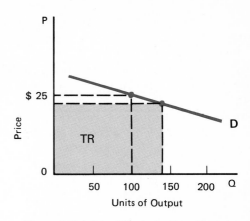

Figure 2.7b Price Discrimination; Market for Clothing (2).

borhoods are shown in Figure 2.7a and b. For simplicity, we have assumed that half of daily sales is made in each market at the $25 price, for equal revenues of $2500 to the retailer.

Now let us vary price in the two neighborhoods and calculate the effect on total revenue. In the first market, price is below the level of maximum total revenue. Increasing price by 10% should reduce quantity demanded by only 5%. (Since $e_d = \%\Delta Q_d/\%\Delta P$, $\%\Delta Q_d = e_d(\%\Delta P)$ $= -.5(.10) = -.05 = -5$ percent.) With price equal to 1.1($25) and quantity demanded equal to .95(100), total revenue in this market now becomes, TR = P × Q = 1.1($25) × .95(100) = $2612.50.

In the second market, price is above the level of maximum total revenue. Reducing price by 10% should increase quantity demanded by $e_d(\%\Delta P)$ $= -1.5(-.10) = .15 = 15$ percent. With price equal to .9($25) and quantity demanded 1.15(100), total revenue in this market now becomes TR = P × Q = .9($25) × 1.15(100) = $2587.50.

The shaded rectangles in Figures 2.7a and b represent the greater total revenue which results from separating markets and setting price according to elasticity. The retailer's new pricing policy

earns total revenues of $2612.50 + 2587.50 = $5200 daily for an increase of $200. Equal percentage changes in price cause quantity demanded in the first market to fall by less than quantity demanded increases in the second, and total sales increase to 210 units.

This practice is known as *price discrimination*. Frequently, retailers practice price discrimination, reducing price and accepting losses on some items and increasing price for others. The pricing decision is based on differences in price elasticity in the markets for various goods.

Another form of price discrimination takes place when firms separate consumers even more finely and set different prices for different segments of the demand curve. Differential pricing is common for attendance at cultural and sporting events. The basis for separating consumers may be location of the seats or the age or sex of the consumer!

Many of the nation's airlines have been experimenting with price changes as a means of increasing total revenues. In the late 1970s airlines were faced with rising costs for labor, fuel, and capital equipment. Revenues were not increasing fast enough to pay a satisfactory return on funds invested in the industry. The decision was made to reduce fares for any passengers who were willing to give up some service; the airline hoped that enough new passengers would fly to offset the lower price each paid. Figure 2.8 shows a hypothetical market for seats on an airplane. There are 200 seats and the firm would like to "sell" its seats at prices that will produce the greatest revenue. Let 50 seats be designated "First Class" and provide passengers with plenty of comfortable leg room, champagne and lobster for dinner, and attentive stewards. Some riders will be willing to pay $100 for First Class service. Designate the remaining seats "Tourist Class" and serve passengers baked chicken at a price of $75. Total revenue is $100 × number of First Class passengers (maximum 50) plus $75 × number of Tourist Class passengers (maximum 150), for a maximum of $16,250.

Notice that total revenue is represented by the shaded rectangles under the curve in Figure 2.8. Total revenue is price times quantity sold, shown by the height and width of the two rectangles.

With less than the expected number of passengers, revenue will be much lower. In fact, if demand is relatively inelastic over this price range, only a certain number of tickets will be sold regardless of the price difference in fares. In Figure 2.9 only 30 First Class and 100 Tourist passengers yield total revenue of ($100 × 30) + ($75 × 100) = $10,500. Notice the smaller shaded area for 130 seats.

Consider the situation if demand is relatively elastic at lower prices. Let the regularly scheduled passengers fly at the stated rates and then open the remaining seats to "No Frills" passengers at a price of only $50. "No Frills" passengers are unceremoniously dispatched to the rear of the plane and served no food or drink at all. If all remaining seats are filled at the lowest rate, revenue increases by $50 × 70 = $3,500, for a total of $10,500 + 3,500 = $14,000. Unless the firm can fill its planes with First Class and Tourist passengers, it would seem to be an advantage to provide "No Frills" tickets. Total revenue would increase by the added rectangle in Figure 2.9.

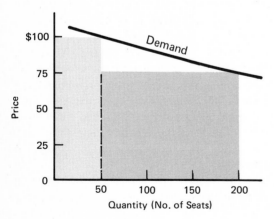

Figure 2.8 Airline Revenues with "First Class" and "Tourist" Fares.
The firm hopes its demand curve is as shown above. Maximum total revenue is the area of the two rectangles.

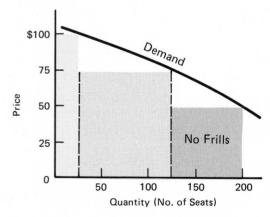

Figure 2.9 Airline Revenues with "No Frills" Passengers.
By offering lower fares the firm takes advantage of more elastic demand at low prices.

The experiment in demand elasticity turned out well for some firms. The results seemed to show that demand for flights is relatively inelastic at high prices and elastic at low prices. Regular customers must travel from place to place regardless of price, and continued to ride at the usual rates. But many new passengers decided to take a trip just because air fares were reduced. (Why? Recall the factors that determine elasticity.) The airlines were able to fill all their seats with passengers paying various rates, and revenues increased.

Experiments with elasticity may be profitable!

WHY IS THERE A TAX ON CIGARETTES?

Government considers elasticity of demand when it attempts to raise money through an excise tax on a consumer good. Generally the taxed item should have inelastic demand. Otherwise, consumers will not buy at the higher price and the government will collect no tax!

How would you describe the elasticity of demand for cigarettes? Are smokers likely to respond to price changes by buying either substantially more or fewer cigarettes?

It is generally believed that the demand for cigarettes is fairly inelastic. The demand curve in Figure 2.10 is drawn on the assumption that smokers will not respond very much to price changes. In Figure 2.10 equilibrium price is $4 per carton and equilibrium quantity is 4,000 cartons. Notice the rectangle representing total expenditure at $4: total expenditure = quantity sold × market price = 4,000 × $4 = $16,000.

Suppose the government imposes a tax which adds $1 per carton to price. At the new price of $5, quantity demanded is 3,500 cartons. Notice the rectangle representing total expenditures: 3,500 × $5 = $17,500. Mark off the rectangle that represents government receipts from the tax: government receipts = quantity sold × tax = 3,500 × $1 = $3,500.

With the new excise tax, total revenue going to producers has dropped slightly. Producers still receive $4 per carton, but sell only 3,500 rather than 4,000 cartons, for revenue of 3,500 × $4 = $14,000. While total expenditure increased by $1,500 (from $16,000 to $17,500) when price was increased, producers' share of revenue fell from $16,000 to $14,000. Mark off the rectangle representing producers' old revenue and the rectangle representing *total expenditure*.

(Test yourself: Compare government receipts from a cigarette tax with that from a tax on a good with more elastic demand, like cheese. How might the demand curve for cheese differ from the demand curve for cigarettes? How would you describe the government receipts rectangle?*)

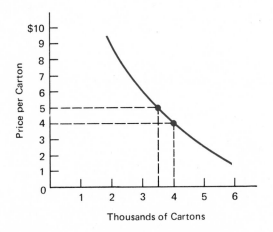

Figure 2.10   A Hypothetical Demand Curve for Cigarettes.
A tax adds $1 to the price of a carton of cigarettes. Because demand is fairly inelastic, smokers do not cut back their purchases very much.

---

* If demand for cheese is relatively elastic, the higher price will cause a proportionally greater decrease in quantity demanded. The result will be smaller total expenditures for cheese and reduced tax revenues for government.

SUMMARY

1. Adam Smith developed the body of theory that explains economic activity under competition. When markets are free and competitive, society will achieve the largest output from its limited resources.
2. Perfect competition requires a) many small buyers and sellers; b) perfect knowledge of market conditions; c) ease of mobility to favored locations; and d) products that are identical.
3. The free market system is based on the preferences of consumers who evaluate the usefulness of goods and services. The result is many consumer demand schedules that are added together to form market demand. Demand curves slope downward because more units will be bought only at lower prices.
4. Elasticity of demand measures the responsiveness of consumers to price changes. Elasticity depends on the availability of substitutes, the importance of the item in the consumer's budget, and the time it takes to develop a substitute.
5. Changes in income, tastes, number of buyers, prices of related goods, and expectations of price changes cause shifts in market demand.
6. Maximum total revenue occurs at the price and quantity on the demand curve where $e_d = 1$. A revenue-maximizing firm might observe the following pricing rule: If $e_d > 1$, reduce price for greater total revenue; if $e_d < 1$, increase price for greater total revenue.
7. Some firms practice price discrimination in separate markets to take advantage of differences in price elasticity and increase total revenue. Government must consider elasticity of demand when it imposes a tax. Because demand for cigarettes is relatively inelastic, cigarettes are often taxed.

TERMS TO REMEMBER

microeconomics: the study of how individual economic units help answer the questions *What?*, *How?*, and *For Whom?*

the law of demand: the relationship between price and quantity demanded is inverse. As price increases, quantity demanded decreases; as price decreases, quantity demanded increases.

demand schedule: the amounts consumers are willing and able to buy at various prices.

quantity demanded: the quantity a consumer would buy at a particular price.

market demand: the quantities all consumers would buy at various prices.

substitute goods: goods which can easily be used in place of one another (hamburger or pizza). As the price of one good changes, demand for the substitute good changes in the same direction.

complementary goods: goods that are normally used together (beer and pretzels). As the price of one good changes, demand for the complementary good changes in the opposite direction.

elasticity of demand: the responsiveness of quantity demanded to changes in the price of a good.

TOPICS FOR DISCUSSION

1. Which of the following markets are likely to be most competitive? Explain your answer. Barbershops, hair stylists, T-shirts, alligator shirts, electric power, concrete.
2. What are the characteristics of a competitive market?
3. Explain why it is important to draw a demand curve for a particular period of time. Then explain how demand curves are likely to change as the period of time lengthens.
4. List substitutes and complements for each of the following items: movies, motorcycles, gold chains, wallpaper.
5. Demonstrate graphically the effect of high gasoline prices on demand in other related markets.
6. A certain auto manufacturer reduced the price of its compact model because of a bad safety record, but still sales fell. Does this result contradict the law of demand? Explain.
7. Old Reliable Air Service reduced its intercity fare from $37.50 to $35.00 and increased ticket sales

from 120 to 160 for the week. Compute Reliable's demand elasticity. Was this a wise move? Explain. Should Reliable continue to reduce price? Why or why not?

8. What circumstances must be true for price discrimination to benefit a retailer? Why?

9. What considerations might affect a city's decision to levy a sales tax? Why might the city decide to exempt food from the tax? medicine?

SUGGESTED READINGS

"The Airlines Hit a Downdraft," *Business Week,* November 5, 1979, p. 104.

"Detroit's New Sales Pitch: Is It On The Right Road?" *Business Week,* September 22, 1980, p. 78.

Gray, Ed, *Levi's,* Boston: Houghton Mifflin Co., 1979, pp. 31–34.

"The Graying of the Soft-Drink Industry," *Business Week,* May 23, 1977, p. 68.

Kiechel III, Walter, "Two Income Families Will Reshape the Consumer Markets," *Fortune,* March 10, 1980, pp. 110–14.

Linden, Fabian, "Extra! The $150 Billion Market for Luxuries," *Across the Board,* April 1981, pp. 47–49.

Linden, Fabian, "A Nation at the Pump—Who Uses all that Gas?" *Across the Board,* March 1980, pp. 68–70.

CHAPTER 3

Supply and Market Equilibrium

or the Case of the Invisible Hand

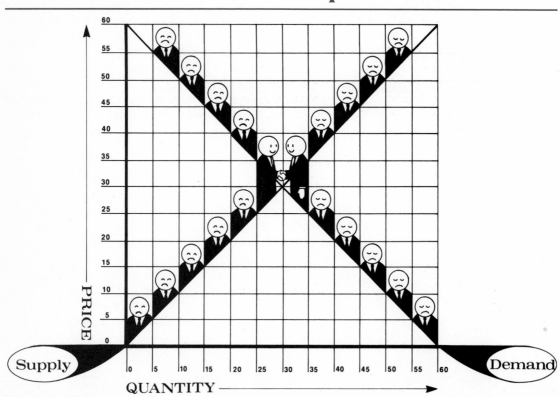

Tools for Study

Learning Objectives

After reading this chapter, you will be able to:

1. explain and illustrate the law of supply.
2. list factors affecting supply and illustrate their effects.
3. explain why producers respond differently to price changes for different goods.
4. define and illustrate market equilibrium using a market model.

Issues Covered

What are the effects of government price supports?
What are the effects of government price ceilings?

In the preceding chapter we began to construct a model of the market for a particular good. We focused on the demand side of markets and showed how consumer tastes, incomes, and other prices help determine consumer demand for a good or service. Of course, our market model is not complete without a full discussion of supply. It is the response of producers to consumer demand that ultimately provides the benefits Adam Smith described. Supply forms the other side of the market model.

MARKET SUPPLY

A producer's response to consumer demand is shown by his or her *supply schedule*. A supply schedule shows the quantity of a good or service that would be offered for sale at every price. Every firm in the industry may be expected to have a supply schedule which, together with supply schedules of all other firms, constitutes market supply. When a supply schedule is plotted on a single graph, the result is a supply curve.

Deriving a Firm's Supply Curve

Production cannot be carried on for long unless revenue from sales is sufficient to pay a firm's costs of operation. This makes an understanding of economic costs essential for understanding a firm's supply curve.

Economic Costs and Economic Profit

Economic costs are defined as the necessary payment to those who provide resources for use in production:

> workers must receive *wages* and *salaries;*
> owners of land must receive *rent;*
> owners of capital must receive *interest;*
> managers or entrepreneurs must receive *profit.*

Economists distinguish between the necessary profit required for entrepreneurship and a payment over and above the necessary profit. Some level of profit is necessary to compensate for assuming the risks of remaining in a particular business. The necessary profit is called **normal profit,** and an extra profit over and above the necessary amount is **economic profit.** Since normal profit is a necessary payment to the entrepreneurial resource, it is considered a part of production costs; thus, when we speak of costs, we will be speaking of wages and salaries, rent, interest, and normal profit. If a firm's revenue from sales should exceed total costs, we will indicate that the firm has received economic profit.

A firm will make its supply decisions on the basis of total economic costs and expected revenue from sales. Most firms have as an objective to maximize economic profit, the difference between total revenue and total costs. They will choose to produce the quantity of output that achieves this objective. *A profit-maximizing firm will expand production until production of the last unit increases total revenue by just enough to offset the increase in total costs.*

Let us illustrate this principle in more detail. Economic costs can be classified in two ways depending on their behavior relative to quantity of

output: **fixed costs** and **variable costs.** Fixed costs are the same regardless of the quantity of output produced; variable costs vary with output.

Fixed Costs

Supply decisions are made in the short run when certain of a firm's resources are fixed. Buildings and equipment are owned or leased for a particular period of time; managerial personnel have contracts for work over a particular period. Whether or not the firm supplies any output at all, charges for its fixed resources must still be paid. Expanding production above zero means that fixed charges can be spread over larger and larger quantities, resulting in a smaller average, or unit, fixed cost.

The concept of fixed costs is illustrated in Figure 3.1, using Metro Music, producer of tape

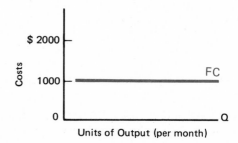

Figure 3.1a   Fixed Costs.

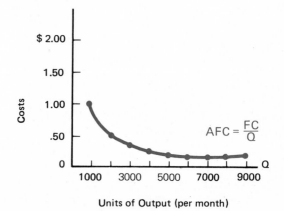

Figure 3.1b   Average Fixed Costs.

cassettes, as an example. Metro Music owns fixed resources for which charges of $1000 must be paid each month, as shown on Figure 3.1a. For any quantity of tape cassettes produced during the month, average or unit fixed costs are AFC = FC/Q, as shown in Figure 3.1b. Average fixed costs continue to diminish for larger quantities of output Q.

Variable Costs

Metro Music's production processes require use of variable resources along with the firm's existing fixed resources: labor, materials, electric power, and water. Expanding production above zero tape cassettes means that additional variable resources must be purchased. However, there is some range of total output for which additional units of output require proportionally smaller additional quantities of variable resources. The reason has to do with the design of existing plant and equipment, such that a particular range of operation uses smaller amounts of variable resources per unit of output. Over this range of operation, average variable resource requirements are low, and average variable costs are low as well. If production is expanded beyond this range of operation, variable resource requirements will increase more than proportionally, and average variable costs will increase.

The typical behavior of average variable costs is illustrated in Figure 3.2. The most efficient, lowest cost level of operation appears to be around 3000 tape cassettes per month.

When average fixed costs in Figure 3.1b are added to average variable costs in Figure 3.2, the result is average total costs, shown as Figure 3.3. If the firm is to earn economic profit, price of output must be greater than average total costs. (In fact, price must be at least as great as average variable costs if production is to be carried out at all. We will have more to say about this concept later.)

Cost Data

The data for drawing Figures 3.1, 3.2, and 3.3 are listed in Table 3.1. Column (2) lists Metro Music's constant fixed costs for all levels of output (Q) shown in Column (1). Column (3) shows how av-

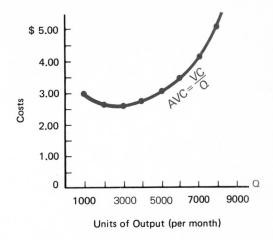

Figure 3.2   **Average Variable Costs.**

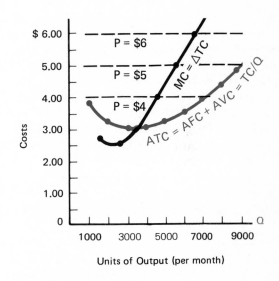

Figure 3.3   **Average Total Costs.**

erage fixed costs decline for larger quantities of output during the short run. Column (4) shows total variable costs for various levels of cassette production, and Column (5) shows average variable costs AVC = VC/Q.

Notice that average variable costs decline to a production level of 3000 units; the design of fixed

Table 3.1   Metro Music's Cost Data.

(1) Q Output per mo.	(2) FC Fixed Costs	(3) AFC Average Fixed Costs	(4) VC Variable Costs	(5) AVC Average Variable Costs	(6) TC Total Costs	(7) ATC Average Total Costs	(8) MC Marginal Costs
1000	1000	1.00	2900	2.90	3900	3.90	
							2.60
2000	1000	.50	5500	2.72	6500	3.25	
							2.50
3000	1000	.33	8000	2.67	9000	3.00	
							3.00
4000	1000	.25	11,000	2.75	12000	3.00	
							4.00
5000	1000	.20	15,000	3.00	16000	3.20	
							5.00
6000	1000	.17	20,000	3.33	21000	3.50	
							6.00
7000	1000	.14	26,000	3.71	27000	3.86	
							7.00
8000	1000	.125	33,000	4.13	34000	4.25	
							8.00
9000	1000	.11	45,000	5.00	46000	5.11	

plant and equipment appears to favor most efficient production at around 3000 units per month. Beyond production of 3000 units plant operation is less efficient, and unit variable costs rise. Total costs in Column (6) are the sums of Columns (2) and (4), and average total cost in Column (7) is ATC = TC/Q or AFC + AVC. Note the behavior of average total cost. The decline and eventual rise of ATC results from the effects of continuously declining AFC and eventually rising AVC.

Average fixed and variable costs are significant for determining a firm's economic profit (or loss) per unit of output. The difference between price and average total cost is average, or unit profit: average economic profit (or loss) = P − ATC.

Marginal Costs
Column (8) in Table 3.1 introduces a cost concept that is significant for determining the quantity of output the firm will produce in the short run: marginal costs. **Marginal costs** are defined as the change in total costs associated with producing a single additional unit of output: MC = ΔTC/ΔQ. The values in Column (8) are calculated by subtracting successive TC values in Column (6) and dividing by ΔQ = 1000 units from Column (1). Since MC is associated with *changes* in levels of production, data are entered between the lines in the table.

A marginal cost curve has been added to Figure 3.3. Notice that MC declines as the level of operation approaches the most efficient, lowest cost quantity of output at Q = 3000. Over this range MC is less than ATC and pulls ATC down. When production expands beyond the most efficient level, MC rises above ATC and begins to pull ATC up. The behavior of MC reflects the variable resource requirements associated with operation at less than or greater than the optimum design capabilities of the firm's fixed resources.

Marginal Revenue and Quantity Supplied
Now we are ready to derive Metro Music's supply curve for tape cassettes. Metro Music is a profit-maximizing firm, basing production decisions on whether or not additional production will increase or reduce the firm's economic profit. Marginal cost is significant in this decision, since marginal cost represents additional costs. Production decisions that involve greater marginal cost than additional revenue would reduce Metro Music's profit for the month and should not be undertaken. In fact, a profit-maximizing firm like Metro Music should continue to increase production as long as the marginal cost of additional units is less than their additional revenue.

We may define a firm's additional revenue from sales as its *marginal* revenue. **Marginal revenue** is the change in total revenue associated with production and sale of a single additional unit: Marginal Revenue = MR = $\Delta TR/\Delta Q$. For firms in competition, the additional revenue from increased production is price. This is because in competition price is set by the market, and no firm is large enough to affect price by its production decision. This allows us to say:

> additional revenue = marginal revenue = price and MR = P.

Comparing marginal cost with marginal revenue enables Metro Music to make its production decision. In fact, if MC > MR, Metro Music should reduce production. Marginal cost greater than marginal revenue indicates that the last unit sold adds *more* to total cost than it adds to revenue. Therefore, producing the last unit causes profit to fall. On the other hand, if MC<MR, Metro Music should increase production. Marginal cost less than marginal revenue indicates that the last unit sold adds *less* to total cost than it adds to revenue. Therefore, producing another unit would cause profit to rise. And finally, only if MC = MR is Metro Music producing the profit-maximizing quantity of output. Marginal cost equal to marginal revenue indicates that the last unit sold adds just enough revenue to cover its additional costs. This is the profit-maximizing quantity of output.

To summarize:

> If MC>MR, reduce production.
> If MC<MR, expand production.
> If MC = MR, continue to produce at this level.

Look again at Figure 3.3 and Metro Music's MC curve. Horizontal lines drawn at $4, $5, and $6 indicate possible prices for tape cassettes when tapes are sold in competitive markets. The profit-maximizing quantity at each price is indicated by the corresponding quantity shown on the MC curve where P = MR = MC. Thus, at a price of P = $4 Metro Music should produce Q = 4500 tape cassettes; when P = $5, Q = 5500; and so forth. For any other price not indicated by a horizontal line (P = $6.50, $5.75, $4.25, etc.) the profit-maximizing quantity may be read from the MC curve.

The Shut-Down Point

Reading quantity from the MC curve enables us to treat MC as Metro Music's short-run supply curve. This is not entirely true, since certain points on the MC curve would involve unacceptable losses. For instance, a price of P = $2.50 is less than ATC≈$3.12 at this level of production, and the firm would experience economic loss of $2.50 − 3.12 = − $.62 for each unit produced and sold.

Losses may be acceptable in the short run if price provides sufficient revenue to cover average variable costs.* Remember that fixed costs must be paid during the short run, regardless of whether production is profitable. To produce zero output would involve short-run losses of FC = $1000. However, production of any quantity of output for which price at least covers AVC would yield some revenue for reducing the loss associated with fixed costs. Therefore, a price of $2.50 < $3.12 is not necessarily unacceptable in the short run. The question is whether P = $2.50 does, in fact, cover Metro Music's average variable cost.

Look at Table 3.1 at Q = 2500 where MC = $2.50. Production of 2500 units per month would involve variable costs of between $2.67 and $2.72. This means that in addition to losses of FC = $1000, Metro Music would incur losses of between $.17 and $.22 per unit, attributable to average variable costs. Therefore, production should not be carried on. The lowest price for which Metro Music should produce tapes would be $2.67, a price that just covers variable costs, so that the maximum economic loss would be FC = $1000.

We might identify P = $2.67 as Metro Music's **shut-down point** in the short run. Production will be carried on only for prices greater than $2.67, with the profit-maximizing quantity identified by the MC = Supply curve. Prices greater than $3.00 would enable Metro Music to earn economic profit. Prices between $2.67 and $3.00

---

*A number of firms experienced short-run losses in 1980: Chrysler, Ford, Pan Am.

would involve economic loss, but short-run losses would not exceed FC = $1000. This makes Metro Music's supply curve its MC curve down to a minimum acceptable price at its shut-down point.

At the end of Metro Music's short run, for which certain resources are fixed, the firm would want to re-evaluate its performance in this market. If short-run losses have occurred and are expected to continue, the firm should consider discontinuing operation. Continuing losses should be an indication that resources might be better employed elsewhere. On the other hand, if short-run operation has produced economic profit, Metro Music might want to expand operations. These kinds of decisions are referred to as long-run decisions, since they require decisions to expand or contract a firm's capacity to produce. Long-run decisions involve increasing or decreasing the firm's fixed resources consistent with expectations of market conditions in the long run.

The Market Supply Curve

Metro Music's MC = Supply curve has been drawn again as Figure 3.4a. The firm will supply 3000 tapes per month at a price of $2.67. It will supply as many as 7500 tapes if price is at least $7.00.

Figure 3.4b shows Jive Town's supply. A better quality of resources or better management permits Jive Town to produce more cassettes at every price level.

Finally, Figure 3.4c shows the quantities that all firms in the industry would supply for sale at various prices. At a price of $8, 55,000 tapes would be supplied in the market as a whole. At a price of $3, only 12,000 tapes would be supplied. Data for drawing all these figures are listed in Table 3.2.

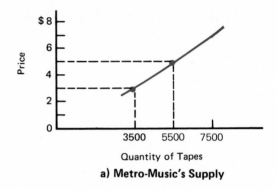

a) Metro-Music's Supply

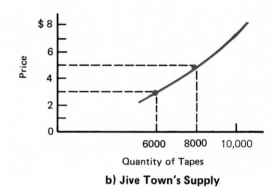

b) Jive Town's Supply

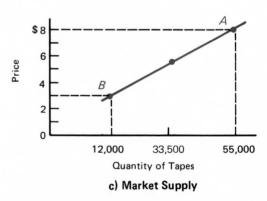

c) Market Supply

Figure 3.4   The Supply of Tape Cassettes.

The Law of Supply

We have seen that there is an inverse relationship between price and the quantity that would be demanded by consumers. We now see that there is a *direct relationship* between price and the quantity that would be supplied by producers. At low prices, few units would be supplied. At high prices, a larger quantity would be supplied. The direct relationship between price and quantity supplied is known as the law of supply.

Table 3.2 Hypothetical Supply Schedules for Tape Cassettes (per month).

Price	Metro Music's Supply	Jive Town's Supply	Sum of Firm Supply = A + B + ... + n = Market Supply
$8	8500	11,000	55,000
7	7500	10,000	45,000
6	6500	9000	35,000
5	5500	8000	25,000
4	4500	7000	15,000
3	3500	6000	12,000
2.67	3000	5500	10,000

SUPPLY VERSUS QUANTITY SUPPLIED

As with demand, it is useful to distinguish between *supply* and *quantity supplied*. A change in the price of a good would cause a change in **quantity supplied,** shown on the graph as a movement along the supply curve. In Figure 3.4c a change in price from $8 to $3 would cause a movement along the market supply curve from point *A* to point *B*. The change in supply is from 55,000 to 12,000 units.

Factors other than price also affect a firm's decision to supply goods for sale. Other factors affecting supply must be held constant while drawing a single supply curve. Changing the other factors will cause *changes in supply* and *shifts in market supply curves*.

Some other factors that affect supply are: (1) the number of firms in the industry; (2) the costs of resources used in the industry; (3) the state of technology used by firms in the industry; (4) prices of related goods; and (5) expectations of future price changes. How do these other factors affect the supply curve?

Suppose the cost of an important variable resource increases. As a result, the cost of producing all units increases so that Metro Music would produce fewer units at every price level. The old and new supply schedules are shown in Table 3.3.

Both supply schedules are plotted on Figure 3.5. (See page 50). The graph shows that there has been a change in supply. The new supply curve lies to the left of the old curve because there has been a *decrease* in supply. (An *increase* in supply would be shown by a shift to the right.) At every price Metro Music would supply fewer units than before.

Table 3.3 Metro Music's Supply Schedule for Tape Cassettes (per month).

Price	Old Supply Schedule	New Supply Schedule
$8	8500	7500
7	7500	6500
6	6500	5500
5	5500	4500
4	4500	3500
3	3500	2500
2.67	3000	2000

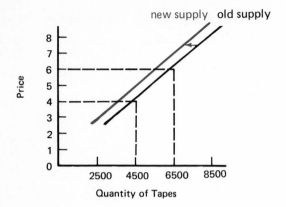

Figure 3.5 Change in Supply.
An increase in the cost of electric power reduces Metro Music's supply of tapes at every price level. A decrease in supply is shown by a shift of the entire supply curve to the left.

A change in quantity supplied refers to a movement along the supply curve, brought about by a change in the good's price. A change in supply is a shift of the entire supply curve to a new position, brought about by a change in a factor other than the good's price. (Test yourself: A rise in the price of American grain has increased the cost of producing beef cattle. Did higher grain prices cause a change in quantity supplied or a change in supply of beef in the supermarket?*)

How do the other factors affect supply? If the number of firms in the industry should increase, we might expect the supply of a good to increase. Remember how the profitability of pocket calculators led to the movement of many new firms into this industry in the 1970s. As a result, the market supply curve for pocket calculators shifted to the right. A change in technology will also affect supply. A new technique for extracting sugar from cellulose, for example, might lead to lower production costs and an increase in the supply of sugar.

What about other prices and expectations of price changes? Falling wheat prices would proba-

* a change in supply

bly cause the supply of soybeans to increase, as farmers replant their fields with the higher-priced crop. On the other hand, *expectations* of falling wheat prices would probably cause the supply of wheat to increase, as farmers try to unload their existing stocks before prices fall.

ELASTICITY OF SUPPLY

An important principle in studying supply is elasticity of supply. **Elasticity of supply** is defined similarly to elasticity of demand:

elasticity of supply $= e_s = \%\Delta Q_s / \%\Delta P.$

Since quantity supplied in the short run depends on marginal cost, the responsiveness of producers to price changes depends strongly on the behavior of marginal cost. For some goods, marginal cost rises fairly quickly as more units are produced. For these goods, larger quantities can be supplied only if price rises substantially; percent change in quantity supplied is low relative to percent change in price. Economists describe supply for such goods as *price inelastic:* quantity supplied is not very responsive to price changes. When supply is inelastic, supply curves slope upward rather steeply.

For other goods, quantity supplied can be increased with little increase in marginal cost and relatively smaller increase in price; percent change in quantity supplied is large relative to percent change in price. When producers respond readily to price changes, supply is said to be *price elastic.* Supply curves slope upward less steeply for price elastic goods.

Determinants of Supply Elasticity

Elasticity of supply of a good or service depends on how quickly firms can change output when price changes. We have seen that responsiveness of producers depends strongly on the marginal cost of increasing production in existing firms. Other factors also affect supply elasticity: (1) the time firms require to add or abandon productive capacity or to enter or leave the industry; and (2) the storability of the item (i.e., whether it can be stockpiled when price is low and brought to market later when price is higher).

Consider the following groups of items. How would you describe elasticity, or *responsiveness*, of supply to changes in price? Ask yourself: Will firms produce much more if price rises, or less if price falls? How flexible are production plans of suppliers? Is the product easily storable?

1. Strawberries, milk, eggs, beef.
2. Sweaters, autos, potato chips.
3. Gold, coal, lumber.
4. Transistors, screwdrivers, stained-glass windows.
5. Autos in the 1920s and autos in the 1970s.

MARKET EQUILIBRIUM

In free markets the interaction of demand and supply determines the price of a good. In our example, many consumers (demanders) enter the market to purchase tapes. Many producers (suppliers) respond by offering tapes for sale. Consumers and producers must agree on a market price for tapes. When a price is established at which all the tapes offered for sale are bought, we say the market has reached **equilibrium.**

Through a process of bargaining, bidding, and asking prices, a price is determined which just "clears" the market. It is the only price at which all the quantity offered for sale will be bought.

Figure 3.6 is a model of the market for tape cassettes. Consumer demand and producer supply are shown together in the market for tapes. At a price of $5, 25,000 tapes would be supplied and 25,000 tapes would be demanded. The *equilibrium price,* the price that clears the market, is $5. The *equilibrium quantity*, the quantity that clears the market, is 25,000 tapes. Buyers of the 25,000 tapes are satisfied with the price of $5. Firms producing tapes are willing to supply 25,000 tapes at a price of $5.

Surpluses and Shortages

What would happen at a price higher or lower than the equlibrium price of $5? As shown on Figure 3.7, at a price of $7, quantity supplied would be 45,000 tapes. However, quantity demanded would be only 17,000 tapes. There would be a **surplus**

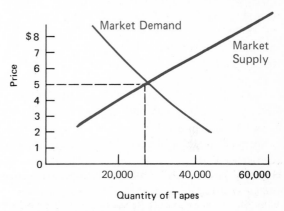

Figure 3.6 Market Equilibrium.
At a price of $5, quantity demanded (25,000 tape cassettes) equals quantity supplied. There are no surpluses or shortages. The market is in equilibrium.

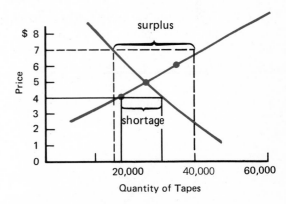

Figure 3.7 Surpluses and Shortages.
When the market price is higher than equilibrium price, quantity supplied will be greater than quantity demanded and there will be a surplus. When the market price is lower than equilibrium price, quantity demanded will be greater than quantity supplied, and there will be a shortage.

of 28,000 tapes (45,000 supplied − 17,000 demanded = 28,000 surplus). Suppliers would compete with one another to sell their product, thus price would be driven down to the equilibrium level.

Figure 3.7 shows that at a price of $4, quantity supplied would be 15,000 tapes. However, quantity demanded would be 29,000 tapes. There is a **shortage** of 14,000 tapes (29,000 demanded − 15,000 supplied = 14,000 shortage). This time consumers would bid against each other for the available product, driving price up to its equilibrium level.

Only at a price of $5 are there no surpluses or shortages. Quantity demanded equals quantity supplied, and the market is in equilibrium. Each consumer will purchase the quantity at which his or her personal desire for the good is high enough to justify the market price. Each producer will supply the quantity at which market price just offsets the added cost of producing the last unit.

Changes in Equilibrium

Changing conditions in the market will cause changes in demand and supply. Changing consumer tastes or incomes may shift demand curves to the right or left. Lower production costs or improved technology may increase supply, moving supply curves to the right. Changes in the number of firms or consumers may also shift supply and demand curves. As curves shift, the market moves toward a new equilibrium price.

Figure 3.8 shows how changes in demand or supply have affected equilibrium price in various markets. Can you cite other examples of changes in supply or demand from current news? What is the effect of each change on equilibrium price?

The remainder of this chapter will consider demand and supply conditions in major markets in the United States. In particular, we will examine the effects of government intervention in markets and differences in elasticities among markets.

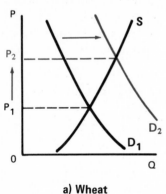

a) Wheat

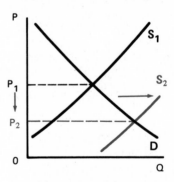

b) Pocket Calculators

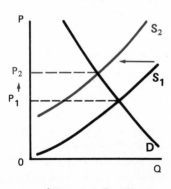

c) Chemical Fertilizers

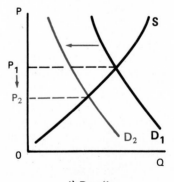

d) Bowling

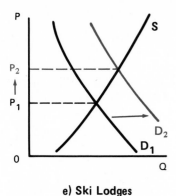

e) Ski Lodges

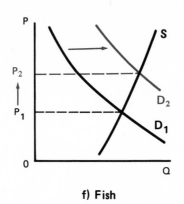

f) Fish

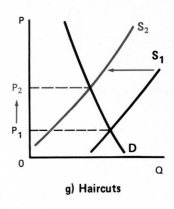

g) Haircuts

Figure 3.8   Changes in Equilibrium Price and Quantity.

a) The demand for wheat increased as Russian and Chinese buyers entered the U.S. market for grain. Producers attempted to satisfy the increased demand, but production costs rose and prices rose also.

b) Improved technology reduced costs of producing pocket calculators and increased supply. Consumers moved down their demand curves and purchased more calculators at lower prices.

c) Increased price of imported oil raised the costs of producing chemical fertilizers and reduced supply. Farmers moved up their demand curves and purchased less at higher prices.

d) Consumers' tastes changed and they preferred roller skating to bowling. The demand for games of bowling dropped and price fell.

e) Higher incomes allowed more Americans to take vacation trips. The demand for rooms in ski lodges increased and price increased.

f) The high price of beef caused consumers to shift to more fish in their diets. Increased demand for fish pushed its price up, too.

g) Changing hair styles reduced the profitability of barber shops. Many barbers left the market, causing a decrease in supply. Consumers purchased fewer haircuts at the higher price.

Self-Check

1. **Economic costs include all but which one of the following:**
   a. charges for repairing the firm's truck.
   b. interest on a loan from the company president's father.
   c. rent on a warehouse owned by the company president.
   d. a required payment to the entrepreneur who set up the company.
   e. an extra return resulting from abnormally high product prices.

2. **Which of the following statements is correct?**
   a. If MC>MR, the firm should expand production.
   b. As long as MR>MC, the firm should expand production.
   c. Production should not be carried on if P<ATC.
   d. Shut down will occur if P falls below AFC.
   e. A firm may decide not to pay fixed costs in the short run.

3. **An increase in quantity supplied may result from:**
   a. an increase in the number of firms in the industry.
   b. a decline in the cost of a variable resource.
   c. an improvement in the technology of production.
   d. a fall in the market price of another product firms might produce in-stead.
   e. an increase in the product's price.

4. **XYZ Pizza Parlor's supply of pizza is price elastic. This probably means:**
   a. it has facilities for producing large quantities.
   b. supply is responsive to price changes.
   c. it would cut back production significantly if price falls.
   d. increasing production would not significantly affect unit costs.
   e. all of the above.

5. **At equilibrium in the market for a good:**
   a. producers are supplying the greatest possible quantity.
   b. there is no incentive to change output plans.
   c. consumers are exploited by producers.
   d. price is necessarily higher than costs.
   e. price is lower than full costs.

6. **Changes in market equilibrium:**
   a. occur rarely.
   b. result from shifts in supply only.
   c. result from shifts in demand only.
   d. might mean higher price and smaller quantity.
   e. none of the above.

Theory in Practice

The laws of demand and supply are the means by which free markets allocate scarce resources among many alternative uses. They help us answer the fundamental question *What?* to produce. The many individual decisions of consumers and producers interact and lead to the final answer: *What?* is to be produced, how much, and what price.

THE EFFECT OF GOVERNMENT INTERVENTION IN THE FREE MARKET

In reality, most markets are not entirely free. Our economic system is actually a *mixed* system: primarily a free market, but with some elements of command (and even some tradition). Government intervenes in the market in a number of ways to influence the prices and quantities of goods and services produced. Much of government intervention is directed toward frictions and immobilities that slow down the process of automatic adjustments toward market equilibrium. *Frictions and immobilities* result from resistance to change and difficulties in movement from declining industries to growing ones.

Frictions and immobilities are particularly common in the housing and agricultural sectors. Rapid population growth, for example, increases the demand for housing. But new construction takes time, during which prices of homes may skyrocket. Improved farming procedures reduce the cost and increase the supply of agricultural products. But the larger supply may cause prices to nosedive. In both cases, resources may not move fast enough into or out of the market to cause prices to settle down at a level that just covers full costs of production.

Very high prices for housing and low prices for farm products impose particular hardships on certain groups. Government intervention has occasionally seemed necessary to protect these groups. In the first case, government may set a *price ceiling* above which housing prices may not rise. In the second, government may set a *price floor* below which farm prices may not fall.

Price Ceilings

In the mid-1950s the U.S. government became concerned about rising prices for natural gas produced in the central United States. It was felt that high prices would impose hardships on households and industrial users of this clean fuel. A price ceiling was established to hold down the price of all gas traded in interstate commerce.

The market for natural gas is shown in Figure 3.9. According to Figure 3.9 the market equilibrium price for natural gas would be $1.50 per thousand cubic feet, but price was not allowed to rise

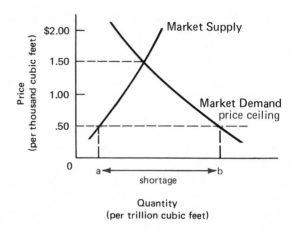

Figure 3.9   The Market for Natural Gas.
A price ceiling creates a shortage of natural gas.

above the price ceiling set at $.50. At the low ceiling price consumers wanted to buy larger quantities of natural gas for heating; business firms wanted to buy larger quantities for heating and power and as a chemical component in manufactured goods. Quantity demanded was equal to *Ob*. However, at the low ceiling price, producers of natural gas would supply a quantity equal to only *Oa*. The market could not move toward equilibrium. The result was a **shortage,** shown in Figure 3.9 as *ab*, the difference between quantity demanded *(Ob)* and quantity supplied *(Oa)*.

Some Americans grew accustomed to a cheap supply of natural gas and used it wastefully. Others could not buy any gas at all. At the low price ceiling, producers of gas were unable to earn enough revenue to cover full costs, and many closed down. The effects of price ceilings can be disastrous shortages!

Other side effects resulted from the low price of natural gas. Some users of natural gas were unable to buy sufficient quantities and turned to other fuels, increasing the demand for other valuable resources. (Test yourself: Are natural gas and other fuels substitutes or complements?*)

When prices are held down by government,

* substitutes

the smaller quantity supplied must often be rationed among the large numbers of would-be buyers. Rationing requires a large bureaucracy and raises many questions regarding fairness of distribution.

In 1978 Congress and the President decided to work toward eventual removal of the ceiling price on natural gas. Immediate decontrol would have sharply raised prices for many consumer and industrial users of gas. It would have transferred large amounts of purchasing power from consumers to owners of existing supplies of natural gas. The final decision was to raise the ceiling price by some amount each year until by 1985 the ceiling could be removed entirely. Rising natural gas prices were expected to encourage suppliers to produce more and consumers to demand less.

Price Floors

In the Depression of the 1930s American farmers experienced severe hardships because of the sharp drop in farm prices. New scientific techniques and advanced equipment had increased food production faster than the American public wanted to buy. As a result, prices and farm incomes fell.

The voting power of the farming sector was strong. Congress passed laws supporting the prices of certain farm commodities including corn, wheat, rice, cotton, tobacco, and peanuts.

The market for corn is shown in Figure 3.10. According to Figure 3.10, the market equilibrium price would be $2.00 per bushel, but price was not allowed to fall below the price floor set at $4.00. At the high support price, consumers wanted to buy less corn; livestock producers wanted to buy less corn for feed. Quantity demanded was equal to *Oa*. However, at the high price producers of corn were willing to supply a quantity equal to *Ob*. Many farmers converted their fields from other crops to the production of corn. The result was a surplus of corn, shown on Figure 3.10 as *ab,* the difference between quantity supplied *(Oa)* and quantity demanded *(Ob)*.

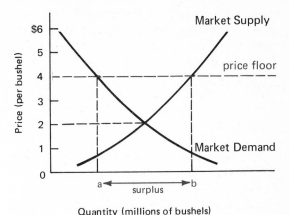

Figure 3.10   The Market for Corn.
A price floor creates a surplus of corn.

American farmers grew accustomed to government-supported prices for their grains. They continued to expand output or, at least, failed to cut back production or leave farming for occupations that would earn sufficient income at free-market prices. Government made crop loans to farmers based on the artificially high support price. Farmers who were unable to sell their grain at that price defaulted on their loans and turned their crops over to the government. The effects of a price floor can be embarrassing surpluses!

Surplus crops were bought and stored by the government at great expense to taxpayers. However, surpluses were used up in years of international food shortages. Stored food supplies were depleted during war years and in years when crop failures brought on famine in other nations. By the mid 1970s, surplus grains in the United States had practically disappeared.

Grain stocks began to build again in 1977. Farmers had taken advantage of rising worldwide demand to expand production significantly. Many borrowed heavily to purchase high-priced land and equipment. When grain prices failed to keep up with their rising costs, farmers grew angry. There was much unrest and a farmers' strike was threatened.

Existing farm legislation expired in 1977, and

Congress established a new farm policy. The objective was to help stabilize farm incomes while interfering as little as possible with pricing in farm markets. The new farm legislation included "target prices." Target prices were set to be just below equilibrium prices in normal crop years and were designed to cover basic costs of seed, fertilizer, labor, and machinery. In years of high demand relative to supply, farmers would sell their grain in free markets, pay their costs, and earn a profit. In years of low demand relative to supply, price would fall below the target price; then government would pay farmers the difference between the low market price and the target price. Government payments would enable farmers to pay their costs, but consumers could continue to enjoy low food prices at the supermarket.

A second part of the 1977 farm law was aimed at controlling the supply of farm commodities. Under the "set-aside" provision of the law, farmers were asked not to cultivate a portion of their land when particular crops were expected to be in surplus. A food grain reserve was established to purchase surplus grain in years of plenty for resale in years of scarcity. By regulating supplies of farm commodities, government hoped to smooth out the wide fluctuations in food prices and farm incomes.

Has Government Price Setting Been a Blessing or a Curse?

Certainly government intervention originated under the best intentions. Our political system helps ensure that government policies reflect the wishes of voters. Often, however, price ceilings and price floors have benefited particular groups of voters while at the same time reducing efficiency for the economy as a whole.

Look again at the market for natural gas in Figure 3.9. A higher free-market price for gas would have discouraged nonessential uses, conserving this valuable resource. The higher price would have also encouraged new and existing firms to seek out and develop new sources of gas.

This would have helped bring prices down in the future. The result of free market pricing might have been more balanced production and use of all available fuel in American homes and businesses.

In the farming sector, lower free-market prices on farm commodities would have meant temporary hardships for some farmers. Some would have left farming to seek better jobs in industry. With fewer farmers in the market the supply of farm commodities would have fallen. Prices would have risen until finally the remaining farmers could earn sufficient income from their crops.

Free-market prices help ensure economic *efficiency* in the use of our scarce labor and other resources: to produce the most of what we want with the least use of scarce resources. Occasionally, there may be need for temporary intervention in the market to ease temporary hardships for particular groups. But over the long run, the free market generally provides a better answer to the question *What?*

Price setting can have other side effects. Artificially low prices can encourage excessive use of a commodity. Throughout most of the 1970s crude oil produced in the United States was sold at a price set by law. The price ceiling made gasoline cheap to American drivers and encouraged the use of private automobiles. In addition, the price of parking in downtown areas is often held below equilibrium by department stores. The cost of building highways is often paid by the federal government at little cost to local taxpayers. Low prices for all these complementary goods have contributed to the rise of automobile traffic in the United States.

Remember that the *opportunity cost* of using land as a parking lot or highway is the other things for which the land could have been used (department stores, restaurants, factories, homes, parks, and so forth). It is not incorrect to say that in part the artificially low prices on gasoline cost us the opportunity of using land to provide more homes, businesses, and recreational areas.

Elasticity Considerations in Price Fixing

When government sets prices, it is important to consider elasticity of demand and supply. Consider our two examples of price fixing: natural gas and farm commodities. How has elasticity affected markets under price fixing? How would removal of price controls affect markets?

In the market for natural gas, the artificially low price moved buyers down their demand curves. Users responded to lower prices by demanding substantially larger quantities. We would say that demand was relatively elastic. When demand is elastic, removal of the price ceiling would sharply curtail quantity demanded, limiting sales to only the most urgent users. (Test yourself: What characteristics of natural gas affect elasticity of demand? See Chapter 2.)

Elasticity of supply is important, too. Price ceilings on natural gas have clearly reduced incentives to increase production of this clean, efficient fuel. Would a free market price encourage greater production? No one really knows for certain how much natural gas remains in underground reservoirs or how much it would cost to get it out. This makes a clear answer impossible. To the extent that convenient sources exist, supply will be elastic and a free market price would not be substantially above current ceiling prices. However, as sources become depleted, supply will eventually become highly inelastic and price may rise sharply. At the higher price, little additional fuel would be available and only the most urgent needs would be satisfied.

(Test yourself: Illustrate graphically the market for natural gas under the assumption of fairly elastic demand and inelastic supply. Show government's price ceiling. Then show the expected result of decontrolling price.)

Elasticities are different in the markets for farm commodities. Demand for farm products is relatively inelastic. The response to price changes is not as great as for natural gas. This is because families must buy food items in roughly stable quantities regardless of price. High support prices do not substantially reduce quantity sold—at least in the immediate period. Nor would lower free market prices increase food purchases very much.

Modern technology has made supply of farm products relatively elastic over time periods sufficiently long for grain to ripen, calves to mature, and so forth. The artificially high support price encourages substantial excess production. What would be the result of free market prices? A small drop in prices from support levels would probably sharply reduce production. Many farmers would leave the farm for jobs in industry. The fewer remaining farmers would have to supply our entire food requirements in good years and bad. Widespread crop failures in any one year would make supply curves quite inelastic and lead to significant price increases.

(Test yourself: Illustrate graphically the market for farm products under the assumption of fairly inelastic demand and elastic supply. Show government's support price. Then show the expected result of decontrolling price.)

All these considerations and more are involved in government's decision to fix prices—or to remove controls. The issue of price fixing is not a simple one.

Supply Elasticity in Home Building

The prices we pay for the essential things of life depend strongly on supply. The location and the shape of supply curves depend on decisions to produce goods and services. Many firms assemble the resources and organize production for the market. They offer goods for sale as long as price is sufficient to cover costs of production.

Production costs behave differently depending on the time period involved. This is particularly true in the home building industry. Most homes are built by small, privately owned firms. Their capacity to increase production substantially is limited—at least in the immediate time period. Their managerial staff would be stretched too thin; their skilled workers would have to work overtime; and their capital equipment would be overworked and subject to breakdowns. As a result, an increase in the market price for housing would bring forth little immediate increase in quantity supplied. With inelastic supply, prices in the housing market would be subject to wide swings.

Over a longer time period, conditions are likely to be different. If higher prices persist, more small firms will enter the housing industry. More houses can be offered for sale and prices will not rise as much. We would say that supply is more elastic over the long run.

What about supply over a *very* long time? The housing industry is a good example of what can happen to supply curves if there is plenty of time for responding to price changes.

In recent years, wide fluctuations in housing costs have brought on major changes in the housing industry. The structure of the industry has been changing from a fragmented industry of many small firms to one of fewer, larger firms. Larger firms can use modern production techniques and equipment for producing more houses at lower costs. For example, a large firm can assemble roof sections and wall panels at a centrally located factory. On an ordinary assembly line, low-skilled workers can nail building sections according to a standard pattern. Even electric wiring and plumbing may be installed at a central location. Then flatbed trucks can carry the preformed parts to building sites over a wide area. Only a few skilled workers would be needed to complete the construction. Finally, appliances can be delivered to an entire tract of houses at one time.

Technological development of this sort can make supply curves even more elastic over the *very* long run. Figure 3.11 shows a range of hypothetical supply curves for the immediate time period, a longer time period, and a very long time period. Notice the effect on price as the time for adjusting to increased housing demand lengthens.

Could a supply curve ever slope downward to the right? Under what conditions might this occur? (Refer to the factors that determine supply elasticity.)

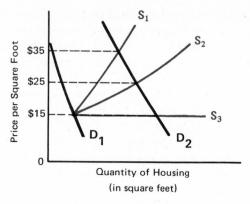

S_1: Supply over a short time-period
S_2: Supply over a longer time-period
S_3: Supply over a very long time-period

Figure 3.11   Hypothetical Supply Curves in the Market for Housing.

SUMMARY

1. A firm's supply schedule is based on economic costs, including necessary payments to owners of all productive resources. Economic profit is extra profit above the necessary normal profit to people who supply entrepreneurial ability.
2. Payments to fixed resources are necessary in the short run, regardless of quantity produced; payments to variable resources depend on quantity produced. Quantity supplied can be read from a firm's marginal cost curve, since MC = MR = P defines the profit-maximizing quantity for a firm in competition. The shut-down point occurs where price is equal to average variable costs.
3. Supply curves slope upward because more units will be produced only at higher prices. Changes in the number of firms in the industry, the costs of resources used in the industry, the state of technology, related prices, and price expectations cause supply curves to shift to the right or left.
4. Elasticity of supply measures the responsiveness of producers to price changes and reflects the behavior of marginal costs.

5. Market equilibrium is reached at the price at which the quantity demanded by consumers is just equal to the quantity supplied by producers. At prices higher than the equilibrium price, quantity supplied will be greater than quantity demanded, and there will be a surplus. At prices lower than the equilibrium price, quantity demanded will be greater than quantity supplied, and there will be a shortage.

6. Government intervenes in free markets to ease temporary hardships created by market adjustments. Government may establish price ceilings or price floors when market price is believed to be too high or too low. A price ceiling is likely to cause a shortage. A price floor is likely to cause a surplus.

7. Elasticity of demand and supply will influence the range of price and quantity changes in particular markets.

8. For most goods and services, elasticity of supply increases over longer time periods.

TERMS TO REMEMBER

economic costs: necessary payments to owners of productive resources.

normal profit: necessary payment for the use of entrepreneurial ability.

economic profit: a payment greater than normal profit to entrepreneurs.

fixed costs: costs which are constant in the short run, regardless of quantity produced.

variable costs: costs which vary with quantity of output produced.

marginal costs: changes in costs associated with changes in quantity produced.

marginal revenue: changes in revenue associated with changes in quantity offered for sale; in competition marginal revenue is the same as price.

supply schedule: the amounts firms are willing to supply at various prices.

quantity supplied: the amount firms would supply at a particular price.

market supply: the quantities all firms would supply at various prices.

shut-down point: the quantity at which price is equal to average variable costs.

the law of supply: the relationship between price and quantity supplied is *direct:* as price increases, quantity supplied increases; as price decreases, quantity supplied decreases.

elasticity of supply: the responsiveness of quantity supplied to changes in price.

market equilibrium: a condition in the market at which price is satisfactory to buyers and sellers; the only point at which quantity supplied is equal to quantity demanded.

surplus: a condition that occurs when price is set too high so that quantity supplied is greater than quantity demanded.

shortage: a condition that occurs when price is set too low so that quantity demanded is greater than quantity supplied.

price ceiling: a price set by government above which market price is not allowed to rise.

price floor: a price set by government below which market price is not allowed to fall.

TOPICS FOR DISCUSSION

1. Explain why it is important to draw a supply curve for a particular period of time. Then explain and demonstrate market changes which could cause changes in the position and/or slope of market supply.

2. Complete the table below. Then perform the exercises on page 62:

Q	FC	AFC	VC	AVC	TC	ATC	MC
1	100	100	10	10	110	110	10
2	——	——	18	——	——	——	——
3	——	——	24	——	——	——	——
4	——	——	34	——	——	——	——
5	——	——	48	——	——	——	——
6	——	——	66	——	——	——	——
7	——	——	90	——	——	——	——
8	——	——	118	——	——	——	——
9	——	——	150	——	——	——	——
10	——	——	186	——	——	——	——

(1) The firm's shut-down point occurs at a price of _____ .

(2) Economic profit is received for any price greater than _____ .

(3) The profit-maximizing quantity for price of $14 is _____ . Economic profit would be _____ .

(4) The profit-maximizing quantity for price of $32 is _____ . Economic profit would be _____ .

(5) Draw the firm's supply curve.

3. During the 1974 period of rising food prices, I went to the supermarket for a head of lettuce. The lettuce bin was not sporting its customary price tag. Since lettuce prices had been fluctuating between 39 and 69 cents, I asked the produce manager what the price was that day. He almost whispered the answer, "Thirty-nine cents." Of course, I took advantage of the low price to buy several heads. Then the produce manager explained to me the reason he hadn't put a sign over the bin.

"If I put out a sign saying '39 cents' I'd be all out of lettuce before noon," he said. "If I had plenty and the price was 69 cents I'd put out a big sign. But this way I can save what I've got and make it last all day."

Was this grocer using the price system to ration a scarce commodity among his customers? Why do you suppose he behaved the way he did? Can you suggest a better approach to his problem?

4. Consumer boycotts are occasionally used to protest high prices on food items. An effective boycott can be shown as a backward shift in the demand curve. The theory of free markets should give us some clues as to the reaction of suppliers to lower demand (and lower prices). How do you think a boycott will affect food prices after several months during which farmers will have time to adjust to the new conditions? How will the "invisible hand" change farm output? Show graphically.

5. In September 1973, *Newsweek* reported that changing lifestyles and the changing age mixture of the population have brought on an increase of 57 percent in wine sales over the last five years. As a result, prices have risen from 25 to 200 percent (depending on the quality of the wine). California vintners have expanded cultivation of grapes by 95,000 acres and it is hoped (among wine lovers!) that prices will soon stabilize.

Comment on the information given. Use a series of graphs to illustrate changes in consumer demand and in equilibrium price. Then show how producers will adjust to changes in market conditions.

6. Since World War II the electronics industry has supplied many of our most exciting and innovative new products. The most recent has been the video recorder for recording television programs. Initially, only two Japanese firms supplied the entire market. How would you describe elasticity of supply in the immediate period, over a five-year period, and over a twenty-five-year period? What price behavior would you predict?

7. Some local governments in the United States have imposed rent controls on city apartments. Discuss the intent of this kind of price ceiling and list as many effects as you can.

SUGGESTED READINGS

"Adapting to Energy Uncertainty," *Economic Report of the President*, Washington: Government Printing Office, January 1981, p. 90.

Adelman, Morris A., "The Case for Decontrol," *Challenge*, July/August 1979, pp. 38–40.

Arrow, Kenneth J., "The Limitations of the Profit Motive," *Challenge*, September/October 1979, pp. 23–27.

Bergland, Bob, "Oats, Peas, Beans, and Barley Grow," *Challenge*, September/October 1978, pp. 26–31.

Berman, Lewis, "A New Case for that Ever-Normal Granary," *Fortune*, April 1976, p. 96.

"Blessings and Problems of 1977's Bumper Crops," *U.S. News and World Report*, September 19, 1977, p. 32.

Breckenfeld, Gurney, "A Decade of Catch-Up for Housing," *Fortune*, April 7, 1980, p. 96.

"The Construction Boom: More Business Than the Process Builders Can Handle," *Business Week*, September 29, 1980, p. 82.

Davidson, Paul, "The Economics of Natural Resources," *Challenge*, March/April 1979, pp. 40–46.

Davidson, Paul, "What is the Energy Crisis?" *Challenge,* July/August 1979, pp. 41–46.

Downs, Anthony, "The House in the Sky," *Across the Board,* April 1979, pp. 35–45.

"Energy Conservation: Spawning a Billion-Dollar Business," *Business Week,* April 6, 1981, p. 58.

"Farm-Price Pinch: Carter to the Rescue," *U.S. News and World Report,* September 12, 1977, p. 72.

Loving, Rush, Jr., "The Pros and Cons of Airline Deregulation," *Fortune,* August 1977, p. 209.

Moore, Thomas Gale, "Energy Options," in *The United States in the 1980s,* Peter Duignan and Alvin Rabushka, eds. Stanford University: Hoover Institution, 1980, p. 221.

Rivlin, Alice, "Incentives for Exploration and Development," *Challenge,* July/August 1979, pp. 34–35.

Schultz, Charles L., "The Oil Price Decontrol Debate: The President's Plan," *Challenge,* July/August 1979, pp. 28–34.

Tavoulareas, William P., "U.S. Crude Oil Pricing—A Proposal," *Challenge,* July/August 1979, pp. 36–38.

Thurow, Lester, *The Zero-Sum Society,* New York: Basic Books, 1980, Chapter 2.

Tracy, Eleanor Johnson, "In Search of Super-Cow," *Fortune,* December 29, 1980, p. 57.

Uttal, Bro, "TI's Home Computer Can't Get in the Door," *Fortune,* June 16, 1980, p. 139.

CHAPTER 4

Market Adjustments With and Without Competition

or What's Good for GM Is Good for GM

Tools for Study

Learning Objectives

After reading this chapter, you will be able to:

1. explain how adjustments in competitive markets work to eliminate economic profit or loss.
2. define monopoly, oligopoly, and monopolistic competition and give examples of each.
3. explain how the absence of competition may mean the persistence of economic profit.
4. discuss legislation aimed at preserving competition.

Issues Covered

How does monopoly affect us?
How do public utilities determine rates?

Adam Smith and the classical economists who followed him described how the market system would work when there is perfect competition. As you learned in Chapters 2 and 3, perfect competition depends upon: many buyers and sellers, each too small to affect market price; products so similar that no one producer can insist on a higher price; complete information about market conditions; ease of movement into the most favorable markets. In perfect competition, many individual firms compete for the consumer's dollar. An "invisible hand" guides firms to produce the goods and services consumers want.

In Chapters 2 and 3 we developed the market model that illustrates the classical theory of free markets. In the classical theory, individual consumer demand schedules combine to yield a market demand curve. Individual firms' decisions to supply goods and services combine to yield market supply. The interaction between market demand and market supply yields market equilibrium. At equilibrium, market price is such that quantity demanded is equal to quantity supplied and there is no surplus or shortage.

In the short run, the market equilibrium price may mean economic profits or losses for firms in the industry. Economic profit or loss is possible because of the existence of fixed resources and the difficulty of substantially expanding or contracting production in response to price changes. Thus, price may be greater or less than average total cost. Over the long run, however, fixed plants and equipment can be expanded or abandoned, so that supply curves can shift to the right or left. Price may fall or rise to the level of average total cost, eliminating economic profit or loss.

In this chapter, we will consider long-run adjustments in the theoretical market model of competition. Then we will look at conditions in noncompetitive markets and show how the absence of competition may affect market adjustments. Much of our discussion in this chapter will involve economic profit.

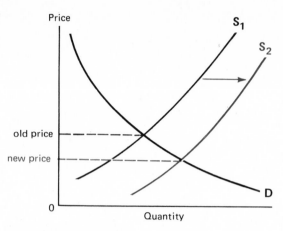

Figure 4.1   An Increase in Supply in the Competitive Market.
New firms enter the industry. Market supply increases and price falls until economic profit is eliminated.

PRICE AND OUTPUT DETERMINATION IN COMPETITION

Adam Smith showed that in competitive markets, economic profit serves as an "invisible hand" encouraging new firms to enter an industry. As new firms add their output to that of existing firms, market supply will grow. The larger market supply will push price down, eliminating economic profit.

Figure 4.1 shows what happens when new firms enter an industry. The greater total supply is shown as a rightward shift of market supply, creating a surplus at the current price. As firms compete to sell their output, price falls and a new, lower equilibrium price is reached. If the new price includes economic profit, still more firms will enter the market, continuing to push price down until price is equal to average total cost. When P = ATC, there is no economic profit and no further incentive for new firms to enter the market. The new price will be just enough to cover full costs, including normal profit but not economic profit.

In competition, firms rushing in to take advantage of economic profit will force prices down to their lowest possible level. Why is this so? Firms in the industry will be compelled by compe-

tition to construct their plants so as to achieve maximum technical efficiency. And they will operate their plants at the best possible rate for holding down unit costs. This result is ideal in terms of both technical and allocative efficiency. Efficient production is certainly important in view of the problem of scarcity. *In competition, consumers' wants are satisfied at prices that just offset the minimum necessary cost of scarce resources.*

The process of adjustment also works in reverse. It may be that in some industries market price is not high enough to cover full unit costs. Total revenue from sales will be less than total costs, and firms will be receiving negative economic profit or loss. Negative economic profit should serve as an "invisible hand" encouraging firms to leave an industry. As firms leave, output falls.

Figure 4.2 shows what happens when firms leave an industry. The smaller total supply is shown as a leftward shift of market supply, creating a shortage at the current price. Buyers will bid against each other for the limited supply, forcing price up. Finally, a new equilibrium is reached with a higher price and smaller quantity sold. The

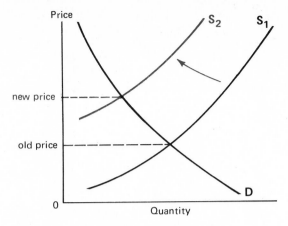

Figure 4.2   A Decrease in Supply in the Competitive Market.
Firms leave the industry. Market supply falls and price rises until negative economic profit (loss) is eliminated.

new equilibrium price will be just high enough to cover full costs, including normal profit but not economic profit. Again, the new equilibrium price will be the minimum price for which this good can be produced.

We say that firms in competition are *price takers*. Every competitive firm faces an equilibrium price which it is too small to affect. It can sell any quantity at the market equilibrium price, but it can sell *nothing* at a higher price. Normally, the competitive firm will continue to supply output in the long run as long as market price is at least as great as average total cost. When all firms follow this rule, price will be forced to a level that includes neither economic profit nor loss.

It is understandable that Adam Smith should regard the free market with a kind of reverence. In free markets, consumers communicate their preferences to producers through demand. Producers, in turn, seek the least costly means of satisfying consumer wants. The result is efficient production: the minimum expenditure of limited resources and the maximum production of goods consumers want. When production is efficient, opportunity costs are reduced to the minimum.

But Adam Smith realized that competition might not be perfect in the real world. Business firms might try to gain control over the output of particular goods. They might look for ways to maintain high prices so that they could continue to receive economic profit. They might prefer not to "flood the market" but would cut down on output so as to maintain high prices. To the extent that the real world differs from the free market ideal, our market system has lost some of the benefits Adam Smith described.

MONOPOLY

Remember that one of the characteristics of competition is many small sellers producing identical products. In the real world, some markets are characterized by a *few large* sellers producing *differentiated* products. In such markets, the conclusions of Adam Smith's theoretical model may not be valid.

If there is only one large seller in a market, the firm is said to be a **monopoly.** There are few examples of *pure* monopoly, but many where a few large firms *behave* like a monopoly and achieve results similar to monopoly. When we speak of monopoly in this text, we will be referring to groups of noncompeting firms with power to affect price.

Monopoly can be achieved in several ways. The monopoly may be the first firm (or firms) in the industry, it may buy out all rival firms, or it may drive its competitors out of business. The monopoly firm must keep out price-cutting competitors in order to maintain control over supply. And it will try to increase demand so that there will be buyers at profitable prices.

A country fellow in the rural South had learned this lesson quite well—without ever attending business school! Some tourists were driving along a detour off the main road when they became hopelessly mired in the mud. A humble shack was the only sign of civilization, and the farmer's tractor was available (at a price) to pull their car from the ditch. As he handed the fellow a twenty, the tourist observed, ''I'll bet you're busy night and day pulling cars from this mud, aren't you?''

''Nope,'' replied the farmer. ''Night's when we haul the water.''

(Single supplier—control of demand! It would be hard to beat that!)

Gentlemen's Agreements

When there are a few large firms in the industry, they may agree among themselves to behave like monopolists. They may make ''gentlemen's agreements'' not to compete. They may agree not to reduce prices, and they may establish market shares for each firm. In this way, each individual firm will enjoy total control over supply in a protected market area. Firms like these are said to be **price makers.** Price makers are distinguished from price takers (competitive firms) because they have some degree of power to affect price.

(Gentlemen's agreements are a little like the cartoon showing two donkeys tethered at either end of a strong rope. Each donkey is struggling to eat a bale of hay just beyond his reach at the end of the rope. But when they agree to cooperate, they are able to eat first one bale and then the other, and both are satisfied.)

Horizontal and Vertical Integration

Firms may combine, through formal merger or informal agreement, in two ways. A monopoly may consist of firms which provide the same good or service. This type of combination is called **horizontal integration:**

supermarket—supermarket—supermarket
auto plant—auto plant

Or a monopoly may consist of firms that process a single good from start to finish—from its raw form

to its distribution to the final consumer. This type of combination is called **vertical integration:**

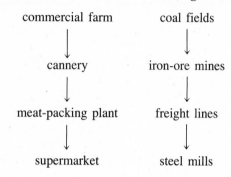

OLIGOPOLY

Whereas monopoly is rare in U.S. markets, **oligopoly** is more common. An oligopoly industry is an industry in which a few large, independent firms supply most of industry output, but small firms may operate in particular markets. Oligopoly is typically found in industries requiring large capital investment. In these industries, initial costs may be too high for small firms to establish themselves, or market demand may be too small for many firms to operate efficiently.

When a few large firms dominate an industry, the results are often similar to monopoly. Oligopoly firms may not actually agree to limit output and raise price, but because they are subject to similar cost patterns, they may arrive at similar price and quantity decisions even without actual agreement. Like monopolists, they become price makers.

Some examples of industries long dominated by a few large firms are the automobile industry (dominated by General Motors, Ford, Chrysler, and American Motors), the steel industry (dominated by U.S. Steel, Bethlehem, and Republic), the rubber-tire industry (dominated by Goodyear, Uniroyal, Firestone, Goodrich, and General), and the meat-packing industry (dominated by Swift, Armour, Wilson, and Cudahy).

MONOPOLISTIC COMPETITION

Other markets in the U.S. are described by a term that suggests characteristics of monopoly and competition: **monopolistic competition.** Monopolistic competition is similar to monopoly because each individual firm claims to produce a distinctly unique product: the *only* socially accepted toothpaste or haircream, the *only* truly tasteful soft drink, the *only* fully nutritious breakfast cereal.

In monopolistic competition, products may be fairly similar, but producers try to make them *seem* different. Differences can be achieved by frequent style or packaging changes or simply through clever advertising. In any case, firms have some control over price. They can raise price somewhat above the competitive level and still hold on to customers who are completely loyal to their product. They are price makers, but in a more limited sense than true monopolists or oligopolists.

Monopolistic competition is similar to competition because there are many firms in the industry. There are so many firms that each may produce a smaller volume than is economically efficient. The best example is when four fast-food restaurants crowd into a single block. Each one may promise special "service with a smile," but they divide a market which might be served more efficiently by only two larger enterprises.

Industries characterized by monopolistic competition include retail-trade and personal-service industries such as delicatessens, fabric shops, laundries, and barber shops. Initial capital requirements for these industries are low, making it easy for many small firms to enter.

The three major market structures can be summarized as follows:

Monopoly
    One seller
    Difficulty in entering
    Unique product
    Influence over price
    Higher price, lower quantity

Oligopoly
    Few sellers
    Not very easy to enter
    Homogeneous or differentiated product
    Price leadership
    Somewhat higher price and lower quantity

Monopolistic Competition
    Many sellers
    Ease of entry
    Differentiated product
    Little influence over price
    Slightly higher price, frequently excessive quantity

PRICE AND OUTPUT DECISIONS IN THE ABSENCE OF COMPETITION

Without competition, the automatic adjustment mechanism of the market system will not work as Adam Smith predicted. *Firms will not be forced by competition to supply output at a price just high enough to cover full costs of production.* Monopolistic firms may be able to continue to receive economic profit by preventing the entry of new firms.

Entry into some markets is difficult. Established firms may own patented information or essential equipment unavailable to newcomers. Or a monopoly firm may control the supply of an important resource or component part. Dealership arrangements may be closed to new firms. And finally, the secure market position of an old, established firm may be almost impossible to penetrate.

Remember that firms in perfect competition are price takers, selling any quantity at the market equilibrium price. Without competition, firms become price makers. Facing the entire demand curve for its product, a monopoly firm can set any price on the curve and sell the corresponding quantity. Selling a larger quantity requires a movement down the demand curve and a lower price. A higher price will mean a smaller quantity.

Viewpoint

TWO MONOPOLIES IN AMERICAN HISTORY

During the earliest stages of industrialization following the Civil War, there was cut-throat competition among American business firms. (The donkeys were still struggling to get at the hay.)

In the building of the railroads, early industrialists like Cornelius Vanderbilt fought ruthlessly to drive their competitors out of business. Where a competing parallel line served the same two cities, Vanderbilt would lower his rates below costs. He would make up the loss on other routes where he faced no competition. When the competing line was forced into bankruptcy, Vanderbilt would buy it cheaply. Eventually the Vanderbilt network took control of freight service over most of the industrialized Northeast.

In the petroleum industry, John D. Rockefeller began with several small oil refineries. However, he realized he could make more profit if he controlled the oil from well to final distributor. Rockefeller's Standard Oil was able to buy the major pipelines and establish a monopoly in the transport of crude oil. As the only buyer of crude oil from well owners, he would pay a low price. Then the oil would be transported over Rockefeller pipelines. Finally, as the only seller of oil to refiners, he could demand a high price. Economic profits were substantial.

As well owners were forced out of business on the one hand and refiners and distributors on the other, Rockefeller's Standard Oil could buy them up. In this way a major part of the petroleum industry was brought within one enterprise. Whenever rivals could not be forced out of business or could not be merged with the dominant company, cooperative agreements were often made. (The donkeys agreed to share the hay!)

These two cases illustrate *vertical* and *horizontal* combinations to achieve monopoly. Can you identify each?

What price will the monopoly firm set? The answer depends, first, on the effect of price on total revenue and, second, on the effect of quantity on total costs. (These topics were the subject of Chapters 2 and 3, respectively.)

To illustrate, suppose your monopoly firm is selling 100 widgets a week at a price of $3.50. You could sell 110 units if you reduced price to $3.00 or 90 units if you raised price to $4.00. How many widgets would you decide to produce and sell? In this case, your firm would increase its total revenue by *reducing* the number of units sold. In fact, if price elasticity of demand is less than 1 at the current price, raising price will always produce an increase in total revenue.

Maximum total revenue is not generally the goal of the monopoly firm, however. Like a competitive firm, a monopoly must consider production costs as well, if it is to achieve maximum economic profit. Since economic profit is the difference between total revenue and total costs, the monopoly firm will try to set a price that maximizes the difference between total revenue and total costs. It will look for the point on its demand curve at which price and quantity sold satisfy this objective.

Selecting price and quantity in the monopoly firm is similar to competition in one respect: like the competitive firm, the monopoly selects quantity where MC = MR. When MC = MR, the last unit produced adds just enough revenue to cover its additional costs, and economic profit is maximum. The difference between pricing in competition and without competition has to do with marginal revenue. Whereas marginal costs of production may be the same for both types of firms, marginal revenue is not. Because the monopoly firm faces the entire market demand curve, selling additional output requires a reduction in price. Selling all units at the lower price means that marginal revenue is lower than price.*

When a monopoly firm compares marginal cost with marginal revenue, the profit-maximizing quantity is less than the profit-maximizing quantity in competition. Furthermore, with MC = MR < P, price must be greater than in competition.

Twentieth-century economists have studied noncompetitive markets carefully and found these results to be true for monopoly, oligopoly, and monopolistic competition. The significant characteristic in all these markets is the firms' power to set price. The strength of a particular firm's pricing power depends, in turn, on the relative dominance of the firm in its market. The degree of dominance is reflected in the shape of the firm's demand curve and, in particular, the elasticity of demand at the current price. Firms with greater market power face demand curves that are relatively *price inelastic:* percentage changes in price yield smaller percentage changes in quantity demanded. Firms with less market power face demand curves that are relatively *price elastic:* percentage changes in price yield larger percentage changes in quantity demanded. In the first case, many consumers want the product so badly they are willing to pay a noncompetitive price. In the second, consumers have greater choice and can decide to buy or not, depending on price.

THE RESULTS OF MONOPOLY

Monopolistic behavior in industry can have harmful effects, both in the immediate period and for the future. With monopoly, oligopoly, or monopolistic competition, prices tend to be higher than in competition and quantity sold tends to be lower. Barriers to entry prevent new firms from responding to market signals. When consumers must pay more for wanted goods, they have less income left to make other purchases, holding back the development of other industries.

Often, firms that sell to monopolies must accept low prices for their products. Workers and suppliers of materials and component parts may

---

* Suppose 10 shirts sell for $25 for total revenue of $250. If selling 11 shirts requires a price of $24, total revenue is $264. The change in total revenue associated with a one-unit increase in quantity sold is $14: thus, MR < P.

have no choice but to accept low pay from the single monopoly firm.

Higher prices and lower quantity mean that our economy is less *efficient* than it might be. Moreover, unless a firm faces competition, it is doubtful that it will use its economic profits to improve its production techniques or its product. The result may be slower growth and lower productivity for our economic system as a whole.

The harmful effects of oligopoly are especially damaging in international trade. Higher prices and lower incentives to improve product quality have caused U.S. auto and steel manufacturers to lose markets to foreign suppliers. Monopolistically competitive industries have expended valuable resources for trivial product changes while neglecting major innovations. In all these cases, the U.S. potential for technological progress may have been harmed.

ANTIMONOPOLY LEGISLATION

Organized monopoly was not a problem early in our economic development, but toward the end of the 1800s a great merger movement swept American industry. Corporations were formed in the transportation industry and in industries producing and processing raw materials.

Under the corporate form, firms would sell shares of stock to large numbers of investors. Holders of stock become the owners of the business and receive a share of corporate profits. In theory stockholders have the power to select managers and decide on company policy. In fact, few stockholders exercise their voting rights in corporate policy, leaving actual power in the hands of a few active stockholders. This makes it possible for a small group to control several firms just by buying a small portion of the outstanding stock of each. Such organizations were called **trusts** or **holding companies** and were able to monopolize production in particular industries: sugar, meat-packing, steel, rail transport, tobacco, and oil.

Farmers were often harmed by trusts. With a monopoly in the production of a good or service, a trust could charge high prices to its customers and pay low prices to its suppliers. Farmers' incomes were squeezed by high fuel and transport charges and low prices for farm products. Opposition to the trusts developed in the agricultural regions of the Midwest. Farmers began to pressure Congress for legislation to outlaw trusts. Finally, in 1890 Congress passed the Sherman Antitrust Act.

The Sherman Antitrust Act

The Sherman Antitrust Act forbade any "contract, combination . . . or conspiracy, in restraint of trade." Any act to "monopolize, or combine or conspire . . . to monopolize" any market was prohibited.

The act was so vague that it was difficult to decide precisely what actions were forbidden. This left plenty of room for interpretation by the courts. Also, while the act prohibited cooperative agreements among companies, it did not prevent outright purchase of companies. This fact contributed to a great round of business mergers.

Except for court action against the Standard Oil Company and the American Tobacco Company, the act was used primarily against labor unions—which were regarded as monopolies of labor markets.

The Clayton Antitrust Act

In 1914, the Clayton Antitrust Act was passed. This law more precisely defined certain specific actions harmful to competition. For example, the Clayton Act forbade *price discrimination;* some firms had been setting prices below costs in areas where they faced competition in order to force rival firms out of business.* The law also forbade *tying contracts,* which required the buyer of one of

---

* They would make up the loss by setting prices higher than costs in other markets.

a firm's products to buy a full line of products and thus closed out other suppliers, and *interlocking directorates,* in which a single director would serve on the boards of several related corporations. Interlocking directorates had allowed firms to coordinate their price and output policies and avoid competition.

The Clayton Act also forbade a firm to acquire voting stock in related corporations in order to operate them as one large firm. The act was later amended to forbid outright purchase of competing firms. Firms wishing to purchase or to merge with a related firm now must request permission from the Antitrust Division of the U.S. Department of Justice.

Difficulties of Enforcement

Enforcement of the antitrust laws has been uneven and has depended on the particular philosophy and loyalties of the administration. Over the first seventy years of antitrust law, not one businessman was sent to jail for violation. Fines were commonly imposed, but fines were small compared to the expected profits from a "gentlemen's agreement."

In 1959, for the first time, business executives were sent to jail under the antitrust laws. Again in 1961 respected officials of major firms were imprisoned for conspiring to fix prices on electrical generating equipment.

In the early 1970s executives of large corporations were found guilty of making illegal contributions to political campaign funds. It was suspected that the contributions were aimed at forestalling antitrust prosecution. The most publicized case involved the purchase of several small companies by International Telephone and Telegraph Company. Following a large campaign pledge, ITT was allowed to keep the largest of its new acquisitions.

Recently the Antitrust Division has moved more vigorously to examine the pricing policies of highly concentrated industries. Investigations have been made of the American Telephone and Telegraph Company and of major producers in the sugar industry. In 1981 executives of firms producing certain kinds of transparent paper were found guilty of price fixing and sentenced to jail terms.

CONGLOMERATES

The courts' crackdown on horizontal and vertical mergers has led business firms to combine in new ways. In recent years corporations have formed **conglomerates,** in which the merging firms are from totally unrelated industries. A giant conglomerate may combine firms producing such diverse products as dog food, whiskey, aerospace equipment, and Chinese food. Because the merging firms are in different industries, a conglomerate does not technically reduce competition. Still, it may represent a dangerous concentration of financial and political power. What are the dangers associated with, say, an airline owning a motel chain?

The popularity of conglomerate mergers poses new questions regarding enforcement of the antitrust laws.

Viewpoint

THE DEBATE OVER BIGNESS

There is some disagreement over whether bigness in business is actually harmful. On one side of the argument, economist John Kenneth Galbraith sees benefits from large-scale enterprises. He believes that large firms may provide more funds and facilities for research and development. Furthermore, unit costs of production tend to fall as volume increases. This could mean lower prices for consumers. Galbraith would permit large firms to operate, but he recommends careful government regulation of price and output policies. All of this, of course, would add considerably to government bureaucracy and costs.

On the other side of the argument, economist Milton Friedman worries about excessive power, however it is used. He believes that individual freedom may be threatened by concentrations of financial (and political) power. Friedman recommends vigorous enforcement of the antitrust laws. He favors breaking up established market power and preventing further concentrations of power from developing.

For many decades government relaxed its prosecution of the antitrust laws. The philosophy was: bigness is not necessarily bad. As a result, concentration increased in many industries.

In 1945 a new philosophy took over. Alcoa Aluminum Company was forced to separate some of its subsidiaries into competing firms. Alcoa was not accused of outright illegal practices—just growth through good management! The new approach seemed to be to stop monopoly before it develops.

The case of the Brown Shoe Company is an example. In 1962 Brown Shoe Manufacturing Company applied for permission to merge with Kinney Shoe Stores. Together they would have made up only a very small part of the shoe market. It was felt, though, that the merger would be a dangerous start down the road to monopoly, and it was not permitted.

A more recent antitrust issue has involved parallel practices: cooperative industry policies which shut potential competitors out of the market. The breakfast food industry, for example, includes three large firms whose combined power works to deny shelf space to small cereal manufacturers. Antitrust prosecutors would like to break up the firms into competing divisions, but the cereal firms are resisting the effort.

Self-Check

1. **Firms in perfect competition:**
   a. will be producing identical products.
   b. will enter an industry in which there are economic profits.
   c. will expand or contract supply until price is equal to average total cost.
   d. will produce output at the lowest unit costs.
   e. all of the above.

2. **Monopolization is likely to result from:**
   a. ''gentlemen's agreements.''
   b. repeal of the patent laws.
   c. economic theory.
   d. low initial capital requirements.
   e. growing numbers of consumers in the market.

3. **Which of the following is not characteristic of oligopoly?**
   a. a few large firms in the industry
   b. generally high capital requirements
   c. similar cost patterns
   d. ease of entry of new firms
   e. similar pricing policies

4. **A product sold by a monopolistically competitive firm:**
   a. will be lower in price than under competition.
   b. will be identical with others in the industry.
   c. is produced by a few large firms.
   d. may experience frequent model changes.
   e. will have characteristics similar to oligopoly.

5. **Antitrust laws now forbid:**
   a. tying contracts.
   b. interlocking directorates.
   c. price discrimination by firms among customers.
   d. mergers harmful to competition.
   e. all of the above.

6. **When there is monopoly in industry:**
   a. excess economic profit will serve as a signal attracting new firms.
   b. price is the minimum for which the good can be produced.
   c. output will be greater than under competition.
   d. a larger volume of sales may mean a smaller total revenue.
   e. new firms can enter the industry with ease.

Theory in Practice

HOW DOES MONOPOLY AFFECT US?

The most nearly monopolized industry in America is probably the automobile industry. Actually it is an oligopoly industry, with three firms supplying more than 90 percent of domestic output. Antitrust laws prevent the three firms from collaborating to raise price, restrict output, or establish market shares. Still, after long years in the business, each auto manufacturer knows pretty well how the oth-

ers will behave in any market situation. As a result, their pricing and output decisions are generally similar.

How does imperfect competition affect equilibrium price and quantity?

Figure 4.3a illustrates a hypothetical demand curve for Cruisers. In a free market, many sellers would supply Cruisers, producing a market supply

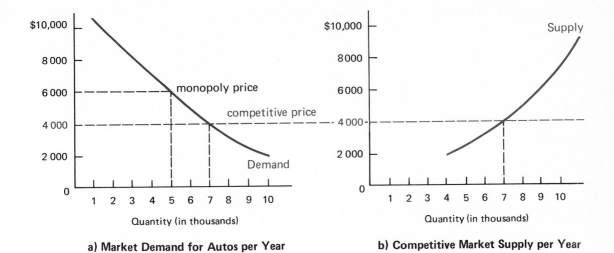

a) Market Demand for Autos per Year

b) Competitive Market Supply per Year

Figure 4.3   The Market for Cruisers.

curve like the one shown in Figure 4.3b. Each seller would be forced by competition to charge the market price of $4000. The price would be just enough to cover all costs of production including normal profit. It would also be the price where quantity supplied equals quantity demanded. (Test yourself: What would be the equilibrium quantity at a price of $4000?*)

If one firm has a monopoly in the market for Cruisers, it need not fear competition. The monopoly firm may decide to charge a price of $6000. At a price of $6000 the quantity of autos demanded is less than at the free-market price, and production is lower in the automobile industry. (Test yourself: What is the quantity demanded at a price of $6000?**) Furthermore, *the monopoly price may include excess economic profit over and above full costs of production. Without competition, however, economic profit cannot serve as a signal attracting new firms into the industry.*

Look at Table 4.1. (See page 78.) The first two columns provide hypothetical data about market demand. If Cruisers are selling for $10,000,

* 7000 units

** 5000 units

only 1000 units can be sold, for total revenue of $10 million. At a price of $3000, 8000 Cruisers can be sold, for *total revenue* of $3000 × 8000 units, or $24 million. The third column contains hypothetical cost data. One thousand Cruisers can be produced for an average total cost of ATC = $10,000. *Total costs* to the firm are $10,000 × 1000 units, or $10 million. Four thousand Cruisers could be produced for an average cost of $5000, or a total cost of $20 million.

The last column in the table allows us to compare total revenue with total costs at each level of output. The difference between *total revenue* and *total costs* is *economic profit*.

Suppose you control a monopoly firm producing Cruisers. What quantity of output would you decide to produce? You could achieve maximum economic profit by producing 5000 units and selling them for $6000 each. How much economic profit would you earn on each Cruiser?

Now suppose this is a competitive industry. The existence of economic profit would encourage other firms to enter this market. Production and sale of Cruisers would increase. New firms would cut price in order to sell more Cruisers. What is the lowest price for which firms will agree to produce

Table 4.1 Hypothetical Demand and Cost Schedules for Cruisers.

No. of Units Per Year	Price	Average Unit Cost	Total Revenue (millions)	Total Cost (millions)	Economic Profit (millions)
1000	$10,000	$10,000	$10	$10	$ 0
2000	9000	8000	18	16	2
3000	8000	6000	24	18	6
4000	7000	5000	28	20	8
5000	6000	4000	30	20	10
6000	5000	4000	30	24	6
7000	4000	4000	28	28	0
8000	3000	5000	24	40	− 16
9000	2000	7000	18	63	− 45

and sell Cruisers? How many units will be sold at this price? Why is it not a good idea to produce more Cruisers than this number?*

How does the economy suffer from monopoly? Price is higher and output of goods and services is lower than under competition. Too much of consumer spending power goes into the monopolized industry and too little is left for spending in other industries. The economy suffers a loss of technical and allocative efficiency. Furthermore, without competition the market system is less able to send out the signals necessary for quick and smooth adjustment to changing consumer demand.

OLIGOPOLY IN CIGARETTES

The four largest tobacco companies in the United States were once a single very large firm: the American Tobacco Company. In 1911 the Supreme Court dissolved the American Tobacco Company and formed four separate firms: American Tobacco, Reynolds Tobacco, Liggett and

Myers, and Lorillard. Sales of cigarettes grew steadily after that, and by 1976 per capita consumption was twenty-five times what it had been in 1911. Sales of all four firms increased with the increase in demand so that in 1977 they controlled 84% of the U.S. market.

Today's cigarette industry would be characterized as oligopoly. Like most oligopolies, the four firms avoid price competition. Price is decided through a process of price leadership, with Reynolds Tobacco Company the leader. Reynolds has the power to resist price cutting by another firm. If another firm reduces price, Reynolds cuts below and captures a larger share of the market. If another firm raises price, Reynolds refuses to follow and gains sales. The result is a tendency for all firms to set the same price.

Price leadership is possible because the major brands are regarded as good substitutes. Customers can easily switch back and forth if prices are different. Price leadership enables the firms to enjoy economic profits. Profits have averaged more than 6 percent of sales, somewhat above profits in other industries. When production costs rise and profits fall for the four tobacco firms, pressure builds up for a price increase. Normally the three other firms wait for Reynolds to make the first move. When Reynolds raises price, the other firms follow quickly.

* Lowest price is determined by minimum average cost: ATC = $4000 with production of between 5000 and 6000 units. Producing more units would force price down below ATC. Firms might produce for a price lower than ATC in the short run only if price at least covers average variable cost.

Because of their control of supply, oligopoly firms may react to changes in demand differently from competitive firms. *Competitive firms respond to an increase in demand by producing more at a higher price. They respond to a drop in demand by producing less at a lower price. Price changes tend to moderate the change in equilibrium quantity so that production and employment remain fairly stable. In oligopoly more of the adjustment to demand falls on quantity of output. Price is stable, and production may be increased or decreased by the full amount of the change in demand.*

This presents some problems for the economy as a whole. It means that production and employment will fluctuate more widely than in competition. Workers in oligopoly firms may be subject to alternating periods of heavy overtime work followed by lay-offs. Furthermore, the power to maintain stable prices during recession may add to inflation and slow recovery.

WHAT ABOUT NATURAL MONOPOLIES?

Although we have stressed the economic efficiency associated with competition in many markets, production of some services may be better carried out by one large firm. Utilities, for example, are considered *natural monopolies*. Most are privately owned, but their prices are regulated by public commissions to prevent them from behaving like monopolists!

A public utility must invest millions of dollars in productive equipment. However, once plant and equipment are in place, the utility can provide larger amounts of service with little or no additional cost. Large-scale production allows a utility to spread its fixed costs over many units of service, so that average unit costs are very low.

Let us imagine a market demand curve for electric power. Market demand includes demand from households, commercial establishments, and factories. A hypothetical market demand curve is shown in Figure 4.4.

What price and level of output would be fair to customers and also fair to the owners of the power company? It is important to be fair to the owners or they will refuse to reinvest their funds in the enterprise. Then the firm's productive capacity cannot grow with the needs of the community.

Users whose need for electric power is most urgent may be willing to pay as much as 10¢ per kilowatt hour (KWH). This might include some homeowners and many manufacturing firms. According to Figure 4.4, at a price of 10¢, a total quantity of 1 trillion KWH would be demanded per month.

Most homeowners and businesses would be willing to pay in the range of 5¢ per KWH for some power. If the rate were as low as 2¢, they would increase their usage considerably. The result is a market demand curve that slopes downward like a typical demand curve.

A *rate schedule* allows the power company to charge different rates to different groups of customers, based on the amount of power used. The company can then collect *all* the revenue under the demand curve within the permitted range. Price discrimination of this sort might be illegal for an unregulated monopoly, but the regulatory commission may permit price discrimination if it helps the

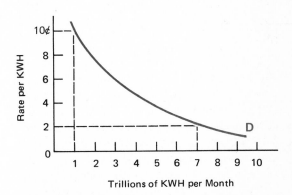

Figure 4.4   Market Demand for Electric Power.
Some users are willing to pay as much as 10¢ per KWH for electric power. If the rate falls to 2¢ per KWH, quantity demanded will be much greater.

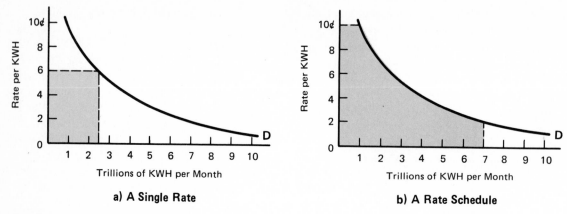

Figure 4.5   Total Revenue.
A rate schedule allows the company to collect all the revenue under the demand curve within the rate schedule.

utility cover full costs. Figure 4.5 shows the total revenue collected with a single rate for power and with a rate schedule. The figure assumes that the rate schedule ranges from 2¢ to 10¢ per KWH.

A single rate would yield revenues equal to a rectangle formed under the demand curve at the established rate. A rate schedule yields a much greater total revenue. Also, it permits customers far out at the right of the demand curve to enjoy the service even if their rate is less than the cost of production! In effect, users at the left of the curve are helping pay for the service used by those at the right.

The revenue collected by the power company is used to pay operating expenses and to compensate all those who help finance the firm's investment in plant and equipment: banks and holders of utility stocks and bonds. When operating and capital costs rise, the power company must ask the public regulatory commission for permission to raise its rate schedule. If the increase is approved, all users will pay more for the power they use. Some users will decide to use less power and move upward along their demand curves. If the power company has calculated correctly, however, it will have larger revenues to meet its higher costs.

Agreeing on a "fair" rate schedule is not easy. There are many users of electric power, all seeking low rates. There are relatively few owners of stocks and bonds seeking higher returns on their invested capital. The voting strength of the first group may influence elected commissioners to hold down rates. Or power companies may seek higher rates by making campaign contributions to commissioners.

If rates are held down, so that the return on invested capital falls, bondholders may decide to lend their funds elsewhere. Service will deteriorate. New plants and equipment will not be constructed. With revenues insufficient to cover full costs, a utility may need government help. Government help could be in the form of tax credits, subsidies, or outright government ownership of utilities.

Government intervention has some disadvantages. Utility managers may be less concerned about costs if they expect government to bail them out of a financial bind. Also, a tax-supported subsidy is financed by all taxpayers while the benefits go only to users of the service. Perhaps a more equitable solution might be for the costs to be borne by users in the form of higher rates.

Viewpoint

MONOPOLY IN MONOPOLY

It's not whether you win or lose; it's how you name the game!

That's the problem in the antitrust dispute over Monopoly.

You won't meet many Americans who aren't familiar with the game of Monopoly. Legend has it that the game was devised around the turn of the century by a Virginia Quaker, Elizabeth Magee. It was known as "The Landlord's Game." For years, several versions were played on painted oilcloth.

In 1933 a retired hotel manager from Georgia became interested in the game and bought rights to the idea. After some updating and standardizing, the patent and trademark were eventually sold to Parker Brothers. Today Parker Brothers is the world's largest producer of games and Monopoly is its star. More than 80 million games have been sold worldwide.

Such success could not forever go unchallenged. Many other manufacturers have come up with similar ideas hoping to grab a share of the market, but Parker Brothers has fought them all. Generally the company has been successful in preventing other firms from using any ideas similar to the original, one-and-only Monopoly. It was successful, that is, until 1973 when an economics professor from California came out with a new game he called Anti-Monopoly.

Professor Ralph Anspach is a specialist in antitrust law. His game is similar to the original, but instead of **building** monopoly its objective is to break it up. His idea caught on, and in the first two years he sold 280,000 games for revenues of about a million dollars. This was after investing only $5000 to set up his own company!

By law the Monopoly trademark belongs exclusively to Parker Brothers. Theirs is a **legal** monopoly. Therefore Parker Brothers is suing Professor Anspach for illegal use of their property. In turn, the professor is suing Parker Brothers over the validity of the trademark itself. He points out that some trademarks eventually become a part of the language itself and are free to be used by any firm. Kleenex, Kodak, aspirin, and even checkers are examples of brand names which now have meanings far broader than a single firm's product. And besides, he says, Anti-Monopoly does not involve competition with Monopoly at all.

Once the trademark case is settled, the right to a monopoly on Monopoly will probably be contested under the Sherman Act. The outcome cannot be considered of tremendous importance in the development of antitrust policy. But it's bound to be of interest to Monopoly lovers everywhere!

SUMMARY

1. Economic profit is an excess return over and above the full costs of resources used in production. Economic profit serves as a signal attracting new resources into an industry. Negative economic profit, or loss, signals resources to leave an industry. As firms enter (or leave) price falls (or rises) until economic profit is gradually eliminated.

2. The free movement of resources is difficult to achieve in the real world. Some industries become monopolized when conditions prevent the entry of new firms.

3. Pure monopoly is rare in American industry. However, several firms have occasionally made "gentlemen's agreements" not to compete against each other.

4. Other forms of imperfect competition are: oligopoly, dominance by a few large firms; and monopolistic competition, many small firms producing similar products.

5. A monopoly firm may reduce output and raise price above the competitive level. It will continue to collect economic profit if there are no competitors to force prices down.

6. In the late 1800s political pressure was put on Congress to outlaw vertical and horizontal monopolies. The Sherman Antitrust Act of 1890 and the Clayton Antitrust Act of 1914 forbade certain practices aimed at reducing competition. More recently, competition has been threatened by conglomerates, mergers of unrelated companies.

7. Very large-scale firms may be an advantage in some types of production. This is because of the low unit costs associated with high volume. Firms in these industries are called natural monopolies.

8. Where large-scale firms are desirable, public commissions have been established to regulate price and output practices. The job of regulating prices and profits is not an easy one.

TERMS TO REMEMBER

monopoly: an industry supplied by one firm, or by a group of firms acting as one.

price makers: firms that can raise their prices and still sell some output.

horizontal integration: a combination of firms all producing the same type of output.

vertical integration: a combination of firms each involved in one stage of production of a particular good.

oligopoly: an industry supplied by a few large firms.

monopolistic competition: an industry supplied by many small firms each producing a slightly different product.

conglomerate: a combination of firms each producing an entirely different good or service.

price takers: firms that can sell any quantity at the market price but no quantity at a higher price.

TOPICS FOR DISCUSSION

1. Make sure you understand the difference between the following pairs of terms:

   vertical mergers and horizontal mergers
   free-market pricing and monopoly pricing
   price takers and price makers

2. How is each of the following involved in the problem of enforcing the antitrust laws?

   natural monopolies
   price leadership
   conglomerates

3. One area in which monopoly power may be of particular concern in American democracy is the news media. The situation is especially threatening in towns where there is single ownership of newspaper, radio, and television facilities. The Antitrust Division of the Department of Justice has been pressuring the Federal Communications Commission to draw up rules to deal with this problem. One proposal would require owners to sell or swap properties in order to increase competition in local markets.

   Can you suggest any advantages in single ownership of the news media? What are the disadvantages? What position would you take with respect to the proposal before the regulatory commission?

4. In the late 1800s, farmers of the Midwestern states complained they were being squeezed between monopoly suppliers and monopoly buyers. They had to pay high prices to suppliers of agricultural

machinery, freight service, and fuel; and they had to accept low prices from meat packers, grain dealers, and the sugar trust.

Do such problems exist today? How can the courts help reduce them? How is the American citizen affected?

5. Public utilities often face the problem of "peak loads" at particular times of the day or year. Power usage is greatest during the day (industrial plants) and in the summer (air conditioning). Telephone usage is greatest on weekdays (business calls). Mass-transit usage is greatest in the morning and evening rush hours. A public utility must invest in additional capital necessary to fill exceptionally high demand, but capital may be idle during other times of the day or year. Costs may also be higher during peak periods if old, obsolete equipment is brought into service to fill the need.

How might a public regulatory commission deal with this problem? Would you approve of price discrimination in these situations? How would price discrimination work?

6. Explain how the goal of technical and allocative efficiency is served under competition and without competition.

SUGGESTED READINGS

Backman, Jules, "The Steel Industry: Problems and Solutions," *Challenge,* July/August 1978, pp. 7–12.

Baker, Donald I., "Price-Fixers, Beware!" *Across the Board,* February 1977, p. 37.

Bock, Betty, "New Numbers on Concentration: Facts and Fears," *Across the Board,* March 1976, p. 18.

Bock, Betty, "No Fault Monopoly," *Across the Board,* November 1979, pp. 55–63.

Burck, Charles G., "A Comeback Decade for the American Car," *Fortune,* June 2, 1980, p. 52.

"Flexible Pricing," *Business Week,* December 12, 1977, p. 78.

Hayes, Linda Snyder, "Scripto Erases Its Past," *Fortune,* November 17, 1980, p. 95.

"Kellogg: Still the Cereal People," *Business Week,* November 26, 1979, p. 80.

Kiechel, Walter, III, "The Soggy Case Against the Cereal Industry," *Fortune,* April 10, 1978, p. 49.

Kindkead, Gwen, "Heileman Toasts the Future with 34 Beers," *Fortune,* June 18, 1979.

Little, Royal, "How I'm Deconglomerating the Conglomerates," *Fortune,* July 16, 1979, p. 120.

Louis, Arthur M., "The $150-Million Cigarette," *Fortune,* November 17, 1980, p. 121.

Loving, Rush, Jr., "The Pros and Cons of Airline Deregulation," *Fortune,* August 1977, p. 209.

"No-frills Food: New Power for the Supermarkets," *Business Week,* March 23, 1981, p. 70.

"An Oil Giant's Dilemma," *Business Week,* August 25, 1980, p. 60.

Poe, Randall, "Letter from Mad. Ave.," *Across the Board,* February 1979, pp. 49–58.

Quirt, John, "Putting Barbie Back Together Again," *Fortune,* September 8, 1980, p. 84.

"Trans World Corp.: The Strategy Squeeze on the Airline," *Business Week,* May 19, 1980, p. 104.

Uttal, Bro, "The Animals of Silicon Valley," *Fortune,* January 12, 1981, p. 92.

CHAPTER 5

Labor Markets and the Labor Movement

or You've Come a Long Way, Maybe

Tools for Study

A first-grade teacher struggled through a long, rainy day to keep her squirmy dears quietly and constructively occupied (with no recess period for the children to release energies while the teacher regained hers). At last, it was dismissal time, and appropriate mittens, hoods, and galoshes (last year's small-sized) had to be fitted, then exchanged, and often exchanged a second time. This was all accomplished amid great hilarity and confusion. One little boy amused himself in the hubbub by exploring the contents of the teacher's desk. He found the brown window envelope containing her paycheck and asked what it was. Upon hearing the answer, he queried, ''Oh, do you work someplace?''

Learning Objectives

After reading this chapter, you will be able to:

1. explain how supply and demand work in resource markets.
2. explain the basic rule of employment for deciding how many workers will be employed and at what wage.
3. discuss the history of the labor movement.
4. distinguish between craft and industrial unions.
5. define closed shop and secondary boycott.

Issues Covered

How do resource markets adjust to changes in supply and demand?
How may labor unions interfere with free-market adjustments?
How does the collective bargaining process work?
How is labor changing?

THE NATURE OF WORK

Most of us ''work someplace'' whether or not we receive a paycheck. Indeed, in Western society the nature of the work performed by a person is probably the most important mark of his or her social status. Our work is essential to our emotional health and to the progress of our society. But in a more immediate sense, work is essential to our

Viewpoint

THE PROBLEM OF ALIENATION

There was a parlor game making the rounds several years ago in which the players were asked to answer the question, "Who are you?" with three responses. Supposedly, deep psychological insights could be derived from the answers and their sequence. For example, a man who answers "I am an engineer, I am a Republican, I am a golfer" reveals much of his personal conception of self.

How frightening it would be to have no answers to the question! Without identity, one almost ceases to exist. And most of us in Western culture achieve our identifies from our work. We *do,* therefore we *are!*

When modern manufacturing jobs became simplified, workers began to lose some of the self-identity associated with particular skills. Repeating one simple operation over and over reduces a worker's sense of pride of creativity and involvement in a finished product. At one time it may have been possible to reply in answer to the parlor question, "I am an automaker." But it is hardly uplifting to admit "I am a lever operator," or a "wrench twister," or a "windshield lifter."

Karl Marx called this problem *alienation.* Alienation is the separation of a worker from the product of his or her work. It diminishes a worker's sense of self-worth and the capacity for creative expression and personal growth. Also, alienation often leads to boredom, poor quality production, and reduced worker productivity.

These ill effects have produced a deliberate turnabout in some manufacturing firms, from the increasing simplification of jobs back to complexity. (Some might say it is contrived complexity.) In some plants, teams of workers are allowed to organize total production of a product as in the "old days" before the assembly line. The team is rewarded according to the quantity and quality of production. Total output may be less than under the assembly-line method, but there are compensating psychological benefits in improved employee morale and, frequently, better quality products as well.

---

material well-being and survival. Lacking sufficient banana trees beneath which we can repose as ripened fruit continuously satisfies our hunger, we are compelled to "rise and shine" and "put our shoulders to the wheel." We must cooperate to produce the goods and services we need for existence. Someone must cultivate the grain, weave the cloth, distill the drugs, and yes, even bury us.

The change from individual self-sufficiency to cooperation marked the beginning of economic development. As communities began to divide the necessary work, and individuals began to specialize in particular tasks, they found they could produce more than they could working alone. Adam Smith's famous story of a pin factory showed the benefits of specialization. When workers were assigned specific subtasks on an assembly line, they could produce many times more pins than if each concentrated on producing finished pins.

During the early 1900s two American businessmen, Frederick Taylor and Frank Gilbreth, expanded the concept of specialization. Their studies of *task management* centered around **division of labor;** they broke jobs down into simple operations requiring little special training or effort. Division of labor was soon applied by Henry Ford in his first auto assembly lines.

The effect of specialization and division of labor is to expand dramatically the output produced per hour of work—it enables societies to produce not only the necessities but also some of the luxuries that enrich life. Thus modern consumers can enjoy an abundance of autos, ice makers, and what-have-you!

LABOR SUPPLY AND DEMAND AND THE EQUILIBRIUM WAGE

In this chapter we will focus on labor as a productive resource. Resources are bought and sold in markets similar to the markets for finished goods and services. Morever, the principles that govern supply and demand of land, capital, and entrepreneurial ability apply as well to supply and demand of labor resources.

Resource supply is the quantity resource owners would offer for sale at various market prices. Like any other supply curve, resource supply must be drawn for a certain period of time over which factors other than price are assumed to remain constant. Thus, the *supply of labor* is the units of labor which would be offered at various wage rates over a certain period of time. When the individual supply curves of all workers in a particular market are added together, the result is a market supply curve.

In general, the supply of labor obeys the *law of supply:* workers will tend to offer more units of labor at higher wages.

Likewise, the *demand for labor* obeys the *law of demand:* firms will tend to hire more units of

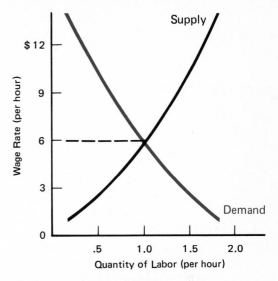

Figure 5.1a A Market for Labor.
Hours of labor supplied increase as the wage rate increases. Hours of labor demanded fall.

labor at lower prices. Market demand for labor is the sum of all individual firms' demand curves. As we found in product markets, the intersection of supply and demand shows equilibrium price and quantity: the wage and the units of labor employed during the time period for which supply and demand curves are drawn.

The supply curve in Figure 5.1a shows the quantities of labor that will be offered for employment in a particular market at various wage rates. The supply curve slopes upward showing that larger quantities will generally be offered at higher wage rates. The demand curve slopes downward because larger quantities will be employed only at lower wages. The equilibrium wage rate on Figure 5.1a is $6 per hour. At a wage of $6, a total of one million units of labor will be hired in this market.

Opportunity Cost

In any resource market, equilibrium price reflects the *opportunity cost* of using the resource in a particular way. Equilibrium price is higher when there

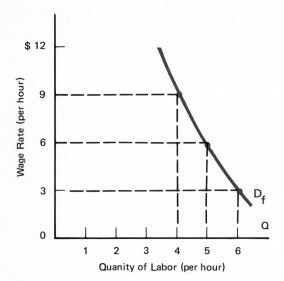

Figure 5.1b   A Firm's Demand for Labor.
A firm's demand curve for labor slopes downward because of the law of variable proportions.

are competing uses for a resource and lower when the resource is limited to one use. Likewise, equilibrium price is higher when the resource is particularly scarce and lower when the resource is plentiful.

In labor markets, equilibrium wage determines another result. For an individual firm, the market wage determines the most *efficient* combination of labor to use with the firm's own capital resources for producing goods and services.

A Firm's Demand for Labor

A firm employs two kinds of resources for producing output: **fixed resources** and **variable resources.**

Fixed resources are those which the firm cannot easily change over a certain period called the short run. For example, the amount of land and the number of plants with productive equipment in use usually cannot be altered in the short run. Fixed resources cannot be increased or cut back in the short run, but a firm can vary the quantity of output

produced by using them more or less intensively. A firm varies its rate of production by adding different quantities of variable resources to its fixed resources. Variable resources are such things as labor, raw materials, and the electric power necessary for operating the fixed plant.

The Law of Variable Proportions or the Law of Diminishing Returns

As the proportion of variable resources to fixed resources changes, total production tends to change also. The first units of variable resources increase production by larger and larger amounts; total product increases at an increasing rate. Eventually, however, adding more variable resources increases production by smaller and smaller amounts; total production increases at a decreasing rate. At some point, the addition of more variable resources may even cause production to fall.

This principle is known as the **law of variable proportions** or the **law of diminishing returns.** It recognizes that there is some ideal proportion of variable resources to fixed resources where production is most efficient. Beyond this most efficient range of variable resources, each additional unit of variable resource adds less to total product than the one before.

Equilibrium Wage and Employment

There appears to be some efficient range of variable resources to be employed with a firm's fixed quantity of land or capital. If the firm employs too few variable resources, it loses the value of the output that could have been produced by their addition. If the firm employs too many variable resources, production will be inefficient; unit costs will rise as fixed resources are overused.

Within its ideal employment range, a firm must decide precisely how many units of variable resources to employ. That employment decision rests on two kinds of market prices: (1) the price of

Table 5.1 Resource and Production Data (per hour).

(1) Number of Workers Q_L	(2) Total Product (per hour) TP	(3) Value of Total Product TP $\times$ p	(4) Value of Additional Production Δ(TP $\times$ p)	(5) Wage Rate (per hour) w
1	2	6	6	6
2	5	15	9	6
3	9	27	12	6
4	12	36	9	6
5	14	42	6	6
6	15	45	3	6
7	14	42	-3	6

final output and (2) the price of the variable resource. If a firm is to employ the most efficient proportion of variable resources, it will follow the basic rule of employment: *continue to employ additional units of a variable resource up to the point where the value of the output of the last unit hired is just offset by the cost of hiring it.* As long as this rule is honored, a firm is using its fixed and variable resources most efficiently.

Let us use a hypothetical example to illustrate the rule of employment. Table 5.1 provides hypothetical data for a Grumpet firm that sells grumpets for $3 each. The firm owns a certain quantity of fixed plant and equipment and may employ various quantities of labor at an hourly rate of $6. Column (1) lists quantities of labor, and Column (2) shows total product at various levels of employment per hour. Notice that increasing employment of variable resources causes hourly production to increase first at an increasing rate, then at a decreasing rate, and finally if as many as 7 workers are employed, to diminish.

Column (3) lists the value of hourly production at various quantities of variable resources, and Column (4) shows the value of the *additional* output associated with hiring *additional* workers during the hour. Column (5) lists the hourly wage.

How many workers should the firm hire? To hire 1, 2, or 3 workers would enable the firm to sell its grumpets and pay the workers' wages.

However, hiring only 1, 2, or 3 workers would sacrifice the gain from hiring the fourth worker at $6 and selling his or her additional output for $9. In fact, the firm should hire up to the fifth worker, whose additional production is just sufficient to pay the hourly wage.

Now, suppose the wage rate should fall to $3. At a wage of $3 a sixth worker adds enough to total product to pay the wage. (Test yourself: How many workers would be hired at a wage of $9?*)

Have you noticed that, given the behavior of production when variable resources are employed, the quantity of labor demanded depends on the wage rate? In fact, we have just located 3 points on this firm's demand curve for labor: w = $9 and Q_L = 4; w = $6 and Q_L = 5; w = $3 and Q_L = 6. These points have been plotted on Figure 5.1b and connected to form a demand curve.

We may summarize these results as follows. Adding variable resources to a certain quantity of fixed resources eventually causes total production to increase at a decreasing rate. A firm calculates its own demand curve for a resource by measuring the value of the resource's contribution to total production. Then the firm hires the quantity for which the value of additional production is equal to the price of the resource. The firm's demand curve slopes downward because of the law of variable

*4

proportions (or the law of diminishing returns). Thus, smaller additions to total production mean that more resources will be employed only at a lower resource price.

Derived Demand

We say that demand for labor is a *derived demand*. Firms hire labor because there is demand for the products labor can produce. Workers are hired up to the point where the cost of hiring the last worker is just offset by the value of the worker's output. This means that workers will be paid a wage equal to the value of the goods or services produced by the **last** worker hired. In fact, all variable resources will be paid according to the value of the output produced by the last unit.

After all variable resources are paid, the remainder of the revenue from sale of output goes to the owners of the fixed resources used. This ensures that each type of resource is rewarded according to its contribution to production. Furthermore, it ensures that total income received during any production period is just enough to purchase all the goods and services produced.

LABOR'S SHARE

Look again at Figure 5.1a. Can you show on Figure 5.1a the space that represents the share of total output paid to labor? How does the size of the space reflect labor's productivity and market demand for labor's output?*

Of the four types of productive resources, labor receives the largest share of total output. One reason for labor's large share is the size and quality of the labor force. More and better workers have contributed to a growing economic pie and a growing share for labor. From only 60 percent of total

production in 1929, labor's share grew to 75 percent in 1980.* Rental income declined over that period from 6 percent to 2 percent, while interest earnings rose from 5 to 8 percent. Income of unincorporated enterprises, corporate profits, and farm income also declined, from 29 to 15 percent of total production.

Differences in resource shares are the result of different supply and demand conditions in resource markets. For an especially productive resource in limited supply, share of output might be relatively great. Less productive resources in plentiful supply would receive smaller shares. Likewise, changes in resource supply and demand produce changes in resource shares. Whether resource shares increase or decrease with change depends on elasticities, much as price changes in product markets depend on elasticities of demand and supply.

CHANGES IN DEMAND FOR LABOR

Growth in job opportunities has been uneven among industries. More workers have been needed in state and local government, retail trade, transportation and public utilities, and services. The demand curves in these industries have been shifting to the right over the last decade, contributing to a rising equilibrium wage.

Employment opportunities have grown more slowly in the federal government, mining and construction, and certain manufacturing industries. The demand curves in these sectors have shifted very little so that their wage rates have not increased much in real terms.

Some examples of average hourly wage rates for workers before taxes for 1971 and 1981 are in Table 5.2. Figures are from the *Monthly Labor Review,* published by the U.S. Department of Labor. The third column in the table shows the gain in real wages—wage gains corrected for inflation—over the decade.

---

* Labor's share is the rectangle formed beneath the demand curve at the equilibrium wage. It is determined by the quantity of output produced by labor and the price of output along with the supply of labor curve.

*Labor's increasing share is in part the result of a movement away from self-employment, where earnings would be reported as profit, to work for hire.

Table 5.2 Average Hourly Wages.

	Hourly Wage 1971	Hourly Wage 1981	Change in Real Wage
Mining	$4.00	$7.04	− 18%
Construction	5.56	9.84	− 17
Lumber and Wood Products	3.06	6.85	30
Furniture and Fixtures	2.84	5.77	9
Stone, Clay, and Glass Products	3.55	7.86	27
Primary Metal Products	4.09	10.44	61
Fabricated Metal Products	3.67	7.90	21
Machinery, except Electrical	3.90	8.61	27
Electrical and Electronic Equipment	3.43	7.39	21
Transportation Equipment	4.44	9.89	29
Instruments and Related Products	3.48	7.22	13
Miscellaneous Manufacturing	2.94	5.81	4
Food and Kindred Products	3.32	7.22	23
Tobacco Products	3.02	8.35	82
Textile Mill Products	2.54	5.33	16
Apparel	2.48	4.89	3
Paper Products	3.58	8.28	37
Printing and Publishing	4.08	7.94	1
Chemicals and Allied Products	3.84	8.75	34
Petroleum and Coal Products	4.49	11.18	55
Rubber and Miscellaneous Plastics	3.32	6.96	16
Leather Products	2.58	4.86	− 6
Transportation and Public Utilities	4.08	9.38	36
Wholesale and Retail Trade	2.83	5.81	11
Finance and Real Estate	3.24	6.21	− 2
Services	2.95	6.28	19

HISTORY OF THE LABOR MOVEMENT

In the early years of the Industrial Revolution, two groups competed for larger shares of the economic pie: a small, well-organized, property-owning class of capitalists and a large, unorganized class of workers. The unequal power of these two groups resulted in a great gap between the living standards of the "propertyless proletariat" and the owners of the new factories. According to Karl Marx, a nineteenth-century political and economic theorist, private ownership of capital leads to class conflict and, ultimately, revolution. Revolution is followed by movement to a higher stage of historical development. Marx believed that the first great revolution moved Western nations from feudalism to capitalism, and the next would move capitalist nations to socialism. The greatest revolution of all would finally move socialist nations to communism.

When Marx was living, the possibility of class warfare was a real concern. In England, the birthplace of the Industrial Revolution, tenant farmers were forced off the land during the period of the enclosures; large landowners "enclosed" their land in order to raise wool for the new textile industry. Forced into the towns in great droves, the peasants became labor power for factories and mines. Marx told pitiful stories of women and young children working long hours underground and dying of disease or malnutrition at an early age.

During any period of rapid industrial development, workers are needed to build the capital for producing more goods and services in the future. Production of consumer goods and services must be cut back in order to produce the necessary capital equipment. Sacrifices are most easily obtained from unorganized and desperate groups, for whom any employment at all is better than starvation.

According to Marx, workers' hardships would eventually create class consciousness and rebellion. Violent revolution would overthrow the ruling class, and workers would seize the mines and factories. Afterward, all capital resources would be operated in the interests of the working class alone.

Radical Unionism and Business Unionism

The first European labor unions were looked upon by radical Marxists as the beginnings of a new international brotherhood of labor. The new unions were expected to overthrow capitalism and replace it with socialism.

In the United States, however, revolutionary unions were soon challenged by **business unions,** concerned more with improving the material conditions of workers than with revolutionary politics. A strong consensus of cooperation developed between labor and management. Emphasis was on *job* needs rather than *class* demands. Workers generally remained aloof from revolutionary politics.

The most successful unions in the United States have emphasized specific problems of work: wages, hours, sick leave, retirement, seniority, and fringe benefits. Unions have sought solutions to problems within the capitalist system. Too, contrary to Marxian expectations, the American sys-

tem has provided higher standards of living both for the capitalist class and for the "propertyless proletariat." It has also allowed many workers to become owners of capital themselves, something else that Marx did not foresee.

Craft Unions and Industrial Unions

Eighteenth-century labor unions in the United States were **craft unions,** similar to the guilds of the Middle Ages. Their members specialized in skilled crafts such as shoemaking, carpentry, or printing. The unions were generally small, and they quickly disbanded if employers objected to their existence. Until 1842, unions were considered illegal conspiracies in restraint of trade.

As industry spread in the nineteenth century, craft unions grew in number and size. But a question arose over the nature of union membership. Craft unions were *exclusive* organizations, limited to skilled craftsmen. Some new unions were more *inclusive.* They invited all wage earners in an industry to join together under a single banner. An example of this type of **industrial union** was the Knights of Labor, which planned a nationwide federation of unions of skilled and unskilled workers alike.

In 1886, the exclusive, craft formula won out when the American Federation of Labor was organized, with cigarmaker Samuel Gompers as president. Many local craft unions joined the AFL. At the turn of the century, union membership comprised 750,000 workers, roughly 3 percent of the labor force. By 1920 membership had grown to five million, 12 percent of the labor force.

The 1930s

Union growth slowed during the 1920s because of general prosperity and economic progress. It declined further with the unemployment of the Depression years. (Can you suggest a reason?*)

* When jobs are scarce, finding a job becomes more important than maintaining union wage scales.

By the mid-1930s the federal government was struggling with the problem of falling income, output, and employment. The Roosevelt administration was sympathetic to the problems of labor unions and, in 1935, Congress passed the Wagner National Labor Relations Act. The act gave labor the right to organize and to bargain collectively with employers.

In that same year, the lingering conflict between the skilled, exclusive craft philosophy and the unskilled, inclusive industrial approach to organization again divided the labor movement. Unions of skilled workers remained with the AFL. Unions of unskilled workers formed the more inclusive Congress of Industrial Organizations in 1935 under mineworker president John L. Lewis. The CIO became a national union for unskilled mass production workers in modern automated industries.

By 1945, total union membership included almost one fourth of the civilian work force.

Postwar Labor Problems

Unions generally refrained from strikes and demands for large increases in wages during World War II. But after the war ended, unions demanded raises to offset rising inflation, and a wave of strikes broke out. Congress reacted by passing the Taft-Hartley Act of 1947 to restrict the power of unions. The law retained the bargaining rights formerly guaranteed to unions but placed limits on strikes and certain "unfair labor practices." The law granted the President the right to obtain an 80-day injunction to postpone a strike and outlawed practices such as the *closed shop* and *secondary boycotts*.

Closed shop rules had required employers to hire only union members. Hiring had been carried out only through the union at union wages. The Taft-Hartley Act replaced closed shop with *union shop,* in which workers may be required to join a union after they are hired.

A *boycott* is a refusal to do business with a firm because of its policies and is generally legal. However, **secondary boycotts** are sympathetic boycotts against a firm because of its policies toward *another* union and are illegal.

Perhaps the most controversial part of the Taft-Hartley Act is Section 14B. This section allows individual states to pass "right-to-work laws." Right-to-work laws forbid union shop within the state and weaken a union's influence on the work force. About twenty states, mostly in the South and Midwest, have such laws.

In 1955, the AFL and the CIO buried their differences and merged into a single organization—the AFL-CIO. It was felt that the combined organization would be better able to deal with growing public opposition to unions. Later, several unions, such as the Teamsters and United Auto Workers, broke apart from the AFL-CIO. (The Auto Workers returned in 1981.)

Corruption in national unions in the 1950s prompted congressional investigation by the McClellan Committee. New laws were passed to regulate the internal affairs of unions. The Landrum-Griffin Act of 1959 required democratic election of union leaders and called for detailed reporting of union finances.

UNIONISM TODAY

Total union membership in the United States has grown slowly in recent years. In 1950 about 15 million workers belonged to unions. By 1981 union membership had increased to 20.2 million. However, this represents a diminishing share of the work force—from one-third in 1950 to less than one-fifth today.

In part, declining union power is a result of the changing structure of the U.S. economy. We are becoming increasingly a service economy. Almost half of consumer expenditures go for health, education, recreation, housing, and other services. Three fourths of the labor force now work in the service industries: transportation and public utilities; trade, finance, and real estate; and government. These white-collar, highly skilled, and professional workers have traditionally been the most difficult to organize.

In one sense, labor's weakening position is a result of past successes. Pay increases won by unions have frequently priced their members out of the market. High union labor costs have pushed some firms out of business and disrupted entire industries. The automobile industry in the U.S. suffers from high United Auto Workers' wages relative to low wage costs abroad. In many cases, nonunion workers have taken over jobs lost by high-cost union workers. This is particularly true in the building construction industry.

As their strength has diminished, unions have turned their attention to establishing a political climate favorable to labor's goals. They support goverment policies promoting high employment, federally supported job training, union wage scales for federal contractors, a legal minimum wage law, and national health insurance.

The largest unions are the Teamsters, the United Auto Workers, and the Steelworkers, each with more than 1 million members. Other strong unions are the Brotherhood of Electrical Workers, Retail Clerks, and Communication Workers. The fastest growing union today is the Association of State, County, and Municipal Employees, with more than 1 million members.

Self-Check

1. A significant force for economic development is:
   a. specialization.
   b. division of labor.
   c. interregional trade.
   d. all of the above.
   e. none of the above.

2. The employment level of a variable resource is based on:
   a. its price.
   b. the price for which the final product sells.
   c. the existence of some quantity of fixed resources.
   d. both (a) and (b).
   e. All answers are correct.

3. Karl Marx predicted that:
   a. tenant farmers would revolt against landowners.
   b. violent revolution would redistribute property.
   c. unions would make peaceful gains.
   d. labor and management could work together profitably.
   e. employment of labor would increase with advances in technology.

4. Which of the following laws is most harmful to union interests?
   a. Wagner National Labor Relations Act
   b. Clayton Antitrust Act
   c. Taft-Hartley Act
   d. Landrum-Griffin Act
   e. None is harmful to union interests.

5. In 1981, union membership in the United States amounted to:
   a. about one third of the labor force.
   b. about one fourth of the labor force.
   c. about one fifth of the labor force.
   d. an insignificant fraction of the labor force.
   e. a large force of radical revolutionaries.

Theory in Practice

CHANGES IN RESOURCE SUPPLY AND DEMAND

We have focused on labor as the largest class of productive resource. Other resources are subject to the same kinds of demand and supply conditions that affect labor. Throughout the economic system, changes are constantly taking place in the availability of resources (supply) and in their productivity and the value of their output (demand).

Markets must constantly adjust to changes in equilibrium price and quantity of land, capital, and entrepreneurial ability.

Figure 5.2 illustrates an increase in resource supply and a fall in equilibrium price. How will a lower equilibrium price affect the economic system? In general, we would expect a lower price to encourage firms to use more of this resource; they will move down their demand curves and employ more of the more plentiful resource. For example,

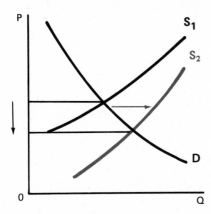

Figure 5.2   Increased Supply, Lower Price.

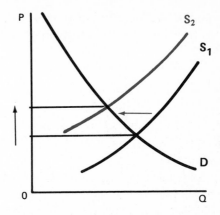

Figure 5.3   Decreased Supply, Higher Price.

larger supplies of skilled labor, new sources of mineral resources, and more readily available capital equipment should result in greater use of these resources.

Figure 5.3 illustrates a decrease in resource supply and a rise in equilibrium price. A decrease in the supply of a particular resource will generally cause a rise in price. The higher price will discourage firms from using this resource; they will move up their demand curves and employ less of the resource. Throughout the economy, firms will substitute more plentiful (and cheaper) resources for the scarcer (and more expensive) resource. For example, reduced supplies of certain types of labor, poorer sources of mineral resources, and scarcer capital equipment should reduce the employment of these resources.

Are price changes helpful to the economy in terms of the efficient use of scarce resources? Are price changes helpful in encouraging the owners of resources to supply larger or smaller quantities for hire? Trace the effects on resource supply of an increase in demand and a higher equilibrium price. How are the results helpful to the economy? Now trace the effects on resource supply of a decrease in demand and a lower equilibrium price. What are the results in terms of production of resources in the economy as a whole?

What productive resources are you developing as a student? Was your decision influenced by supply and demand in a particular resource market? How would changes in supply or demand affect your decision?

Test yourself: consider the following examples. Explain the adjustments that would follow each of these changes in market conditions. Then graph the resource market or markets affected and demonstrate the change in price and quantity employed.

1. The Defense Department increases its orders for military aircraft. What labor markets will be affected? Will there be shifts in demand or supply? What other resource markets may eventually be affected?

2. A saturated market causes a reduction in the price of instant photographic equipment. How does lower product price affect the demand for resources used to produce cameras?

3. Jamaica, a substantial producer of bauxite used in manufacturing aluminum, reduces its shipments to U.S. aluminum manufacturers. How does this affect the market for aluminum used in the production of automobiles? What substitute or complementary markets may also be affected?

4. World famine raises the export price of American grain. How will higher grain prices affect the market for U.S. farmland and implements? Will there also be effects in markets for suburban homes?

A BACKWARD BENDING SUPPLY CURVE

The supply of any resource depends on the willingness of resource owners to offer it in the market. The supply of labor resources is unique because labor is inseparable from its owner! This sometimes makes for a peculiar supply curve.

We have said that the price of a resource reflects its *opportunity costs:* the resource's alternative employments in other kinds of production. But *labor's* opportunity costs include also the cost of not working at all. Deciding to supply labor in production requires a wage that is high enough to offset the worker's own sacrifice of *leisure time.*

In general, we find that supplying small quantities of labor involves such a small sacrifice that a low wage is sufficient. Supplying larger quantities involves greater sacrifice and requires a higher wage. The result is a typical upward-sloping supply curve like the one we saw in Figure 5.1. But suppose a worker reaches such a high level of material comfort that leisure becomes more valuable than additional earnings, whatever the wage. When a worker reaches an income level adequate for his or her desired standard of living, the worker's supply curve may bcome very steep and may even *bend backward* to the left.

Figure 5.4 illustrates a backward-bending supply curve. At a wage of w_1 a worker would offer h_1 hours of work for total income of $Ow_1 \times Oh_1$. If wages rose to w_2, workers could enjoy a higher income of $Ow_2 \times Oh_2$ by supplying more hours of work. But working only Oh_3 hours would yield the same income as before and leave more hours for leisure. Thus the higher wage has the effect of reducing quantity supplied!

What is the actual level of wages at which workers will begin to reduce hours worked? Of

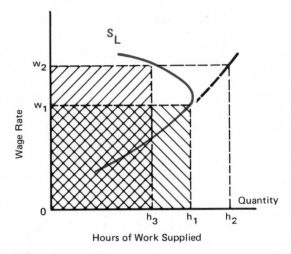

Figure 5.4   A Backward Bending Supply Curve of Labor.

course, this wage level would be different for different workers. It depends on their current living standards relative to their desired living standards; and it depends on their attitudes toward work and leisure. For "workaholics" the bend would occur at a very high level of w. It is generally believed that workers in tropical climates experience the bend in labor supply at a low level of w. Can you explain why? Can you identify groups in the U.S. economy for which the bend might occur at a lower level than others? Might other resources also be subject to backward-bending supply curves? Why?

LABOR UNIONS AND FREE MARKET ADJUSTMENTS

Unions affect resource markets in much the same way that monopolies affect product markets. In both cases, the goal is to control supply and keep price higher than it would be in free markets.*

* Economist John Kenneth Galbraith believes that the trend toward union organization was a reaction to monopoly in product markets. He describes unions as "countervailing power," labor power to balance the power of industrial giants.

Union Wage Rates

As we saw earlier in this chapter, a craft union is composed of all workers with a particular skill, like the International Brotherhood of Electrical Workers. In effect, members of a craft union represent the entire supply of this type of labor.

Historically, craft unions have tried to limit their membership, much as the American Medical Association and the American Bar Association have tried to limit the number of doctors and lawyers. Unions limit supply by establishing long apprentice programs and controlling who can enter them; though many former discriminatory practices are now illegal, unions still control the number of apprentices who are accepted.

The result is that there are fewer craftsmen than there probably would be under free-market conditions. There is no free-market supply curve like the one in Figure 5.1. Instead, the supply curve for this type of labor is a vertical line drawn at the quantity of labor made available by the union. Look at Figure 5.5 and note the effect on the equilibrium wage rate for craftsmen. Whereas the free market wage rate would be about $7 per hour, the rate for unionized workers is about $11 per hour in this market.

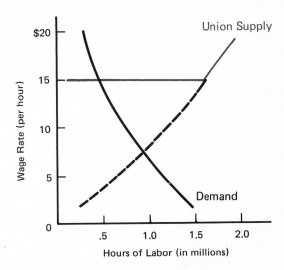

Figure 5.6 An Industrial Union and Equilibrium Wage.

In contrast to a craft union, an industrial union represents all workers in an industry, whether skilled or unskilled. Again, control of the supply of labor enables the union to establish a higher level of wage rates. The union determines its wage rate through bargaining with management, keeping as an ultimate threat the possibility of a strike if a satisfactory wage agreement cannot be reached. Once a contract is signed, no labor will be supplied at a rate lower than the agreed-upon price. Thus, the supply curve becomes horizontal at that level, as shown in Figure 5.6. Firms can hire any number of workers shown on the horizontal portion of the supply curve. Larger quantities might be hired by moving up the free-market supply curve and paying a higher wage. Control of supply pushes the wage rate from a free-market wage of $7 to a union wage of $15.

Notice the level of employment in Figures 5.5 and 5.6. Union control of supply prevents many willing workers from entering certain markets. The result is a lower level of employment and higher labor costs of production. Lack of free competition interferes with the free flow of labor resources and reduces the efficiency of industry. Test yourself: in Figure 5.5, what is the difference in employment at a wage rate of $11 and that of $7? In Figure 5.6,

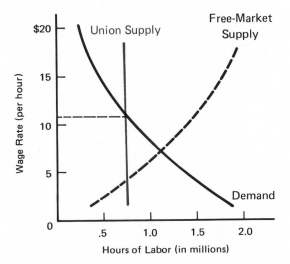

Figure 5.5 A Craft Union and Equilibrium Wage.

what is the difference in employment at a wage rate of $15 and that of $7?*

Actual Experience

How have labor unions actually affected the level of wages and employment in the industrialized nations? The answer depends to some extent on the character of the unions and the type of society in which they exist. In the United States, generally reasonable demands from labor and a flexible social environment have helped ease conflicts between labor and management and have moderated the effects of unionism.

It is difficult to separate the economic effects of unionism from the effects of other tendencies in the economic environment. For example, rising wages may result not only from union power but also from:

1. a greater willingness of business firms to grant wage increases;
2. government policies promoting full employment at any costs;
3. administered pricing, where large firms pass on higher wage costs to consumers in the form of higher prices;
4. the end of rural to urban migration, which formerly provided cheap labor and held wage demands down.

The combination of unionism with these other factors has kept wages higher during recessions than they would otherwise have been. For example, while prices tumbled during the Great Depression, wages of union members fell only slightly. When economic activity is on the upswing, contract negotiations may lag behind price inflation, so that unionism may actually slow the pace of wage increases. In both these cases, unionism may contribute to a more stable level of income and spending.

During periods of sustained growth and full employment, union wages may rise more rapidly

than the prices of finished products, squeezing profits and discouraging new business investments. This is a particularly serious problem when productivity growth slows and labor cost per unit of output is increasing.

The most powerful unions are those of skilled craftsmen for whom there are no clear substitutes. Highly skilled craftsmen can insist on higher wages with little fear of unemployment. This is because the demand for skilled labor is relatively inelastic: firms will continue to employ necessary workers at higher and higher wage rates. Over the long run, however, substitutes may be developed for high-priced labor, and labor demand will become more elastic. Also, consumers may find lower-priced substitutes for goods produced by high-priced labor, and labor demand will become more elastic, further reducing the derived demand for labor.

The best example of this development is the bituminous coal mining industry. A strong mineworkers' union in the 1940s and 1950s drove wages up to a point where mineowners sought substitutes; they were finally able to develop capital equipment to substitute for high-priced union labor. Morever, consumers and business firms were able to substitute cheap oil and gas for high-priced coal. The result was more coal miners forced out of work.

When high wages cause unemployment in unionized industries, workers must shift into non-unionized jobs. This will increase the supply of workers in these industries and cause wages there to fall. The result may be lower wages in the nonunion sector, keeping average wages for the economy as a whole lower than they might be otherwise.

COLLECTIVE BARGAINING AND THE UNION CONTRACT

As a worker in American industry, you may be invited (or required) to join a union. Periodically, your union leaders will negotiate a contract with management; this negotiating process is known as

* about .4 million workers; about 1.1 million workers

collective bargaining. The contract will cover wages, hours, fringe benefits, pension and insurance plans, and other conditions of employment. It will probably include a no-strike provision for the life of the contract (generally from one to three years).

The wage clause will guarantee a wage scale for various job classifications. Wage differentials will be provided for night work, supervisory responsibilities, hazardous or dirty work, and overtime work. Workers will also be guaranteed certain paid holidays and paid vacations depending on length of service. The firm may agree to collect union dues through automatic deductions from workers' paychecks. This is called a union *check-off clause* and it enhances the strength of the union.

Beginning in the 1950s, high levels of inflation began to threaten the purchasing power of workers' pay scales. This was a particularly serious problem when the life of a contract extended over several years. Unions began to insist that escalator clauses be added to contracts, guaranteeing cost-of-living wage increases* when prices rise. For example, a contract might provide for a one-cent-per-hour increase in wages for each .5 percentage-point increase in the consumer price index.

A typical union contract provides for pension and insurance funds to be financed by employers with regular contributions from employee paychecks. The employer's contribution is a tax-deductible expense—a cost of production similar to depreciation and other capital costs.

Firms in the auto, steel, and aluminum industries (and some others) have agreed to establish Supplemental Unemployment Benefits, funds financed solely through employer contributions. Within certain limitations, these funds provide cash benefits to workers laid off because of production cutbacks.

A union contract also includes provisions for job security. Generally, preference in layoffs and rehiring must be given to workers with greater seniority (longer length of service). Seniority is less

important in promotions, however, which are usually made on the basis of merit.

A union will generally establish procedures for disciplining or discharging workers for specified "good and proper" reasons. Proper reasons might include violation of company rules, excessive absenteeism, incompetence, or intoxication. If a worker claims he or she was unjustly disciplined or discharged, the dispute may be taken to a grievance committee. Members of the union will attempt to settle the question fairly through discussion with management.

During the process of negotiating a union contract a *mediator* may be called in to help resolve differences between the bargaining parties. A mediator is an outsider whose impartiality may help achieve a compromise on particular issues; however, his or her recommendations are not binding.

If a conflict arises during the life of a contract, an arbitrator may be called in to settle the dispute. An arbitrator is an expert in the field of industrial relations. He or she is registered with the Federal Mediation and Conciliation Service and is expected to judge the situation impartially. The judgment of the arbitrator is binding on both sides.

There is no clear evidence to prove whether or not unions have actually raised the level of wages in American industry. (It is impossible to know what wages might have been without unions.) It is probably correct to say that unions have contributed to stability of wages and employment. To the extent that union leaders understand that increases in *real* wages depend on increases in productivity, they may persuade union members to work for *productivity* gains rather than higher money wages.

LABOR PRODUCTIVITY

Increased productivity is important for two reasons. First, it enables us to enjoy higher standards of living, and second, it holds down production costs and thus reduces inflation. Since World War II, productivity of workers in private business has

* Cost of Living Adjustments are called COLAs.

been increasing about 2.5 percent each year. Gains in productivity are the result of more and better tools, more efficient use of resources, better management, and a better educated work force. All these factors contribute to higher productivity growth.

Over the years, productivity growth has varied among industries, chiefly because of differences in the level of mechanization and standardization of production. Highest gains have occurred in communications, electric power, gas, and sanitary services. Utilities like these are characterized as **capital-intensive** because each worker has enormous capital equipment for increasing his or her output. An industry is **labor-intensive** if there are few opportunities for mechanizing production. Services like finance, real estate, and insurance fall in this category.

Table 5.3 shows the value of output produced (minus materials used) per dollar payroll costs for various industries. Identify the capital-intensive and labor-intensive industries.

Future gains in productivity may be harder to achieve than in the past. More women and young people are joining the labor force; often these groups have had fewer opportunities for education and skill development and their job performance may be low. The quality of our capital stock is changing, too. New legislation requiring installation of environmental and safety equipment reduces the measured output of material goods per unit of capital investment. And finally, U.S. industry is becoming dominated by service industries. Production of services is highly labor-intensive, offering few opportunities for productivity growth.

As productivity growth slows, workers face the possibility of slower growth in material standards of living. Price inflation may be a worsening problem, too, as rising labor and energy costs push up prices. For these reasons it is important always to seek new methods for increasing productivity.

EVERYONE A CAPITALIST?

''Workers of the world unite. You have nothing to lose but your chains.''

That was Karl Marx's message to industrial workers more than a century ago. It was a call for revolution to overthrow the capitalist owners and managers of productive capital. Marx believed that history would move economic society inevitably to *communism*, when the tools of capitalism would be owned ''in common'' and operated in the interests of workers. What has been the actual outcome for capitalism? How correct were Marx's predictions?

The twentieth century has brought tremendous changes in manufacturing processes. Mass production has permitted greater industrial specialization and all the benefits of economies of large scale. Citizens of industrialized nations have enjoyed more and better goods at lower relative prices than ever before in history.

But the news has not all been good. Mass production has aggravated some of the problems that Karl Marx predicted. Remember that Marx predicted that large-scale production would lead to *alienation* of the working classes. As mere cogs in

Table 5.3   Value Added Per Dollar of Payroll.

Value of output (net of materials cost) per dollar of labor input.

	1947	1973
Tobacco	$3.10	$5.20
Petroleum	2.70	4.51
Chemicals	2.75	3.80
Food	2.35	2.90
Instruments	1.60	2.55
Paper	2.25	2.35
Rubber	1.65	2.30
Lumber	1.80	2.25
Nonelectrical Machinery	1.60	2.05
Transportation Equipment	1.55	2.01
Textiles	1.85	1.98
Furniture	1.70	1.90
Apparel	1.75	1.90
Leather	1.75	1.85

an impersonal productive system, workers would lose the drive to achieve high levels of craftsmanship, and their productivity would fall. They would grow bitter toward the system which they felt oppressed them.

Fortunately—and not predicted by Marx—Western nations have been flexible enough to adjust to the needs of working people. Democratic political institutions have provided the means for individuals and groups to express their job dissatisfactions in constructive ways.

Workers in large European firms were the first to seek remedies to problems at the workplace. In West Germany, coal and steel firms organized worker councils to consult with management on all decisions affecting jobs. Employees are represented along with stockholders on the board of every major corporation in the nation. Labor-management co-responsibility has long been in effect in other European nations, including socialist Yugoslavia. One result of joint decision making has been that the national government has not intervened in industrial crises; another is a high level of industrial peace. Workers have generally shown moderation in wage demands and strike activity.

Is the United States ready for this type of industrial democracy? An important change in labor-management relationships in the United States has been an idea popularized by Louis O. Kelso. Kelso's motto is "make every worker a capitalist"—but not in the way Marx predicted. Kelso's way is to enable workers to invest their own savings in industrial corporations.

In Kelso's *universal capitalism,* a firm establishes an Employee Stock Ownership Trust—**ESOT,** for short. The ESOT obtains funds through bank loans and through the sale of stock to employees. Then the ESOT buys stock in the firm itself. Stock dividends are used first to pay interest and principal on the bank loan and, ultimately, are paid to worker-owners. In the meantime, workers and their representatives accumulate greater power to influence company policy and to share in profits.

The scheme has several advantages for a business firm and for the economy as a whole. The firm benefits from a work force that feels committed to increased production; workers realize that their prosperity depends on the company's prosperity and are less likely to make excessive wage demands. The economy benefits from a more equal distribution of income; modern technology can be capital-intensive without depriving workers of adequate income.*

Now the question: Was Marx right? Or wasn't he?

SUMMARY

1. People earn their identity and status through participation in work. Primitive society took a large step forward when specialization and division of labor allowed great increases in production.
2. Labor is a variable resource. Firms hire labor to use along with fixed resources for the production of goods and services. The profit maximizing firm will employ labor up to the point where the cost of hiring the last unit of labor is just equal to the value of its output.
3. Two conflicting types of unions sought to organize American workers. Craft unions were exclusive, each one consisting only of workers of a particular skill. Samuel Gompers' American Federation of Labor is an example of this type of union. An alternative approach was industrial unions, which were inclusive and aimed at organizing all skilled and unskilled workers. The Knights of Labor is an example.
4. In 1935, the Wagner National Labor Relations Act was passed, guaranteeing labor's right to organize and bargain collectively. Also in the thirties, workers under the leadership of John L. Lewis broke away from the AFL and organized unskilled, mass-production workers into the Congress of Industrial Organizations.
5. After World War II, public sentiment turned against unions. The Taft-Hartley Act, which limited strikes and restricted compulsory union membership, was passed in 1947.

* A disadvantage to workers is that their investment is concentrated in one firm, with increased risk of loss.

6. The supply and demand for resources will affect equilibrium prices. A high equilibrium price will discourage the use of a relatively scarce resource and encourage its production. A low equilibrium price will encourage use of a relatively plentiful resource and discourage further production.
7. Labor unions interfere with the smooth adjustment of supply in resource markets. The result may be a wage level that is higher than the free market equilibrium wage. At the higher union wage there is likely to be some unemployment of labor resources.
8. Through a process of collective bargaining, a union draws up a contract with management. Provisions of the contract may include no strikes for the life of the contract, a guaranteed wage rate, an escalator clause, and pension and insurance plans.
9. Changes are taking place in the productivity of labor and of new types of capital equipment; labor is becoming more active in the ownership and control of business.

TERMS TO REMEMBER

division of labor: a system of production in which a job is divided into small tasks and workers specialize in a small portion of the total job.

fixed resources: resources (such as land and capital) that are fixed in quantity over a certain time period.

variable resources: resources (such as labor) whose quantities can be varied, changing the rate of operation of fixed resources.

law of variable proportions or **law of diminishing returns:** as more and more variable resources are added to a fixed quantity of plant and equipment, total production eventually increases by smaller and smaller amounts.

business unions: unions that are concerned with job needs such as wages, hours, and working conditions rather than with radical politics.

craft unions: unions whose members specialize in a particular craft or skill.

industrial unions: unions whose members include all workers in a particular industry, skilled and unskilled alike.

closed shop: an agreement made by a firm to hire only workers who are union members; outlawed by the Taft-Hartley Act of 1947.

secondary boycott: a boycott by a union against a firm because of its policies toward another union; outlawed by the Taft-Hartley Act.

collective bargaining: the negotiating process between a union and management in order to reach an agreement on the union contract.

capital- or **labor-intensive:** a way to describe production processes using substantial quantities of capital or labor resources per unit of output.

ESOT: Employee Stock Ownership Trust

TOPICS FOR DISCUSSION

1. Make sure you understand each of the following expressions and how it is significant in the use of labor resources:

   specialization and division of labor
   alienation
   opportunity cost
   countervailing power

2. Distinguish between each of the following groups of expressions:

   craft unions and industrial unions
   fixed and variable resources

3. How did each of the following pieces of legislation contribute to the growth of the labor movement?

   Wagner National Labor Relations Act
   Taft-Hartley Act

4. The energy crisis of the 1970s was particularly hard on workers in the automobile industry. This may be a long-range problem which will require major adjustments in labor markets over the coming decades. What adjustments can you foresee? Explain in terms of demand, supply, and equilibrium price (wage). Include markets for other types of labor in addition to automobile workers.

5. Some of the blame for declining productivity in the United States has been placed on labor. Even with all the advantages of large-scale technology, we have failed to motivate American workers to contribute their maximum effort to production.

This is in sharp contrast to management techniques in Japan which have apparently earned the loyal enthusiasm of workers for their jobs. It has been suggested that business firms should hire industrial engineers to be used as "vice-presidents of human productivity."

Imagine that you had accepted such a position in a large American firm. How would you approach the problem of motivating workers? What production data would you need and how would you use it? What new programs or policies would you initiate?

6. Can you think of any disadvantages of joining a union? What are the advantages? Compare the advantages and disadvantages of unionism as a whole. What are the effects on society? Does your answer depend on the type of union and the quality of union leadership? Explain.

7. The energy crisis of the 1970s caused some policy makers to turn to new "soft" energy sources: sun, wind, and biomass (organic material). Discuss the implications in terms of the derived demand for resources.

8. Only about 30 of the nation's 15,000 banks are unionized. A small Minnesota bank suffered a long strike when eight female employees formed a union to protest discriminatory employment practices. Why do you suppose banks have been slow to unionize, and what do you expect will be the effect on other banks of the strike in Minnesota?

9. What do pecan rolls in Alaska's Westward Hotel have to do with traffic on the New Jersey turnpike? If you're the hotel pastry chef and you're offered double wages to leave the hotel and follow construction crews at work on the Alaskan pipeline so as to help provide Eastern commuters with gasoline—well, you are well aware of the connection! At a cost of at least $4.5 billion, the Alaskan pipeline turned out to be the largest construction job ever attempted.

Discuss the probable effects of the pipeline project on other markets:

pick-up trucks and hardware
crane operators
housing and linens
movies and radios
transportation services
illicit activities

SUGGESTED READINGS

Burck, Gilbert, "A Time of Reckoning for the Building Unions," *Fortune*, June 4, 1979, p. 82.

"Can Labor's Tired Leaders Deal with a Troubled Movement?" *New York Times Magazine*, September 4, 1977, p. 8.

"An Economic Dream in Peril," *Newsweek*, Special Report, September 8, 1980, p. 50–69.

Ewing, David W., "A Bill of Rights for Employees," *Across the Board*, March 1981, pp. 42–49.

Fraser, Douglas, "Beyond Collective Bargaining," *Challenge*, March/April 1979, pp. 33–39.

Geiger, Theodore, "The Movement for Industrial Democracy in Western Europe," *Challenge*, May/June 1979, pp. 14–21.

Guzzardi, Walter, Jr., "Demography's Good News for the Eighties," *Fortune*, November 5, 1979, p. 92.

Hamermesh, Daniel S., "Substitution and Labor Market Policy," *Challenge*, January/February 1980, pp. 44–47.

"Hard Work on the Way Out?" *U.S. News and World Report*, January 23, 1978, p. 47.

Lecht, Leonard, "The Labor Force Bulge Is Temporary," *Across the Board*, December 1977, p. 15.

Leontief, Wassily, "Is Technological Unemployment Inevitable?" *Challenge*, September/October 1979, pp. 48–50.

"Public Employees vs. the Cities," *Business Week*, July 21, 1975, p. 50.

Raskin, A. H., "Big Labor Strives to Break Out of Its Rut," *Fortune*, August 27, 1979, p. 32.

Raskin, A. H., "Coal Dust Darkens the Bargaining Table," *Fortune*, April 24, 1978, p. 47.

"Robots Join the Labor Force," *Business Week*, June 9, 1980, p. 632.

"The Ruins Gave Rise to Big Labor," *Business Week*, September 3, 1979, p. 26.

"Trends in Industrial and Labor Markets," *Economic Report of the President*, Washington: Government Printing Office, January 1981, p. 123.

Ways, Max, "The American Kind of Worker Participation," *Fortune*, October 1976, p. 168.

Weber, Arnold R., "In the 1980s a Dramatically Different Labor Force," *Across the Board*, December 1979, pp. 24–32.

CHAPTER 6

Measuring Economic Activity

or How to Prove Anything with Statistics

Tools for Study

Learning Objectives

After reading this chapter you will be able to:

1. describe the circular flow of spending, production, and income.
2. define national income, personal income, and disposable income.
3. define Gross National Product and explain how it is calculated.
4. define aggregate demand and aggregate supply.
5. show how changes in total spending affect the circular flow.

Issues Covered

How is a price index used to calculate *real* growth in GNP?

How do social costs affect economic welfare?

How can we measure GNP?

How has the level of government spending changed over the years?

How do consumers spend their incomes?

We have used the concepts of supply and demand to describe individual markets for finished goods and for productive resources. The study of individual markets is called *microeconomics*. Now we turn to investigation of the total production of all goods and services in the economy. The study of all markets taken together is called **macroeconomics.** Our concern is to measure the value of all goods and services produced during the year as a means of judging our economy's performance in satisfying the needs of its people.

THE CIRCULAR FLOW OF SPENDING, PRODUCTION, AND INCOME

It is helpful to view the economic system as two continuous flows:

1. Money expenditures flow into business firms in return for the goods and services desired by households.
2. Incomes flow into households in return for the use of productive resources— land, labor, capital, and entrepreneurial ability—used in business firms.

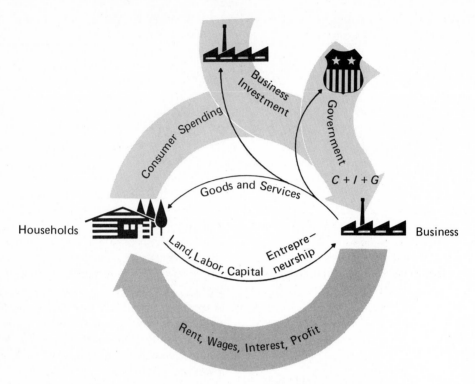

Figure 6.1   The Circular Flow of Spending, Production, and Income.

The circular flow of spending and incomes is shown in Figure 6.1.

Spending

The upper loop of the circular flow in Figure 6.1 shows total spending in all the markets for goods and services. These are the kinds of markets we described in Chapters 2, 3, and 4. In all these markets, money expenditures flow in one direction. Goods and services flow in the opposite direction.

Notice the largest part of the spending flow comes from households. Households purchase consumer goods and services, such as autos, appliances, food, clothing, and recreation and health services.

Business firms also spend. They purchase raw materials, parts, equipment, buildings, and services from other businesses. Business spending for plants, productive equipment, and inventory is called *investment*.

The third major spender is government. Governments purchase goods and services to be used in the operation of government agencies and for government programs. Only government expenditures for goods and services are included in the circular flow. Not included are **transfer payments**— government income-support payments such as welfare checks, unemployment compensation, food stamps, and veterans' benefits.

Foreigners also purchase goods produced by American business, and we buy from foreigners. The net value of these transactions may be called *net exports*. Net exports are becoming an increasingly important component of aggregate demand. The complexity of international economics, however, calls for separate treatment. Therefore, we will omit net exports from our discussion at this point and consider them in detail in Chapter 14.

Total spending by all these domestic groups is a measure of all goods and services produced: consumer expenditures plus business investment expenditures plus government expenditures = C + I + G = total output. Total spending is also a measure of the total income received by business which is then distributed to resource owners in return for their contribution to production.

Production and Income

Business uses its income from sales to hire productive resources. Productive resources are owned by people in households who provide their land, labor, capital, and entrepreneurial ability to business in return for income. The lower loop of Figure 6.1 shows all the markets for productive resources. We discussed resource markets in detail in Chapter 5. We found that demand for a resource depends on the value of its production, and supply depends on the willingness of resource owners to supply the resource at various prices.

In resource markets, land, labor, capital, and entrepreneurial ability flow in one direction. Incomes in the form of rent, wages, interest, and profit flow in the opposite direction. Not all spending received by business is actually paid to households as income, however. A portion of business revenue is paid in taxes, and a portion is set aside in the form of business saving, including allowances for depreciation of capital equipment. Only the remaining revenue—after taxes and business saving—is used to pay productive resources.

The sum of rent, wages, interest, and profit is the **national income.** Strictly speaking, national income is income *earned* by productive resources. Thus, government transfer payments are not included, since they are not earned payments for current economic activity. Income *received* by individuals, including transfer payments, is called **personal income.** Personal income minus personal taxes (income tax, property tax, and inheritance tax) leaves the measure known as **disposable income.**

Most households save a part of their disposable income. However, they use the largest part to purchase more consumer goods and services. Their new spending returns to the circular flow and becomes part of spending in the next period. The circular flow is complete.

GROSS NATIONAL PRODUCT

The circular-flow diagram is a visual representation of a concept which is familiar to most of us: *Gross National Product* or GNP. Gross National Product is the final value of all goods and services produced for sale during the year: trucks, stereos, jeans, eggs, dentistry, mail service, and so forth. It also includes final goods and parts produced for inventories, to be sold in later years.

Note that GNP includes only *final* value, leaving out intermediate goods such as steel for autos and flour for bread. Including intermediate goods would overstate GNP. An auto, for example, may sell for $5000. But it may include a chassis worth $2000; an engine worth $2000; $100 worth of paint; $300 worth of rubber, glass, and plastic; $100 worth of electrical equipment; and a transmission worth $500. Including all these parts along with the car's final value would be double-counting.

GNP also leaves out sales of goods produced in earlier years. This means that sales of used cars, sales of houses built in earlier years, and sales from last year's inventory are not included. Stocks and bonds are not included either because they are not goods or services. The same is true of sales of unimproved land.

Government transfer payments are not included in GNP because they are not payments for producing goods and services. (However, when individuals use their transfer payments to purchase consumer goods and services, those purchases *are* counted in GNP.) Nonmarket exchange of goods and services is also omitted from GNP: home-grown vegetables, volunteer work, and the unpaid services of housewives. (It has been said that a man who marries his housekeeper reduces the level of GNP.)

GNP can be measured in two ways:

1. *Output*. GNP is the total value of expenditures on output. We have seen that expenditures are made by consumers, business firms, and governments. Thus, GNP is the sum of spending flows in all product markets, as shown in the upper loop of Figure 6.1. It represents total demand in the economy, or **aggregate demand:** Aggregate Demand = $C + I + G$.

2. *Income*. GNP is also the total income received from production of goods and services. Remember that a portion of the business revenue from sales must be used to pay taxes and to save for future investment. But the largest part is divided among resources used in the production of goods and services for payment of rent, wages, interest, and profit. Thus GNP is also the sum of income flows in all resource markets, as shown in the lower loop of Figure 6.1. Taken together business revenue from sales measures the value of all resources used in production and is, therefore, the value of total production or **aggregate supply:** Aggregate Supply = $w + r + i + p$ + business taxes and savings.

*We can express these relationships with a simple formula: aggregate demand (output) = GNP = aggregate supply (income).**

CHANGES IN THE CIRCULAR FLOW

Macroeconomics is concerned with the size of the circular flow. Many citizens favor a steadily rising GNP for the rising levels of living it provides. In their view, GNP should grow in line with our growing population and resource productivity. If GNP grows too slowly, workers will be unemployed, and incomes will be low. We will be operating *inside* our production possibilities curve and failing to make efficient use of our scarce re-

* The expression AD = GNP = AS is actually an identity; that is, the sides of the expression measure essentially the same thing, approached through different means.

sources. When GNP fails to grow for two consecutive quarters, we say the economy is experiencing *recession*.

There are some potential problems with GNP growth, however. If GNP grows too fast, the demand for goods and services may exceed increases in resource productivity. We will be trying to produce *outside* our production possibilities curve. Too rapid growth could mean shortages of materials and skilled labor, with a tendency for prices and wages to rise. The result of too rapid growth in GNP may be *inflation*.

What determines the actual level of GNP and its rate of growth?

The level of total production is determined by aggregate demand. Aggregate demand is total spending from consumers, business investment, and government $(C + I + G)$. If spending from any of these three sources should rise, the entire circular flow will tend to *expand*. Profit-seeking business firms will increase production in an effort to satisfy the higher demand for goods and services. If spending should fall, the circular flow will *contract*. Business firms will cut back production to avoid losses on unsold merchandise.

An Increase in Aggregate Demand

A rise in total spending might begin with changes in consumer spending *(C)*. Consumers may go on buying sprees and purchase a variety of new durable goods: campers, videotape machines, and hot tubs. If many consumers become optimistic about the future, they may cut back on their saving in order to enjoy the "good life" with little fear of hard times ahead.

A rise in spending might also begin with changes in business investment spending *(I)*. Business firms may increase their investment in new products or new technical processes. Or population growth may encourage business to build new factories, rail lines, and power plants to satisfy expected growth in consumer demand.

Finally, a rise in spending might begin with

changes in government spending *(G)*. The federal government may decide to spend more for national defense or for research and development of new technologies. Or perhaps voters may demand increased state and local government expenditures for schools, roads, or parks.

Whatever the source of higher spending, the result will be greater incentives to produce goods and services, so as to satisfy the higher demand. More workers will be hired, materials ordered, and factories built. The higher level of spending will circulate throughout the economy, raising incomes of workers and suppliers. Workers and suppliers will spend their higher incomes for consumer goods and services, and their higher spending will cause other incomes to rise also. Thus, the initial increase in spending will be magnified as higher incomes spread throughout the economy. Greater spending increases the size of the circular flow, producing more goods and services and employing more of the nation's productive resources.

A Decrease in Aggregate Demand

Eventually the spending which began the upward swing in incomes may begin to slow down. Unsold goods will pile up in retail stores. As demand declines, stores order less from manufacturers, and new factories become idle. Manufacturers lay off workers, and the economy enters a slump. Cutbacks in spending circulate throughout the economy. More workers are laid off and must cut back their own spending for consumer goods and services. The entire circular flow of spending and production contracts.

A lower level of spending may begin with any of the three major groups of spenders. Consumers may decide to spend less of their incomes. They may be overstocked with consumer goods. They may be pessimistic about the future and cut down on spending in order to accumulate savings for hard times ahead.

Business firms may decide to reduce their plans for new investment. They may have com-

pleted all necessary new projects and have no need for new productive capacity.

Government may decide to reduce spending on government programs or projects. Government expenditures are geared to construction of public services and defense. Since these needs come about irregularly, government spending may fluctuate widely from year to year.

Whatever the source of a drop in spending, the result will be a decline in the production of goods and services. Business firms will try to avoid losses on unsold goods. They will cut back on materials ordered and lay off workers. They will cancel plans for new buildings and equipment. Incomes of workers and suppliers will fall.

Households will be forced to reduce their spending for consumer goods and services. As a result, more business firms will cut back production. The initial decrease in spending will be magnified as lower incomes spread throughout the economy.

INFLOWS AND OUTFLOWS

Changes in spending may be described in terms of flows into and out of the spending stream. Spending by consumers, business firms, and governments constitutes *inflows* into the circular flow. Expenditures included in aggregate demand are received by business firms as shown in the upper loop of Figure 6.2. (See page 112.)

Spending flows received by business firms are then paid to households as income. Households use their incomes in any of three ways. Taxes must first be paid *(T)*, a portion of income is saved *(S)*, and the remaining income is spent for consumer goods and services *(C)*. Consumer spending remains in the flow and continues to circulate. Taxes and saving constitute *outflows* from the circular flow.

Outflows represent the part of consumer income not spent: autos, appliances, and clothing not bought, trips not taken, homes not bought. In order for the circular flow to remain stable at the current

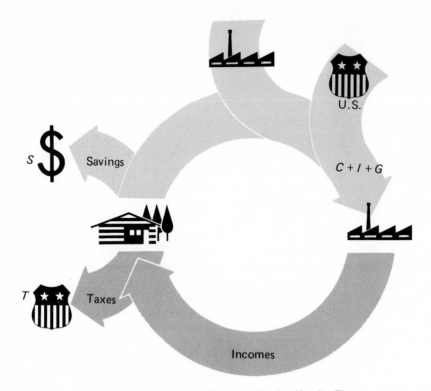

Figure 6.2   Inflows and Outflows in the Circular Flow.

level of income, some other groups must spend an amount equal to what consumers fail to spend. Government or business must purchase the goods and services that are not bought by the household sector. Outflows from the household sector must be balanced by new inflows from business or government.

There are several ways outflows from spending might be replaced. Saving outflows *(S)* may be returned to the circular flow by new investment spending *(I)* on the part of business firms, or tax outflows *(T)* may be returned by new government spending *(G)*. Or saving and tax outflows may be offset by new investment and government spending: $S + T = I + G$.

If all outflows from spending are returned as new inflows, the circular flow will remain stable. Aggregate demand *(C + I + G)* will be equal to aggregate supply *(C + S + T)* at the current in-

come level. But if outflows are not balanced by new inflows, there will be changes in the entire circular flow.

If inflows of new spending *(I + G)* are greater than outflows from the spending flow, the level of GNP will increase. The higher level of aggregate demand will encourage an increase in aggregate supply, and the circular flow will *expand*. If outflows *(S + T)* are greater than inflows, GNP will fall. Lower aggregate demand will cause a drop in aggregate supply, and the circular flow will *contract*.

When inflows and outflows balance, we say the economy has reached *equilibrium*. There is no tendency for GNP either to expand or to contract.

In the next chapter we will develop an economic model that explains how aggregate demand determines the equilibrium level of spending, production, and income.

Self-Check

1. Which of the following is included in GNP?
   a. an appendicitis operation
   b. an antique table
   c. wood flooring in a new house
   d. purchase of a U.S. Treasury bond
   e. a gift of homemade cookies

2. The major groups of spenders are:
   a. consumers, savers, and investors.
   b. consumers, business, and government.
   c. land, labor, capital, and managers or entrepreneurs.
   d. savers, investors, and government.
   e. aggregate demand and aggregate supply.

3. Productive resources:
   a. flow in return for consumer expenditures.
   b. are outflows from the circular flow.
   c. flow from households to business firms.
   d. flow from business to government.
   e. are rent, wages, interest, and profit.

4. GNP is likely to grow if:
   a. consumers are pessimistic about the future.
   b. business has completed all desired investment projects.
   c. consumers are well stocked with goods.
   d. the government cuts back on its defense program.
   e. population growth causes higher aggregate demand.

5. The circular flow will stabilize at the level of spending and income at which:
   a. aggregate demand is equal to aggregate supply.
   b. $C + I + S = C + T + G$.
   c. new inflows of spending = outflows from income.
   d. all of the above.
   e. both (a) and (c).

6. Changes in consumer, business, or government spending:
   a. have no effect on production plans.
   b. are a subject of microeconomics.
   c. may cause recession or inflation.
   d. constitute aggregate supply.
   e. all of the above.

Theory in Practice

Table 6.1 Summary Data from National Income Accounts, 1980 (billions of dollars).

Personal Consumption Expenditures	$1670	Rental Income	59
Gross Private Domestic Investment	395	Wages and Salaries	1596
Government Purchases of Goods and		Interest Income	180
Services	535	Profit Income	241
Indirect Business Taxes (Sales and		Government Transfer Payments	294
Excise Taxes)	212	Business and Personal Taxes	382
Business Saving	312	Personal Saving	104

Source: *Economic Report of the President,* January 1981.

CALCULATING GNP

Table 6.1 lists the components of GNP and income for 1980. (Figures are altered slightly for simplicity.) Pencil the figures into the appropriate places in the circular flow shown on Figure 6.3. Then answer the following questions. (Answers can be found at the end of Topics for Discussion.)

1. Calculate upper-loop spending on output to find *aggregate demand:* _____ .

2. Calculate lower-loop income from production (including business taxes and saving) to find *aggregate supply:* _____ .

3. Now calculate *national income,* income earned by productive resources: _____ .

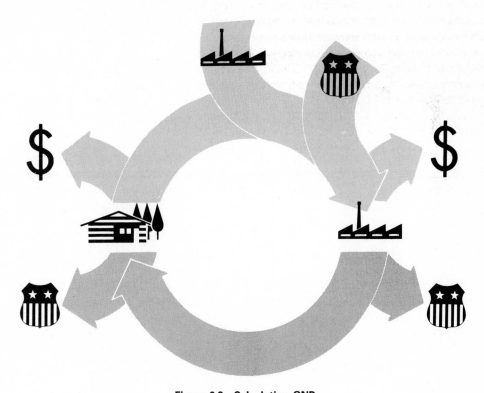

Figure 6.3 Calculating GNP.

4. In addition to income from production, some households receive transfer payments from government. Transfer payments are payments to individuals to increase their disposable income. Add transfer payments to national income to find *personal income:* _____ .

5. Now compute the following percentages: consumer spending as a percent of aggregate demand: _____; government purchases as a percent of aggregate demand: _____; wages as a percent of income earned in production: _____; profit as a percent of income from production: _____ .

6. What percent of personal income was saved in 1980? _____

7. What was the total value of the outflows for 1980? _____ What was the value of new inflows? _____ (For this purpose include government transfer payments along with government purchases as a new inflow.)

These calculations should give you a better idea of how GNP is measured and of the quantities involved. *The Economic Report of the President,* published in January of each year, supplies these figures for the last thirty-five years. You may be interested in comparing data for the current year with earlier years.

MEASURING GROWTH IN GNP

Over the long term, rising GNP has brought rising income to the United States. Greater production of goods and services has permitted higher material standards of living. This is true both in terms of the total volume of production and on a *per capita* (per person) basis.

Money GNP and Real GNP

Not all increases in GNP bring these kinds of benefits, however. In fact, the dollar value of GNP may grow even if there is no real increase in the quantity of goods and services produced. This happens when general price inflation places higher price tags on most items.

Economists distinguish between money GNP and real GNP. *Money GNP* is the value of GNP stated in dollar values of the current year. *Real GNP* is GNP stated in dollars of constant purchasing power. If prices have risen, money GNP must be "deflated" to determine real GNP, the real value of goods and services produced. For example, total dollars spent on GNP may increase from $10 billion to $11 billion in one year. But if prices over that year rose by 10 percent, the *real* quantity of GNP has not changed. With prices 10 percent higher, the $11 billion in expenditures has bought only $10 billion in goods and services. Money GNP has increased by $1 billion; real GNP has not changed.

Correcting money GNP for price changes requires the use of a *price index.*

Using a Price Index

A price index is a percentage comparison of current prices to prices in a base year. To illustrate, suppose that a dollar's worth of goods in the base year included a loaf of bread, a bus ticket, and a pair of socks. Then suppose that five years later the same collection of goods sells for $1.25. The price index for the current year would be PI = (current year price)/(base year price) = $1.25/$1.00 = 1.25 = 125 percent. With prices 25 percent higher, a worker must now earn 125 percent of what he or she earned in the base year in order to enjoy the same standard of living.

Suppose a worker can live comfortably in the base year on an income of $6000. Five years later

Table 6.2   Gross National Product in (1) Current Dollars and in (3) Constant Dollars of 1972.

Year	(1) Money GNP ($ billions)	(2) Price Index	(3) Real GNP ($ billions)	(4) Personal Consumption Expenditures ($ billions)	(5) Gross Private Domestic Investment ($ billions)	(6) GNP per capita (in 1972 dollars)
1929	103.4	32.87	314.7	215.6	55.9	2584
1933	55.8	25.13	222.1	170.7	8.4	1769
1939	90.8	28.40	319.7	220.3	33.6	2443
1945	212.3	37.99	559.0	271.4	27.8	3995
1950	286.2	53.64	533.5	338.1	93.7	3813
1955	399.3	60.98	654.8	395.1	104.1	3946
1960	506.1	68.67	736.8	453.0	105.4	4078
1965	688.1	74.32	925.9	558.1	150.1	4765
1970	982.4	91.36	1075.3	668.9	154.7	5248
1972	1171.1	100.00	1171.1	733.0	188.3	5607
1973	1306.6	105.80	1235.0	767.7	207.2	5869
1974	1412.9	116.02	1217.8	760.7	183.6	5747
1975	1528.8	127.18	1202.1	775.1	141.6	5629
1976	1706.5	133.88	1274.7	821.3	173.0	5925
1977	1890.4	141.32	1337.6	860.3	195.6	6169
1978	2156.1	150.05	1436.9	904.8	229.7	6569
1979	2413.9	162.77	1483.0	930.9	232.6	6721
1980	2627.4	177.45	1480.7	933.0	204.0	6646

Source: *Economic Report of the President,* January 1978 and January 1981.

the price index has risen to 125. Income of $6000 will be worth (current income)/*PI* = $6000/125 percent = $6000/1.25 = $4800. In order to live as comfortably as before, the worker must now earn 125 percent of what his or her income was in the base year: 1.25 × $6000 = $7500. (Test yourself: Suppose the price index *falls* to 90 percent. This means that a worker needs only $.90 to buy what a dollar bought in the base year. How much is income of $6000 worth now?*)

Economists calculate the *consumer price index* from prices on a "market basket" of goods

* $6000/90 percent = $6000/.90 = $6666.67

and services purchased by a typical family. They also calculate a *producer price index* based on industrial commodities purchased by business. The *GNP deflator* is another price index based on all goods, services, and industrial commodities.

Growth in Real GNP

You can use the following formula to calculate real GNP: real GNP = (money GNP)/(Price Index). Using this formula, you can set up equations for measuring the growth of real GNP over time. Table 6.2 provides data on GNP and its components in selected years since 1929. Data are expressed both in *current dollars* of each year and in *constant dollars,* dollar values corrected for inflation.

In the table, 1972 is used as the base year for calculating the price index. Notice that money GNP and real GNP for 1972 are identical at $1171.1 billion. This is understandable, since the price index for 1972 is PI = (current year price)/ (base year price) = $1.00/$1.00 = 1.00 = 100 percent. The price index for 1929 is only 32.87. This means that prices in 1929 were about one-third of prices in 1972. The price index for 1980 is 177.4, indicating prices more than 75 percent higher than in 1972.

Table 6.2 shows fairly steady real growth except for the Depression of the 1930s and six recessions since World War II. Real GNP grew from an estimated $12 billion in 1869 to $1481 billion in 1980 (both expressed in dollars of 1972). In per capita terms this represents a real increase from $269 in 1869 to $6446 in 1980.

NET ECONOMIC WELFARE

There are some problems with the use of GNP as a measure of a nation's well-being. GNP measures goods and services produced. It doesn't, however, consider the "bads" which may also be produced! Our nation's business firms also produce polluted air and water, scars on the landscape, and junk piles.

In computing the cost of its output, a firm deducts the prices of all resources used in production: land and buildings, intermediate materials, machinery, labor, and management services. However, many kinds of production involve the use of resources that have no price in the market: clean air and water, quiet and pleasant surroundings, and even vacant land for eventual disposal of the product itself.

Economists refer to the costs of using these resources as *external costs* because they are imposed on the community *outside* the business firm.

They are *social* costs, as opposed to the *private* costs that appear on a firm's expense statements. The community as a whole pays for a business firm's use of resources in the form of air and water pollution, noise, and so on.

A business firm is not presently required to pay for its external costs since they are not included in its costs of production. However, as communities become aware of the scarcity of such valuable resources as pure air and water, some payment may be required. A tax or fine levied against a polluting firm would have the effect of reducing the value of the firm's net contribution to GNP. It would make GNP a better measure of actual improvements in well-being.

Some economists have defined a new measure, net economic welfare or *NEW,* which would take into account external costs. Computing NEW would require that "bads" be deducted from the measured value of GNP. Thus, NEW would more correctly measure improvements in the quality of our lives.

The problem of measuring such things as polluted air and water is a difficult one. Still, efforts are now being made to shift social costs back to the firms producing them. Coal-burning utilities, for example, have been required to install "scrubbers" in their smokestacks to remove impurities from their discharge. Firms guilty of water pollution have been required to clean up their discharge. In some cases, daily fines of thousands of dollars have been imposed, with the revenue to be used by government for operating purification facilities.

Concern for the environment is certainly healthy—and many communities are requiring business firms to assume responsibility for their external costs to the community. However, some problems remain. If rigid antipollution laws are established, many firms will be forced out of business. Some will decide not to locate in areas with strict antipollution laws. This could mean a loss of jobs and income to the community. Furthermore, as firms are required to pay for all resources used, their costs will rise. Prices to consumers will rise

Table 6.3   Percentages of National Output Used for Public Purposes.

Year	Government Purchases of Goods and Services % of GNP	Total Taxes State, Local, and Federal as % of GNP	Government Transfer Payments as % of GNP
1929	8.3	11.0	1.0
1933	14.3	16.6	2.7
1939	14.3	16.9	2.7
1945	38.7	25.1	2.7
1950	13.3	23.5	5.0
1955	18.6	25.2	4.0
1960	19.8	27.8	5.3
1965	20.0	27.6	5.4
1970	22.5	31.0	7.6
1974	22.1	32.6	9.6
1977	21.0	31.8	10.9
1978	20.1	31.6	10.4
1979	19.6	31.7	10.3
1980	20.3	31.7	11.2

Source: *Economic Report of the President,* January 1978 and January 1981.

and sales will fall. Consumers must be willing to pay the full costs of "cleaner" production if they are to have the goods and services they want.

TRENDS IN GOVERNMENT EXPENDITURES

Over the years, several factors have combined to increase the government spending *(G)* component of aggregate demand: (1) the more threatening nature of international relations and the growing role of the United States in world affairs; (2) our growing prosperity which has made us want a better quality of public services; and (3) social and technical changes in ways of life that require collective action (our population has shifted from farm life to crowded cities; we are living longer and are dependent for more years after retirement; modern industry is more complex and requires a longer period of technical education for the young).

As a result, by 1980 net tax receipts and total government outlays had grown to almost one third of national output (GNP). This fraction has drifted upward over the last forty-five years, showing the greatest increase in years of unstable international conditions or economic crisis. Table 6.3 shows the percentages going to various purposes for selected years.

The percentages in Table 6.3 may overstate the actual shift in resources toward the public sector. Much of government spending goes for services, the costs of which have risen faster than the costs of consumer goods. Also, in earlier years, resources may have been used for public services without having a price tag attached.

Column (1) includes only government purchases of goods and services. The table shows the greatest jump in expenditures from 1939 to 1945. The increase was due to federal defense expenditures for World War II.

Not shown in Column (1) is the distribution of expenditures between federal and state and local governments. In 1980 state and local spending constituted 13% of GNP and federal spending, only 8%.

Column (2) shows the percentages of total spending which have been paid to governments in business and personal tax payments. Taxes include state, local, and federal government tax receipts: personal income taxes, corporate profits taxes, indirect business taxes, and contributions to Social Security. Total taxes claimed almost one third of spending on GNP in 1980. Again, the greatest jump was in 1945.

Column (3) lists transfer payments as percentages of GNP. Transfer payments have grown from only a small part of total spending during the 1930s to more than 10 percent in 1980. The high level of payments in 1980 was partly a result of the business recession. Real GNP actually fell in 1980, and government outlays for unemployment compensation increased as more workers became unemployed.

SPENDING TRENDS

Crystal balls grow cloudy when it comes to predicting consumer behavior in the market. Who in the 1960s could have predicted the popularity of electronic games or the disappointing sales of luxury automobiles in the 1980s? Consumers are influenced by such a wide range of circumstances that it is impossible to know for certain what products will sell, what businesses will be profitable, and what training will earn you the highest income.

It is possible, however, to note some long-range trends that have been affecting markets since World War II. Increased productivity has given American consumers more income to spend and more leisure time to enjoy the things we buy. But nowadays we are spending a smaller share of our earnings for the ordinary necessities of life. Nondurable consumer goods like food, clothing, gasoline, home heating oil, and so forth, consumed more than half (57.5%) of consumer spending in 1946. By 1980 the typical family spent only 38% of its total budget on these necessary items. While

real spending for all goods grew about 3% annually, consumer spending in these markets grew much more slowly. The only exception was spending for gasoline and oil, which grew at the rate of almost 14% a year in real terms. These changes have meant declining employment opportunities for workers in industries producing food, textiles, shoes, and other nondurable consumer goods.

During these years of rising consumer spending, an increasing share of the consumer's budget was being spent for durable consumer goods. Automobiles, furniture, and household appliances rose from 11% of consumer purchases to more than 14% in 1980. Workers employed in industries producing dishwashers, stereos, and pleasure boats, for example, enjoyed better employment opportunities and higher wage rates as a result.

The greatest change in consumer spending habits has been the spectacular rise in spending for services. In 1980, services consumed 47% of the typical family budget compared with only 31.5% in 1946. The greatest gain occurred in spending for housing and household services, which increased about 12% a year in real terms.

Another important part of the gain in service spending has been spending for medical treatment, in part a result of government programs like Medicare and Medicaid. Because supplies of healthcare resources are limited, this field offers many new opportunities for workers and even provides some government support for education and training.

Recreation, including travel and entertainment, is also a fast-growing service industry. Hotel and restaurant chains are taking advantage of rising consumer incomes and increased leisure time. The effects of early retirement and an increasing elderly population have also been favorable for recreation services. The outlook is less favorable for education. Slower population growth has reduced demand for primary and secondary education, but community colleges and adult education programs are continuing to grow.

The tremendous growth of service industries has important implications for the national economy. Probably most important is the fact that services are relatively labor-intensive. In contrast to manufacturing, many services involve a greater use of labor resources than of capital equipment. There are fewer opportunities to increase productivity when machines cannot be used to supplement human labor. This means that production costs cannot be reduced very much; rising demand for services is likely to mean rising prices.

There is a positive side to this problem, however. Advances in technology are likely to reduce jobs in the more capital-intensive industries, like manufacturing. As new machines replace workers in manufacturing, service industries will offer new job opportunities. Shifts of workers into service jobs will help hold down labor costs.

Some other favorable results are possible. To provide certain services requires a higher level of skills than many manufacturing operations do. Service jobs may be more challenging than routine manufacturing work, helping to develop individual creativity. If this is the case, then job satisfaction should improve for most workers.

Finally, production of many services is relatively nonpolluting. Services involve few smokestacks, result in little chemical discharge, and are generally free of industrial blight.

SUMMARY

1. The economic system can be described in terms of flows of spending and income: spending flows *paid* from households to buy consumer goods and services, from business to purchase capital investments, and from governments to purchase goods and services; and spending flows *received* as income in the form of wages, rent, interest, and profit.
2. Gross national product is the final value of all goods and services produced for the market. GNP can be measured as total expenditures on output or as total income received from the sale of output.
3. When consumer, business, or government spending increases, the total flow of production and in-

come expands. When spending decreases, the total flow of production and income contracts.
4. An increase in spending can be seen as an increase of new spending inflows into the circular flow; inflows are investment spending and government expenditures. A decrease in spending can be seen as an increase of outflows from the circular flow; outflows are savings and taxes.
5. Measures of GNP must be corrected by the use of a price index to take account of price changes. The result is real GNP, a value that reflects the real quantities of goods and services produced.
6. GNP is not a perfect measure of well-being. It does not include production carried on outside the market, and it does not reflect the unfavorable environmental changes which may be the result of production.
7. Over recent years government expenditures have risen as a percentage of total spending. This is partly a result of our rising demand for public services and partly a result of the prominence of the United States in world affairs. Consumer spending has shifted toward increased purchases of consumer services.

TERMS TO REMEMBER

macroeconomics: the study of the economy in the aggregate, or total, sense; all markets taken together.

transfer payments: government income-support payments to individuals, including welfare benefits, veterans' pensions, food stamps, social security benefits, and unemployment compensation.

national income: income *earned* by productive resources after business taxes are paid and after a portion of income is set aside in the form of business saving and allowances for depreciation of capital equipment.

personal income: income, including transfer payments, actually *received* by people.

disposable income: personal income minus personal taxes.

aggregate demand: total spending on output by consumers, business, and government.

aggregate supply: the value of output produced by all business firms.

recession: a period of decline in GNP when the demand for output falls below the productive capacity of our resources.

inflation: a general increase in prices.

Money GNP (current dollars)	Price Index (1972 = 100)	Real GNP (constant dollars of 1972)
1929 103	33	_____
1940 100	29	_____
1958 449	66	_____
1972 1171	100	_____
1977 1890	141	_____
1980 2627	171	_____

TOPICS FOR DISCUSSION

1. What would be the effect on GNP of each of the following? Would *C, I,* or *G* be affected? Discuss the chain of spending and production that would follow from each:

   a. Population growth increases so that the average age of the population falls from roughly thirty-three to twenty-eight. There are more young marriages and more teenagers.

   b. An inventor develops a process for converting cottonseed into a milklike drink, high in nutritional value.

   c. The U.S. government signs nonaggression pacts with other nations and promises to limit the production of offensive weapons.

   d. The public becomes convinced that the American way of life is too materialistic. People return to a simpler life-style and cut down on modern conveniences.

   e. Strict eligibility requirements reduce the number of families receiving transfer payments from government.

2. Distinguish clearly between each of the following pairs of terms:

   money GNP and real GNP
   microeconomics and macroeconomics
   inflows into and outflows from spending flow

3. Explain how each of the following terms is related to the others:

   GNP
   national income
   personal income

4. Use the information below to compute real GNP for the years shown (figures are in billions of dollars):

5. Explain the concept of social or external costs. Who should pay the social costs of production? (Careful!) How is it possible to shift social costs to the proper party?

   There is a parallel concept of social benefits. It refers to benefits received from production, for which the community doesn't have to pay. Some examples of social benefits are higher skill levels of workers and the movement of new supplying firms to an area, resulting in higher levels of employment. Does your community benefit from the actions of some business firms? How can firms be encouraged to provide more social benefits?

6. Do you know of polluting business firms? Have antipollution regulations been imposed on them? Under what circumstances might a community reduce its pollution standards?

(Answers to *Calculating GNP*) 1. 2600; 2. 2600; 3. 2076; 4. 2370; 5. 64, 21, 77, 12; 6. 4%; 7. 1010, 1224.

SUGGESTED READINGS

"Blessings and Problems of 1977's Bumper Crops," *U.S. News and World Report,* September 19, 1977, p. 32.

Collins, Lora S., "The Service Economy," *Across the Board,* November 1980, pp. 17–22.

"The Economy: Review and the Prospects for 1981 and 1982," *Economic Report of the President,* Washington: Government Printing Office, January 1981, pp. 131 and 165.

Ehrbar, A. F., "The Upbeat Outlook for Family Incomes," *Fortune,* February 25, 1980.

"Farm-Price Pinch: Carter to the Rescue," *U.S. News and World Report,* September 12, 1977.

Hayes, Linda Snyder, "How Americans Turned into Spendthrifts," *Fortune,* April 7, 1980, p. 60.

Hein, John, "The Quality of Well-Being," *Across the Board,* October 1979, pp. 42–47.

Hom, Joan, "Adhesive Bandages to Zippers," *Across the Board,* June 1977, p. 45.

Klein, Lawrence R., "Econometrics," *Across the Board,* February 1979, pp. 49–68.

Linden, Fabian, "The Six Ages of Economic Man," *Across the Board,* November 1977, p. 74.

Meadows, Edward, "A Close-Up Look at the Productivity Lag," *Fortune,* December 4, 1978, pp. 82–85.

Meadows, Edward, "Tracking the Ever-Elusive Gross National Product," *Fortune*, May 22, 1978, p. 100.

CHAPTER 7

Cycles
in Economic
Activity

or What Goes Up
Must Come Down

Tools for Study

Learning Objectives

After reading this chapter, you will be able to:

1. use a consumption function to describe consumer spending.
2. show graphically how total spending determines the equilibrium level of GNP.
3. explain how increases in total spending may lead to an inflationary gap.
4. explain how decreases in total spending may lead to a deflationary gap.
5. show how the multiplier works to bring on upswings and downswings in economic activity.

Issues Covered

How has the American economy performed in recent years?
What are the effects on GNP of government expenditures for public projects?
How do aggregate demand and aggregate supply affect prices?

As we saw in the preceding chapter, GNP will tend to stabilize at the level of production at which total spending for goods and services for the year is just equal to the value of goods and services produced: aggregate demand = aggregate supply. If total spending increases during the year, business firms will be encouraged to increase output; thus, rising aggregate demand means an increase in aggregate supply and GNP. If total spending declines during the year, business firms will cut back output to avoid losses; falling aggregate demand means a decrease in aggregate supply and GNP. Only when total spending is just equal to production for the year will GNP remain stable at the current level of income.

Changes in aggregate demand are communicated to business firms through unwanted changes in inventory stocks. An increase in aggregate demand, for instance, will cause inventory stocks to fall below customary levels and encourage a speedup in production to rebuild stocks. A decrease will cause stocks to build up and encourage production cutbacks until inventories fall to their desired level. If aggregate demand is equal to aggregate supply, there will be no unwanted change in inventories, and GNP wil remain stable.

A perfectly stable, unchanging GNP may not always be desirable. Ideally, GNP should grow steadily in line with the growing productive capacity of our nation's resources. Unfortunately, we have seldom enjoyed steady growth. We have experienced frequent periods of too rapid growth followed by a drop in total spending.

Irregular growth creates either of two kinds of problems. A too rapid rise in aggregate demand and GNP may bring on inflation. Too slow growth in aggregate demand can cause widespread business failures, with unemployment and hardship for many groups. These alternating ups and downs in the level of economic activity are known as **business cycles.** In this chapter we will study the Keynesian explanation of business cycles, developed by John M. Keynes (1883–1945). Then in the next two chapters we will learn about government economic policy designed to deal with the problems of too fast or too slow growth in GNP.

We have described GNP in terms of flows of spending, production, and income. Now, we will translate our simple discussion of flows into a more sophisticated economic model.

CONSUMER SPENDING (C)

Changes in GNP growth can be explained in terms of the Keynesian *model of income determination.* The Keynesian model focuses first on consumer spending, then on total spending in the economy as a whole. Economists refer to consumer spending as *Consumption (C).*

The Marginal Propensity to Consume

The largest part of total spending comes from the household sector. Consumers plan their spending in relation to their incomes. In fact, it has been estimated that American consumers spend an average of about $.93 of each dollar of disposable income they receive.

The amount a consumer will spend of each additional dollar of income is called the **marginal propensity to consume** *(MPC)*. For example, if a consumer's income rises from $10,000 to $12,000

a year, he or she may increase spending for goods and services from $9500 to $11,000. Out of $2000 in additional income, the consumer would have increased spending by $1500. On the average, his or her spending would have increased by (change in spending)/(change in income) = $1500/$2000 = 3/4 of each additional dollar. Thus:

$$MPC = \Delta\text{spending}/\Delta\text{income} = 3/4.$$

The *MPC*s of different people will vary. A wealthy person may spend a smaller portion of each additional dollar than a poorer person. His or her *MPC* might be *MPC* = (change in spending)/(change in income) = $5000/$10,000 = 1/2. A poor person would probably spend a much larger portion, possibly even the entire amount: *MPC* = $100/$100 = 1. Some people may have an *MPC* even greater than 1. An *MPC* greater than 1 is possible by borrowing or using past savings. (Test yourself: How do you think your own *MPC* would differ from your professor's? From your parents'? Why?)

The Consumption Function

The consumption plans of all households in the economy can be combined to describe the consumption plans of the nation as a whole. Table 7.1 shows hypothetical spending data for the nation as a whole at various levels of income. Column (2) shows total consumption *(C)* > GNP if national income is low, *C* = GNP at some middle income level, and *C* < GNP if national income is high. The change in total consumption at each successively higher income level is $75 billion out of income change of $100 billion. Thus, the *MPC* for this hypothetical nation is *MPC* = (change in spending)/(change in income) = 75/100 = 3/4.

Figure 7.1 is a graph of total consumer spending as shown in the table. GNP = Income is measured on the horizontal axis, and consumption *(C)* on the vertical axis. The line representing consumer spending is called a **consumption function.** The consumption function in Figure 7.1 is drawn

Table 7.1   Expenditures and Aggregate Demand (billions of dollars).

(1) Income = GNP	(2) Consumption	(3) Investment	(4) Government Expenditures	(5) Aggregate Demand
0	125	100	100	325
100	200	100	100	400
200	275	100	100	475
300	350	100	100	550
400	425	100	100	625
500	500	100	100	700
600	575	100	100	775
700	650	100	100	850
800	725	100	100	925
900	800	100	100	1000
1000	875	100	100	1075
1100	950	100	100	1150
1200	1025	100	100	1225
1300	1100	100	100	1300
1400	1175	100	100	1375
1500	1250	100	100	1450

to show that consumers spend on the average 3/4 of each additional dollar of current income.

Notice the 45° line drawn from the origin an equal distance from the horizontal and vertical axes. The 45° line enables us to compare consumer spending with GNP = Income at all levels of income. Thus, $C >$ GNP if national income is low and $C <$ GNP if national income is high. Because points on the 45° line are an equal distance from both axes, consumer spending is equal to income at the point where the consumption function crosses the 45°. At that point, consumer spending alone is just equal to the total value of goods and services produced. In Figure 7.1 consumer spending is equal to income at $500 billion. Refer to Table 7.1 and verify that $C =$ GNP at GNP = 500 billion.

TOTAL SPENDING $(C + I + G)$

Now let us combine consumer spending with spending by business firms and government. Economists refer to business investment spending as (I)

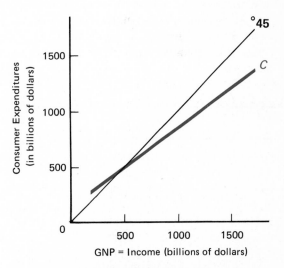

Figure 7.1   The Consumption Function.
Consumer spending depends on income. This consumption function is drawn with the assumption that consumers as a whole will spend 3/4 of each additional dollar in disposable income: $MPC = 3/4$.

and government expenditures as *(G)*. Business investment may be assumed to be fairly stable in any one period. Investment is based on plans made months or even years in the past. It does not rise and fall quickly in response to changes in current income. Table 7.1 shows investment of $I = \$100$ billion. Investment of $100 billion is shown on Figure 7.2 by adding a parallel line $100 billion above the consumption function.

Government expenditures are also independent of income in any one period. Government spending is based on our needs for public services and defense needs and does not depend on changes in current income. Thus, government spending is listed as $G = \$100$ billion on Table 7.1 and shown by the addition of another parallel line above the consumption function in Figure 7.2.

Adding investment *(I)* and government expenditures *(G)* to the consumption function *(C)* produces an aggregate demand function, showing aggregate demand associated with every level of current income: $AD = C + I + G$. All possible levels of aggregate supply, or total income, for the year are shown on the horizontal axis. All possible levels of aggregate demand, or total spending, for the year are shown on the vertical axis. The interaction between aggregate demand and aggregate supply determines the level of GNP toward which the economy will tend to operate.

EQUILIBRIUM GNP *(AD = AS)*

Figure 7.2 represents the Keynesian *model of income determination*. It enables us to measure the components of aggregate demand and illustrate their effects on aggregate supply and GNP. We have found that the actual level of GNP for any year will tend toward the level at which aggregate demand equals aggregate supply. At this income, the demand for output is just enough to purchase the total supply of goods and services: $AD = AS$. This is the level of GNP at which economic activity tends to stabilize: **equilibrium GNP.**

Look again at the 45° line drawn from the origin in Figure 7.2. The line marks all possible

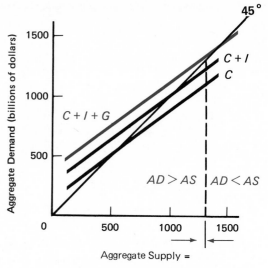

Figure 7.2   Model of National Income Determination.

The economy stabilizes at the level of spending, production, and income where *AD=AS*. In this figure the equilibrium level is $1300 billion.

equilibrium levels of GNP and income. At what income on Figure 7.2 is aggregate demand just sufficient to purchase aggregate supply? It is the point where $C + I + G$ crosses the 45° line. At an income of $1300 billion, aggregate demand = $C + I + G = \$1100 + \$100 + \$100 = \$1300 =$ aggregate supply. Business firms will be encouraged to produce at this level of GNP.

For all levels of production less than $1300 billion, total spending would be greater than the value of output. $C + I + G$ lies above the 45° line; $AD > AS$. With aggregate demand greater than aggregate supply, sales would have to be made from inventories. Business firms would want to expand production to fill the higher demand and maintain their inventory stocks.

For all levels of production greater than $1300 billion, total spending would be less than the value of output. $C + I + G$ lies below the 45° line: $AD < AS$. With aggregate demand less than aggregate supply, unwanted inventories would begin to accumulate. Business firms would want to cut back production to avoid losses on unsold inventories.

Only at an income of $1300 billion are the combined spending plans of all buyers equal to the production plans of producers; $AD = AS$. GNP is in equilibrium.

These results are easy to read from Table 7.1. For all levels of income less than $1300 billion, $AD = C + I + G > AS$, and GNP would tend to expand. For incomes greater than $1300 billion, $AD = C + I + G < AS$, and GNP would tend to contract. At incomes of $1300 billion, $AD = C + I + G = AS$, and GNP would be stable.

What can we learn from the Keynesian model of income determination? The model helps us locate the equilibrium level of spending, production, and income. It does not tell us whether this is an *efficient* equilibrium:

1. Is the equilibrium level too low to employ all available resources? A low level of spending, production, and income could mean that we are failing to use our scarce resources productively. This cannot be considered an *efficient* equilibrium level of GNP.
2. Is the equilibrium level so high that we are pushing against the limits of our resource capability? A high level of spending, production, and income could mean rising prices as business firms encounter scarcities of particular resources. This cannot be considered an *efficient* equilibrium level of GNP. If equilibrium income is neither so low as to cause unemployment nor so high as to cause inflation, we would say the economy is operating efficiently.

Changes are constantly taking place in spending plans, moving the economy to new equilibrium levels of GNP. Economic analysis helps project and evaluate future equilibrium levels of GNP. If the projected equilibrium level is not an efficient one, policy may be proposed to correct it. Macroeconomic policy to correct business cycles is the subject of Chapters 8 and 9.

CHANGES IN EQUILIBRIUM GNP

What lies behind changes in aggregate demand which move the economy to new equilibrium levels? Remember that changes in total spending can come from any of the three groups of spenders. Consumers, business firms, or government may decide to increase or decrease their spending in any particular year.

Increases in Total Spending

Consumers may decide to spend more for household appliances, recreation equipment, or personal services. They may save less from their current incomes, spend from past savings, or borrow against future earnings. An increase in consumer spending will shift the C component of aggregate demand upward. Total spending will increase and business firms will expand production and employment.

The same result would follow an increase in the investment plans of business. For example, production of a nonpolluting, low-energy-using automobile engine would require substantial new investment spending, shifting the I component of aggregate demand upward. Figure 7.3 (see page 130) shows additional new investment expenditures of $50 billion, causing a change in equilibrium GNP from $1300 billion to $1500 billion.

Government expenditures (G) may increase, perhaps in response to a military threat from abroad or through a massive program to provide free health care to every man, woman, and child in the United States.* If government expenditures jump from $100 billion to $200 billion, the new equilibrium GNP will be $1700 billion. Figure 7.4 shows this increase in G.

---

* Government expenditures may be financed at least in part by new taxes. New taxes would reduce disposable income and consumer spending. Thus, the C component of aggregate demand would shift downward and partially offset the rise in G.

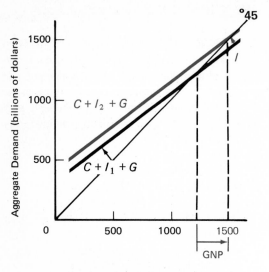

Figure 7.3   An Increase in Investment Spending.
An increase in *I* causes a greater increase in spending, production, and income. Compare the increase in *I* with the increase in GNP.

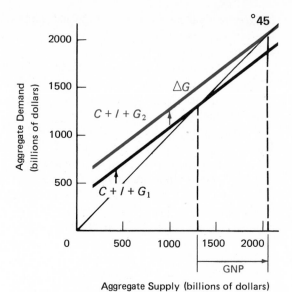

Figure 7.4   An Increase in Government Spending.
An increase in *G* causes a greater increase in spending, production, and income. Compare the increase in *G* with the increase in GNP.

The Multiplier Effect

Have you noticed that $50 billion additional investment spending in Figure 7.3 caused equilibrium GNP to increase by $200? And that $100 billion additional government expenditures in Figure 7.4 caused equilibrium income to increase by $400? In both cases, equilibrium income increased by more than the additional new spending. The greater increase in equilibrium GNP was a result of what economists call the **multiplier effect.**

The multiplier effect results from the fact that persons who receive as income the additional investment or government spending tend to *respend* a portion of their own receipts. Furthermore, persons who receive the respending enjoy a gain in income which they also spend. Finally, many individuals will have received additions to income, such that the total of all new income will be greater than the initial change in spending.

An illustration may be helpful. Remember

that the tendency to spend additional income is called the marginal propensity to consume and that the *MPC* for our example is $MPC = 3/4$. Of the $100 billion in new government expenditures shown on Figure 7.4, the initial amount of respending will be $MPC \times \Delta G = 3/4(100) = \$75$ billion. The $75 billion will be received by others and respent in the amount of $MPC(MPC \times \Delta G) = 3/4(75) \approx 56$. Other individuals will receive a total of $56 billion and spend $MPC[MPC(MPC \times \Delta G)] = 42$. The process of spending and respending will continue until the total of all changes in income is a multiple of the initial change. The value of the multiplier for measuring the change in income is determined by the formula: Multiplier $= k = 1/(1 - MPC)$, or in our example $k = 1/(1 - 3/4) = 1/(1/4) = 4$. The total change in income is $\Delta GNP = k \times \Delta G = 1/[(1 - MPC)] \times \Delta G$, or in Figure 7.3 $\Delta GNP = k \times \Delta I = 1/[(1 - MPC)] \times \Delta I$. Substitute the values from our examples into the formula and verify the results.

The result of multiplier analysis is that changes in *C, I,* or *G* can be shown to have substantially greater effects on the equilibrium level of GNP. Is this *efficient* in terms of the careful use of our nation's scarce resources?

The answer depends on the current level of resource use. Whenever there are idle resources available to be drawn into production, it is generally efficient to use them. Multiple effects of new spending on equilibrium GNP would be welcome. On the other hand, if the economy is already producing at full employment, further increases in *C, I,* or *G* will only aggravate the problem of scarce resources and may bring on inflation.

Inflationary Gap

We can use the Keynesian model of income determination to illustrate the problems associated with unwanted increases or decreases in equilibrium GNP. Figure 7.5 illustrates an upward shift in *C + I + G* of $200 billion. The increase in spending causes incomes to rise from $1300 billion to $1300 + 4(200) = $2100 billion. However, suppose available productive resources can produce only $1300 billion worth of goods and services when fully employed; that is, maximum production potential is $1300 billion. The full-employment level of output is shown by a vertical line drawn across Figure 7.5 at GNP = $1300 billion.

Aggregate demand of $2100 billion yields spending beyond the capacity output of the economy. The nation's business firms will produce $1300 billion worth of goods and services for which $2100 billion will be spent. Result: inflation!

The excess of aggregate demand above the 45° line at full employment is a measure of excess spending. The difference between total spending and total production at full employment has been called an **inflationary gap.** Any excess spending over and above the productive capacity of our economy cannot be considered *efficient,* in terms of the careful use of our nation's resources.

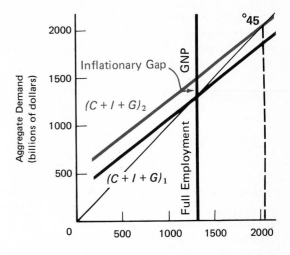

Aggregate Supply (billions of dollars)

Figure 7.5   Inflationary Gap.
Aggregate demand is greater than aggregate supply at full employment. Follow the line up from the full-employment level of $1300 billion. The portion of the line above the 45° line measures the inflationary gap when equilibrium GNP is $2100 billion.

Decrease in Total Spending

Downward changes in *C, I,* or *G* may produce other inefficient results. If any of the components of total spending should fall, there will be a multiple decline in incomes. Spending *not* received as income is *not* spent and *not* respent!

If consumers decide to save more because of uncertainty about the future, the *C* component of aggregate demand will fall. Unsold inventories will pile up, and manufacturers will reduce production. Likewise, if business decides to invest less, the *I* component will fall. Equipment orders will be canceled and construction workers will be laid off. Or finally, the *G* component of aggregate demand may fall as public projects are completed or stopped. For example, when the government ended the program to put a man on the moon, *G* fell sharply. As a result, production was cut back, and many aerospace engineers lost their jobs.

Figure 7.6 illustrates a multiple downward shift in incomes. If investment or government spending plans fall from $100 billion to $10 billion, the equilibrium level of output and income in Figure 7.6 will fall from $1300 billion to only $940 billion.

Deflationary Gap

Compare the lower equilibrium level in Figure 7.6 with the full-employment capacity output of $1300 billion. Then look at the aggregate demand line at the full-employment level of spending. The difference between aggregate demand and the 45° line at full employment is a measure of the deficiency of spending. The difference between total production and total spending at full employment has been called a **deflationary gap.** As long as aggregate demand is less than aggregate supply at the full-employment level of output, resources will be idle and workers unemployed.

A deficiency of spending relative to the productive capacity of our economy cannot be considered *efficient* in terms of the careful use of our scarce resources.

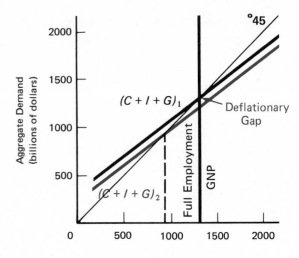

Figure 7.6 A Decrease in Investment or Government Spending and a Deflationary Gap.
A decrease in *I* or *G* causes a greater decrease in spending, production, and income. Compare the drop in $(C + I + G)_1$ with the drop in GNP. Follow the line up from the full-employment level of $1300 billion. The portion of the line from $(C + I + G)_2$ to the 45° measures the deflationary gap when equilibrium GNP is $940 billion.

CUMULATIVE UPSWINGS AND DOWNSWINGS

Even small changes in any of the components of aggregate demand can produce much larger changes in the level of GNP. A small increase in *C, I,* or *G* may send the economy into a strong upward swing in employment, income, and production. A small drop may start the economy into a deep slide of worsening unemployment, falling incomes, and declining production.

The United States experienced many swings in production and income over its first hundred years as a nation. Many economists finally came to believe that some form of government intervention might be necessary to help correct business cycles, with their alternating periods of unemployment and inflation. They decided that government taxing and spending might be used to adjust aggregate demand so that equilibrium would tend toward a full-employment, noninflationary level of GNP.

In the remainder of this chapter we will investigate the actual performance of the American economy in recent years. Then, in the next two chapters, we will examine the federal government's two instruments for influencing aggregate demand: fiscal policy and monetary policy. *Fiscal policy* involves the use of government spending and taxing powers to affect total spending. *Monetary policy* involves control of the supply of money to affect business investment spending.

Viewpoint

ANOTHER EXPLANATION FOR
BUSINESS CYCLES?

Some early economists blamed business cycles on sunspots! According to their theory, sunspot activity produced a favorable climate and good crops, increasing the incomes of farmers and encouraging spending for the products of manufacturing industries. Industrial capacity would then be enlarged, raising the number of jobs and generally stimulating a rise in incomes and expenditures throughout the economy. As sunspots receded, the process would go into reverse. Incomes and spending would decline, followed by bankruptcies, general pessimism, and lower rates of economic growth.

Indeed, in years past, there did seem to be some correlation between the highs and lows of economic activity and the eleven-year cycles of sunspots. The farming sector is no longer dominant in the U.S. economy, however, and can hardly be blamed for cycles in a modern industrialized nation. (Still, the worldwide economic recession of 1973–75 was certainly worsened by climatic changes and crop failures in many of the world's farming areas.)

Self-Check

1. **An individual's marginal propensity to consume may depend on all but which of the following:**
   a. the quantity of goods already owned.
   b. the level of consumer debt outstanding.
   c. plans for future spending.
   d. the portion of total income spent.
   e. the backlog of saving already accumulated.

2. **Equilibrium GNP:**
   a. is determined where aggregate demand is equal to aggregate supply.
   b. may leave workers unemployed and factories idle.
   c. may exceed the nation's productive capacity.
   d. may change if $C + I + G$ changes.
   e. all of the above.

3. **You carry mail for Uncle Sam during the Christmas season and use your earnings for a skin-diving trip to Florida. This is an example of:**
   a. noneconomic behavior.
   b. recession.
   c. the multiplier effect.
   d. a business cycle.
   e. the sunspot theory of economic activity.

4. **Enrollment increases at your college and a hamburger chain enlarges its restaurant nearby. This is an example of:**
   a. technological advance.
   b. inflation.
   c. the multiplier effect.
   d. an increase in investment expenditures.
   e. excess saving.

5. **In 1975, Queen Elizabeth II decided that "in view of the economic situation" she would postpone redecorating her vacation home. The queen must have believed there was:**
   a. excess saving in the British economy.
   b. an inflationary gap.
   c. a deflationary gap.
   d. a high level of unemployment.
   e. excess capacity in industry.

6. **In 1975, Congress voted to send taxpayers a rebate on their 1974 income taxes. Congress must have believed there was:**
   a. too much business investment spending.
   b. an inflationary gap.
   c. a deflationary gap.
   d. too much demand in relation to our productive capacity.
   e. a cumulative upswing in GNP and income.

Theory in Practice

HOW HAS THE AMERICAN ECONOMY PERFORMED IN RECENT YEARS?

Since World War II ended in 1945, the United States has experienced six recessions. A recession is defined as a period in which real GNP (GNP corrected for inflation) fails to grow for at least two quarters. Figure 7.7 is a time series graph showing real GNP for each of the years since 1945. (Money GNP has been corrected for inflation through the use of a price index with base year 1972.) The six post-war recessions are marked by the shaded bars.

The first postwar recession followed the war by about three years. Unemployment rose from 3.8 percent in 1948 to 5.9 percent in 1949 as civilian industries were unable to employ the large numbers of returning servicemen.

There were two recessions in the 1950s, one immediately following the Korean War in 1954 and one in 1958. A contributing factor was too optimistic production of consumer goods invento-

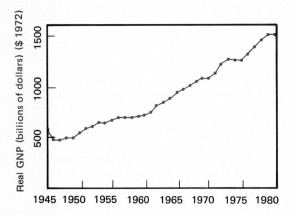

Figure 7.7   Growth of Real GNP Interrupted by Six Recessions.

The usual definition of recession is two consecutive quarters of negative real growth of GNP.

ries which could not be sold. Many business firms were forced to cut back production and lay off workers. In the recessions of the fifties, unemployment rose to 5.5 percent in 1954 and 6.8 percent in 1958.

Unemployment remained high until 1961 when increases in government spending began to be effective in stimulating total spending and production. The Vietnam buildup beginning in 1965 absorbed much of the slack in the labor force, and unemployment dropped to 3.5 percent (1969). But by 1971 unemployment again reached 5.9 percent, almost five million workers.

Unemployment continued at a high level, with the unemployment rate reaching more than 9 percent during the recession of 1974–75. The output of industry fell by a total of 2 percent in real terms.

After three years of strong growth, expansion weakened in 1979 and a new recession seemed imminent. But a single quarter of negative real growth in 1979 failed to satisfy the usual definition of recession. A similar pattern occurred again in 1980, and analysts finally declared a brief recession. By early 1981, the economy seemed to be floundering again, with some economists predicting no growth for the year.

What are the common elements in all these recessions? Each followed a period of heavy new spending: for military purposes, inventory investment, or social programs. Heavy spending raised incomes and consumer spending for goods, stimulating factory construction and employment. Eventually new spending slackened; incomes failed to rise further, new factories were not needed, and unemployment spread.

Changes in total spending have been partly a result of irregular investment spending. Real investment expenditures declined by 21 percent during 1975, but grew by 19 percent in 1976, 16 percent in 1977, 8 percent in 1978, and 1 percent in 1979. In 1980 real investment expenditures declined by about 12 percent. A slowdown in the growth of consumer spending from earlier highs was largely to blame for cutbacks in business investment. Scarcities and high prices for food, industrial commodities, and imported oil also discouraged investment spending in 1980.

It appears that irregular spurts in investment spending contribute significantly to changes in aggregate demand. During good years, inflows of business investment spending are generally high enough to offset the personal savings that drain from the spending flow. But unless business spending continues at high levels, investment will not be high enough to offset the outflow caused by saving. Total spending will fall.

Once a decline in total spending is felt, other changes take place that reduce chances for recovery. During the late 1970s, much consumer spending was financed by borrowing. Both mortgage and consumer debt grew faster than 10 percent during those years. Fear of hard times ahead makes large debt seem especially burdensome. Consumers tend to cut back drastically on new spending and pay off old bills instead. This is particularly true in the market for "big ticket" items, durable goods whose purchase can be postponed.

When spending falls, business inventories will begin to pile up and business firms will decide to cut back on their new orders. Manufacturers will postpone plans for building new capacity. All of this will aggravate the problem of declining total spending and worsen unemployment.

THE MULTIPLIER IN ACTION

Many large American cities are planning mass-transit systems to reduce the use of private automobiles in urban areas. One Southern city decided on a plan for mass transit with an estimated cost of $2.1 billion. The U.S. Urban Mass Transportation Agency agreed to contribute part of the cost, perhaps as much as 80 percent. The remainder was to come from city tax revenues.

Local economists predicted that as a result of the construction project, personal income across the entire state will increase an average of $475 million a year over the ten years required for construction. An estimated 35,300 new jobs will be created, and tax collections will go up by an average of $16.2 million per year.

Construction projects like this illustrate the multiple effect new spending can have on GNP. Contracts are signed with designers, landowners, earth-moving companies, equipment manufacturers, electricians, and builders. Firms hire new workers, order steel and cement, and install new machinery. Incomes grow throughout the area. Rising incomes enable consumers to increase their spending for homes, furnishings, and recreation. All these expenditures add a further push to incomes and GNP.

Occasionally, though, things don't turn out so well. Britain and France have long dreamed of a connecting tunnel under the English channel. The project finally got under way in the 1970s and was dubbed the ''Chunnel.'' For several years many millions of British pounds were spent for planning and construction costs. Early in 1975 British planners decided the project was impractical and too costly, and the ''Chunnel'' was abandoned.

Remember that the multiplier works in reverse also. What will be the probable result of the reduction in government spending? What are the effects of orders *not* made, money *not* spent, workers *not* hired? Trace through the chain of events and their effects on Britain's and France's GNP.

AGGREGATE SUPPLY AND AGGREGATE DEMAND

Throughout this text we have been concerned with supply and demand. Demand reflects the willingness of people and organizations to spend their dollars for certain goods and services. Demand for a particular good depends on its price. Normally, quantity demanded is greater at low prices so that a typical demand curve slopes downward from left to right. The demand curves in Chapters 2 through 5 were drawn according to this fundamental law of demand.

In this chapter we have been concerned with *aggregate demand*—the total of spending for all goods and services taken together. We have expressed aggregate demand as a function not of price but of income; that is, we assumed that consumer spending depends on a family's income. The aggregate demand curves in this chapter are drawn as a function of income.

Aggregate demand may also be thought of as a function of price, however. In this case we would assume that business and consumer spending depend on changes in the price level. An *aggregate demand curve* would look very much like a single demand curve, sloping downward from left to right according to the law of demand.

The reason has to do with the effect of price changes on the value of money. Rising prices reduce the value of money income and savings. Many consumers will attempt to rebuild their purchasing power by spending less for consumer goods and services. Rising prices also raise the interest cost of borrowing and discourage business investment spending. When prices are rising, lower consumer and investment expenditures mean lower aggregate demand. On the other hand, falling prices increase the value of money and cause interest rates to fall. The result is higher consumer and investment spending when prices are falling.

Figure 7.8   Aggregate Demand.

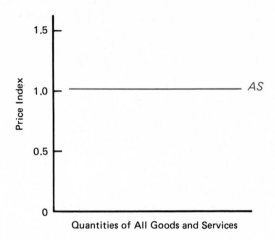

Figure 7.9   Aggregate Supply.

In Figure 7.8 the vertical axis measures price in terms of a price index, varying from zero to 1.50. The curve labeled *AD* represents aggregate demand for all goods and services. At prices higher than 1.00, quantities sold of all goods and services are smaller than quantities sold at prices less than 1.00.

Aggregate Supply can also be drawn in relation to a price index. Aggregate supply represents the sum of all production plans in all business firms. For a single firm, supply obeys the law of supply. Larger quantities will be supplied only at higher prices; individual supply curves slope upward from left to right because of rising marginal costs in the short run.

Aggregate supply curves may behave differently. Larger quantities may be produced with no increase in price. This is because new firms are constantly entering the market, putting their output into competition with existing firms' output. Over a wide range of output, quantities sold may increase substantially without upward pressure on the price index. Aggregate supply may actually be flat as drawn in Figure 7.9.

A flat aggregate supply curve is important for all of us. It makes it possible to consume larger quantities of goods and services without experiencing inflation. In fact, as our population increases and as our wants for goods and services grow, aggregate demand will shift to the right. With a flat aggregate supply curve, larger quantities can be provided at constant prices. (Pencil in a series of aggregate demand curves on Figure 7.9.)

Of course, the picture is not yet complete. We know that supply cannot increase indefinitely at constant prices. New firms cannot continue to enter the market producing larger output without eventually experiencing rising costs. As resources become fully employed, their prices will rise and firms must raise their prices for finished goods. The aggregate supply curve will begin to slope upward. At the absolute limit of productive capacity, aggregate supply would become very steep. No additional quantity is possible, but sharply rising prices are indeed possible.

Figure 7.10 combines a shifting *AD* curve with an *AS* curve that becomes very steep at full employment. Increases in consumer spending, business investment spending, and government purchases are not inflationary as long as there are unemployed resources. But as resource markets tighten, the price index must rise. Aggregate de-

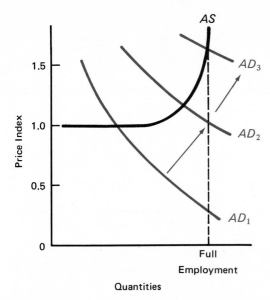

Figure 7.10 Aggregate Supply and Demand at Full Employment.

mand may continue to increase, but the actual quantity of goods sold cannot increase. The result is an inflationary gap.

Fortunately, there is more to the story. Aggregate supply may also change with time. Improvements in the quantity and quality of resources are increasing our productive capabilities. The full-employment limit to supply has moved to the right fairly steadily from year to year. We may hope that it continues to do so. (Pencil in a new aggregate supply curve and comment on the implications.)

AGGREGATE SUPPLY AND PRODUCTIVITY

An average worker's share of total output is measured by productivity: worker productivity = (total output or GNP)/number of workers. If output grows faster than employment, we say that worker productivity has increased and, likewise, each worker's share can grow. Through much of the

1960s and early 1970s, worker productivity did grow, but by the end of the decade the reverse was true. In 1974, 1978, and 1979, employment grew faster than GNP, so that worker productivity fell.

There are many causes for the decline in worker productivity. Some of the causes have to do with the level of business investment spending. Rising energy costs during the 1970s reduced business profits and discouraged new capital investment. Also, new environmental and safety regulations added to business costs and increased the risk of new investment. Three recessions in the 1970s contributed to a decline in business confidence and worsened the outlook for investment. Other things affected the savings rate during the 1970s. Members of the "baby boom" generation born in the years 1948–1961 required a high level of consumption expenditures during their young years. A generally higher marginal propensity to consume left less savings for investment and helped keep interest rates high. Also, persistent inflation moved many households into higher tax brackets, increasing their tax bills and further discouraging saving for investment.

Changes in the quality of the work force may also have affected productivity. Many new entrants to the work force during the 1970s were young and inexperienced. In particular, a rise in female employment raised the fraction of workers whose skills were not highly suited for jobs in modern industries. Much of the earlier gains in productivity had been a result of a movement of labor out of agriculture (where worker productivity was relatively low) to mechanized industry (where worker productivity was relatively high). Lately, this process has slowed and will contribute less to productivity gains in the future. This may be true also for the productivity gains that have resulted from improved worker health and education.

What is the outlook for worker productivity in the future? And, in turn, what is the likely course of aggregate supply for the nation? High energy costs will continue to challenge business firms to develop new, less costly technical processes. New government regulation must be geared to only the most critical environmental and safety problems and toward the least costly solutions to these problems. The "baby boom" generation will eventually mature, become more productive, and reach an age where saving is possible. Finally, tax laws should be changed to encourage saving and investment for improving productivity.

In terms of aggregate supply, all these hoped-for changes should increase our nation's capacity to produce goods and services. The result may be a flat aggregate supply curve over a longer range of output. If more goods and services can be produced per worker, then aggregate demand can grow without causing prices to rise. Might increased worker productivity cause the aggregate supply curve to shift downward? (Pencil in the effect of increased worker productivity on the aggregate supply curve in Figure 7.10.)

SUMMARY

1. A rising GNP means more goods and services for the population. But if spending for GNP rises faster than our capacity to produce goods and services, inflation may result. A falling GNP, or one that rises too slowly, may mean unemployment and low production. Alternating periods of rising and falling GNP are called business cycles.
2. Consumer spending at various levels of income is shown graphically by the consumption function. Consumer spending is based on the marginal propensity to consume *(MPC)*. *MPC* measures the fraction of additional income that consumers will spend.
3. The economy will tend to stabilize at an equilibrium level of GNP where aggregate demand is equal to aggregate supply. At equilibrium there is no tendency for production either to expand or contract.
4. If aggregate demand is greater than aggregate supply at the full-employment level of GNP, there will be an inflationary gap. If aggregate demand is less than aggregate supply at the full-employment level of GNP, there will be a deflationary gap.

5. Small changes in aggregate demand produce cumulative changes in income because of the mutiplier effect. Changes in total spending have been a result partly of irregular business investment spending.
6. Increases in aggregate demand may be satisfied by increases in aggregate supply at constant prices. However, as resources become fully employed, prices will begin to rise.
7. Slow growth of worker productivity in recent years can be attributed to factors affecting capital investment and to the quality of the work force. Future developments may reverse the trend so that worker productivity can increase, and the aggregate supply curve may remain flat over a longer range of output. The hoped-for result is that aggregate demand can increase without a price increase.

TERMS TO REMEMBER

business cycle: recurring upswings and downswings in the level of economic activity.
marginal propensity to consume *(MPC):* the fraction of each additional dollar of income that consumers will spend.
consumption function: the graph showing consumer expenditures for every level of GNP and income.
equilibrium GNP: the level of GNP at which aggregate demand is equal to aggregate supply; total spending is equal to the value of output.
inflationary gap: an excess of aggregate demand over aggregate supply at full employment.
deflationary gap: a deficiency of aggregate demand below aggregate supply at full employment.
multiplier effect: the multiple change in income that results when an initial change in spending is spent and respent many times.

TOPICS FOR DISCUSSION

1. Explain and illustrate each of the following pairs of terms:

   aggregate demand and aggregate supply
   inflationary gap and deflationary gap

2. Trash collectors in a large American city were interviewed during the recession of 1974–75. They reported a noticeable drop in the appearance of usable items in trash collections, even from wealthy neighborhoods: fewer pairs of shoes, pieces of furniture, and repairable small appliances. Does this suggest anything about the rate of consumer saving in hard times? What does this imply about the chances of recovery from recession?

3. Producers of most goods suffer declining demand during recessions. Others may enjoy *rising* demand. How would you explain the increasing sales of the following goods during the recession of 1974–75: white bread, beer, home freezers, sewing machines, movie tickets, dehydrated foods?

4. During the inflation-recession of 1975, economic analysts were worried about the high level of inventory accumulation in business. What "signals" does a business firm receive from an exceptionally high level of inventory stock in relation to its monthly sales? Discuss this situation in terms of flows of spending and income. What implications do you foresee for the levels of: employment, production, investment, prices?

5. Droughts in the Midwestern states beginning in 1974 reminded many weather scientists of the historical pattern of dry spells that have often damaged American agriculture. The dustbowl days of the 1930s and the long dry spell of the 1940s are examples. There were fears that the 1974 drought signaled a new prolonged period of reduced output from American farms. The drought was believed by some to be related to sunspot activity and, if past experience is repeated, could last from three to eight years.

Discuss the implications of this situation for the American economy. How would prolonged drought affect the output of other sectors of the economy, real income of workers, the federal government budget, and technological progress?

6. Explain the origins of inflation and recession as summarized in Chapters 6 and 7. What are the characteristics of each? How is each related to the rate of growth of GNP? What rate of growth of GNP would be ideal?

7. Using the multiplier developed in this chapter, compute the effect on GNP of a $20 billion drop in government expenditures, ceteris paribus. Can you explain why the marginal propensity to consume is incorporated in the formula for the multiplier?

SUGGESTED READINGS

"America in 1929: The Illusion of Prosperity," *Business Week,* September 3, 1979, p. 6.

Daane, J. Dewey, and Morley, Samuel A., "Supply Chic," *Across the Board,* November 1980, pp. 45–49.

Evans, Michael K., "The Bankruptcy of Keynesian Econometric Models," *Challenge,* January/February 1980, pp. 13–19.

Fiedler, Edgar R., "Capital," *Across the Board,* September 1977, p. 40.

Heller, Walter W., "Can There Be Another Crash?" *Challenge,* March/April 1980, pp. 31–36.

"The Runaway Economy," *Business Week,* March 10, 1980, p. 102.

"The Slow-Investment Economy," *Business Week,* October 17, 1977, p. 60.

"Vanishing Innovation," *Business Week,* July 3, 1978, p. 46.

CHAPTER 8

Government Finance and Fiscal Policy

or How to Spend Money
When You Don't Have Any

Tools for Study

Learning Objectives

After reading this chapter, you will be able to:

1. explain three ways through which government can finance its expenditures.
2. define three classes of taxes.
3. explain how government fiscal policy helps stabilize economic activity.
4. discuss some advantages and disadvantages of fiscal policy.
5. explain the origins, composition, advantages, and disadvantages of the national debt.

Issues Covered

How well has fiscal policy worked?
What were the major points of President Reagan's 1981 fiscal program?
What is the fiscal outlook for the future?

Nobody loves the tax collector. The story is told of how Saint Peter stood at the "Pearly Gates" checking the qualifications of all who wanted to enter Paradise.

First, a politician convinces Saint Peter of his good intentions during life. But he is told he must pass a test before entering. "Spell 'God'," he is told, and upon answering correctly he is ushered in.

Next a policeman tells of his sufferings in life, carrying out his duties as preserver of the peace while he is ridiculed and spat upon by law-breakers. Likewise, he must be tested. "Spell 'God'," he is told, and likewise, he passes through the pearly gates.

Finally, a tax collector tells of his tribulations in a thankless and friendless job. Saint Peter agrees that he is also worthy. But he, too, must pass a test. "Spell 'asafoetida'," he is told.

ALLOCATION OF RESOURCES: PUBLIC OR PRIVATE?

In our nation's early years, settlers willingly combined their energies and talents to construct public projects: roads, meeting houses, fortresses, and even stockades. Later, as the nation grew, citizens continued to contribute a few days each month to maintain the community's property. There was a direct and visible relationship between citizen participation on the one hand, and the security and growth of the society on the other. Direct citizen involvement created bonds of satisfaction often lacking today. Today a taxpayer merely fills out and signs a Form 1040 and thus assigns a portion of his or her production to the U.S. Treasury. The citizen often feels not a *part* of the government but a *victim*, struggling to escape its clutches!

Taxes represent a major form of government intervention in the market system. Through taxes, resources are channeled away from private purposes toward public purposes, the production of goods and services used by the community as a whole. When you pay your dollars for sales and property taxes, income and social security taxes, you have fewer dollars to spend for autos, appliances, clothing, and trips to the shore. Government casts some of your "dollar votes" for you— for schools, highways, and national defense.

Our final choice of private goods and public goods can be shown on a production possibilities curve like the one in Figure 8.1. The two axes represent private goods—for the consumer's own use—and public goods—for the use of the community as a whole. Our willingness to give up part of our income in taxes permits the use of some of our nation's scarce resources for production of goods and services to be enjoyed by the community.

As a nation, we try to achieve the correct balance between production for private enjoyment and production for the use of the entire community. Given a fixed quantity of productive resources, we try to determine the most efficient allocation of resources that will best serve the objectives of the community and its citizens.

Production of some goods and services is clearly an individual's responsibility; others can be provided best by group action. In the United States, the first group includes the production of consumer goods and food. The second includes

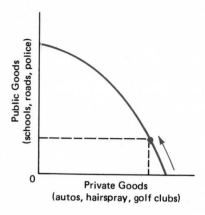

Figure 8.1 Private Goods and Public Goods.
The government channels some of our resources into production of public goods.

defense and international relations, highway systems, and regulation of interstate and foreign commerce. In a gray area, where public and private responsibilities mingle, are education, health and nutrition, housing, and the arts.

SPENDING FOR PUBLIC GOODS AND SERVICES

Federal government outlays in the United States for fiscal year 1980 totaled about $600 billion. Shares of the budget allocated to specific purposes are shown in Figure 8.2.

National defense and defense-related expenditures comprised the largest portion of the budget. National defense consumed nearly $136 billion, or about 23 percent of the total. Defense-related expenditures—international affairs, space research and technology, interest on the public debt, and veterans' benefits and services—consumed an additional $102 billion (17 percent). Health, education, housing, commerce and transportation, agriculture, and rural and natural-resource development took about $145 billion (24 percent). *Revenue sharing,* federal payments to state and local

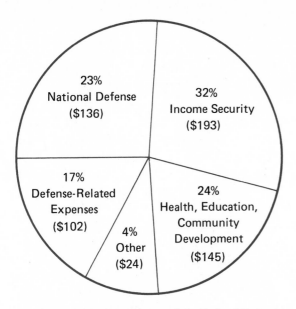

Figure 8.2   Allocative Shares of the Federal Budget for 1980 (dollar figures in billions).

Source: *Economic Report of the President,* January 1981.

governments, amounted to only $8.6 billion (1 percent). Income-support payments to individuals (such as social security benefits, welfare, and unemployment compensation) were about $193 billion (32 percent).

Shares of government expenditures going for various purposes have remained fairly constant over the years. An exception has been the greater emphasis on military expenditures in wartime. Emphasis on public services such as education and health has varied also, depending on the philosophy of the administration in power and on the mood of the public, expressed in political pressure.

State and local government expenditures focus primarily on community services. Education is highest on the list of local government expenditures, with highways an important second. Fire and police protection, water and sewage, and parks and recreation are other local government responsibilities.

GETTING THE MONEY

How does government obtain the money it needs to pay out? Outlays can be financed in three ways: (1) by printing new money; (2) by borrowing from the public; or (3) by taxing the public. Let us look at each of these methods in more detail.

Printing Money

Printing new money sounds like a relatively safe and easy way for government to finance its expenditures. In fact, it is the poorest way to obtain funds and is not now used by the U.S. Treasury. The reason has to do with its effect on total spending. If government prints more money for its own spending without taking any money away from consumers, consumer spending will continue at the same level. However, now individuals will be competing with government for the limited supply of output. As government and individuals bargain and bid for the available goods and services, prices will rise and all money will be worth less. The result of printing new money can be serious inflation.

During the 1920s, the German government needed money to make its reparations payments to the victors in World War I. Many of its debts were paid by printing new money. The money supply increased by almost 10 billion times in four years! The result of money growth was inflation so severe that workers had to be given time off during each day to spend their pay before prices could rise again.

Borrowing from the Public

A better way to raise money would be to borrow from the public. Government can sell bonds to individual consumers and business firms. (Remember that when you buy a government bond, you are, in effect, lending your money to government!) If consumers purchase bonds with money that they otherwise would have spent, consumer spending will fall by the amount government wants to spend. If buyers of bonds use money that they otherwise would have loaned to banks or other businesses, investment spending will fall by the amount government wants to spend.

A problem with this method is that at times it may be difficult to persuade the public to buy government bonds, unless interest rates are allowed to rise. Interest charges on U.S. Treasury bills and bonds rose from around 5 percent in 1972 to almost 13 percent in 1980. Higher interest rates made total interest expense on the federal debt jump from only $20 billion in 1972 to $65 billion in 1980!*

Taxing the Public

Perhaps the best way to finance government spending is through taxation. Other spending will be reduced by the amount government needs to spend. And it isn't necessary to persuade taxpayers to cooperate!**

In 1980 total federal tax receipts were $520 billion. Personal and corporate income taxes were the major source of federal tax revenue, making up about 60 percent of the total. The U.S. Treasury ran a deficit of $60 billion which was financed by borrowing.

A CLOSER LOOK AT TAXES

Because taxes make up the major portion of government revenue, we will look at them in more detail. The various taxes levied by government are often classified by comparing the amount paid in taxes with the taxpayer's income base.

---

* Interest rates of 16 percent were expected to cost the Treasury $80 billion in 1981.

** Citizens in some cities and towns have lately begun to resist new tax measures, however. Passage of Proposition 13 in California is an example of what some analysts have called a "taxpayers' revolt."

Regressive Taxes

A tax which takes a larger percentage of income base from low-income earners than from high-income earners is a **regressive tax.** Examples are:

1. any uniform "head" tax such as the (now outlawed) poll tax, which takes a stated amount from every citizen regardless of income.
2. social security taxes, which take a portion of an employed person's earnings up to a certain amount, above which earnings are not taxed.
3. and even sales taxes.

The regressivity of numbers 1 and 2 above is easy to see. But why is a sales tax regressive? A sales tax is a fixed percentage of expenditures for goods. However, a sales tax is considered regressive because low-income families generally spend a larger percentage of their income on taxed goods than do higher-income families. Upper-income families generally spend more of their incomes on untaxed services, and they save more. (Excluding such necessary items as food and medicine from the sales tax makes it less regressive.)

There is some difference of opinion on the proper classification of the property tax. Most agree that low- and middle-income families are likely to use a larger portion of their incomes for housing than are high-income families. This would make the effects of the property tax regressive.

Proportional Taxes

A tax which takes an equal portion of income base from all taxpayers is a **proportional tax.** An example is Illinois personal income tax, which is 2 1/2 percent for all income levels (however, exemptions for dependents have the effect of reducing the proportional effect of the tax).

Progressive Taxes

A tax which takes a larger percentage of income base from high-income earners than from low-income earners is a **progressive tax.** The federal corporate and personal income taxes are the best examples. Tax rates increase as the taxpayer moves into higher tax brackets. For a typical married parent with two children, the tax on the 8000th dollar earned above deductions and exemptions is $.19; the tax on the 8001st net dollar is $.22.

The Tax Structure as a Whole

State and local taxes, dominated by sales and property taxes, are considered **regressive.** It is generally agreed that the federal tax structure, dominated by income taxes, is *progressive.*

The progressivity of the federal tax structure is affected also by the existence of **negative taxes.** Negative taxes are payments to individuals or groups and are also known as transfer payments. (Transfer payments were discussed in Chapter 6.) Remember that transfer payments are not payments for goods or services, but additions to the disposable incomes of particular groups. When negative taxes received from government are subtracted from taxes paid to government, the result is *net taxes:* the net amount withdrawn from private income by government.

The effect of net taxes is to increase the progressivity of the federal tax structure. This is because low-income families who pay a lower tax rate will be more likely to receive government transfer payments of some kind. The receipt of negative taxes may make their net tax rate very low or even less than zero. High-income families who pay a higher tax rate receive fewer transfer payments. This makes their net tax rate high.

The progressive rate structure is weakened at very high income levels by certain tax advantages designed to improve economic incentives. At very high income levels, where steep tax rates would take as much as 50 percent of additional income, many taxpayers take advantage of legal means to reduce their tax bills. This is done by increasing their deductions from taxable income. Some possible deductions are: losses from side business ventures; contributions of stocks or works of art to

nonprofit organizations; fast depreciation of business equipment or facilities; and entertainment and other expenses related to business (though these latter deductions are being carefully scrutinized by the IRS).

A taxpayer may also arrange to have a portion of his or her income treated as a *capital gain.* A capital gain is the difference between the cost of an asset and its selling price when sold by the taxpayer; it is taxed at less than half the rate of the tax on the taxpayer's earned income.

A study by the Brookings Institution examined the effects of the tax structure at various income levels. Except for the 10 percent of families having the lowest incomes and the 3 percent having the highest, almost all families pay between 20 and 25 percent of their income in federal, state, and local taxes. Persons with the lowest incomes actually pay a higher percent of their income in taxes (mostly sales taxes) than the 87 percent of the population in the middle range. The same is true of persons with the highest incomes (who pay mostly income taxes).

If these findings are correct, we may conclude that our tax structure as a whole is *regressive* at low levels of income, *proportional* over a wide range of middle income, and *progressive* for a small group at the top of the income scale.

FISCAL POLICY

The U.S. government uses its tax receipts to provide public goods and services to citizens. But government taxing and spending policies also have important consequences for the level of economic activity.

The Keynesian Revolution

The Great Depression of the 1930s awakened our elected representatives to the dangers of unstable growth of GNP. They searched for ways to correct unemployment and to protect against unemployment (or inflation) in the future. In the late 1930s the British economist, John Maynard Keynes, presented his ideas on economic stabilization to President Franklin Roosevelt.

Keynes's basic proposition was simple. Any time aggregate demand was too low, bringing on high levels of unemployment and recession, government should increase its spending and reduce taxes to increase aggregate demand. If aggregate demand was too high—over and above the capacity of existing resources to produce—government should reduce its spending and raise taxes to avoid a boom of inflationary spending. In this way, government **fiscal policy** would offset changes in private spending. (The word *fiscal* evolved from "fisc," which referred to a money basket carried by tax collectors in the days of the Roman Empire. The term refers to the taxing and spending activities of the U.S. Treasury.)

According to Keynesian proposals, there need be no relationship between taxes and government expenditures; the federal government did not need to balance its expenditures with its tax collections. In times of too little private spending, government spending should exceed tax revenues. This would funnel more purchasing power back into the spending flow than the government took out through taxes. Operating "in the red" would tend to cause a government **deficit:** $G - T$ = deficit.

In times of too great private spending, tax revenues should exceed government spending. This would drain out more purchasing power from the spending flow through taxes than the government put back through spending. The result would be a tendency toward a government **surplus:** $T - G$ = surplus.

In deficit years, extra government spending could be financed by the sale of bonds. Then in surplus years, bonds could be redeemed. If by some coincidence government borrowing during deficit years should be offset by loan repayments in surplus years, there need be no permanent increase in total federal debt. In any case, according to Keynes, minor increases in government debt would be a small price to pay for maintaining an efficient level of employment and production.

Keynes's ideas were considered revolutionary.

For several decades, public officials hesitated to recommend that government spend more than it collected in taxes. The budget often was in deficit during recessions anyway when incomes (and income tax receipts) fell. It was not until the early 1960s that the federal government actually *planned* a budget deficit. (The first *planned* deficit is discussed in more detail in the second part of this chapter.)

Some features of fiscal policy are *automatic,* with built-in tax and spending changes which take effect automatically when private spending changes. Other features are *discretionary*. They require the action of Congress before they can be put into effect.

Automatic Fiscal Policy

Automatic fiscal policy consists of the progressive net tax structure, including tax rates that rise with income and *negative taxes* like farm subsidies, unemployment compensation, welfare benefits, food stamps, and veterans' pensions.

The progressive tax structure ensures that, as incomes rise for individual taxpayers, they move into higher tax brackets. They must pay higher taxes and thus must cut back spending to a smaller portion of their higher incomes. On the other hand, as incomes fall, lower tax rates go into effect and help keep consumer spending stable.

Negative taxes have the same result. As incomes rise, welfare benefits, subsidies, food stamp allotments, and unemployment compensation tend to fall. Smaller transfer payments tend to slow the rise in incomes and stabilize the level of consumer spending. On the other hand, when incomes fall, these payments rise, stabilizing consumption near its desired level.

Guarding Against Unemployment
The progressive net tax structure helps prevent widespread unemployment of the nation's productive resources. If spending drops, unemployment could increase, and the economy could spin lower

and lower into recession. But the tax structure helps cushion the effects of a drop in spending because:

1. reduced incomes are taxed at lower rates.
2. transfer payments increase as more families move down the income scale.

The result is to pump purchasing power into the pockets of low-income households particularly likely to spend it. This cushions the downward slide of spending and helps keep employment and production from falling as far as it might otherwise. It also tends to produce an automatic *deficit* in the federal budget.

Guarding Against Inflation

If spending increases too rapidly, higher incomes may cause rising prices. Again, the tax structure helps dampen the effects of a jump in spending:

1. As families move into higher income brackets, they are taxed at higher rates.
2. They are entitled to fewer government transfer payments.

The result is to drain some of the excess purchasing power from the spending stream. This brakes the upward thrust of spending and helps hold prices down. It also tends to produce an automatic *surplus* in the federal budget.

Discretionary Fiscal Policy

Automatic fiscal policy is removed from the fallible judgment of public officials. (This may be seen as an advantage or disadvantage, depending upon one's confidence in public officials!) Occasionally, however, automatic fiscal policy may not be enough to hold spending at a full-employment, noninflationary level. Additional changes in the entire rate structure and in spending appropriations may be needed. This makes it necessary to use *discretionary* fiscal policy, deliberate action by government to affect spending plans. Discretionary fiscal policy can be expansionary or contractionary.

Guarding Against Unemployment

In times of high unemployment, *expansionary fiscal policy* may be necessary to increase aggregate demand. Congress might decide to reduce tax rates for individuals and corporations. Lower personal income taxes would leave households with more money to spend for consumer goods and services. Lower corporate income taxes would leave business firms with more money for investment spending.

Congress might also decide to increase government expenditures. Expenditures could be increased for public projects like dams and highways, education and health services, or scientific research and resource development. Higher government expenditures would increase aggregate demand, production, and income. Finally, Congress could decide to distribute more funds as transfer payments. Larger transfer payments would increase incomes and increase the level of private spending.

Guarding Against Inflation

In times of inflation, *contractionary fiscal policy* may be needed to reduce aggregate demand and hold down the level of resource use. Congress might decide to raise tax rates or impose a *surtax* on tax bills. (A surtax is an extra tax, a tax on a tax.) Higher taxes would leave families with less money for consumer expenditures and would leave business firms with less money for investment plans. (Of course, if families and businesses cut back on their saving in order to pay their higher taxes, they may be able to continue spending at the same level.)

Congress might also decide to reduce government expenditures. Reducing expenditures may be difficult if essential public projects are under way and must be continued. Congress may be reluctant to cut back transfer payments, since the payments generally go to low-income groups who suffer severely from inflation.

The best remedy for unemployment or inflation might be some *combination* of discretionary actions that avoid the disadvantages of a single policy. For example, during the recession of

1974–75, President Ford recommended that Congress: (1) reduce personal and corporate tax rates; (2) increase unemployment compensation; and (3) appropriate funds for public-service jobs in highway maintenance, library and hospital services, and other public projects. And during the inflationary expansion of 1979, President Carter recommended that Congress: (1) allow taxes to increase automatically; (2) reduce the growth of federal outlays; and (3) encourage labor-management cooperation in a voluntary program of wage and price restraint.

Evaluating Discretionary Fiscal Policy

An important weakness of discretionary fiscal policy is the lack of well-planned and needed projects on which to spend government funds. A major energy research and development effort or a space program may come up only once in a generation—make that a century! Moreover, massive government expenditure programs tend to be difficult to administer without waste and duplication. And occasionally, projects completely fail to achieve their intended aims.

They are also slow to put in place. Ideally, economic advisors would maintain a backlog of desired projects, engineered and ready to go. The plans could be begun quickly when needed, and in spending amounts ranging from very small to rather large. This would permit more long-range planning and flexibility in the injection of new spending.

Economic Planning
Another serious problem with discretionary policy is the lack of immediate economic information. Economic forecasting and planning is not as exact a science as, perhaps, horticulture. The story is told of a New York apartment dweller who was caring for a collection of cacti and needed a precise indicator to tell her when they should be watered. She solved her problem by subscribing to an Arizona newspaper. Whenever the paper reported rain, she watered her plants!

Unfortunately, Congress has no equally precise indicator that signals when to inject or hold back new spending, and there are no generally reliable means for accomplishing the needed results. Proposals must be debated and compromised, voters must be informed and persuaded and, finally, administrative procedures must be designed and put into operation. All in all, it is a frustratingly difficult and time-consuming process. By the time any decision is put into effect the problem may be much worse (or it may have disappeared).

Economics and Politics
The most serious disadvantage of discretionary fiscal policy stems from political considerations. Tax and spending proposals often depend more on current politics than on what is best for the nation's long-range health. For instance, spending for rural development or for supersonic transport will affect different groups of voters differently. Each legislator will want to pass a spending or tax proposal that provides the most help for his or her own constituents. It is very difficult to separate economics from politics!

Political considerations mean that discretionary fiscal policy will tend to have an inflationary bias. Congress finds it fairly easy to turn on the faucet and allow more spending power to flow into the system. Appropriations bills and tax reductions receive little objection from voters and maintain a legislator's popularity back in his or her district.

The reverse is not so agreeable. Closing off spending, through reductions in grants and increases in taxes, doesn't secure one's seat in the next legislative session! The result is that expansionary fiscal policy to fight unemployment will be favored at the expense of contractionary fiscal policy to fight inflation.

Viewpoint

THE POLITICS OF ECONOMICS

The American political mechanism provides a voice for the interests of many groups, no matter how small. There are some disadvantages to this. Decision making in a democracy requires consensus from many groups before action can be taken. Problem solving cannot proceed smoothly from *description* to *analysis* to *policy*. The interests of different groups must be considered and compromises must be made. The result may be economic policies that are too little or too late—or just plain wrong!

Voters disagree about the types and amounts of government spending programs. In general, each of us tends to favor spending policies that will increase our own spendable income, whether or not those policies promote the general economic welfare.

This is especially true with respect to spending for national defense. Spending for national defense raises the incomes of some groups and raises the tax bills of many others. Particular regions or occupational groups often use their legislative power to benefit proportionally more from defense expenditures. (A distinguished senator from Georgia was for many years chairman of the Senate Armed Services Committee. It was sometimes said that if his state received one more defense installation it would sink into the Atlantic!)

What is politically desirable for some, however, may turn out to be undesirable for the economy. A region's economic growth may be slowed if resources are diverted from long-range economic development to short-range military purposes. Also, when defense spending is cut off, those areas may suffer severely from the loss of jobs and income.

The farming sector is another that is strongly affected by government spending decisions. Farmers generally favor free markets and oppose price fixing for the equipment they must buy. At the same time, they may demand price supports for the farm commodities they sell. In the end, farm price supports increase the costs to consumers of many other goods. Strong farm lobbies in Congress can exert political pressure (some even contribute campaign funds) in support of policies that benefit farmers.

Economic decisions must be made in light of political realities. What is politically popular may at times outweigh what is economically efficient. It is little wonder, then, that the study of economics was originally known as *political economy*.

THEN THERE'S THE NATIONAL DEBT . . .

The result of Keynesian economic policy is that the federal government may often spend more than it collects in taxes. Whenever spending from the private sector is not sufficient to buy the full-employment supply of output, government spending should absorb the difference. If consumer spending and business investment spending fall short, government spending and lower taxes will help keep resources employed. According to Keynesian economic policy, *a balanced federal budget is desirable only if private spending alone will achieve full employment.*

Spending more than taxes means that government may often need to borrow. Deficits in the federal budget must be financed by the sale of bonds to individuals, business firms, financial institutions, and state and local governments. Fortunately, government bonds are seen by many as a safe way to store money assets. Bonds provide interest income generally sufficient to offset the effects of inflation, and they provide security for an individual's retirement years.

The first major increase in the national debt accompanied World War II when the debt jumped from $45 billion to more than $250 billion. Obviously this great increase in government spending was not all due to deficit financing to achieve full employment! The increase in debt was necessary to finance military expenditures.

Since the 1940s, government debt has continued to grow at an annual rate of about $10 billion. The rate of increase was understandably greater during the years when we were at war. At the end of 1980, the total national debt amounted to more than $900 billion. Debt of $900 billion was 35 percent of GNP for the year, down from 40 percent of GNP in the late 1960s and 125 percent of GNP in 1946! Government debt has declined as a percent of GNP primarily because of economic growth, which has contributed to a faster increase in total production.

Who Holds the Debt?

The gross amount of federal debt is somewhat misleading. Much of the debt is held by agencies within the federal government itself. Many government agencies receive payments for long-term special purposes and then buy government bonds temporarily as interest-earning assets. For example, the U.S. highway trust fund receives gasoline tax revenues which it holds to allocate for interstate highway construction. The social security trust fund receives employee and employer contributions from which disability and pension payments are made. In all, almost $200 billion of the national debt was held by such agencies of the government in 1980.

Of the remainder, the largest single owner of government bonds is the Federal Reserve System with more than $120 billion. Federal Reserve banks receive interest on these assets, but by law they are required to return most of the interest to the U.S. Treasury. Private commercial banks, savings banks, and insurance companies together hold about $125 billion in government bonds. Other corporations hold about $25 billion, and state and local governments, about $73 billion.

Another $250 billion is held by miscellaneous holders such as nonprofit institutions, pension funds, foreign agencies, and individuals. Foreigners hold an increasing percentage of the debt— $134 billion, or 14 percent in 1980. This figure has leaped from $20.6 billion in December 1970. As foreigners earn more U.S. dollars— from the sale of petroleum, for example—they often use their dollars to buy Treasury bills. This leaves about $123 billion in the hands of private individuals in the United States.

Some Advantages

An important advantage of the national debt is that it provides government a means for stabilizing economic activity through variations in government spending. Furthermore, the purchase and sale of government bonds is a means of changing the quantity of money in circulation, as the Federal Reserve buys and sells bonds from its own holdings. (This subject is discussed more fully in the next chapter.)

Government bonds provide financial security to many small investors. Many individuals and institutions regard U.S. government bonds as a convenient and safe way to store their savings for future needs.

Since the U.S. government is a continuing operation, it is never necessary to repay the debt completely. As older people cash in bonds for their retirement needs, younger people will want to buy bonds for their long-range security. Because only a relatively small part of the debt is held by foreigners, cashing in bonds does not normally cause a serious outflow of dollars to other nations.

Some Disadvantages

To repay the debt in its entirety (which is not being suggested!) would require that taxes be increased by the amount of the debt in order to pay cash to bondholders. The effect would be a major redistribution of wealth within the country. All income earners would be taxed to pay the smaller group of bondholders. Furthermore, since bondholders are likely to be among the higher income groups, they would tend to spend a smaller proportion of their receipts. The result might be a decline in total spending and a resulting decline in economic activity. Nevertheless, to repay the national debt would not significantly affect the *total* wealth of our economic system.

A similar disadvantage applies to the collection of tax revenues used to pay interest on the national debt. All income earners are taxed to pay interest charges to bondholders—$65 billion in 1980 and $80 billion projected for 1981. This amounts to about 10 percent of all federal outlays (but only 2 percent of GNP). Holders of debt gain

from interest payments, of course, but many gainers are also taxpayers whose tax payments cancel out their gains. The extent to which some groups gain and others lose from the effects of the federal debt has not been precisely measured.

It is often argued that the large national debt places a burden on future generations who, it is said, must tax themselves to pay interest charges or to repay the debt. We have seen that total repayment is not necessary or desirable. Interest charges are necessary and are "inherited" by future generations. But the interest income, as well as the bonds themselves, are also inherited by those future generations.

A significant disadvantage of the debt has to do with government's competition with private borrowers for a limited quantity of funds for lending. Whether the national debt imposes a net gain or loss on the economic system depends on whether borrowed funds spent by government help produce a safer more efficient national and international environment than would have been produced by private use of the same funds.

Supply-Side Economics

The Keynesian model of income determination dominated economic theory for a quarter of a century. Economic policymakers tended to follow Keynesian recommendations; in particular, they suggested that increased government spending should be used to raise aggregate demand and correct tendencies toward recession and unemployment. Through the 1970s and into the 1980s, however, analysts began to question the validity of certain Keynesian principles. Keynesian policy concentrated too much on demand, they said, expecting that higher total spending would itself generate the investment spending necessary to produce higher levels of output. They argued that high consumption spending and high taxes to finance government spending programs had, in fact, stifled the capacity to save, such that borrowing costs were too high for adequate new investment. Without additional capital investment, increases in aggregate demand would mean accelerating inflation.

A new group of economists called for a rejection of demand-side economic policy and acceptance of policies to stimulate the supply side. **Supply-side economics** concentrates on tax reductions along with cuts in government spending programs:

1. Personal income tax reductions are expected to increase incentives to work and save.

2. Corporate tax reductions are expected to increase capacity to invest.

3. Cuts in government spending are expected to free up productive resources for more efficient employment in private industry.

The result of supply-side economic policies was expected to be increased productive capacity and a reduction in inflation.

President Reagan campaigned on a platform that emphasized supply-side solutions to economic problems. Reduced tax and spending policies were put in place late in 1981.

Self-Check

1. **The largest single federal outlays go for:**
   a. health, education, and welfare.
   b. revenue-sharing to states.
   c. national defense and defense-related expenditures.
   d. interest on the national debt.
   e. highway construction.

2. **The federal net tax structure:**
   a. is generally regressive.
   b. includes primarily sales and excise taxes.
   c. is considered roughly proportional.
   d. requires low-percentage tax rates on high incomes.
   e. includes some negative taxes.

3. **Automatic fiscal policy depends on:**
   a. changes in net taxes as incomes change.
   b. lower tax payments during inflation.
   c. lower transfer payments during recession.
   d. congressional action to change tax rates.
   e. the consent of voters.

4. **Discretionary fiscal policy:**
   a. will never create a government deficit.
   b. is a fool-proof instrument of economic policy.
   c. requires congressional action.
   d. is easiest to accomplish during inflation.
   e. focuses on welfare payments and subsidies.

5. **As a result of the national debt:**
   a. the United States is heavily indebted to foreign banks.
   b. many private investors are dependent on risky assets.
   c. we must tax ourselves heavily to pay bondholders as bonds mature.
   d. there is some redistribution of spending power.
   e. we have placed an unfair burden on our grandchildren.

6. **The federal government provides funds for industrial development in areas of high unemployment. This is an example of:**
   a. automatic fiscal policy.
   b. discretionary fiscal policy.
   c. expansionary fiscal policy.
   d. contractionary fiscal policy.
   e. both (b) and (c).

7. **Which of the following would be an appropriate way to deal with inflation?**
   a. build a dam
   b. increase farm subsidies
   c. reduce social security taxes
   d. run a deficit in the federal budget
   e. run a surplus in the federal budget

Theory in Practice

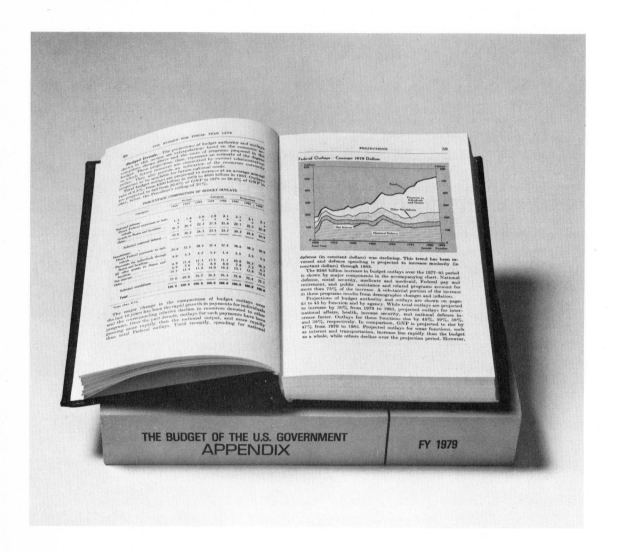

HOW WELL HAS KEYNESIAN FISCAL POLICY WORKED?

During the Depression of the 1930s, Keynesian fiscal policy was still a new and untried idea. Government spending was not undertaken vigorously enough to offset the decline in private spending. Keynes joked that it might be a good idea to bury jars of money around the countryside and encourage people to dig them up! In that way, consumers would receive spending power which, when spent, would increase someone else's income and spending. Ultimately there would be *multiple* increases in spending and income and, finally, increased employment.

Instead of such schemes, some government funds were used for public works projects under the Public Works Administration, Civilian Conservation Corps, and Works Progress Administration. Unemployed people were hired to work on public roads, bridges, parks, and so forth. Still, the total government expenditure was rather skimpy.

Total federal, state, and local government expenditures did not rise substantially from 1929 to 1933. Tax revenues fell, however, so that by 1940 the federal government had incurred automatic deficits averaging almost $4 billion a year for seven years. Fear of growing federal debt led to attempts by policymakers to cut spending. In 1940, there were still 10 million people unemployed.

During the recessions of the Eisenhower years (1954–55 and 1958–59) the balanced-budget philosophy was in control. The idea of using expansionary fiscal policy to offset declines in private spending was abandoned. It was not until the early 1960s that Keynesian economic policy was actively applied. It was then that a conscious decision was made to unbalance the budget in order to stimulate economic activity. Walter Heller, chairman of President Kennedy's Council of Economic Advisors, convinced the President to ask Congress for a tax cut at a time when the federal budget already showed a deficit!

Heller reasoned that the deficit was a result of *high* tax rates! High tax rates kept consumer and business spending low. This meant low levels of employment and income and, hence, low tax revenues. A reduction in tax rates would leave consumers and business firms with more spending power, permitting higher aggregate demand. This would increase job opportunities and earnings and finally enable the Treasury to collect *higher* tax revenues.*

The tax cut was implemented under President Johnson in 1964, and Dr. Heller's prediction proved correct. The budget went from a $3 billion deficit in 1964 to a $1.2 billion surplus in 1965. Tax revenues for 1965 were nearly $10 billion higher than revenues in 1964, before the tax cut!

The success of *expansionary* fiscal policy (along with increases in the money supply) led to some self-satisfaction among economic policymakers. But toward the end of the 1960s, economic conditions changed from recession to inflation. The new inflation called for *contractionary* fiscal policy.

This period illustrates the principal weakness of Keynesian fiscal policy. It is a weakness that follows from political realities.

When Vietnam expenditures began to overheat the economy, the high level of spending brought on inflationary pressures. Keynesian fiscal policy called for higher taxes to channel spending away from private purposes and move resources into military production. But the unpopular war and insecure political position of the President and Congress precluded a tax increase until 1968. By this time inflation had been built into public expectations and had accelerated beyond the point where simple policy tools would have substantial effect.

The end to the war and the slowing of government expenditures in the early 1970s brought ris-

---

* Similar reasoning lay behind supply-siders' proposed tax cuts in 1981. Keynesian critics pointed out that there was less slack in the economy in 1981, however, so that higher consumer spending might aggravate inflation.

ing unemployment (although inflation continued at high levels). The problem of unemployment called for *expansionary* fiscal policy, with relatively lower taxes and higher government outlays. From 1970 through the fiscal year ending in 1980, federal budget deficits amounted to $372 billion, roughly $37 billion per year. During the preceding twenty years the average annual deficit had been only $4.3 billion.

In spite of this substantial increase in government spending relative to tax revenues, there was no significant reduction in unemployment. Unemployment reached a peak of 9.2 percent in 1975 and was still more than 7 percent through much of 1980.

Continuing inflation has also been a disturbing problem for policymakers. Keynesian remedies for unemployment seem only to aggravate the problem of inflation, which reached levels of over 13 percent during 1981.

Some economists believe that it is impossible to control both unemployment and inflation at the same time. Lately it seems to be impossible to control *either!*

PRESIDENT REAGAN'S FISCAL PROGRAM

President Reagan came to office on a broad wave of disillusionment with Keynesian economic policy. High inflation and unemployment, weakening influence in world affairs, and faltering economic growth seemed to call for new approaches. Congress appeared willing to cooperate in the new administration's efforts to correct longstanding economic problems.

We have referred to President Reagan's economic program as ''supply-side economics.'' Critics of familiar Keynesian economics pointed out that ''aggregate demand economics'' had focused too much on consumption, assuming that a high level of consumer spending would create incen-

tives for investment and healthy growth. But, critics said, high taxes and government spending for social programs had been withdrawing so much spending power from the economy that investment had suffered. Without substantial new investment spending, job creation had slowed and low productivity had fed inflation.

Proposed Policy Changes

The new administration recommended a series of actions to change policies that they believed contributed to the current crisis:

1. *Reducing the Role of Government in the Economy.* Throughout the 1970s total federal government outlays (including purchases and transfer payments) amounted to almost 22 percent of GNP, and taxes to 21 percent. Fearing growing dominance by government in allocation of resources, the administration proposed significant cuts in taxes and government spending programs.

2. *Personal Tax Cuts.* Personal income taxes were to be cut substantially, with the greatest savings going to high income persons who pay proportionally greater taxes. Tax cuts were expected to increase work incentives, thus raising income and ultimately increasing tax revenues. Higher disposable incomes were expected to increase savings, making available increased funds for investment and contributing to rising productive capacity.

3. *Business Tax Cuts.* Business firms were to be allowed larger tax deductions, leaving greater retained profits for financing expansion and modernization of obsolete production processes.

4. *Government Spending Cuts.* Tax cuts would initially reduce government revenues, making for a larger deficit, at least for the immediate

future. Government programs which were judged to be wasteful or not essential had to be cut back or eliminated. Some targets were: (1) The Economic Development Administration (EDA), which administers development funds for depressed areas: (2) Trade Adjustment Assistance, which pays benefits to workers unemployed as a result of foreign competition; and (3) food stamps, which may have been distributed to people who do not need them.

5. *Increased Defense Spending.* A perception of military inferiority relative to the Soviet Union and a fear of growing world tensions led to recommendations for significant increases in defense spending.

6. *Decreased Government Regulation.* Environmental health and safety regulations of the 1970s were believed to have increased the risks of investment and stifled innovation. Therefore, regulatory agencies were asked to reduce the level of new regulatory activity and consider carefully the economic impact of existing regulations.

Some Criticisms

The gravity of the economic situation ensured substantial support for the President's proposals. However, critics pointed to some potential problems. First, unless proposed new tax cuts were fully offset by spending cuts, higher levels of total spending would aggravate already high inflation. Second, the administration's recommended tax cuts tended to favor high income earners while spending cuts would harm low income workers. Third, some of the proposed spending cuts might save dollars currently but worsen long-range problems and require greater spending in the future. Fourth, spending for defense production increases incomes while producing no consumer goods, thereby contributing to inflation. Finally, tax cuts could not generate additional taxable income soon enough to avoid extremely large government deficits.

Despite these fears, many elected representatives were willing to consider carefully the "supply-side" proposals and give the administration a chance to test its theories for the sake of economic recovery.

THE FISCAL OUTLOOK

The federal budget is closely tied to changes in the level of economic activity. Certain classes of federal expenditures rise with a growth in spending and incomes. Social security benefits are tied to consumer price increases; Medicare and Medicaid payments are tied to the cost of medical services; and interest on the debt is influenced by interest rates in the economy. Also, tax revenues are particularly sensitive to changes in income as taxpayers move into higher or lower tax brackets.

Table 8.1 shows changes in the quantities of federal expenditures and receipts for selected years. The deficit in 1939 can be attributed to the

Table 8.1 Federal Budget (in millions of dollars).

Year	Receipts	Outlays	Surplus or Deficit
1929	3862	3127	734
1939	4979	8841	− 3862
1943	23,649	78,533	− 54,884
1951	51,646	45,546	6100
1959	79,249	92,104	− 12,855
1968	153,671	178,833	− 25,161
1975	280,997	326,092	− 45,095
1980	520,050	579,613	− 59,563
1982*	711,780	739,296	− 27,516

Source: *Economic Report of the President,* January 1981.

* 1982 figures are estimated.

Table 8.2   Projected Federal Budget (in billions of dollars).

Year	1978	1979	1980	1981*	1982*	1983*	1984*
GNP							
Current $	2099	2413.9	2627	2928	3312	3718	4156
Constant $							
(1972)	1400	1483.0	1481	1493	1545	1600	1659
Budget							
Tax Receipts	400.4	465.9	520.0	607.5	711.8	809.2	922.3
Outlays	462.2	493.6	579.6	662.7	739.3	817.3	890.3
Surplus or							
Deficit	− 61.8	− 27.7	− 59.6	− 55.2	− 27.5	− 8.0	+ 32.0

Source: *The United States Budget in Brief, Fiscal Year 1982.*
*projected

severe drop in tax revenues during the Great Depression; in 1943, to the large World War II defense expenditures. The recession of 1958–59 again reduced federal tax revenues, and Vietnam expenditures contributed in large part to the deficit in 1968. Deficits in the mid-1970s were primarily a result of the lower level of incomes and tax receipts during the prolonged recession. Finally in 1980, an inflationary recession pushed up federal outlays faster than the growth of tax revenues.

Projections of economic activity for future years permit some tentative forecasts about the size of federal expenditures and revenues. Many government programs continue over several years, making it possible to predict expenditures fairly accurately. Projected figures for selected years are shown in Table 8.2.

Between 1980 and 1986, government outlays are expected to increase an average of 9.2 percent a year. Tax receipts will grow an average of 13.7 percent because of rising personal and corporate incomes over the period and because of inflation, which pushes workers into higher tax brackets. Social security tax rates are expected to rise again also.

Since the late 1960s federal government payments to individuals have been rising steadily as a percent of the total budget, and defense spending has declined. Some reversal of this trend began in

the mid-1970s. Still, domestic assistance programs are expected to constitute 42 percent of federal outlays in 1983; defense expenditures will be about 25

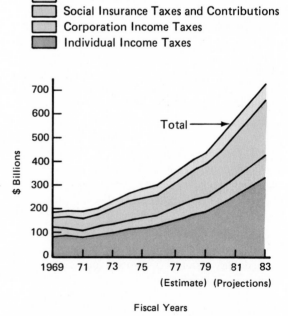

Figure 8.3 **Budget Outlays and Receipts as a Percent of GNP.**

percent. Other federal expenditures will include payments for projects begun and appropriations made in earlier years and new energy research and development projects.

Figures 8.3, 8.4, and 8.5 illustrate budget projections to 1983. Figure 8.3 shows that the large deficits of the 1970s are expected to diminish as a percent of GNP. If these projections are correct, the federal budget would be in surplus by 1984. Figure 8.4 shows the budgetary effects of rising social security contributions and of higher incomes and income taxes. Figure 8.5 shows the recent behavior of defense spending and income support payments.

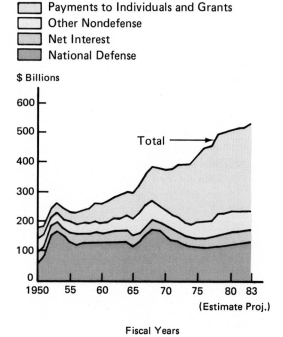

Figure 8.4   Budget Receipts: 1969–83.

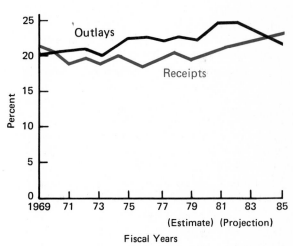

Figure 8.5   Federal Outlays—Constant 1979 Dollars.

Viewpoint

LETTING GOVERNMENT DO IT

If you are ever in Beaver Creek, Minnesota, on Saturday night, don't miss the big dance at the community recreation center just outside town. There, in a massive Quonset hut, a contribution of $2 will buy you an evening of foot-stomping music and a rousing good time. Just about everyone in town will be there, for in many ways this is the center of the town's social, economic, and political life.

It also illustrates an important relationship between citizens and their government. The people of this small, isolated community agreed to combine their resources for construction of their community recreation center. In effect, they decided to "tax" themselves $2 a week, and in return they enjoy the recreation services at the hall. Ticket sales have long ago paid off the original borrowing to build the center and are now paying for new tennis courts on adjacent land.

This is the way it has always been in the United States. Citizens have perceived needs for community services; they have chosen representatives to plan programs to fill the needs. In the beginning most services were provided by local government—usually on a limited scale. But since the Great Depression of the 1930s, the federal and state governments have been providing more services for their citizens.

How well does the system work? The answer depends in part on the level of government involved. Some needs can be perceived and filled at the local level. Public education and local law enforcement are examples. Services like these can be provided on a small scale, and the administrative costs may be very small. Other needs, like dam construction, agricultural research, and forest conservation, are more complex and extend over larger areas. Plans must be made and carried out at the level of the state or even the federal government.

When broader programs are drawn up to deal with these more complex needs, there are some advantages and some disadvantages. Providing services for a large area may be cheaper than when each community provides services separately. Large volume purchasing and large-scale production often cost less and are more efficient. But large-scale production sometimes means higher administrative costs which may offset these gains.

In terms of overall productivity, it is probably correct to say that the government sector is far behind the private sector. One reason is mechanization. Gains in productivity are generally the result of mechanization, but government services are not easily mechanized. The high labor content of public services makes it difficult to cut costs. Moreover, at the local level especially, it is difficult for government to establish clear goals and to use scientific management for planning programs.

How can government be helped to perform better? Critics have offered some suggestions:

1. Local governments might be combined into metropolitan or regional units. Larger units could use professional management techniques for a more systematic approach to broad area-wide problems. Higher levels of government could provide technical help with budgeting, accounting, and reporting procedures. Links between government workers at various levels would help coordinate programs and avoid waste.

2. Another way to improve government's performance might be to hire private firms to produce some public services. Private business firms have long experience in cutting costs. Garbage collection, school lunch programs, data processing, fire protection, and even law enforcement are examples of services that might be provided more efficiently by private firms.

3. Finally, if public services are to be provided efficiently, they must be performed at the level of government which can do the job at lowest cost. This may mean that taxes should be collected by one level of government and revenues spent by another level. The federal government appears to be better at collecting taxes than state and local governments. This is partly a result of the progressive income tax which yields more revenues as national income grows. On the other hand, spending programs conducted at the federal level have often been inefficient. State or local governments may be better able to tailor spending programs to their particular needs. In fact, the federal government now collects tax revenues for redistribution to states under the revenue-sharing program begun in 1972. Federal grants to states now comprise more than a fifth of total state and local government spending, amounting to $75 billion in 1979.

In the United States we ask government to do for us what we cannot do for ourselves. Unfortunately, some jobs may be too complex even for government! When government programs fail to accomplish their objectives, it is unfair to compare the results with some ideal standard. A truer evaluation would be to compare results with results at some other level of government—or with no government action at all.

SUMMARY

1. Civilized communities have always depended on the cooperative efforts of their citizens to provide the facilities and services enjoyed collectively by the community at large. Nowadays, production of public services is indirectly provided for through the payment of taxes, which are used by government for the purposes the community wants.

2. Nearly one third of total spending goes to satisfy collective demand for community services and national defense. About 20 percent of national income and output is used by the federal government and about 10 percent is used by state and local governments. The largest single purpose of federal expenditures is defense and defense-related expenditures. State and local governments provide community services.

3. Taxes are classified as regressive, proportional, or progressive depending on the percentage of income paid at various income levels.

4. A progressive tax structure provides a degree of automatic stability in the level of economic activity. It helps moderate a tendency toward too rapid growth or recession. Stability is accomplished by withdrawing more net taxes from the spending stream when incomes rise and withdrawing less net taxes when incomes drop.

5. When the automatic changes in tax payments are not sufficient to prevent unemployment or inflation, discretionary changes in tax rates or government spending may be necessary. Discretionary action is difficult because of the time required to plan, debate, and, finally, put new proposals into effect. Furthermore, political pressure may favor types of government projects or tax policies that do not serve the long-range interests of the nation.

6. When government spending exceeds tax revenues, the Treasury must borrow by selling bonds. Treasury bonds are held by individuals, businesses, financial institutions, and local governments and are considered a safe way to store purchasing power. Because the debt is held largely within the United States, the interest costs on the bonds are paid by Americans to Americans. If borrowed funds are used wisely, they can represent an investment in the quality of life for our nation.

7. Disillusionment with the results of Keynesian economic policy in the 1970s led to the emergence of supply-side economics with the election of President Reagan. Supply-siders recommended cuts in federal tax and spending programs and increased incentives to business investment. These programs were implemented late in 1981.

TERMS TO REMEMBER

deficit financing: government expenditures in excess of tax revenues, financed by borrowing.

regressive tax: a tax that takes a larger percentage of income from low-income earners than from high-income earners.

proportional tax: a tax that takes the same percentage of income from all taxpayers.

progressive tax: a tax that takes a larger percentage of income from high-income earners than from low-income earners.

net tax: the tax paid by income groups after allowance is made for payments *received* from the government.

negative taxes: government income-support payments to individuals; transfer payments.

fiscal policy: use of the federal government's taxing and spending powers to promote economic stability.

deficit: an excess of spending over revenues.

surplus: an excess of revenues over spending.

Keynesian economic policy: emphasis on government tax and spending policies to affect the level of aggregate demand.

supply-side economics: economic analysis and policy that stresses the ability of free markets to increase total production in the absence of government intervention.

TOPICS FOR DISCUSSION

1. Explain the effects of each of the following on national income and expenditures:

   negative taxes and net taxes
   revenue sharing
   federal deficits and surpluses

2. What is meant by the statement that our tax system is:

> regressive at low levels of income, proportional at medium levels of income, and progressive at high levels of income?

3. Subjects for debate:

> What is the proper allocation of economic responsibility to the public sector and to the private sector?
>
> What is the proper allocation of economic responsibility to the federal government and to state and local governments?

4. A respected British economist, the late Barbara Ward (Lady Jackson), once called for an "international fiscal policy." What do you think she meant by that? How do you suppose her suggestion might be carried out?

5. In contrast with government, private enterprises must attempt to balance their budgets each financial period. Can you envision a time when a large, healthy corporation might spend more than it collects in revenues? How might such a condition come about? Where would the corporation get the extra funds to spend? Would you like to be a stockholder in such a company? Explain your answer.

6. Some analysts view the growth of government debt as less a threat than the growth of consumer installment debt. In what ways is growing consumer debt a threat to economic stability? What policies might be useful in managing the level of consumer debt?

7. The author suggests that lower tax rates may actually *increase* tax revenues collected by the government. Explain this paradox. Is the reverse also possible?

SUGGESTED READINGS

Asimakopulos, A., "The Incidence of Taxation," *Challenge*, March/April 1979, pp. 47–51.

"Behind the Campaign Rhetoric: What the Candidates Really Believe About Economic Policy," *Business Week*, November 3, 1980, p. 74.

Bosworth, Barry, "Economic Policy," in *Setting National Priorities: Agenda for the 1980s*, Washington: The Brookings Institution, 1980, p. 35.

Brimmer, Andrew F., "The Political Economy of Limitations on Federal Spending," *Challenge*, March/April 1980, pp. 6–11.

Cameron, Juan, "The Tax Education of Jimmy Carter," *Fortune*, January 16, 1978, p. 54.

"Campaign Politics Rule Economic Policy," *Business Week*, October 22, 1979, p. 130.

Ehrbar, A. F., "A Tax Strategy to Renew the Economy," *Fortune*, March 9, 1981, p. 92.

Greenspan, Alan, "Economic Policy," *The United States in the 1980s*, Hoover Institution: Stanford University, 1980, p. 31.

Harriss, C. Lowell, "Reduce Personal Tax Rates! Wipe Out the Corporate Tax! But Don't Diminish Government Revenues!" *Across the Board*, October 1977, p. 19.

"The Integration of Demand-Side and Supply-Side Policies," *The Economic Report of the President*, Washington: Government Printing Office, January 1981, p. 78.

"Interventionist Government Came to Stay," *Business Week*, September 3, 1979, p. 39.

Levy, Frank, "The Biography of Proposition 13," *Across the Board*, January 1980, pp. 26–38.

Levy, Michael E., "Carter's Budget," *Across the Board*, April 1978, p. 66.

Meadows, Edward, "How Congress Ought to Cut Taxes," *Fortune*, December 31, 1979, p. 36.

Meadows, Edward, "Laffer's Curveball Picks Up Speed," *Fortune*, February 23, 1981, p. 85.

Okun, Arthur, "The Balanced Budget Is a Placebo," *Challenge*, May/June 1980, p. 3.

Okun, Arthur, "The Great Stagflation Swamp," *Challenge*, November/December 1977, p. 6.

Quirt, John, "'Jaws II' vs. the California Tax Bite," *Fortune*, May 19, 1980, p. 102.

"Reagan's Top Problem: Braking Inflationary Expectations," *Business Week*, December 1, 1980, p. 104.

Splow, Robert M., "Jobs, Jobs, Jobs," *Across the Board*, January 1977, p. 38.

CHAPTER 9

Banking and Monetary Policy

or Money Isn't
Everything—
Most of the Time It Isn't
Even Enough

Tools for Study

Learning Objectives

After reading this chapter, you will be able to:

1. explain the disadvantages of barter.
2. list the three functions of money.
3. describe how banking developed and explain how banks create and destroy money.
4. explain the functions of the Federal Reserve System.
5. describe the financial services performed by nonbank financial institutions.
6. explain how monetary policy aims at stabilizing economic activity and discuss some of the problems.

Issues Covered

What is the controversy over the quantity theory of money?
How successful has monetary policy been?
How have changes in bank lending affected monetary policy?
How is monetary policy affected by politics?

Natives of the North Georgia mountains tell about an illiterate country fellow who is particularly ignorant in money matters. According to the tale, this old gentleman is unable to recognize the value of a half-dollar over that of a quarter. When offered his choice between the two coins, he will always choose the quarter. In the fall of the year when it's "leaf-looking" time in the Blue Ridge, they say tourists will line up before his bench on the courthouse lawn for the opportunity to offer him coins. True to legend, he will invariably select the quarter and drop it into his roomy overalls pocket.

We should all be so "ignorant" in money matters as this mountain gentleman!

MONEY IS AS MONEY DOES

The first use of money was a kind of watershed in the ongoing process of economic development. Before money came into use, exchange was possible only through **barter.** In barter, goods are exchanged for other goods. Barter requires a "double coincidence of wants." People have to find someone willing to accept their own goods in exchange for the goods they want (you have a pig and want

Viewpoint

BARTER: ITS TIME HAS COME

Barter requires a double coincidence of wants. This requirement makes barter difficult and time consuming—at least it did before the age of computers!

Certain changes in the U.S. economy have had the effect of reviving barter as a means of exchange. High inflation has frequently reduced the value of receipts from a sale faster than the money can be spent. Barterers receive what they want simultaneously with the sale of what they don't want. High taxes have also discouraged sales for cash and encouraged barter. Barterers are supposed to report their gains as taxable income, but some don't.

And how do computers figure in the growing "barter fever" in the United States? Computers can be used to identify goods for trade. They help identify persons with a "double coincidence" of wants and make barter more convenient.

Throughout the country there are barter clubs, barter newsletters, and barter businesses. Consumers trade legal services for recreation equipment, prime beef for bridgework, and house plans for stereos. U.S. exporters have traded Pepsi Cola for Russian vodka and airplanes for Yugoslavian ham.

There is no way to measure precisely the extent of barter in the United States, but one government agency is trying—the Internal Revenue Service! What do you think about barter? Are there advantages and disadvantages not mentioned here?

cloth; I have cloth and want a pig). Barter makes trade difficult and time consuming.

Payment in the form of tokens or symbols for the goods, rather than the goods themselves, helped overcome the disadvantages of barter. The use of tokens promoted specialization and division of labor. Each worker could develop a particular skill for producing a good or service and receive some type of token as payment. Because tokens represented the same value for every person, workers could use their tokens to purchase items produced by either other workers or other communities.

These tokens served as *money;* they provided flexible purchasing power which could be used for whatever an individual wanted to buy. (Even the word *currency* comes from the Latin word meaning "flow," which describes the free flow of goods when money is widely used.)

Functions of Money

The preceding section implied that, in order for something to serve as money, it must perform certain functions. There are, in fact, three necessary functions of money.

First and most important, money must be a *medium of exchange*. It is accepted as payment for goods and services and, in turn, is used to buy other goods and services.

Second, money must be a *standard of value*. It provides a measure for expressing the worth of goods and services. As such, it also provides a means for comparing value. (For example, in the United States, the standard of value is expressed in terms of *dollars*. A pound of chicken may be worth only fifty cents while a pound of beef may be worth two dollars, or four times as much.)

Finally, money must be a *store of value*. It can be saved and used to purchase goods and services some time in the future.

Bones, Bullion, and Bank Notes

Money can take many shapes and forms. Whatever is generally accepted as money becomes money. Throughout history the functions of money have been carried out by such diverse things as shells, cattle, and bones (even human skulls!).

Gold and silver served well as money because they were *scarce* and *durable*. Also, they were easily divided into small pieces and they had few uses other than as money. Chunks or flat pieces of these precious metals promoted the free flow of trade in the Near East and Europe in ancient times.

Occasionally, cheaters would chip away the edges of these early coins to form more pieces. Eventually it became necessary to make coins round with serrated edges so that any tampering could be detected.

The difficulty of storing and transporting precious metals led to the development of banking in many parts of the world. (Primitive banks may have existed as far back as the seventh century B.C.!) Banks held gold on deposit for their customers and issued *certificates* or *notes* promising to pay gold to the bearer on demand. They charged a small fee for the service.

The earliest banks were unable to earn enough income simply by handling gold for their depositors. By the seventeenth century, banks began to make loans to borrowers for investing in productive enterprises. They issued additional certificates to business borrowers, with the expectation that profits from the business would make it possible to repay the loan with interest.

Although the amount of gold certificates outstanding might exceed a bank's supply of gold, this was not considered a problem. It was reasoned that not all depositors would want their gold at the same time. On any given day while some depositors might be withdrawing gold, others would be depositing gold. As long as holders of bank notes had faith in the bank and did not insist on withdrawing their gold without notice and en masse, lending was reasonably safe.

EARLY BANKING

Banking developed in the United States during the early 1600s. The first banks were unregulated and tended to overissue bank notes. A bank with 1 million dollars in gold would issue several times that much in notes. At first, the notes would be perfectly good as purchasing power. They would circulate freely until holders began to realize the bank would never be able to redeem all its certificates in gold. Many holders would then demand gold for their bank notes. With the loss of its gold the bank would vanish, and along with it, the savings of its depositors.

Some banks were called wildcat banks because they grew up in the wilderness, "out where the wildcats howl." These banks would accept gold deposits from trappers and miners and go through a brief orgy of lending. Finally, many wildcat banks collapsed when note holders insisted on exchanging their gold certificates for the real McCoy.

Centralized Banking

In the late eighteenth century, Secretary of the Treasury Alexander Hamilton helped set up a central bank to regulate bank lending and protect the value of savings. Many members of the general public distrusted centralized government control, however, particularly control by powerful moneyed interests of the Northeast. Southern and Western opposition to regulated banking brought on its collapse in 1836 during the administration of Andrew Jackson.

The problem of overissue of banknotes and frequent bank failures continued until finally, in 1863, the National Banking Act was passed to regulate banks chartered by the federal government. The Act set up cash reserve requirements for national banks and limited their lending. This brought some stability to the supply of bank money. However, the states still had power to charter state banks, and state regulations were much less restrictive than the regulations of the national banking system.

THE FEDERAL RESERVE SYSTEM

The late 1800s were again marked by a series of severe financial crises. Following the Panic of 1907, voters finally began to support the idea of a strong national banking system. It was hoped that regulated banking would earn the confidence of savers and achieve greater stability in the supply of bank money.

In 1913, a new National Banking Act was passed setting up the Federal Reserve system (commonly called the Fed). Commercial banks throughout the nation are now regulated under this system. The system is controlled by a seven-member Board of Governors appointed by the president with Senate approval. Governors serve overlapping terms of fourteen years. This removes them from political pressure and makes it generally impossible for one president to appoint more than two members during a four-year term.

Federal Reserve banks are situated in twelve Federal Reserve districts. They do not deal with the American public, but rather with the Treasury and with commercial banks. Federal Reserve banks hold deposits, or reserves, for commercial banks and act as bankers for the U.S. Treasury, holding tax revenues and paying the bills of the U.S. government.

COMMERCIAL BANKS

Unlike Federal Reserve banks, commercial banks deal with individuals and business firms. They accept **demand deposits** (checking accounts) and **time deposits** (savings accounts) and make loans based on their deposits. They may be chartered by the federal government or by a state government. Of the commercial banks within a Federal Reserve district, all federally chartered or national banks are required to join the Federal Reserve system. State-chartered banks may also join but may leave the system when they desire.

Almost 6000 of the nation's 14,000 commercial banks are members of the Federal Reserve system. While this number is less than half the total, members tend to be among the nation's largest banks, holding on deposit about three fourths of the money supply.

In the beginning, only member commercial banks were required to abide by the rules of the Federal Reserve system, and only members received the benefits. In 1980 Congress extended banking regulations to all commercial banks and other bank-like institutions. According to the Banking Act of 1980, all commercial banks must keep a certain percentage of their deposits as cash in reserve accounts in the Fed, and all must submit to regular supervision and examination. Member banks are required to purchase stock in the Federal Reserve Bank in their district.

In return for their compliance with Federal Reserve regulations, all commercial banks receive these benefits:

1. *A central clearing house for checks*. Commercial banks receive as deposits checks drawn on other banks. The checks are then sent to the

Federal Reserve for return to the issuing bank. This process is called *check clearing*. It allows all banks to record their customers' deposits and withdrawals.

2. *Deposit insurance through the Federal Deposit Insurance Corporation*. Banks pay a small fraction of their deposits into an insurance fund for paying off depositors of failed banks.

3. *A source of borrowed reserves*. Commercial banks may borrow from the Federal Reserve to keep their reserve accounts adequate.

4. *Financial information*.

5. *A 6 percent return on their paid-in stock*.

OTHER FINANCIAL INSTITUTIONS

Commercial banks are important *financial intermediaries*. Intermediaries occupy a position in the market between buyers and sellers of a good or service. For financial intermediaries the good or service provided is money, and the buyers and sellers are borrowers and lenders.

Most of us are both borrowers and lenders. We deal with many financial institutions for our various financial needs. We deal with commercial banks for deposits and short-term loans. In 1981 commercial banks held deposits of $1125 billion and loans of $906 billion.* Deposits included demand and time deposits; loans included real estate loans, loans to business firms and other financial institutions, and installment loans to individuals. Until 1981 commercial banks were prohibited from paying interest on demand deposits. Since demand deposits are subject to immediate withdrawal by check, commercial banks have been obliged to limit their lending to mostly short-term purposes.

Other financial intermediaries perform certain other specialized functions. For instance, savings and loan associations and mutual savings banks

engage in longer-term borrowing and lending. In 1981 these thrift institutions held savings deposits of more than $650 billion, making them second only to commercial banks in size. Until 1981 thrift institutions were not normally allowed to provide checking accounts. Because few of their deposits were subject to immediate withdrawal and because they could pay interest on all their deposits, thrift institutions enjoyed a more stable source of funds. This enabled them to make loans for long-term purposes at rather low rates. In 1981 about $600 billion of their funds were invested in home mortgages. Savings and loan associations and mutual savings banks are essential to the health of the nation's housing industry.

Insurance companies are a third type of financial intermediary. Through insurance policies, savers put aside funds to protect against the ordinary risks of life. These funds are loaned out at interest, earning income to use for paying insurance claims and operating the insurance business. In 1981 life insurance companies had accumulated assets of about $470 billion. Their funds were invested in corporate bonds and stocks and in mortgages for large commercial or industrial projects. Life insurance companies can afford to make long-term loans because they have rather precise estimates of the number of claims that must be paid in any single year. Fire and casualty insurance companies are subject to greater variability in claims. Therefore, their funds are invested in short-term investments, like U.S. government securities and state and local government bonds.

In recent years, credit unions have been emerging as important financial intermediaries. Most credit unions are made up of employees of a particular firm. A credit union collects the savings of members and makes short-term loans and occasionally mortgage loans to other members. Because borrowers are well known to the credit union, there is little risk of default. As a result, interest charges can be kept relatively low. Also, the administrative costs of running the credit union are low, making it possible to pay rather high inter-

---

* Many of the banks' deposits were created in the process of making loans, as we will soon see.

est to savers. In 1981 the total assets of credit unions were about $71 billion.

In the late 1970s a new type of financial intermediary was developed: money market mutual funds. A *mutual fund* is an organization of savers who pool their funds to purchase a diversified collection of investments. A money market mutual fund purchases only short-term securities and pays its shareholders interest at current rates. By 1981 money market mutual funds held assets of more than $140 billion. Their popularity became a disadvantage for other financial institutions when current interest rates rose substantially above what commercial banks and thrift institutions could pay on savings. A drain of savings into money market mutual funds reduced lending ability and reduced profits for many other financial intermediaries.

A well-developed system of financial intermediaries has helped promote U.S. economic growth. Safe financial institutions have encouraged saving and provided funds for business capital investment. Whereas the major intermediaries tend to specialize in particular functions, there is also some overlap in services. When services overlap, there is basis for competition among intermediaries, with the expectation that service will improve and costs fall. The Banking Act of 1980 removed many of the legal restrictions on financial services among financial intermediaries so that now they can compete freely. Savings and loan associations and credit unions are free to offer checking accounts, and commercial banks may pay interest on demand deposits. In the future, banks may be allowed to sell stocks and bonds, and insurance companies might issue travelers checks and money orders.

Increasing competition should improve efficiency and strengthen our financial system. However, competition may also force some firms out of business. Many small and inefficient financial intermediaries will not be able to compete successfully and may be absorbed by more efficient ones. Still, the final result should benefit the nation's economy.

HOW BANKS CREATE (AND DESTROY) MONEY

When banks make loans to consumers or business firms, they are actually *creating* money. Newly created money is expected to stimulate new production and generate profits for repaying the loan with interest.

The money supply is defined most narrowly as the sum total of cash in the hands of the public and demand deposits in commercial banks. All are money because all are acceptable in exchange for goods or in settlement of financial transactions. Currency is a very small part of the money supply, involving only about one fifth of all transactions.

Savings accounts and securities are not generally counted as money because they are less *liquid* than cash or checks; this means that they are not immediately acceptable as purchasing power. They are often referred to as *near money*. (Some near moneys are included in the broader measures of the money supply, as we will see.)

A Bank's Balance Sheet

Commercial banks must hold a certain percentage of their checking accounts as cash in their reserve accounts at the Federal Reserve. *A bank is permitted to make loans in the amount by which its actual reserve account exceeds the required reserve.*

Table 9.1 is a simplified model of a bank's balance sheet. A balance sheet shows the bank's financial position on any date. It is sometimes referred to as a T-account, since items are arranged under the bar of a T.

The bank's *assets* are listed on the left side of the balance sheet. Assets are the things the bank *owns:* its building, cash in the vault, reserve account at the Fed, interest-earning securities, and loans to customers. Loans to customers are assets because they represent promises to pay the bank. They are normally made to credit-worthy individu-

Table 9.1   Balance Sheet for a Hypothetical Bank; December 31, 1981.

Assets		Liabilities	
Cash and Reserves at Fed	250,000	Demand Deposits	1,000,000
Loans to Customers	750,000	Time Deposits	100,000
Securities	200,000	Other Borrowing	50,000
Building	100,000		1,150,000
		Capital Account	150,000
Total Assets	1,300,000	Total Liabilities and Capital	1,300,000

als or business firms who are expected to repay their loans with interest when they come due.

The bank's *liabilities* are listed on the right side of the balance sheet. Liabilities are the amounts the bank *owes*. The checking and savings accounts of its depositors and loans owed to businesses and other banks are its chief liabilities.

Notice that the sum on the asset side is equal to the sum on the liabilities side. This is because any excess of the value of assets over liabilities is added to the liabilities side as the **capital account.** The capital account represents the net amount owned by the bank (amounts owned − amounts owed = capital account). It is the portion of total assets that would remain if all liabilities were paid. Equality of Total Assets on the one hand and Total Liabilities and Capital on the other makes the statement balance; hence, *Balance Sheet*.

Making Loans

Suppose that the bank in Table 9.1 is required to keep 25 percent of its demand deposits in its reserve account. Notice that the bank is complying with Federal Reserve regulations (25 percent of $1,000,000 in demand deposits is $250,000).

Now suppose that the bank receives a new cash deposit of $100. This might be cash from under someone's mattress, proceeds from the sale of a government bond, or cash received from the sale of goods to a foreign buyer. Let us watch what happens to the bank's balance sheet. For simplic-

ity, we will show only *changes* in assets and liabilities. Notice that every change on the asset side requires an equal change on the liabilities side so that the statement will remain in balance:*

1. The $100 deposit adds $100 to Wall Street Bank's cash and $100 to its checking account liabilities.

Assets	Wall Street Bank	Liabilities
Cash $100		Demand Deposits $100

2. Noninterest-earning cash is of little use to the bank, so it sends the cash to its reserve account at the Federal Reserve.

Assets	Wall Street Bank	Liabilities
Cash 0		Demand Deposits $100
Reserves $100		

* or an offsetting change on the same side

3. Before the new deposit was made, the Wall Street Bank was maintaining its required reserve account in the Federal Reserve. But it is required to hold only 25 percent of its new deposit: 25 percent of $100 = $25. The bank can extend loans equal to the amount by which its reserve account exceeds required reserves: actual reserves ($100) minus required reserves (25) equals excess reserves (75). ($100 − 25 = $75). With $75 in excess reserves the Wall Street Bank will normally encourage a creditworthy borrower to take out a loan, possibly at the same time reducing its interest charge.

When the loan is granted, the bank will issue a check for $75 which the borrower will very likely deposit in his or her checking account at the bank. On the left side of the balance sheet, the bank adds the $75 loan; the loan is the borrower's promise to pay and therefore an asset for the bank. On the right side, the bank adds the $75 to the borrower's demand deposit.

Assets		Wall Street Bank	Liabilities
Reserves	$100	Demand Deposits	$100
Loans	$75		+ 75
			$175

Now Wall Street Bank is using its available reserves as an interest-earning loan. It has complied with Federal Reserve regulations and loaned out only the amount by which its reserves exceed the required percentage of its demand deposits.

4. Suppose the borrower now decides to use the $75 to make a purchase. He or she writes a check or withdraws the amount in cash. Whoever receives the check or cash deposits it in his or her own checking account in another bank, say, the Lombard Bank. The Lombard Bank receives the check and sends it to the Federal Reserve to be cleared. The Federal Reserve clears the check by subtracting $75 from Wall Street Bank's reserve account and adding $75 to Lombard Bank's reserve account. When Wall Street Bank reduces the borrower's demand deposit and its own reserve account by $75, actual reserves are precisely equal to required reserves: 25 percent of $100 = $25. Notice that the balance sheet remains in balance.

Assets		Wall Street Bank	Liabilities
Reserves	$100	Demand Deposits	$175
	− 75		− 75
	$25		$100
Loans	$75		

Assets	Lombard Bank	Liabilities
Reserves + $75	Demand Deposits + $75

5. Now the Lombard Bank has excess reserves. The Lombard Bank is required to keep 25 percent of demand deposits in its reserve account: 25 percent of $75 ≈ $19. It can extend loans in the amount by which its reserve account exceeds required reserves: actual reserves ($75) minus required reserves (19) equal excess reserves ($75 − 19 = $56). A new loan may be made and added to the borrower's demand deposit in the Lombard Bank.

Assets		Lombard Bank	Liabilities
Reserves	$75	Demand Deposits	$ 75
Loans	+ $56		+ 56
			$131

6. Again the borrower will probably decide to withdraw the $56 to make a purchase. The check is paid and eventually deposited in a third bank, say, the Peachtree Bank. Peachtree Bank sends the check to be cleared and deposited in its reserve account.

The Federal Reserve adds $56 to the Peachtree Bank's reserve account and subtracts $56 from the Lombard Bank's account. When the Lombard Bank reduces the borrower's account and its own reserve account by $56, actual reserves are precisely equal to required reserves: 25 percent of $75 ≈ $19.

Assets		Lombard Bank	Liabilities
Reserves	$75	Demand Deposits	$131
	− 56		− 56
	19		$75
Loans	$56		

Now look at the Peachtree Bank's balance sheet. Can more loans be made? Will a fourth bank receive a new deposit? A fifth? A sixth?

Assets	Peachtree Bank	Liabilities
Reserves $56		Demand Deposits $56

Let us stop here and calculate the amount added to the money supply as new loans are created. Thus far, the original $100 has led to the creation of $75 + $56 = $131 in additional new money. Presumably, the third, fourth, fifth, and other banks will use the opportunity to extend loans as they receive checks on deposit. Finally, the money supply may increase by as much as $400: the original $100 deposit plus $300 in created money.

How do we know this? With a 25 percent reserve requirement, the initial new reserves of $100 will enable the banking system as a whole to hold deposits equal to four times their reserves. And the banking system will be in compliance with the regulations of the Federal Reserve: new reserves of $100 = 25 percent of $400 in demand deposits.

The original deposit of $100 constitutes part of the increase in demand deposits. The remaining $300 is created money. It is created by extending loans and adding to the checking accounts of borrowers. The banking system as a whole can create money equal to excess reserves times the reciprocal of the reserve ratio:

$$\text{created money} = \text{excess reserves} \times \frac{1}{\text{reserve ratio}}$$

Thus, in our example:

$$\text{created money} = \$75 \times \frac{1}{1/4} = \$75 \times 4 = \$300$$

Reducing Loans

Banks can destroy as well as create money. Banks *must* destroy money when they lose reserves and are failing to maintain the required reserve ratio. The process is the reverse of the process outlined above.

Suppose a bank loses a deposit of $100 in cash. This time it might be a withdrawal of cash to put *under* someone's mattress, cash to *buy* a government bond, or cash to *buy* goods from a foreign seller. As the $100 check clears at the Federal Reserve, the issuing bank loses reserves. It may have to reduce its loans in order to maintain its required reserves.

How does a band *reduce* its lending?

Every day old borrowers repay loans by writing checks to the banks. Every day new borrowers receive new loan checks. If a bank needs to reduce its total demand deposits to comply with reserve requirements, it will accept loan payment checks and not extend new loans in their place. Payment checks will reduce borrowers' checking accounts until demand deposits are the permitted multiple of bank reserves.

In effect, the bank has destroyed (ugly word!) money.

MONETARY POLICY

The Federal Reserve System is responsible for planning and carrying out the nation's **monetary policy.** Monetary policy involves changes in the supply of money to meet the nation's need for purchasing power. Since about three fourths of the nation's money supply is held in commercial banks under the regulatory authority of the Federal Reserve, a decision by the Board of Governors can significantly influence the nation's spending power.

The objective of monetary policy is to achieve the appropriate supply of money for ensuring an efficient level of economic activity. As our capacity for producing goods and services increases, the supply of money must increase also. Money must be available for spending by consumers and business firms so that our productive capacity will be fully utilized.

On the other hand, if spending rises too sharply, it may exceed our capacity to produce goods and services and bring on inflation. In those times, the Federal Reserve System should hold down the supply of money and limit consumer and business spending.

How are changes in the money supply accomplished? It isn't generally practical to fly over cities and towns scattering currency from airplanes!

The Federal Reserve System has three ways to influence the supply of money. All three methods work primarily by changing the level of checking accounts in commercial banks. The level of checking accounts is changed by changing a bank's ability to make loans—i.e., by changing its capacity to create new demand deposits.

A bank's lending ability is affected by: (1) its *required reserves* held in the Federal Reserve; (2) the *discount rate* on borrowed reserves from the Federal Reserve; and (3) *open-market operations* in the purchase and sale of U.S. government bonds.

Required Reserves

The first tool of monetary policy is the ratio of **required reserves** to a commercial bank's holdings of demand deposits. The Federal Reserve establishes a required ratio of total demand deposits that a commercial bank must keep in its reserve account. (The average amount required is about 12 percent.) The bank can lend out only the amount by which its reserve account exceeds the required level.

A bank must be careful not to extend too many loans. Otherwise when its checks are cleared, the bank may lose too much from its reserve account and find that it isn't in compliance with reserve requirements. (How do you like the thought of your bank being "overdrawn"?)

Increasing the Money Supply

Consider a situation in which all banks are maintaining their proper reserve level. We will assume the required reserve ratio is 25 percent. There are no excess reserves, so no new loans can be made.

Now suppose the Board of Governors wants to increase the money supply in order to encourage new spending and increase production and employment. The governors may reduce the required reserve ratio to 20 percent. All banks now have excess reserves available for lending. They will encourage consumers and business firms to borrow by reducing interest charges on their loans. Then new borrowers will deposit their loan checks in their checking accounts.

Eureka! From nothing there is money!

Total demand deposits in the banking system may expand to a level equal to *five* times total bank reserves, whereas the limit before the change was *four* times reserves.

A Numerical Example: Easy Money

Imagine the banking system as a whole has demand deposits of $100 billion. If we ignore cash in the hands of the public, we can regard the $100 billion in checking accounts as the nation's money supply. Under the 25 percent reserve requirement, the banking system must be holding $25 billion in Federal Reserve accounts.

Now the Board of Governors decides on an **easy money** policy: that is, to expand the money supply. It changes the reserve requirement to 20 percent. Banks are now required to hold only $20 billion; immediately the banking system has *excess reserves* of $5 billion.

Loans will be made and loan checks deposited in the accounts of borrowers. As demand deposits expand, the banking system as a whole experiences a growth in checking accounts and therefore a growth in the money supply.

What will finally be the level of deposits in the banking system? With reserves of $25 billion and a 20 percent reserve requirement, the system as a whole may have total deposits of $125 billion: reserves of $25 billion = 20 percent of $125 billion.

The money supply may grow by $25 billion:

$$\text{created money} = \text{excess reserves} \times \frac{1}{\text{reserve ratio}}$$

$$= \$5 \text{ billion} \times \frac{1}{1/5} = \$25 \text{ billion.}$$

Reducing the Money Supply

Of course, this process also works in reverse. Suppose the Board of Governors wants to reduce purchasing power to restrain inflationary spending. It may increase reserve requirements, perhaps to 33.33 percent. Now all banks must reduce their checking-account balances until total deposits are only *three* times reserves.

Banks will collect old loans and make fewer new loans. They will discourage borrowing by raising interest charges on loans. Old borrowers will pay off loans by writing checks, and the value of checking accounts will fall.

A Numerical Example: Tight Money

Again, imagine total demand deposits of $100 billion and a 25 percent reserve requirement. The banking system as a whole is holding reserves of $25 billion.

The Board of Governors decides on a **tight money** policy: that is, to reduce the money supply. It changes the reserve ratio to 33.33 percent. Banks are now required to hold $33.33 billion in reserves. The banking system has *negative excess reserves,* or deficit reserves. Under the new reserve requirements excess reserves are: actual reserves ($25) minus required reserves (33.33) equals excess reserves: ($25 − 33.33 = − $8.33).

Commercial banks must collect old loans, deducting payment checks from borrowers' demand deposits. Throughout the banking system checking accounts will contract and the money supply will fall.

What will finally be the level of demand deposits in the banking system? With reserves of $25 billion and a 33.33 percent reserve requirement, the system as a whole may have total deposits of $75 billion: reserves of $25 billion = 33.33 percent of $75 billion.

The money supply must decline by $25 billion:

$$\text{destroyed money} = \text{excess reserves} \times \frac{1}{\text{reserve ratio}}$$

$$= -\$8.33 \text{ billion} \times \frac{1}{1/3} = -\$25 \text{ billion.}$$

The Discount Rate

Commercial banks may go to their banker, the Federal Reserve Bank, for loans just as individuals go to their commercial banks. A bank may need additional funds to comply with additional reserve requirements, particularly if reserve requirements have recently been raised.

The Federal Reserve Bank charges an interest rate, called the **discount rate**, on funds loaned to commercial banks. The discount rate provides the Federal Reserve a second tool for changing the money supply.

If the Board of Governors favors an increase in bank lending, it will reduce its discount rate in order to enable commercial banks to maintain their required reserve accounts. However, if it wants to discourage new lending, it will raise the discount rate. Banks will be forced to reduce their demand deposits in order to comply with reserve requirements. There will be fewer new loans made and fewer loan checks deposited in borrowers' checking accounts.

Open-Market Operations

The third tool for influencing the money supply is **open-market operations.** This is the tool used most often because it can be carried out quietly and without embarrassing headlines to aggravate ulcers on Wall Street!

The Federal Reserve banks and most commercial banks, as well as many individuals, hold some of their assets in the form of U.S. government securities. U.S. Treasury bills, notes, and bonds are considered a safe investment and provide interest income to their owners. Open-market operations involve the purchase and sale of these securities.

The Federal Reserve Bank of New York is constantly buying and selling securities in the open market. *If the New York Bank buys more securities than it sells, the result is to increase the quantity of money held by the public.* To illustrate, suppose the Federal Reserve increases its holdings of government bonds by $500 million. Individuals, businesses, and banks throughout the country will send their government bonds to the Federal Reserve and receive checks in return. Their checks will be deposited as demand deposits in commercial banks. Local Federal Reserve clearing houses will add a total of $500 million to member bank reserve accounts, and the stage will be set for the expansion of bank loans.

If the New York Bank sells more securities than it buys, the result is to reduce the quantity of money. This time suppose the Federal Reserve reduces its holdings of government bonds by $500 million. Buyers will receive bonds and send their payment checks to the Federal Reserve banks. Federal Reserve clearing houses will reduce commercial reserves, and demand deposits must fall as well.

All these changes take place so quietly one scarcely knows whether the Federal Reserve has been expanding or contracting the money supply.

SOME PROBLEMS

Monetary policy can help achieve economic stability. But it is not always completely successful, and it can create some problems.

If Federal Reserve authorities correctly analyze the state of the economy and quickly prescribe the proper remedy, and if borrowers' investment plans respond as expected, the Federal Reserve's purpose will be accomplished. However, it may be difficult to persuade business to borrow when necessary.

During recessions, when spending, production, and income are low, additional spending would be most welcome. But at those times business firms may very sensibly hesitate to take the risks of borrowing for expanding capacity. After all, who will buy the newly produced goods and services if income and employment are low? This means that monetary policy is least effective for increasing spending during periods of recession and unemployment.

Alas, it may be just as difficult to put the brakes on inflation. Once inflationary expectations become solidly fixed in the minds of business people, higher interest costs may not discourage borrowing for new investment. As long as prices on finished goods are rising faster than the cost of borrowing, new investment may still be profitable. Moreover, business loans can be repaid when due with dollars that are worth less than the dollars originally borrowed. In fact, higher interest charges may even accelerate inflation as manufacturers raise their prices to cover the higher cost of borrowing!

Another problem is the long-term lag between deciding on a new policy and waiting for it to take effect. Delays in policy decisions may cause alternating periods of expanding and contracting the money supply, by turns helping and hurting the problem the policy was designed to correct. An easy money policy may last too long and aggravate a tendency toward overexpansion and inflation. Changing to tight money may cause a severe recession, with worsening unemployment and slow growth.

Critics of monetary policy point out that some borrowers are more seriously harmed by high interest rates than others. For example, small building firms are particularly hurt by a shortage of funds for borrowing for new home building. In contrast, large firms with substantial funds may finance new investment projects without having to borrow. State and local governments are also critically affected by high borrowing costs. High interest rates may cause them to neglect local services, which later must be provided by the federal government.

Other critics claim that the use of monetary policy may seriously damage the nation's long-range economic health. When the Federal Reserve is fighting recession, it will act to increase the money supply and push interest rates down. But lower interest rates in the United States will cause many wealthy individuals, financial institutions, and businesses to lend their funds to foreign borrowers in order to obtain higher interest earnings. Dollars will flow abroad where they will be unavailable for fighting the domestic recession.

On the other hand, when the Federal Reserve is fighting inflation, it will act to reduce the money supply and push interest rates up. Higher interest rates are designed to hold down business investment spending. But business investment is the principal means by which we increase the productivity of our economy!

High interest rates also hurt the U.S. Treasury. The Treasury carries a national debt of about a trillion dollars; interest charges on it are considerable. When the U.S. Treasury is pinched, you can expect an eventual yelp from the U.S. taxpayer!

All these problems suggest that rapid or radical changes in monetary policy may not be wise. It may be better to combine consistent monetary policy with flexible fiscal policy to ensure a healthy level of economic activity.

Self-Check

1. **Which of the following is *not* a true description of money?**
   a. It permitted specialization in production.
   b. It facilitated trade among producing regions.
   c. It provided a standard of value.
   d. It made barter necessary.
   e. It permitted division of labor in production.

2. **Which of the following is *not* a characteristic of monetary gold?**
   a. It serves as a medium of exchange, a store of value, and a standard of value.
   b. It is scarce and durable.
   c. It is easily transported and stored.
   d. It has few uses other than as money.
   e. All are characteristic of gold.

3. **Which of the following is *not* a function of the Federal Reserve System?**
   a. It provides loans to individuals and businesses.
   b. It holds the accounts of the U.S. Treasury.
   c. It provides a system for clearing checks.
   d. It holds reserve accounts for member banks.
   e. It helps stabilize the nation's money supply.

4. **Changes in the money supply:**
   a. aim at influencing the level of total spending.
   b. are accomplished primarily by purchases and sales of securities.
   c. are actually changes in the lending capacity of banks.
   d. all of the above.
   e. none of the above.

5. **An important defect of monetary policy is that:**
   a. low interest rates retard economic growth.
   b. high interest rates cause loanable funds to flow to other countries.
   c. business firms may not respond properly to changes in interest rates.
   d. it is removed from political influence.
   e. high interest charges benefit home builders.

6. **Which of the following policy actions is most appropriate for reducing inflation?**
   a. Federal Reserve purchases of U.S. government securities.
   b. An increase in required reserves for member banks.
   c. Easy money to hold down interest rates.
   d. Encouragement of member banks to borrow from the Fed.
   e. An increase in the growth rate of the money supply.

Theory in Practice

MIND YOUR P'S AND Q'S

Much of monetary theory can be summed up with a simple expression: $MV = PQ$. The left side of the equation measures total spending over a particular period of time: the quantity of money in the system (M) times its velocity (V), or the number of times it is spent. The right side of the equation measures the value of total production over the same period: the prices of all goods and services (P) times the quantity of goods exchanged (Q).

This equation is known as *the quantity theory of money*. The equation must always balance because expenditures (MV) will always equal the value of output (PQ).

Surprisingly, this simple expression is the source of much controversy. The debate concerns the proper conduct of monetary policy. One group of economists, called Monetarists, believes that the supply of money (M) is the most important factor in determining economic activity. A steady increase in M in line with our rising productive capacity will keep production (PQ) growing at a full employment, noninflationary rate.

The leader of the Monetarists is Milton Friedman. Friedman favors automatic increases in the money supply of about 4 percent a year. Regular, systematic increases in the money supply would allow spending to increase consistently with increases in productive capacity, thereby avoiding either rising prices or falling production. Moreover, automatic increases in the money supply would not depend on decisions made by the Board of Governors. Decisions to change money growth, says Friedman, cannot take effect for a year or more, during which time economic conditions may change completely. Without precise information about future economic conditions, policymakers are likely to make major errors.

Another group of economists contends that steady, automatic increases in M will not stabilize total spending if V is changing at the same time. Large-scale unemployment and a decline in consumer confidence could cause a slower turnover (V) of the available money supply. If growth of M is to offset the drop in V, policymakers should increase M faster than normal. On the other hand, inflation could cause faster spending, so that V rises. In this case, policymakers should cut back the growth in M to offset the increase in V.

Before the proper policy is agreed upon, it is necessary to first measure M. The traditional definition of the money supply has been checking accounts plus cash in the hands of the public. This definition of money is called M_{1-A}. At the end of 1980, checking accounts and outstanding currency amounted to $275 billion and $115 billion, respectively, or about $390 in the M_{1-A} definition of money. This amount was only about 3 percent higher than the money stock in December 1979.

Some critics of Federal Reserve policy said that the 3 percent increase in 1980 was not enough to offset the increase in prices during the year and to allow for additional new spending. They charged that *tight money* pushed the economy into recession. Other critics believed that money growth was too *easy,* contributing to increased spending and higher inflation. A tight money policy is needed, they said, to "wring out" the tendency for wages and prices to rise.

Monetary policy was complicated by other problems in 1980. During the 1970s nonbank financial institutions began to offer checkable deposits to their customers. Accounts in savings banks and savings and loan associations became subject to immediate withdrawal by check. All these new forms of purchasing power increased money holdings and led to a new definition of the money supply: M_{1-B}. M_{1-B} includes cash and commercial bank checking accounts plus checkable deposits in nonbank financial institutions. In 1980 M_{1-B} amounted to $415 billion. Other *near moneys* are almost as spendable as these accounts: savings and time deposits and shares in money market mutual funds. Holders of near money probably feel wealthier as a result and probably maintain a higher level of spending than they would otherwise. Including these accounts in the money definition produces M_2 money, which was $1669 billion in 1980. Other long-term time deposits are added to yield the M_3 definition of money, $1964 billion in 1980. (See Table 9.2.)

Table 9.2   Money Forms—December 1980.

M_{1-A}	Cash and Checking Accounts in Commercial Banks	$ 387.7 billion
M_{1-B}	M_{1-A} plus Checkable Deposits in all Financial Institutions	415.6 billion
M_2	M_{1-B} plus Savings and Small Time Deposits and Money Market Fund Shares	1669.4 billion
M_3	M_2 plus Large Time Deposits in all Financial Institutions	1963.5 billion

Controlling the growth of such diverse forms of spending power has grown increasingly difficult, and the Federal Reserve has come under increasing criticism. Worsening inflation has seemed to call for slower money growth, but attempts to reduce bank lending have been ineffective or—if effective—have plunged the economy back into recession.

HOW SUCCESSFUL HAS MONETARY POLICY BEEN?

How closely does the reality of monetary policy conform to the theory? How successfully has the Federal Reserve managed the money supply to promote stable prices and growth of production? Let us look at the experience of the last decade.

During 1969 and 1970, the economy was experiencing a recession in spending, production, and income. To deal with the recession, the Fed bought government securities, increased bank reserves, and allowed the supply of currency and checking accounts to grow about 6 percent annually. By 1972, economic activity had picked up and it seemed proper to cut back reserves and hold down the growth of the money supply. But the money supply continued to grow, by 9 percent that year!

A tight money policy was begun in earnest in 1973, with six increases in discount rates during the year. As a result, the prime rate charged by banks to their best customers rose ten times to reach 12 percent in 1974. Rates on short-term business loans rose to almost 14 percent. Reserve requirements were increased also. Still, business firms expected new investment to be profitable. They continued to borrow, and inflation soared.

In spite of the Federal Reserve Board's efforts toward restraint, the supply of currency and checking accounts continued to grow. The money supply expanded at the rate of about 6 percent in 1973.

Part of the reason for the increase may be attributed to the growing number of banks that were not members of the Federal Reserve System and not subject to its regulations.* It is ironic that the membership requirements for carrying out monetary policy were often the reason a bank would decide not to join the system!

Inflation grew to dangerous levels in 1974, and the Federal Reserve cut money growth vigorously. Finally, business borrowing fell, the business failure rate jumped, and unemployment spread. By February 1975, the money supply was actually *shrinking,* amid vigorous complaints from business and government. Many analysts believed that the drastic reversal in monetary policy would throw the economy into a severe recession. And in fact, the trough of the fifth postwar recession was recorded in March.

The Fed was not entirely to blame for the slowdown in money growth. Evidence suggests that by early 1975 the monetary authorities were trying to relax the earlier tightness. They were adding to reserves by buying U.S. Treasury securities, but banks were not making new loans! General pessimism on the part of lenders and borrowers probably reduced their willingness to take risks.

The situation in 1975 gave economists an opportunity to use one of their old familiar sayings: You can't push on a string. You can pull money out of the economy during inflation. But you can't push money into the economy during recession if banks are unwilling to lend and if credit-worthy borrowers are hard to find.

Recovery from the 1975 recession was slow, in part because of substantial consumer and business debt built up during the previous expansion. Especially virulent inflation and job uncertainty also reduced consumer confidence and held spending down. The Fed struggled to achieve the appropriate monetary policy for aiding recovery without adding fuel to inflation. For the first time the Fed announced its target rate of money growth for the year: a range of 5 to 7 1/2 percent growth of currency and demand deposits. All of the tools of

* Before the Banking Act of 1980, membership was optional for state banks. Because setting aside reserve accounts reduced their ability to make profitable loans, many state banks declined to join the system.

monetary policy were put to use to achieve this goal, but cash and checking accounts grew by less than 5 percent.

Money growth speeded up to 6 percent in 1976, but high unemployment and inflation continued. Hoping to avoid a new recession, the Board of Governors decided to reduce money growth gradually until inflation should subside. Consumer, business, and government spending accelerated in 1977, pushing the U.S. economy closer to the limits of productive capacity. Capital equipment, in particular, grew scarcer relative to the fast-growing labor force. Low rates of return and fear of unfavorable changes in government tax and regulatory policy reduced business incentives to invest. Many business firms were unable to sell their bonds and obtained short-term bank loans. Inflationary expectations increased consumer buying plans too, and heavy credit demand pushed money growth higher (8 percent) than Federal Reserve targets.

Vigorous economic expansion continued in 1978, and inflation accelerated. Higher food and labor costs and declining worker productivity led to a program of voluntary wage and price restraint under President Carter. Nevertheless, beat-the-price-rise psychology continued to increase consumer spending for goods and housing. Too rapid money growth (7 percent) finally called for con-tractionary policy late in the year, continuing into 1979. A second effort to contract money growth was inaugurated in the fall, and interest rates soared. The prime rate charged a bank's best corporate borrowers reached a new high of 20 percent! The new recession hit bottom in the second quarter of 1980, as both M_{1-A} and M_{1-B} dropped by more than 2 percent (annual rate).

Throughout the 1970s M_2 and M_3 grew substantially faster than the more narrow money measures. Rising interest rates encouraged households and business firms to "economize on money balances": that is, to transfer more of their funds to interest-earning accounts and spend their cash and checking accounts faster. The increase in velocity made the Fed's job of regulating total spending more difficult.

The 1970s were characterized by another monetary phenomenon having to do with the relationship between money growth and interest rates. Economic theory predicts that easy money will reduce interest rates and encourage investment; tight money will increase interest rates and retard investment. Indeed, the short-run effects may be as expected. But the long-range results of easy money may be higher incomes and inflation, with *rising* interest rates as lenders insist on protection against inflation. And tight money may reduce employment and incomes so that interest rates *fall*.

Viewpoint

GIBSON'S PARADOX AND REAL INTEREST RATES

A "paradox" is a statement that seems contradictory or absurd, but may actually be true. In the early 1900s, a British statistician named Gibson thought he saw a paradox in the behavior of the money supply, prices, and interest rates.

What happens when the money supply increases? First, banks have more money to lend, and second, people have more money to spend. The first result should cause interest rates to fall, and the second, prices to rise. Thus, falling interest rates would accompany rising prices.

At least this is what we might expect to happen, given our understanding of supply and demand and the effects of shifts in either variable on market equilibrium price. Gibson's paradox was that events did not turn out that way at all. In fact, over the years Gibson observed, prices and interest rates tended to move together, indicating a "contradictory, absurd" result.

The explanation has to do with **nominal** and **real interest rates.** The nominal interest rate is the rate actually paid; nominal rates are frequently quoted in the newspaper and always appear on a loan agreement. The real interest rate is the real purchasing power paid for borrowing; real rates are determined by subtracting the rate of inflation from the nominal rate. If inflation should exceed the nominal rate, the real interest rate is negative. In this case, the lender would be sacrificing more total purchasing power to the borrower than is repaid. The lender is, in effect, paying someone to use his or her own money!

Most lenders take steps to avoid this unhappy result. When prices are rising, they build into interest rates a return sufficient to offset inflation. Thus, high prices—and the expectation that prices will continue to rise—will prompt a move to higher interest rates. On the other hand, stable prices would cause interest rates to fall to the long-run real rate of interest that satisfies lenders. (Historically, the real rate of interest has been about 2 percent.)

Throughout the 1970s, the U.S. economy suffered abnormally high inflation along with interest rates reaching as high as 20 percent. Fast money growth, which was intended to keep borrowing costs low and encourage investment spending, instead contributed to inflation and high nominal rates. Maybe Gibson's paradox was not "absurd" after all!

BANK LOANS AND MONETARY POLICY

Successful use of monetary policy requires that banks adapt to the level of reserves supplied by the Federal Reserve. The level of reserves places limits on a bank's ability to create money through lending. Until the 1960s the system functioned rather well; but then a change took place in bank lending practices that loosened the ties between bank reserves and loan creation.

Remember that a bank's financial assets are primarily its reserves at the Federal Reserve, loans to customers, and securities. Its securities are short-term interest-earning debts issued by private business firms, the U.S. Treasury, and state and local governments. The permitted level of customer loans depends on a bank's demand deposits, required reserves, and reserves.

In the past, if a bank needed more reserves, it could add to its account by shifting its assets. It could sell some of its securities and add the proceeds to its reserves. This would allow the bank to increase lending.

Federal Reserve policy could have substantial influence on banks' willingness to change their holdings of securities. A tight money policy would withdraw money from the system and make it difficult for banks to sell securities. If the banks wished to make new loans, they would have to sell their securities at a loss.* This would discourage banks from selling securities and making new loans—in line with Federal Reserve intentions.

Toward the end of the 1960s banks began to use a new method of expanding their reserves. They turned to the liabilities side of the balance sheet to finance their lending. They offered interest

incentives to depositors for short-term deposits in savings accounts or in certificates of deposit. These borrowed funds were then loaned out, with a comfortable spread between the interest paid to depositors and that received from business borrowers. Loans to business were made under flexible interest terms, to reflect changes in banks' costs of borrowing. Flexible interest charges ensured that lending would be profitable regardless of the interest rate banks had to pay for their borrowed funds.

This new process violated a fundamental rule of banking: borrow "long" and lend "short." Make certain you have long-term control over your funds. Avoid the possibility that your depositors will want to withdraw their money before your business borrowers are ready to repay their loans.

In years past, most commercial bank loans to businesses were short term, to finance production of inventory. As the inventory was sold, loans were repaid regularly. More recently, however, commercial banks have made loans for long-term construction projects, like executive parks and high-rise office and apartment complexes. These loans depend for repayment on the success of the project, with profitable sales and rental income flowing into the borrower's account.

As long as the economy was booming, these loans were safe. High rentals and inflated property values enabled borrowers to pay the rising interest charges on their construction loans. But when the boom collapsed, half-empty office buildings could not produce sufficient rental income to pay off the loans. Loans were foreclosed, and banks became the unhappy owners of a great deal of real estate, much of it worth much less than the loans the banks had carried. These kinds of loan losses made banks reluctant to extend new loans to anyone other than their most secure clients.

The switch to lending based on bank liabilities (rather than assets) and growing apprehension in the financial community have produced wide swings in banks' willingness to make new loans. The result has been that banks are less sensitive to Federal Reserve policy than they formerly were.

---

* Whenever an existing security is sold before maturity, its price must be competitive with new securities being issued currently. If new securities are paying higher interest rates than the existing security, its resale price must fall. A tight money policy will normally cause current interest rates to rise and the prices of existing securities to fall.

This may mean a great increase in lending during inflationary periods and a collapse during recessions—contrary to the wishes of the Federal Reserve.

POLITICS AND THE FEDERAL RESERVE

From time to time there are conflicts between the interests of the U.S. Congress and the president, on the one hand, and the interests of the Federal Reserve Board, on the other.

The president and Congress may want to use expansionary fiscal policy to stimulate spending, production, and income. They may plan larger government expenditures and lower tax rates. Such programs are politically acceptable, but they may cause a deficit in the federal budget which must be financed by borrowing. The U.S. Treasury may have to sell bonds to finance the deficit, and it would prefer to pay low interest rates on its debt.

At the same time, the Federal Reserve Board may believe spending is increasing too fast. It may fear inflation around the corner and feel that the Fed should slow the pace of growth. The Governors may decide on a tight money policy to hold down the level of spending, production, and income. As a result, there will be less money available for lending, and the U.S. Treasury will have to pay higher interest rates if it is to sell its bonds.

Occasionally, the Fed may succumb to pressures from the executive branch and increase money growth. Accusations were made (and denied) that the easy money policy followed in 1972 was in response to election-year politics. The money supply grew at a rate of 9 percent that year compared with only 6 percent in 1971 and 1973. Some critics believe that the excessive money growth spreading throughout the system contributed significantly to the high level of inflation in 1974.

Conflicts between Congress and the Federal Reserve have generally been settled by compromise. When the Treasury desperately needs funds, as it did during World War II, for example, the Fed has been willing to supply money at a faster rate. However, it is important that the monetary authorities protect their power to restrict *all* spending, both business investment *and* government spending, when inflation threatens. Likewise, during the severest recession the monetary authorities should provide the additional money for greater federal spending. Otherwise fiscal and monetary policy might be pushing the economy in opposite directions!

Some members of Congress have been urging new legislation to bring Federal Reserve policy more completely under the control of Congress. The aim would be to guarantee a steady increase in money and to ensure that available funds are allocated for the most pressing needs—housing and productive enterprise rather than speculative buying and inventory accumulation. Many economists are strongly opposed to limits on the power of the Fed. They see the Federal Reserve as an important counterweight to balance the occasionally excessive spending plans of Congress.

Viewpoint

THE THEORY OF RATIONAL EXPECTATIONS

In this text we have been concerned with the *Keynesian Model of Income Determination*. Remember that a model is a simplified view of reality. It summarizes economic behavior and projects the results of policy according to certain assumptions about behavior. Whether projections are correct or not depends upon the correctness of the model's fundamental assumptions.

Certain changes have been taking place in the U.S. economy that have led analysts to doubt some of their fundamental assumptions and, therefore, to question some of the policy recommendations that are dependent on them. Ironically, this new skepticism is the result of more intelligent understanding and awareness of economic conditions among the public at large!

Improved communications have made households and business firms more sensitive to trends in production, employment, prices, and interest rates. Even more important, widespread availability of information about Keynesian economic policy tools has caused people to anticipate government actions before they actually take place. All these factors have worked to change behavior, so that many households and business firms now act according to their *expectations* of *future* economic conditions.

The theory that explains the new type of behavior is called **the theory of rational expectations.** It states that intelligent people will behave according to what they expect economic conditions to be. Rational expectations may have changed the results of Keynesian economic policies, reducing their effectiveness and possibly causing more harm than the situation they were intended to correct.

To illustrate the effect of rational expectations, suppose the growth of spending slows and the economy enters a recession. Unemployment begins to increase, and the automatic stabilizers go into effect to push the federal budget toward an automatic deficit. The relatively low rate of aggregate demand holds down price and wage increases so that inflation slows. What would a rational person expect to happen next?

Having studied economic theory, a rational person would probably expect the use of expansionary fiscal and monetary policy to speed recovery. As expansionary policies take effect, all the current measures of economic activity would reverse themselves. Unemployment would fall, and inflation would begin to accelerate.

A general belief that recessions will be short, and expansion is the usual economic condition, affects behavior significantly. There is less fear of unemployment and easier acceptance of inflation. In fact, households and business firms will tend to behave as if inflation were inevitable and to try to protect themselves against it. They will demand cost-of-living wage increases and target-profit price increases, ultimately bringing on the very inflation they expect.

Now suppose that expansion and inflation accelerate to the point that rational people come to expect the use of contractionary fiscal and monetary policy to slow the boom. As higher taxes, reduced government spending, and slower money growth take hold, the expansion slows and the economy moves toward recession. But rational people understand government's reluctance to allow unemployment to build up, and they will expect expansionary policies to be resumed fairly quickly. Lately, they have been correct in their expectations.

All of which reduces the effectiveness of traditional policies and aggravates tendencies toward an inflationary economic environment. For government policies to change behavior in a certain way, they must be so different from expected policies as to startle people into totally new patterns of response.

The theory of rational expectations implies new problems for economic policymakers. The extreme version of the theory implies that no policy can affect behavior for long in the intended direction. Thus, the theory of rational expectations supports the argument for reduced government intervention in economic life.

SUMMARY

1. The first use of money was a milestone in the process of economic development. Money promoted trade with specialization and division of labor.

2. The development of banking eased the process of exchange and provided credit for expanding investment. Early unregulated banks often caused alternating periods of overexpansion of money followed by bankruptcies and bank failures.

3. In 1913, the Federal Reserve System of banks was established. Through centrally regulated banking, the Fed attempts to influence the supply of money by: (a) expanding the money supply when there are unemployed resources to be brought into production; and (b) contracting money growth when spending exceeds the full-capacity production of our resources.

4. Other financial intermediaries now offer a variety of services including long-term mortgages, loans to state and local governments, and short-term consumer loans. The growth of lending institutions has helped promote economic growth but may have complicated the Fed's money management role.

5. Monetary policy aims at providing stable increases in purchasing power in line with increases in our nation's productive capacity. Monetary policy is carried out through: (a) changes in the required reserve ratio of commercial banks; (b) changes in the discount rate; and (c) Federal Reserve sale and purchase of U.S. Treasury securities (open-market operations).

6. Changes in the level of reserves affect banks' willingness to lend, and thereby affect the interest rate. Changes in the interest rate should in turn affect the expected profitability of new business projects, encouraging (or discouraging) business investment spending.

7. Monetary policy is not always fully effective. If there is recession, business firms may be too pessimistic to risk borrowing for new investment, even if interest rates are low. If there is inflation, business firms may be willing to pay high interest rates in order to avoid even higher costs in the future.

8. Contractionary monetary policy may be particularly hard on small business firms which must depend on credit for investment funds. It also increases the cost of borrowing for state and local governments and for the U.S. Treasury.

9. The quantity theory of money *(MV = PQ)* has been a source of controversy among economists. Part of the controversy stems from the difficulty of defining *M*. The traditional definition of money, M_{1-A} is currency and demand deposits. M_{1-B} includes checkable deposits in all banklike institutions.

10. The results of monetary policy over the last decade have not been completely successful. Money growth has had paradoxical effects on nominal interest rates; banks are less sensitive to Federal Reserve policy; and politics affect decisions. Moreover, rational expectations may interfere with policy effects.

TERMS TO REMEMBER

barter: trade in which goods are exchanged for other goods.

demand deposits: deposits in checking accounts available on demand.

time deposits: deposits in savings accounts, often available only after a stated time period.

capital account: the difference between the value of a bank's assets and the value of its liabilities; a bank's net worth.

monetary policy: deliberate exercise of the Federal Reserve's power to expand or contract the money supply in order to promote economic stability.

required reserve ratio: the percentage of its demand deposits a member bank must keep in its reserve account at the Federal Reserve Bank.

discount rate: the rate of interest a member bank must pay on funds borrowed from the Federal Reserve Bank.

open market operations: Federal Reserve purchases and sales of government securities.

tight money: policies to slow money growth.

easy money: policies to increase money growth.

nominal interest rates: the stated charge for borrowing.

real interest rate: the charge for borrowing, corrected for inflation.

rational expectations: widespread understanding of economic policy which tends to affect behavior.

TOPICS FOR DISCUSSION

1. From your reading of the text can you determine the meaning of the following expressions?

   clearing house for checks
   automatic monetary policy

2. What is meant by the statement, "Monetary and fiscal policy may at times be pushing the economy in opposite directions"?

3. Distinguish clearly among the Federal Reserve's three means of affecting the nation's supply of money.

4. Some critics of monetary policy point out that restricting the supply of money and reducing the growth of production may, over time, *increase* prices. Can you suggest reasons for this result?

5. In late 1974, the Federal Reserve announced a reduction in the reserve requirement on certain large Certificates of Deposit (CDs). CDs are sold by banks to savers and the money is loaned to business. The CDs affected by the ruling were those sold for over $100,000, with maturities of more than four months. In 1974, the banks were handling almost $90 billion of these large CDs with a reserve requirement of 8 percent. The new ruling reduced the reserve requirement to 5 percent. Figure the amount of excess reserves which this new ruling released for new loans. What results would you expect?

6. The problem of balance between growth in spending power and new goods and services is complicated by the fact that the existing supply of money is spent several times. An economy that produces $100 billion in GNP annually may need only $20 billion in money, if it is assumed

that each dollar is spent five times during the year. Economists refer to the number of times money is spent as its velocity. Thus, the quantity of money times its velocity will be equal to the value of GNP: $MV = GNP$. Below are GNP and money-supply data for selected years in the United States. Calculate the velocity for each year. What do you notice about velocity in recent years? What factors may influence the speed with which money is spent?

Year	GNP*	Money Supply: Currency + Demand Deposits*
1947	$ 231	$113
1951	338	123
1955	398	135
1959	484	143
1965	685	171
1969	930	209
1974	1397	284
1978	1890	335
1980	2627	385

*in billions

7. Explain why headlines describing Federal Reserve intentions might "aggravate ulcers on Wall Street!"
8. Consult the *Economic Report of the President* for data on money growth, prices, and interest rates over recent years. Comment on your findings.
9. Explain how following Milton Friedman's prescription for steady money growth might help reduce inflation. Might it also help relieve unemployment?
10. Is Friedman's money growth prescription consistent with a belief in "rational expectations"?

SUGGESTED READINGS

"America's New Financial Structure," *Business Week*, November 17, 1980, p. 138.

Berman, Peter I., "The Basic Cause of Inflation," *Across the Board*, November 1977, p. 23.

Bladen, Ashby, "The Natural History of Money and Credit," *Across the Board*, January 1980, pp. 63–73.

Davenport, John A., "A Testing Time for Monetarism," *Fortune*, October 6, 1980, p. 42.

"The Depression—A Debate That Rages On: Why Did It Happen?" *Business Week*, September 3, 1979, p. 12.

"The Economy: New Look?" *Newsweek*, January 9, 1978, p. 48.

Ehrbar, A. F., "The Reaganites vs. the Fed," *Fortune*, May 4, 1981, p. 287.

Guzzadi, Walter, Jr., "The New Down to Earth Economics," *Fortune*, December 31, 1978, p. 72.

Malin, Steven R., "Money-Watching," *Across the Board*, November 1980, pp. 45–49.

Massaro, Vincent G., "Toward a New Financial Structure for the United States," *Across the Board*, February 1976, p. 18.

Meadows, Edward, "Volcker Takes On the Money Serpent," *Fortune*, November 19, 1979, p. 49.

Minsky, Hyman P., "The Federal Reserve: Between a Rock and a Hard Place," *Challenge*, May/June 1980, pp. 36–38.

"Mutual Funds Resurge in the Chaos of the Financial Markets," *Business Week*, March 31, 1980, p. 68.

Rose, Sanford, "Bank Regulation: The Reforms We Really Need," *Fortune*, December 1977, p. 123.

Rose, Sanford, "More Bank for the Buck: The Magic of Electronic Banking," *Fortune*, May 1977, p. 202.

Sommers, Albert T., "Beyond the Recession," *Across the Board*, January 1980, p. 19.

or Losing Your Assets

Inflation

Tools for Study

Learning Objectives

After reading this chapter, you will be able to:

1. define inflation, identify its causes, and explain its effects.
2. suggest some policy remedies for demand-pull and cost-push inflation.
3. discuss the difficult problem of structural inflation.
4. discuss the price effects of economic and social regulation.

Issues Covered

Who are the gainers and losers in inflation?
How does a wage-price freeze work?
How does price indexing work?

It has been said that if you ask five economists for their opinion on a subject, you will get *six* opinions—one can't make up his or her mind.

This is particularly true of the subject of inflation. Because the sources of inflation are difficult to identify, it is often hard to choose the proper policy for correcting the problem. Before policy alternatives can be evaluated, the problem must be carefully analyzed and the process by which it travels through the system understood. If the problem is approached haphazardly, any action may bring about results opposite from those intended.

Inflation can be defined as a general rise in the price level of goods and services. Some prices are rising and others falling all the time. But if the *average* price level remains the same, there is no inflation. When the average price level for *all* goods and services increases, we have inflation.

A LOOK AT HISTORY

Simpler economic societies or those in early stages of economic development do not have to worry much about inflation. Inflation is primarily a problem of highly industrialized societies.

Primitive Production

Early humans had to struggle just to stay alive. Because primitive tribes were isolated, they had to be self-sufficient. A tribe would produce its entire reserve of game, grain, shelter, and cloth or skins. Later, some tribes began to specialize and trade with neighboring tribes. Specialization made possible greater production so that both tribes could live better. Material gains were accomplished at the expense of self-sufficiency, but that was a small price to pay.

Specialization and trade required the use of money to overcome the difficulties of barter. Primitive tribes used whatever tokens they found at hand as money—special beads and stones and rare shells. As long as spending remained in balance with the supply of goods, there was no problem of rising prices. There was just enough spending to purchase the available goods at their customary prices.

Economic Development

As technical knowledge expanded, however, production grew. More money was needed to symbolize the greater values. A dilemma arose: money had to be of a scarce material so as to prevent cheating, but it also had to be expansible if it was to be exchanged for a growing supply of goods. Gold fulfilled both these requirements for many centuries. But eventually, fewer new sources of gold (as well as the difficulty of hauling gold around in one's pockets) made it necessary to find a substitute. Paper money "tied" to gold was the result.*

Balancing spending with the available supply of goods grew more difficult as economic life became more complex. This might be seen as a problem of *form* versus *substance*. On the one hand, the supply of goods (substance) might grow faster

* Our money is no longer tied to gold. Most of our currency is issued by Federal Reserve banks and is not limited by the supply of gold.

than spending (form). Or, what has been more common lately, spending might grow faster than the real substance of goods.

When spending increases faster than the supply of goods, more buyers will bid for relatively fewer goods. Prices will tend to rise, and the economy will experience *inflation*. When spending increases more slowly than the supply of goods, sellers will compete for buyers' money. Prices will tend to fall, and the economy will experience *deflation*.

Free-Trade Adjustments

Economic theorists of the eighteenth century believed that imbalances between spending and goods would be only temporary and localized. Imbalances would correct themselves *automatically* through free trade.

More spending than goods in one region would bring on inflation. Consumers would look elsewhere for cheaper goods. They would spend their money in regions with the opposite imbalance, because where there was less spending than goods, there would be low prices. Money would flow from *inflating* regions to *deflating* regions until the supply of goods and spending would be in balance in all regions. Then prices would stabilize throughout the trading area.

This happy result might have come to pass if there had been no barriers to the free flow of spending and goods among regions. A free flow was necessary if balance was to be achieved. There was the problem of geographic distance, of course, and there were also political and economic boundaries between nations, each with separate monetary systems, quotas, tariffs, and other limits to free commerce. (The subject of international trade is discussed more fully in Chapter 14.)

Another problem arose with the growth of democracy in Western nations. When democratic governments face domestic problems such as illiteracy, poverty, and unemployment, voters frequently demand new government programs to correct them. Greater government spending calls for creation of new money and adds still more claims against available supplies of goods and services. Unless government programs succeed in increasing production as fast as the growth of spending, there will be inflation.

WHY ALL THE FUSS ABOUT INFLATION?

Why should inflation concern us? A one-dollar bill and a ten look pretty much the same. Why should it matter whether a day's welding, a truckload of soybeans, a college course, or a suit of clothes is counted as ten dollars or one dollar?

It matters if a day's welding *today* at fifty dollars is to be exchanged in ten years for a suit of clothes. By that time the value of the fifty dollars may have shrunk and a suit might cost as much as *five* days' welding. Inflation is especially hard on those people who depend on *stored* money value: savers, the elderly, pensioners. (We'll all be there one day!)

It matters, too, if the price of a college course, for example, rises more slowly than the price of a truckload of soybeans. Those groups who depend on income from the sale of college courses may be unfairly penalized by uneven price changes. Inflation means a lower standard of living for people whose occupations or incomes are relatively *fixed:* teachers, civil servants, and those who depend on government transfer payments.

All these unpleasant effects pertain only to unexpected inflation. If inflation is predicted correctly, welders, retired persons, and college teachers may be able to build into their wage agreements and retirement funds an additional allowance to compensate for inflation.*

Unexpected inflation interferes especially with our ability to plan for the future. We have been taught to save part of our income to provide

* This process creates other disadvantages, as we will soon see.

financial security for our retirement years. Our savings may earn interest of up to, say, 7 percent a year. But suppose the value of our money is declining at the rate of 10 percent a year because of inflation. The unsuspecting saver will actually *lose* 3 percent in purchasing power. The saver may be worse off than the scoundrel who squanders money on riotous living!

What may be even more disturbing is the fact that the saver's interest earnings of 7 percent are taxed as part of his or her personal income. In effect, savers are taxed twice for being virtuous— once through inflation and once by the Internal Revenue Service.

Those who lend or borrow money (creditors or debtors) are also affected by unexpected inflation. In fact, unexpected inflation may benefit the debtor, who pays back less in actual purchasing power than originally borrowed. Lenders lose through unexpected inflation and may become reluctant to lock themselves into long-term loans unless interest rates compensate fully for inflation.

Rampant inflation is often followed by recession or depression. During inflation, there is feverish spending for capital investment and production of goods and services. The result may be overproduction and stockpiling of equipment and inventories. Investment and production will eventually fall off, and unemployment and economic distress follow.

Regrettably, even the *expectation* of inflation can seriously affect economic activity. When prices are expected to rise, speculators may buy and hold goods to sell at higher prices in the future. When speculators withhold goods or raw materials from the marketplace, this in itself will worsen the imbalance between spending and goods. Prices will rise faster, and speculators will make *windfall gains* as they eventually sell their holdings at the higher prices. More importantly, when savings are used for speculation, there is less money available for investment in factories, machines, and vocational training. These are the facilities which equip our society to produce more goods in the future. With fewer facilities with which to increase production, our economic system will be less able to avoid inflation in the future.

Some analysts fear that continuing inflation may bring on serious social and political problems. Strikes, shortages of goods and services, and loss of confidence in government have been linked to inflation and have been a source of public concern. Uncontrolled inflation may even make a country ripe for sharp changes in political philosophy. In times of crisis in the past, nations have turned to demagogues or dictators who promised to solve the problem of inflation. (The best example is Germany in the 1930s.)

Some economists maintain that creeping inflation of about 2 percent a year may help the economy. Slowly rising prices mean higher profits. Higher profits stimulate production, which in turn encourages investment in new manufacturing capacity and creates more jobs. The problem with this theory involves the difficulty of confining inflation to this ideal pace. If business and labor leaders use the 2 percent rate as a base on which to add further price and wage demands, the creep may develop into a headlong lurch!

A CLOSER LOOK AT INFLATION

If we agree that inflation is a serious problem, the next step is analysis. What are the forces producing inflationary pressures in a modern nation? How is inflation transmitted through the system? Finally, what policies can we suggest to deal with the problem?

Demand-Pull Inflation

One explanation of inflation emphasizes the demand side of markets. It is the **demand-pull** theory. Economists moan, "Too much money is chasing too few goods."

Spenders want to buy more goods and services than the economic system is producing. They are trying to purchase a combination of output which is *outside* our production possibilities curve. If there are no unemployed resources to be drawn into production, output cannot increase. The excess spending will start a spiral of bidding for the limited supply of goods. This will raise the prices of finished goods and the labor and material resources used to produce them.

Demand-pull inflation often occurs during wars or during periods of heavy social investment or rapid technological advance. These are times when total spending for goods and services exceeds the productive capacity of resources.

Policy: Cutting Total Spending and Raising Taxes

If excess demand is, in fact, the villain of the piece, what policy would be appropriate?

When wartime spending heats up inflation, Keynesian economists recommend raising taxes and cutting nonessential government programs. Needless to say, this is very unpopular medicine. Few policymakers campaign on a platform promising to enact such harsh remedies.

Political considerations were a serious problem in the late 1960s and early 1970s when the government was spending heavily to finance the war in Vietnam. Tax increases and cuts in other government programs would have been political suicide for many legislators. Consequently, the high levels of wartime spending were allowed to continue. Spending for defense, treatment of urban and rural problems, and consumer goods quickly became translated into ever-rising price levels.

Policy: Stabilizing Money Growth

Another anti-inflation plan is favored by the Monetarists, led by Milton Friedman of the University of Chicago. The Monetarist proposal would avoid the political problems associated with changing federal tax and spending programs.

Friedman emphasizes that if we are to control inflation, we must keep the quantity of money in balance with our growing capacity to produce goods. Our productive capacity has increased an average of about 4 percent each year through growth in the quantity and quality of our resources and improvements in technology. Therefore, the Federal Reserve should allow the money supply to

Viewpoint

HOW TO FINANCE A WAR

It is said that there are three ways to finance a war. (This could be a war on poverty, war on cancer, or war on illiteracy, as well as a conventional war.) The methods are difficult and desirable in the same order:

1. The most desirable and the most difficult is through taxation. Citizens must be *prevented* from spending the amount government wants to spend.
2. Second most desirable and difficult is through bond sales to the public. Individuals must be *persuaded* not to spend their incomes but to lend to government.
3. Least desirable and least difficult (and therefore most often resorted to) is inflation. Avoid prevention and persuasion to reduce private spending, and simply *create* new money to fill government's defense needs. In the preceding chapter we learned how the Federal Reserve banks can enable commercial banks to create new money for lending to government.

Regardless of the means used, a government fighting a war must divert workers and materials away from production of goods for private consumers and to the government's purposes. Creating more money (through the Federal Reserve) will give government the dollars it needs. But creating money may cause inflation, which will reduce the purchasing power of private incomes. When consumer buying power falls, resources will be channeled away from production of private goods in order to produce the goods and services the government needs.

In the end, the public will get fewer goods for their money. Indeed, they are being taxed all along, but in a hidden, less easily measured, and more cruel fashion—through inflation.

---

expand each year only as much as the average expected increase in productive capacity.

Under Friedman's plan, an actual growth of *less than* 4 percent would mean rising unemployment. But the unemployment would be only temporary. If the Federal Reserve continued to supply new money at the rate of 4 percent, the constant addition of new money would be greater than needed to purchase the actual quantity of goods and services. The result would be slightly rising prices, which in turn would stimulate greater pro-

duction and faster economic growth. Furthermore, the larger than necessary quantity of money would cause interest rates to fall. Lower interest rates would encourage borrowing for new investment. Without need for any government decision, production would *increase,* bringing the annual growth rate back up to 4 percent and bringing prices back to normal.

Friedman contends that an actual growth of *more than* 4 percent could not be maintained for long either. At growth rates greater than 4 percent, the economy would bump into the limits of our productive capacity, and inflation could result. If the Federal Reserve continued to supply new money at the rate of only 4 percent, the constant addition of new money would not be enough. Too little money would help hold down prices and discourage consumer spending. The lack of sufficient money for lending would push up interest rates and discourage borrowing for new investment. This time the result would be a *decrease* in production, bringing the annual growth rate back down to 4 percent and bringing prices back to normal.

Thus, a steady yearly increase in the money supply would serve as an *automatic regulator* of economic growth and prices. Without any sort of government intervention, economic growth would tend to stabilize at roughly 4 percent per year and prices would remain stable as well.

Cost-Push Inflation

A second explanation for inflation emphasizes the supply side of markets. This theory bears a somewhat chicken-and-egg relationship to the first but may be a better explanation of recent inflation.

Cost-push (or wage-push) inflation places the blame for the original inflationary push on rising costs of production. Resource owners (generally labor) demand larger shares of income from production. As incomes are increased, the higher costs to business (particularly higher wage costs) create higher prices for goods and services. Higher prices, in turn, create even higher wage demands (or activate cost-of-living clauses in wage contracts).

Of course, rising wages do not necessarily create inflation. Wages may increase every year with no danger of inflation as long as the rate of increase corresponds to the rate of increase in production. If the economic pie expands by roughly 4 percent annually, all incomes can increase by 4 percent without generating cost-push inflation.

On the other hand, if wages rise faster than worker productivity, labor costs per unit of output

will go up. To make up for higher labor costs, business firms will raise prices on final goods. Consumers must then, in effect, pay a bonus to labor for every unit bought. When consumers see their buying power shrinking, they insist upon receiving higher incomes, too, adding another loop to the upward spiral of wages-costs-prices.

The whole problem is complicated because wage costs bear more heavily in certain industries. Labor costs are a small part of production costs in most modern, automated manufacturing plants. But the service industries are less easily mechanized. They need more labor inputs per unit of output. Unfortunately, these are precisely the purchases we affluent Americans want most after our basic material needs are satisfied: health and beauty services, education and environmental services, recreational and travel services, processed foods and custom designs. Increasing wage costs are especially inflationary when consumers spend more of their incomes in the service industries.

Policy: Stabilizing Income Shares

If we accept the cost-push theory of inflation, we must look for ways to moderate the income demands of owners of labor, land, capital, and entrepreneurship. One such program was the Wage Guideposts of the Kennedy administration. During the early 1960s, Guideposts were used to hold down wage demands and preserve the existing relationships among income shares. It was decided that wages should rise only as much as average gains in productivity (3.2 percent). Allowing wages to rise only 3.2 percent annually would keep prices stable. Price increases would be allowed only in industries where funds were needed for capital expansion or modernization and in industries where productivity had grown more slowly than the national average. In industries where productivity had grown faster than the national average, falling prices were expected to offset these price increases.

Attempts to control inflation with the Guideposts were generally successful. This was partly because there was remaining excess capacity in the economy from the recession of 1958–59. Hefty productivity gains in certain industries made up for price increases in others. Also, organized labor seemed willing to cooperate with Wage Guideposts as long as the cost of living remained stable. Unhappily, prices continued to rise in those sectors where the Guideposts were not applied: agriculture and services.

Policy: Increasing Productivity

During the 1960s, programs were also begun to increase productivity and hold down costs of production. Business firms were allowed a tax credit to help pay for new capital investment. In addition, businesses were allowed to deduct larger amounts from taxable income for depreciation of old equipment. Both of these programs reduced tax bills and encouraged business firms to expand and modernize productive capacity. The Economic Development Act was passed in 1965 to encourage the use of modern equipment and techniques in regions of low productivity. Loans, public works projects, and technical assistance were concentrated in depressed areas.

Efforts were also made to increase the productivity of labor. The Manpower Development and Training Act, Job Corps, Neighborhood Youth Groups, and Adult Work Programs provided funds for programs to raise the level of labor skills. Many disadvantaged and unskilled persons were retrained. Such programs are costly, however. In later government programs, on-the-job training in the private sector received greater emphasis.

Structural Inflation and Stagflation

As far back as 1958, a new wrinkle was noticed in the wage-cost-price relationship. The new phenomenon was christened **stagflation,** price inflation accompanied by stagnation, or slower growth of production in industry. (Economists have a tendency to coin new jargon to describe situations that have no theoretical precedents.)

According to traditional analysis of the problem, inflation is the result of: (1) demand-pull, too much spending over and above the capacity of the economy's fully employed resources to produce goods and services; or (2) cost-push, the attempts of resource owners to increase incomes faster than the growth in productivity. In either case, the resulting inflation depends on near *full employment* of labor and material resources.

Recently, however, inflation has been accompanied by a *low* level of resource employment. During the 1970s, unemployment averaged 6.2 percent and the utilization rate of manufacturing capacity only 82 percent. (This contrasts with an average unemployment rate of 4.8 percent and utilization rate of 85 percent during the 1960s and 4.5 and 88 percent during the 1950s.) With so much unused industrial capacity, it is difficult to accept the demand-pull or cost-push explanations for our recent high levels of inflation.

One clue to the cause of the new inflation may be found in the types of commodities whose prices have risen most. On the average, commodity prices in 1968 were 20.8 percent higher than in 1948. Prices increased at an average annual rate of only 1.04 percent, an acceptable rate of increase. However, among some industrial commodities, price increases were between 33 and 75 percent: rubber (37 percent); metals (60 percent); machinery (72 percent); automotive equipment (41 percent); and nonmetallic minerals (40 percent). These industries are generally classified as highly concentrated—i.e., characterized more by monopoly than competition. A few large firms produce 70 to 90 percent of the entire output of these industries.

The effect of concentrated market power has become even more striking in the years since 1968. Between 1968 and 1981 many commodity prices tripled, and fuel prices rose by a factor of seven—a result of the market power of the Organization of Petroleum Exporting Countries (OPEC).*

The apparent connection between price infla-

---

* Consumer prices doubled over the same period.

Viewpoint

A QUESTION TO THINK ABOUT

Which costs push up prices? Labor? Or capital?

What does the record show about the relationship between worker productivity and wage increases? Over the decade of the 1960s productivity per hour of labor rose about 35 percent while real hourly earnings of workers rose only 31 percent. Clearly, it would be difficult to place the entire blame for inflation on labor.

Where did the rest of the economic pie go? What are the other costs which may have started the price spiral?

The increase in productivity was not accomplished by labor alone. In fact, additions to capital stock and the use of scientific discoveries in industry were responsible for much of the increase. Therefore, owners of capital also earned a reward for their contribution. However, if we attempt to blame higher prices on owners of capital resources, we are left with a perplexing question.

At higher levels of personal income, the fraction of income spent on goods and services tends to diminish. The recipient of interest and dividends may spend a smaller portion of his or her income than does the blue-collar wage earner (who may even spend more than 100 percent).

Now the question:

If we accuse owners of capital of demanding more than their share of income from production, and

If it is also true that they tend to spend less of their incomes, then

Who is left to buy the expanding volume of goods turned out by our increased productive capacity?

And, if buyers are lacking, how is it that prices continue to rise?

A larger share of income going to capital would seem to *reduce* inflation. As unspent incomes to capital drain out of the spending stream the lower level of spending would squelch any tendency toward higher prices.

There is no easy answer to this question. The important point is that wages *must* rise. Otherwise goods and services cannot be sold.

Incomes must increase as the economic pie increases. But in general, income *shares* should reflect a resource's contribution to total production. Determining fair income shares is not easy in a complex economy such as ours!

tion and market power suggested a new explanation for inflation. The emphasis shifted to the **structure** of industries: the number and size of firms, the types of material inputs used in production, the types of labor required by modern technology, and the skills of the available labor pool.

Administered Prices

Many economists blamed structural inflation on **administered pricing** in highly concentrated industries. Administered prices are prices set by the major suppliers in a concentrated industry. Smaller firms in a concentrated industry tend to go along with the giants, and inflation accelerates.

In certain industries, pricing agreements may seem necessary because of the large capital investment required and the technical complexity of production. Costly plants and equipment must be operated steadily and the output sold at acceptable prices. Large-scale manufacturers cannot afford price wars. Therefore they agree to set prices high enough to maintain a *target rate of return;* a target rate of return is a certain percentage return on invested capital.

The paradoxical result of target pricing is that when demand falls and plant operation must be cut back, the smaller output must bear a larger per-unit share of the target return. Thus, *falling* sales may mean *rising* prices in order that manufacturers may maintain acceptable levels of profit.

Suppliers of many industrial commodities can demand and get higher prices even when total spending is low and unemployment high. Their market power results from the nature of the commodities in question. They are generally necessary components of manufacture for which there are few substitutes: steel, aluminum, zinc, copper, processing machinery. Alternate suppliers often do not exist, and the higher costs are easily passed on to final consumers anyway.

It is also true that highly concentrated industries are often characterized by powerful labor unions. Unions can insist on higher wage contracts, knowing that large firms can pass on the higher wage costs to the unfortunate consumer.

Policy: Breaking Up Market Power

This rather gloomy analysis leaves the policymaker in a dilemma. If structural inflation results from excessive market power, a policy to reduce or restrain that power is needed. Manufacturers whose pricing policies add to inflation would have to be separated into smaller enterprises or their pricing policies would have to be regulated by public commissions. Neither approach is very satisfactory.

Breaking up large firms through legal action may mean sacrificing large-scale, low-cost production. Also, large firms may be better equipped to conduct research and apply advanced production techniques. Finally, regulatory commissions are costly and often poorly equipped for making policy decisions in a complex manufacturing environment (as we will soon see).

Nevertheless, the Antitrust Division of the Justice Department, the Federal Trade Commission, and the federal courts in various states have been probing into pricing policies of some highly concentrated industries: telephone communications, sugar, bread, coffee, beer, aluminum, breakfast cereals, drugs, and petroleum. If administered pricing can be brought under control, inflationary pressures may be moderated.

Regulation Inflation

Government frequently gets the blame for causing inflation. Sometimes government is not entirely at fault, but there is one instance in which government must certainly accept the blame. That is the area of regulation.

In general, government regulation of business has one of two types of objectives: economic or social. The *economic* objective is primarily to protect competition in particular industries. The *social* objective is to protect workers and consumers. In both cases the result may raise prices.

Regulation for *economic* purposes is generally directed toward a particular broad sector of the economy: agriculture, transportation, communication, banking, or energy. In such capital-intensive industries, there is often a tendency toward greater industrial concentration. In fact, we have referred to some of these industries as natural monopolies. The goal of regulation is to retain a degree of competition in these sectors so as to avoid the harmful effects of monopoly. Even when larger enterprises might be more efficient, regulations protect small competitors by setting prices above the minimum costs of production.

Regulation for social purposes is a more recent form. The objective is to require firms to include *external costs* in their costs of production. External costs are costs generally borne by others outside the business firm which creates them. Some examples of external costs are environmental pollution and the costs of employee health and safety on the job.

Free markets cannot handle external costs well. This is because the benefits of money spent to correct the problems don't necessarily come back to the firm. Like the costs, the benefits of improved health and living conditions are distributed over the entire community. Social regulation forces firms to "internalize" these external costs. Ultimately, the "internalized" costs must be paid by consumers of the products involved, in the form of higher prices for finished goods.

Regulation of any kind has another inflationary effect. To administer rules requires a bureaucratic staff of lawyers, inspectors, accountants, and specialists of all types. They must be paid salaries comparable to those they could earn in private industry, but they produce no good or marketable service. Again, the result is to raise prices.

Policy: Deregulating Industry

In the early days of economic regulation, it seemed necessary to protect small competitors so that a monopoly might not achieve control over output and prices. More recently, technological changes and economic growth have weakened the market power of natural monopolies so that regulation may no longer be necessary. Many firms in the regulated sectors would like to reduce prices and introduce new technologies if the regulatory authorities would let them.

In 1978 Congress and the Civil Aeronautics Board began deregulating the airline industry. Airline firms were allowed to cut prices and cancel unprofitable routes. New small firms sprang up to take advantage of markets abandoned by the giant airlines. By 1980 competition had reduced airline profits substantially, but many analysts believed that the industry was becoming more efficient.

In 1980 Congress and the Interstate Commerce Commission began deregulating the trucking industry. It was hoped that competition would encourage firms to adapt their service and pricing policies to particular markets and operate more efficiently.

Policy: Cost-Benefit Analysis of Social Regulation

Social regulation has not only raised costs of production but has also increased the risks of investment, so that new capital construction and productivity growth have slowed. Aside from the inflationary effects, however, regulation yields many benefits which our society values and for which citizens are willing to pay: healthy working conditions and clean air and water are obvious examples. Still, it is important to weigh these and other benefits against their costs and impose regulations only when the expected benefits clearly justify the costs paid.

Congress has mandated a new benefit-cost approach to social regulation. Social regulatory agencies are now required to assess the benefits of proposed new regulations and compare with all the costs: the *enforcement costs* for government, the *compliance costs* of business, and the long-term *economic costs* for our economic system. Making such calculations is difficult and imprecise, but consideration of benefits and costs should increase the efficiency of social regulation.

Self-Check

1. **Trade will adjust the balance between money and goods:**
   a. if nations restrict the flow of money over their borders.
   b. as money flows into nations experiencing inflation.
   c. if democratic governments carry on large spending programs.
   d. helping to achieve price stability.
   e. if consumers buy from high-price producers.

2. **Inflation is hardest on:**
   a. those who borrow money to be repaid in future years.
   b. speculators who hoard basic commodities.
   c. fixed-income recipients and retired persons.
   d. workers with escalator clauses in wage contracts.
   e. the federal government, whose tax revenues must decline.

3. **The main cause of demand-pull inflation is:**
   a. excessive production of goods and services.
   b. heavy sale of government bonds to the public.
   c. excessive saving by consumers.
   d. a high level of total spending in relationship to available goods and services.
   e. a substantial increase in the productivity of resources.

4. **According to the Monetarists, a steady increase in the supply of money should:**
   a. give politicians more control over monetary policy.
   b. be in line with the average growth in production.
   c. increase spending during inflation.
   d. reduce spending during recession.
   e. none of the above.

5. **In order to avoid inflation, wages must:**
   a. rise only as much as productivity.
   b. be distributed equally among wage earners.
   c. rise faster than the return to owners of capital.
   d. be taxed at lower rates.
   e. be controlled by the government.

6. **Concentration in industry:**
   a. allows monopolistic industries and labor unions to maintain high prices.
   b. may cause high prices even when employment drops.
   c. permits firms to establish a target rate of return.
   d. has no simple policy remedy.
   e. all of the above.

Theory in Practice

GAINERS AND LOSERS IN INFLATION—MOSTLY LOSERS

Inflation shrinks your dollar and erodes the value of your income and savings. A 7 percent annual rate of inflation will halve the value of your dollars in ten years. A 10 percent annual rate will halve the value in only 7 years. (Hint: Divide the rate of inflation into 70. The answer is the number of years before the value of money is cut in half if inflation continues at the same rate. Thus, for a 2 percent annual rate of inflation: 70/2 = 35 years. This is known as the "Rule of 70.")

In 1958, average per capita income in the United States was $1831 after taxes. In 1980 it was $8176, an impressive increase; but when the 1980 figure is corrected for inflation and translated into 1958 dollars, it is worth only $3145. Almost two thirds of the apparent gain reflected only higher prices.

The inflation of 1979–80 was especially hard on production workers. Weekly earnings averaged $204 in 1978. By 1980 earnings had risen to $245. But in real terms weekly earnings had actually *fallen* by almost $9.00. Without cost-of-living escalator clauses in wage contracts, workers are relatively helpless against inflation.

Savers and owners of productive capital haven't fared any better. High-grade, low-risk corporate bonds were earning between 7 and 10 percent during the 1970s. Short-term commercial loans earned somewhat less. Tax-exempt municipal bonds earned between 5 and 7 percent. The safest U.S. government securities earned less than 7 percent. Thus, on the average, owners of capital increased their dollars in absolute amount somewhat more than 7 percent over the period.

How much were these dollars worth?

For the period 1970 to 1980, consumer prices rose 120 percent, or more than 10 percent per year. This means that many owners of America's capital resources also saw their incomes eroded by inflation. Furthermore, they had to pay income tax on their interest earnings in addition to their losses to inflation.

Who does gain from inflation?

The biggest gainer is government! The federal government's income tax revenues soar with inflation, as taxpayers move into higher tax brackets and pay higher tax rates. Inflation leaves the U.S. government with an increasing share of income to use for government projects: social programs, public works, defense. Thus, inflation channels more and more resources into production for government purposes and away from private purposes.

Is this what we want? Whatever we decide, we may discover that control of inflation requires some *political* decisions as well as economic ones.

WAGE-PRICE CONTROLS

A politically acceptable and widely debated antiinflationary tactic has been wage-price controls. (The popular assumption is that *your* wages are controlled but not necessarily mine. Prices I *pay* are controlled but not necessarily those I receive.) Economists generally oppose price controls except possibly as a means of affecting inflationary psychology and ending inflationary expectations. Recent experience with wage-price controls illustrates some of the advantages and disadvantages.

The Vietnam war left the U.S. economy in a shambles. In the late 1960s heavy government spending for military purposes brought on inflation. Contractionary fiscal policy was not used promptly or vigorously enough to hold down civilian spending. The Federal Reserve was obliged to use strongly contractionary monetary policy to slow the inflation.

By 1971, the shortage of money had pushed the economy into recession. Unemployment was more than 5 percent and real GNP was declining. It began to appear that *expansionary* fiscal policy should be used, but fears of again setting off inflation stood in the way.

Finally, in August 1971, President Nixon and the monetary authorities agreed on a package of policies known as Phase I:

1. fiscal policy to stimulate spending, production, and incomes through tax incentives for business investment, a cut in excise taxes on automobiles, and a reduction in personal income taxes;
2. an increase in the rate of growth of the money supply;
3. temporary wage-price controls to slow wageprice inflation.

Most nonfarm wages and prices were controlled for ninety days. Then in December 1971, Phase II began, during which wage and price increases were to be monitored and regulated. A Pay Board was set up to review wage increases, which were generally to be limited to 5.5 percent. (This allowed for an expected 3 percent increase in labor productivity and a 2.5 percent increase in labor costs and finished goods prices.) A Price Commission was set up to review price increases, which would be limited to "pass-throughs": firms were allowed to pass through higher production costs in the form of higher prices. Profit margins would be held to the average of recent years. Controls under Phase II were lifted in January 1973.

Except for farm prices, which were not subject to controls, wage and price inflation slowed considerably in Phase I and II; the consumer price index rose only 1.9 percent and wages 3.1 percent. After the controls were lifted, there was a slight "bulge" in prices, but then the indexes of wages and prices settled down to a rate of increase that was lower than before controls.

Phase III began in January 1973, with a more relaxed system of voluntary restraint. A Cost of Living Council was set up to review price increases with special emphasis on food and medical care, areas where prices had continued to rise.

In late summer of 1973, inflation heated up a second time. Heavy foreign demand and shortages of food, energy, and industrial commodities pushed up prices. During the last half of 1973, food prices rose 10 percent, services rose 5.4 percent, and industrial commodities rose 6.1 percent. New price controls were put into effect for sixty days. Finally, in August 1973, Phase IV began with stricter controls on pass-throughs and profits.

Particular industries were to be removed from controls in stages in order to avoid another price bulge. Legislation authorizing price controls was allowed to expire in April 1974. The Council on Wage and Price Stability was formed to monitor wage-price behavior.

How successful were controls? Probably the greatest success of controls came at the very beginning of the program when there was excess capacity available in the economy. Expansionary monetary and fiscal policy could be used vigorously with little price increase. Furthermore, in the beginning a change in expectations of inflation reduced the rate of inflation that actually occurred.

Why was this? Expectations of future price increases often prompt labor to demand larger wage contracts; expectations of future cost increases often prompt business firms to advance their prices on finished goods. When inflation is not considered a threat, wage and price decisions

can be made in a climate of moderation.

The chief danger of controls comes when they are lifted. Business firms may fear another price freeze and rush to increase their prices. Similarly, labor unions may demand catch-up wage increases.

Another disadvantage of controls may be shortages, particularly of low-profit items. Firms may cut back on production if the controlled price does not cover their higher costs. (Many Americans remember the slaughter of thousands of baby chicks during the period of price controls.) Black markets and unfair allocation of limited supplies may result. (Remember our discussion of price ceilings in Chapter 3; a price freeze is a price ceiling.)

Intervening in free markets may bring on other long-range effects. The free market depends on flexible prices to send out signals of changes in resource supply and consumer demand. These price signals should stimulate adjustments to changing market conditions. For example, high prices for sugar should stimulate greater production and help bring prices down. High wages for auto mechanics should encourage more workers to learn these skills and help bring wages down. Government restraints on price increases interfere with this adjustment process and prolong shortages of goods and materials. This makes the ultimate price increases even greater.

Furthermore, under a free-market system, improved resource availability and technology may be expected to reduce costs of production in some industries. But when firms are afraid of price controls, they will hesitate to pass these cost savings on to consumers.

Price controls might help control inflation in highly concentrated industries. But there may be other undesirable results. In steel production, for example, presidential pressure has been used to hold down price increases. Low steel prices hold down production costs in the many industries using steel, moderating price increases for automobiles, appliances, and building materials. But low steel prices have the effect of reducing profits in the

Viewpoint

DEALING WITH STAGFLATION

In recent years the United States has been suffering a high level of inflation accompanied by serious unemployment. Policymakers have seemed unable to find a solution. Contractionary monetary and fiscal policy has aggravated unemployment without slowing inflation much—if at all. A new program of wage-price controls has been avoided because of the price distortions controls cause and the scarcities they create.

If we are to deal with the inflation problem, we must first identify its causes. Most economists blame the food and fuel price boosts of 1973 for setting off the current inflationary spiral. Since higher domestic food costs are partly a result of increased foreign sales of U.S. grains to pay for foreign oil, we might identify energy costs as the principal source of the problem.

Higher energy costs must have two important results for the world economy: first, the economic pie will not grow as fast as when energy was plentiful and cheap; and second, the distribution of the pie will change as energy producers demand a larger relative share of total world output. These two developments have seriously affected the U.S. economy. Most of us have been harmed by the first result and we are resisting the second. We have been harmed by the fact that material standards of living are not improving as fast as we would like. And we are resisting a reduction in our *real* purchasing power that would reduce our own relative shares of the economic pie. Instead, we have demanded wage increases to compensate fully for each increase in our living costs. We continue to claim our "fair share" of the pie.

Of course, all our increased claims may not increase the size of the pie at all. The result is only to raise wages and prices all around. If there is no change in the relative share going to energy producers, eventually the price of energy must rise again and the entire process is repeated, one worsening spiral after another.

The problem doesn't seem to have a simple solution. In fact, there may be many partial solutions, each of which helps in only a small way. The most obvious efforts might be toward increased productivity in all industries, reduction of unnecessary government claims on GNP, conservation and development of new energy sources, and persuasion to avoid excessive claims against total output. All these measures would require the willing cooperation of every one of us. Curing stagflation may be the test that determines the survival of a free market economy!

industry and discouraging new investment. The result has been a failure to advance technologically and, finally, even higher prices for steel.

INDEXING

Another anti-inflationary tactic is a procedure known as **indexing,** proposed by Milton Friedman. The procedure has been used with some apparent success in Brazil and works as follows:

Many of the harmful effects of inflation are caused by expectations of future inflation. Businesses and workers demand price and wage increases at least as great as expected inflation; lenders demand interest charges at least as great as expected inflation. Their expectations help to bring about the inflation they expect!

Inflation distorts payments to these gainers and away from other groups. Indexing would establish a cost-of-living ''correction'' which would be added to all incomes. The money value of wages, rent, and interest incomes would be adjusted upward in line with changes in the general price level. This would keep *real* incomes from falling. Indexing would hold down demands for increases in income with the assurance that, *should inflation occur*, all groups will receive their appropriate cost-of-living corrections. There would be no danger of losing one's share of the economic pie just because one makes fewer demands than others.

In the private sector, cost-of-living escalator clauses would be written into all labor contracts. This would guarantee wage earners a fair increase in incomes. Interest rates on loans would vary with the rate of inflation. Lenders would be more willing to make loans to home builders and businesses if they were assured a return high enough to offset inflation. The hope is that indexing would help maintain the existing income relationships among resource owners.

There are disadvantages, of course. Perhaps the most damaging part of this proposal would be its effects on the government budget. Indexing would adjust tax brackets, tax credits, and tax rates so that government could not benefit from continuing inflation. Income tax revenues would not increase automatically with inflation. But at the same time, indexing would adjust government's transfer payments upward, so that budget deficits would soar. Moreover, by maintaining stable income shares, indexing would reduce the effectiveness of resource pricing for allocating resources efficiently and rewarding increased productivity. And finally, to protect all income earners against inflation would probably reduce the will to fight against inflation. The result could be wildly accelerating prices, with unimaginable national and international implications.

SUMMARY

1. Inflation is primarily a problem of modern, highly industrialized societies. The difficulty of keeping spending in balance with a society's output of goods and services may lead to changing prices, usually in the upward direction.
2. An excess of spending in one region will cause the price level to rise. If free trade exists, consumers will then buy more from low-priced foreign producers, causing money to flow out and eventually bringing spending down into balance with the quantity of goods. However, modern nations have erected international barriers and established domestic economic programs that interfere with this automatic adjustment mechanism.
3. Demand-pull inflation results from an excess of spending by consumers, business, and/or government. Spending over and above the nation's capacity to produce goods may be curtailed by: increasing taxes on consumers and business, reducing government spending programs, or restricting the supply of money available for loans.
4. Cost-push inflation results from higher costs of productive resources. Higher costs are passed on to the consumer in the form of higher prices for finished goods. To avoid inflation, wages must not rise faster than productivity. Likewise, returns to owners of capital must not rise faster than productivity.

5. Structural inflation is blamed on highly concentrated industries where firms agree among themselves not to cut high prices. The result has been stagflation—high prices even when unemployment is high. The problem may intensify in the coming years because of the large-scale technical requirements of modern manufacturing and the difficulty of maintaining price competition among large firms.

6. Government regulatory policies may add to costs of production and keep many prices higher than free market prices; however, there are some benefits associated with regulation.

7. Inflation imposes particular burdens on savers, the aged, and people on fixed incomes. It creates distortions which may be damaging to the entire society. Some recent programs to deal with inflation are wage-price controls and indexing.

TERMS TO REMEMBER

inflation: a rise in the general price level.

demand-pull inflation: inflation that results from excess demand, over and above our capacity to produce goods and services.

cost-push inflation: inflation that results from rising costs of production.

stagflation: a condition which results when inflation and unemployment of resources exist at the same time.

structural inflation: inflation that results from the concentration of industry into large firms.

administered prices: prices established by tacit agreement among large firms in concentrated industries.

indexing: changes in incomes to compensate for changes in the general price level.

TOPICS FOR DISCUSSION

1. Explain the following expressions and discuss the implications of each for price stability:

speculative buying
cost-of-living clauses
administered prices

2. Is it correct to say that inflation is the cruelest tax? Explain.

3. What does the author mean by the statement that there is a chicken-and-egg relationship between the demand-pull and the cost-push theories of inflation?

4. A successful American businessman once said, "The best way to prevent higher prices is high prices." Was he out of his head? Explain.

5. The 1978–79 inflation was worsened by lagging productivity throughout the U.S. economy. Over the two years, the United States experienced a .6 percent decline in output per labor hour. Over the same period, wages rose 18.3 percent. Price increases of 16.2 percent eroded the value of the higher wages. These figures complicated the fight against inflation. Workers claim their pay is worth less, and employers point to falling labor productivity. What are the political implications of this problem for policymakers? Do you see any ways to resolve the impasse? What ultimate results would you predict?

6. The *Wall Street Journal* of July 22, 1974, reported on the philosophy of Alan Greenspan, Chairman of President Ford's Council of Economic Advisors and President Reagan's economic advisor. Greenspan was reported to regard the problem of inflation as primarily a political, rather than an economic, problem. According to Greenspan, a policymaker's dilemma results from an emphasis of short-term benefits at the expense of long-term costs. Comment on his assessment of the problem on inflation. Would you agree with his conclusion? What suggestions might you make to ease the problem?

7. A letter to the editor of a local newspaper stated: "Let's put all congressional salaries on a 'reverse' cost-of-living basis. Thus, whenever the cost-of-living index goes up, our senators and representatives would have to take a cut in pay."

What does the writer believe about inflation? Evaluate his or her policy prescription.

8. Discuss the major advantages and disadvantages of regulation.

9. How might the results of indexing differ according to the particular price index used?

SUGGESTED READINGS

Alexander, Magnus W., "Inflation: A Lesson from the Past," *Across the Board,* May 1979, pp. 34–37.

Alexander, Tom, "It's Roundup Time for the Runaway Regulators," *Fortune,* December 3, 1979, p. 126.

Cameron, Juan, "Alfred Kahn's Jesting Is No Laughing Matter," *Fortune,* February 12, 1979, p. 78.

"Carter's Risky Strategy," *Business Week,* January 23, 1978, p. 88.

"Deregulation: A Fast Start for the Reagan Strategy," *Business Week,* March 9, 1981, p. 62.

Eckstein, Otto, "Economic Choices for the 1980s," *Challenge,* July/August 1980, pp. 15–27.

Gramley, Lyle E., "The Role of Supply-Side Economics in Fighting Inflation, *Challenge,* January/February 1981, pp. 14–23.

"Greenspan and Okun Debate How to Stop Inflation," *Fortune,* April 1977, p. 116.

Heller, Walter W., "Shadow and Substance in Inflation Policy," *Challenge,* January/February 1981, pp. 5–13.

"Improving Regulatory Practices," *Economic Report of the President,* Washington: Government Printing Office, January 1981, p. 99.

"Inflation," *Economic Report of the President,* Washington: Government Printing Office, January 1981, p. 32.

"Inflation Is Wrecking the Private Pension System," *Business Week,* May 12, 1980, p. 92.

"Inflation Threat: Prices High in Spite of Spare Capacity," *Business Week,* March 21, 1977, p. 120.

Kahn, Herman, and Leveson, Irving, "How Not to Index the Economy," *Fortune,* November 17, 1980, p. 60.

Lave, Lester B., "Health, Safety, and Environmental Regulations," *Setting National Priorities: Agenda for the 1980s,* Washington: The Brookings Institution, 1980, p. 131.

Levy, Michael E., "We Must Rid Ourselves of the Myth of the Free Lunch," *Across the Board,* May 1979, pp. 29–33.

Linden, Fabian, "Inflation of Price, Price of Inflation," *Across the Board,* December 1977, p. 66.

Marshall, Ray, "The Inflation Battle: Winning Labor's Support," *Challenge,* January/February 1979, pp. 18–25.

Meltzer, Allan, "It Takes Long-Range Planning to Lick Inflation," *Fortune,* December 1977, p. 96.

Minarik, Joseph J., "Who Wins, Who Loses from Inflation," *Challenge,* January/February 1979, pp. 26–31.

Nulty, Leslie Ellen, "How Inflation Hits the Majority," *Challenge,* January/February 1979, pp. 32–38.

Okun, Arthur M., "The Invisible Handshake and the Inflationary Process," *Challenge,* January/February 1980, pp. 5–12.

Okun, Arthur M., "Sticks with Two Short Ends," *Challenge,* July/August 1979, pp. 47–51.

Rees, Albert, "Controls," *Across the Board,* May 1980, pp. 14–19.

Rees-Mogg, William, "Inflation: Can Conservatives Put It Right?" *Across the Board,* August 1980, pp. 30–33.

Seligman, Daniel, "The Year There Was No Inflation," *Fortune,* May 5, 1980, p. 98.

Stein, Herbert, "An Anti-Inflation Policy Cannot Be Incredible 1," *Across the Board,* December 1980, p. 62.

Stein, Herbert, "An Anti-Inflation Policy Cannot Be Incredible 2," *Across the Board,* January 1981, p. 31.

Stein, Herbert, "The Coming Clamor for Price Controls," *Fortune,* January 12, 1981, p. 60.

Tabb, William K., "Government Regulation: Two Sides to the Story," *Challenge,* November/December 1980, pp. 40–48.

Thurow, Lester, *The Zero-Sum Society,* New York:

Basic Books, 1980, Chapters 3 and 6.

Weidenbaum, Murray L., ''Government Power and Business Performance,'' in *The United States in the 1980s,* Peter Duignan and Alvin Rabushka, eds., Stanford University: Hoover Institution, 1980, p. 197.

Weidenbaum, Murray L., ''The High Cost of Government Regulation,'' *Challenge,* November/December 1979, pp. 32–39.

World Research Staff, ''Presenting: The Inflation File'' (a play), *Across the Board,* March 1980, pp. 57–66.

or What Good Is a Raise
If You Don't Have a Job?

Unemployment

Tools for Study

Learning Objectives

After reading this chapter, you will be able to:

1. explain the GNP gap.
2. define frictional, cyclical, and structural unemployment and discuss some remedies.
3. discuss the relationship between unemployment and inflation.
4. list the various programs which have been adopted to deal with unemployment.

Issues Covered

How may a minimum wage actually work against those it is intended to help?

How is the unemployment rate distributed among the population?

What are employment opportunities for the future?

The classical economists believed that unemployment would not be a serious problem in a free-market system. They thought that the markets for resources would operate smoothly and competitively just as the markets for goods would. Many business firms would enter the market to demand labor resources, and many individuals would supply labor to businesses. The result would be an equilibrium price, or wage, and a quantity hired that would clear the market.

The classical theory of labor markets is shown graphically on Figure 11.1. (See page 214.) With the demand for labor shown by D_1, the equilibrium wage rate is $1.50 per hour, and employment is 200,000 workers.

Now suppose total spending in the economy falls and the demand for productive resources declines. The demand for labor shifts to the left, shown as D_2 on the figure. At the old wage of $1.50 per hour, the quantity of workers demanded is now only about 125,000, while the quantity supplied is still 200,000. Surplus workers will compete for jobs, causing the wage rate to fall to a new lower equilibrium wage of $1.25. Again, the market is cleared. At $1.25 per hour, 150,000 workers

Figure 11.1   Wage and Employment Adjustments in a Free Labor Market.
In a free market a decrease in demand would produce a lower equilibrium wage.

will supply labor and 150,000 workers will be demanded by business firms. When wages are flexible, there is no unemployment; all workers who want to work for the going wage will be hired.

The classical economists went a step further. They concluded that the lower wage would not necessarily mean a lower standard of living for workers. The economy would continue to produce its maximum production possibilities given available capital and technology and a number of willing workers. But since goods and services would be produced at lower labor costs, they would sell for lower prices. The worker's lower *money* wage would represent greater *real* purchasing power.

Classical labor market theory depended on competition for these smooth adjustments to take place. Wages would have to be flexible enough to rise or fall in response to changing demand for labor. In periods of slack demand, surplus workers would have to compete for jobs by offering . work for lower wages. In periods of excess demand, employers would have to compete for workers by offering higher wages. According to classical theory, full employment would be the normal condition. Wages and prices would rise and fall

together. Real earnings would depend on the productivity of the economic system as a whole.

These circumstances may have prevailed in the earliest stages of industrialization when classical theory dominated economic thought. But economic development brought changes which interfered with the process of automatic adjustments. Groups of employers and workers organized to gain market power to fix wages and prices. Wages lost their flexibility, and a drop in demand created unemployment rather than a lower equilibrium wage. In addition, structural changes took place in the labor market, creating the problem of prolonged unemployment for particular groups.

MEASURING UNEMPLOYMENT

Failing to employ resources productively has long- and short-range effects—economic, social, and perhaps even political. It is impossible to measure all these effects, but some of the material costs can be measured.

GNP Gap

Do you remember our discussion of the economic problem? The economic problem is concerned with the scarcity of productive resources and the vastness of wants. Unless available resources are used fully, many more of our wants cannot be satisfied. Some homes will not be built, dental services performed, or consumer goods produced.

When resources are unemployed, we say there is a **GNP gap.** The GNP gap is the difference between *potential* GNP and *actual* GNP. It represents the wasted goods and services lost by some part of the population. Over the period 1975–77, estimated GNP gap was more than $200 billion worth of goods and services not produced! (This figure is expressed in current dollars. In constant dollars of 1972 the GNP gap would be around $150 billion, still a substantial loss.) The saddest aspect of this loss is that it can never be recovered. Coal not produced this year may be mined in the next. Trees not cut remain for cutting some time in the future. But hours of labor not used today are gone forever.

Aside from these real, material sacrifices borne by the entire society, unemployment causes particular hardships in certain regions.* Areas with substantial unemployment are often beset by social unrest, high crime rates, and environmental decay. On an individual basis, all of these costs are magnified by personal sacrifices: lower material standards of living, emotional distress, and even more important, the loss of skills and motivation resulting from prolonged idleness.

Unemployment Rate

Another, more direct, measure of employment is the unemployment rate. The unemployment rate is estimated by the government in terms of a percentage of the labor force. The **labor force** is defined as all people sixteen years of age or older who are employed or who are unemployed but actively seeking work.

The government counts you as *employed* if you did any work for pay or profit during a given week, regardless of the amount. It also regards you as employed if you worked in a family enterprise for fifteen or more hours in the week, whether or not you received pay. It counts you as *unemployed* if you were laid off from your latest job or actively sought work within the past thirty days. (Actively seeking work means filling out applications and answering want ads, going to job interviews, or registering with an employment agency.)

The estimated unemployment rate tends to be understated, particularly during periods of rising unemployment. A person who would like a full-time job but can find a job working only ten hours

per week is counted as employed. Moreover, those who have stopped seeking work out of discouragement or failure to find a job are not included among the unemployed.* How can these factors affect the unemployment rate? During November and December of 1980 the unemployment rate dropped from 7.5 to 7.4 percent. Over the same period, total employment also dropped by 57,000 workers. Apparently, large numbers of workers left the labor force and were not counted as unemployed, so that what seemed to be a gain in employment was really a loss.

TYPES OF UNEMPLOYMENT

The Employment Act of 1946 set forth the goal of maintaining maximum employment. The law made it the clear responsibility of the U.S. government to establish policies for achieving this goal.

A correct policy for full employment depends first on a correct analysis of the sources of unemployment. Identifying the sources of unemployment will enable policy makers to design effective programs to correct each type. Economists have classified unemployment into three categories: frictional, cyclical, and structural.

Frictional Unemployment

Economists define normal full employment as that condition when approximately 94 to 95 percent of the civilian labor force is employed. The remaining 5 or 6 percent are unemployed because of **frictional unemployment**—"frictions" in the movement of workers from job to job or among workers entering the labor force for the first time.

Frictional unemployment is necessary and even desirable in a dynamic economy. It is a re-

---

* Examples are Appalachia in the 1960s and Detroit in 1980.

* Discouraged workers constitute what is sometimes called "hidden unemployment."

flection of the healthy growth or decline of different sectors of the economy. Markets and production techniques are constantly changing to reflect changes in consumer demand. Workers must move out of declining industries and into expanding industries.

In recent years, frictional unemployment has come to constitute a larger portion of total unemployment. This is primarily because of the growing numbers of married women and teenagers in the job market, with typically higher rates of entry and re-entry into the labor force than adult male workers.

Frictional unemployment is, by definition, temporary. Its effects may be relieved by job information and aids to worker mobility. For example, workers can be provided job counseling, or payments can be made to finance a worker's move to a new industrial location where jobs are more plentiful.

Cyclical Unemployment

The term "mass unemployment" brings to mind the more awesome evil of **cyclical unemployment**—unemployment associated with *cycles* of economic activity. The Great Depression provides the best illustration of this type of unemployment. During the Great Depression, the rate of unemployment reached as high as 25 percent of the labor force.

Typically, economic activity grows in spurts. Periods of great optimism and growth are followed by slower growth or decline. Once homes are equipped with color televisions, dishwashers, and garbage compactors, opportunities for further retail sales diminish. Retailers cut back on inventories and cancel orders to wholesalers. Ultimately, factory orders are cut, and workers are laid off. The whole economic system seems to pause before the next round of innovations brings on a new outpouring of gadgets and the cycle swings upward again.

Cyclical swings in employment are most severe in the industries producing durable goods.

Purchase of an auto, refrigerator, or machine can be postponed if family heads are worried about their jobs. Cyclical swings are less severe in the production of nondurable goods and services. Purchase of food, clothing, and health services, for instance, cannot be postponed.

When consumer demand declines, blue-collar production workers are more likely to suffer unemployment than professional or supervisory personnel. One reason is the specialized functions of these latter workers, which the firm cannot afford to lose to other firms. Another is the fact that many professional workers are covered by job contracts that protect their jobs.

Federal economic policy to stimulate consumer demand was developed following the Depression as a means of controlling cyclical unemployment. Expansionary fiscal and monetary policy make cyclical unemployment less a threat to our economic system today than in former years.

Structural Unemployment

More threatening to our prosperity and social health is the problem of structural unemployment. **Structural unemployment** is caused by an imbalance between the *structure* of the labor force on the one hand and the requirements of modern industry on the other. Where the available labor skills fail to correspond to the needs of industry, there will be unemployment. Substantial unemployment may persist even though there are job vacancies. Structural unemployment is worsened by the entry of untrained workers (such as teenagers) into the labor force.

The greatest needs in business today are for skilled workers and for workers in the growing service sector. For example, there are extreme shortages of workers in machine trades, engineering, nursing, transport, and finance.

Federal and state programs to train workers in new skills, better job information and counseling, and private on-the-job training should help relieve structural unemployment.

AIDS TO UNEMPLOYED WORKERS

Government has established a number of programs to deal with the problem of unemployment. One such program is the national unemployment insurance system, part of the Social Security Act of 1935. The states administer this program, within federal guidelines. Private nonfarm workers and certain state employees are covered. (Separate programs cover workers not covered under this plan.)

Unemployment benefits are financed by a tax on employers and are available to persons who have lost their jobs and are actively seeking employment. These unemployed persons are normally paid benefits up to a maximum of twenty-six weeks. During the high unemployment years of the 1970s, emergency legislation provided additional benefits for up to sixty-five weeks in some states. Funds for additional benefits come from general federal tax revenues.

Benefits under the insurance program range from one half to two thirds of a worker's average weekly wage. Some states also provide allowances for children or for a nonworking spouse. Weekly benefits in 1980 averaged almost $100.00.

Some union contracts now provide additional private unemployment compensation. United Auto Workers' contracts have established Supplemental Unemployment Benefits (SUBs) financed by employers. Under combined state and private programs, total compensation amounts to approximately 95 percent of regular earnings for auto workers. Because benefits are not taxed, however, the actual purchasing power of unemployment benefits is greater than the numbers suggest.

In addition to income-maintenance programs, public-service employment programs developed by the federal government provide many jobs for the unemployed. The first major program of this sort was the Works Progress Administration (WPA) of the 1930s. During the 1960s, the Neighborhood Youth Corps and Operation Mainstream provided jobs for youths and the elderly. In 1974, the Comprehensive Employment and Training Act (CETA) established training programs, public-service jobs, summer youth programs, and on-the-job training in areas where unemployment was greater than 6.5 percent.

Public-service jobs may help workers maintain or improve their skills as well as help produce useful goods and services. However, when these jobs begin to compete with employment opportunities in the private sector, they should be cut back. Otherwise, excessive demand for labor will push all wages up and add to inflation. In 1981 the Reagan administration proposed to cut many of these programs as part of its program to reduce government spending.

UNEMPLOYMENT AND INFLATION

In years past, the levels of unemployment and inflation have tended to move in opposite directions. High levels of unemployment have been associated with low levels of price inflation; low unemployment has generally meant greater price inflation. Why has this been so?

The answer has to do with the availability of resources. As the economy approaches its full capacity, resources become scarcer and their prices rise. At full employment (zero unemployment), employers must bid resources away from their current employments by offering higher pay. Then higher resource costs become built into the prices of finished goods, increasing inflation. On the other hand, when unemployment is high, resources become more plentiful and their prices tend to drop. Accordingly, the prices of finished goods drop (or at least fail to rise).

The Phillips Curve

A **Phillips curve** illustrates the usual inverse relationshp between unemployment and inflation. The curve was developed by a British economist, A. W. Phillips, to show the results of his studies of unemployment and inflation in Britain. It slopes downward, in keeping with the usual inverse rela-

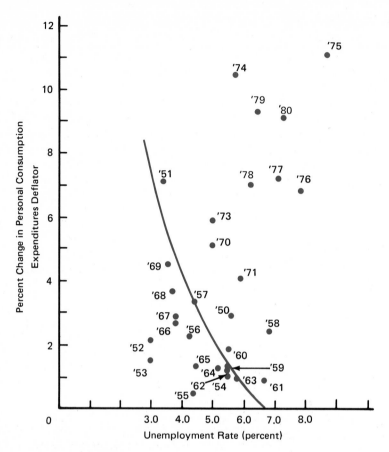

Figure 11.2   Unemployment Rate and Price.
The Phillips curve shows the historical relationship between inflation and unemployment. In the past, as unemployment increased, price inflation tended to fall. In recent years, high levels of unemployment have been associated with high levels of inflation.
Source: *Economic Report of the President,* January 1981.

tionship between the variables. The Phillips curve in Figure 11.2 is drawn to show unemployment and inflation in the United States for the years 1950–80. For the years 1950–69, the relationship between unemployment and inflation was inverse, as expected.

When unemployment and inflation move in opposite directions, an economy may fall within either of the following ranges on the curve:

1. excessive inflation with low levels of unemployment (e.g., 1951);

2. unacceptable levels of unemployment with virtual price stability, i.e., almost zero inflation (e.g., 1961);

3. moderate inflation with moderate unemployment (e.g., 1957).

Our democratic society has tended to favor the third alternative, which imposes fewer hardships on the general public. As a result, most of the points on Figure 11.2 cluster around the center of the Phillips curve. Whenever economic conditions began to move toward either of the extremes, (1) or (2), monetary and fiscal policy have been used to push the economy back toward the center. Test yourself: should expansionary or contractionary policies be used to correct the conditions at (1)? at (2)?

A Shift of the Phillips Curve

More recently, the U.S. economy has experienced a fourth alternative position on the Phillips Curve:

4. excessive inflation *and* unacceptable levels of unemployment!

This situation is represented by a point *off* the historic Phillips curve and is shown by points for the years 1970–80 on Figure 11.2.

Look at the points for the years 1970–80. With extremely high values of both variables, it has been impossible to select monetary and fiscal policies for correcting both problems. Expansionary policies to reduce unemployment would worsen already serious inflation, and contractionary policies to correct inflation would increase already severe unemployment.

The existence of both excessive inflation and unacceptable levels of unemployment has led some analysts to conclude that the curve itself has been shifting to the right. A rightward shift would mean higher levels of inflation associated with each level of unemployment.

How can the shift be explained?

Three explanations have been offered.

Expectations

Many problems of adjustment in economics can be blamed on expectations. If employed workers ex-

pect continued inflation, they may demand excessive wage increases; higher wage costs, in turn, are reflected in future price increases without an accompanying increase in employment. Likewise, if manufacturers expect continued increases in production costs, they may mark up the prices of final goods in order to stay ahead of cost increases. In either case, excessive inflation may continue even when there is substantial unemployment.

Structural Elements

Another explanation blames the shift in the Phillips curve on structural elements in the economy. Advancing technology has changed the type of labor needed in production, but our labor force has been slow to adapt its skills to changing needs. The result is substantial unemployment at the same time that many jobs are unfilled.

Some analysts suggest that there may be some "natural rate" of unemployment that will always exist regardless of government's monetary and fiscal policies. The natural rate has been estimated at about 6 percent; its size depends on the numbers of workers whose skills are inappropriate for employment. If this explanation is correct, the Phillips curve would become roughly vertical at 6 percent. (Note that this is true of many of the recent points on Figure 11.2.)

Other Factors

Financial conditions may also have affected the position of the Phillips curve: the availability of unemployment compensation and other income-support programs; the increased wealth of the labor force; and the higher level of consumer credit. These factors allow workers to maintain their standards of living even while unemployed. Their job search may not be as vigorous as in years past; thus periods of unemployment are longer. Also, since these financial factors allow consumer spending levels to remain fairly stable, total demand for goods and services remains strong, adding to inflationary pressures.

Self-Check

1. The classical economists believed that:
   a. wages would fall when the demand for labor falls.
   b. at lower wages, labor would be fully employed.
   c. competition would make wages and prices flexible.
   d. lower wage rates would not necessarily mean lower real wages.
   e. all of the above.

2. Which of the following is not generally a result of unemployment?
   a. development of new skills during leisure hours
   b. high crime rates and social unrest
   c. loss of material production
   d. lower standards of living
   e. emotional distress

3. Which of the following types of unemployment seems most difficult to correct?
   a. frictional unemployment
   b. cyclical unemployment
   c. structural unemployment
   d. Phillips unemployment
   e. All can be corrected with expansionary fiscal and monetary policy.

4. Public-service employment has all but which of the following advantages?
   a. producing generally useful output
   b. helping maintain worker skills
   c. not competing with the private demand for workers
   d. providing on-the-job training for youths
   e. providing spending power for workers who would otherwise be unemployed

5. Expectations can affect unemployment by:
   a. increasing hiring when wages are expected to rise.
   b. increasing wage demands when prices are expected to rise.
   c. increasing prices when wages are expected to rise.
   d. reducing hiring when wages are expected to rise.
   e. (b), (c), and (d).

6. A Phillips curve shows the relationship between:
   a. employment and prices.
   b. labor force and unemployment.
   c. labor force and prices.
   d. unemployment and prices.
   e. economic growth and prices.

Theory in Practice

MINIMUM WAGES AND UNEMPLOYMENT

Minimum-wage legislation is often presented as a means of improving the incomes of low-skilled workers. A legally enforced minimum wage acts like a price floor to keep wages from falling below a legal minimum.

The first legal minimum wage was established in 1938, when a minimum of 25 cents per hour was set for certain employees. In 1977, Congress voted a new schedule of wage rates which increased the minimum wage from the 1977 level of $2.30 to $3.35 in 1981. The legislation also changed eligibility requirements, making small businesses exempt from the minimum wage law.

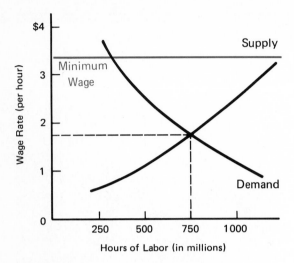

Figure 11.3 Effects of a Minimum Wage.
A minimum wage has the effect of a price floor. A surplus of labor is supplied at the minimum wage rate. A minimum wage may work against those it is intended to help by increasing a firm's costs of production and thereby lowering employment levels.

The result of the legislation was expected to be: (1) pay raises totaling several billion dollars to workers now getting less than the minimum and additional pay increases to other workers to maintain wage differentials; (2) higher prices, particularly in labor-intensive retail and service establishments; and (3) higher property taxes as local governments attempt to offset the rising costs of hiring public employees.

A more serious result, however, may be an increase in unemployment. When wages are set higher than the equilibrium wage, employers will move up their labor demand curves and hire fewer workers. Remember that firms will hire workers only up to the point at which the value of the output of the last worker is just offset by the cost of hiring him or her.

Again, we can illustrate this idea with a graph. Figure 11.3 shows the market for a certain

type of unskilled labor. In a free market, the equilibrium wage is $1.80 per hour, at which 750,000 hours of labor will be demanded and supplied. How many hours will be demanded and supplied when a government-imposed minimum of $3.35 takes effect?

The contractionary effects of the minimum wage may be hardest on those groups least able to find other employment. For example, the demand for unskilled workers and teenagers is highly elastic. Employers can readily substitute away from the use of these workers when their wages rise (although there is a move to set the minimum for teenagers some percentage below the legal minimum). Because of this, people most in need of work may be unable to find employment. This means that the results of the minimum wage may be the opposite of what was intended.

This problem presents a dilemma for the policymaker. Should there be a minimum-wage law if the results include lower levels of employment, higher production costs, and price inflation? Or should labor markets be free, even though the result might be insufficient earnings for some workers?

THE DISTRIBUTION OF UNEMPLOYMENT

Levels of unemployment differ widely among various groups in the labor force. Unemployment is higher among teenagers than other age groups, higher among blacks than whites, and higher among women than men. Table 11.1 shows unemployment rates broken down into these three categories.

Some groups enter and leave the labor force frequently. Their high turnover rate gives them a higher unemployment rate than the national average. Many teenagers and some women, for example, are counted as unemployed if they are seeking a job while working as a student or housewife.

Table 11.1   Unemployment Rates by Age, Race, Sex (1980 figures).

	Unemployment Rate
Whites	6.3
Men, 20 years and over	5.2
Women, 20 years and over	5.6
Teenagers (male)	16.2
Teenagers (female)	14.8
Blacks and Other Minorities	13.2
Men, 20 years and over	13.3
Women, 20 years and over	13.1
Teenagers (male)	34.9
Teenagers (female)	36.9
Total Unemployment Rate	7.1

Source: *Economic Report of the President,* January 1981.

Experienced women who regard employment as permanent have about the same unemployment rate as men. Similarly, teenagers who expect employment to be permanent have lower unemployment rates than students.

High turnover rates for teenagers may reflect the fact that they are changing jobs to achieve advancement and greater experience. Also, higher unemployment rates among low-skilled teenagers may be partly a result of minimum-wage legislation.

Workers with special education or training have relatively lower rates of unemployment than less-educated groups. They are more likely to go directly from one job to another without ever being unemployed. White-collar workers in clerical or supervisory jobs are less subject to cyclical fluctuations in employment than blue-collar workers.

Unemployment among blacks has been about twice that of whites in recent decades. However, when only experienced adult workers are considered, unemployment rates are almost the same for both races. Some of the remaining difference in unemployment rates between races may be ex-plained by discrimination, although state fair-employment laws and the Civil Rights Act of 1964 have helped reduce differences resulting from discrimination.

UNEMPLOYMENT AND THE CAPITAL SHORTAGE

A careful reader of this chapter might think that once and for all we have solved the *Economic Problem!* Remember we began this text by pointing out that every nation faces the problem of *scarce resources* and *unlimited wants*. If there is substantial unemployment, might we conclude that we have *too many* resources?

A more correct conclusion would be that our supply of labor doesn't always exactly match up with other available resources. Labor resources must be used along with capital resources: improved land, buildings, equipment, and inventories. In fact, the average production worker in manufacturing works with invested capital worth more than $50,000. In some manufacturing industries, average invested capital per production worker is much higher: petroleum, $345,000; chemicals, $150,000; tobacco, $115,000. Non-manufacturing industries like transportation, utilities, finance, real estate, insurance, and mining require still higher levels of capital investment per worker.

The United States has been fortunate in the richness of our resource base. Production and incomes have been high, permitting high levels of saving for investing in capital resources. In the last half-century real wealth has grown about 2.5 percent a year. Growth in capital stock has been slightly greater than growth in the labor force, providing more capital for each worker every year.

Nevertheless, our need for capital is increasing. New health, safety, and environmental regulations call for more costly equipment. Technological change has made some existing capital obsolete. If we are to employ our expanding work-

Viewpoint

A FOUR-DAY WORKWEEK?

We have classified unemployment as cyclical or structural. In practice, it may be difficult to separate the two types precisely. On the down side of the business cycle when production starts to fall, the first workers to lose their jobs are often blacks, teenagers, and women. These groups are also most subject to structural unemployment. What is the best way to help these cyclically/structurally unemployed workers?

Some labor unions believe they have an answer. A new proposal being tested in some firms is a four-day workweek. A shorter week would spread the work over more employees and reduce lay-offs. In general, the proposed shorter workweek would involve no cut in wages.

A forty-hour workweek has been the standard in manufacturing since the Fair Labor Standards Act was passed in the 1930s. In recent years, some firms have been experimenting with four ten-hour days as a means of reducing employee transportation costs. Other firms have cut hours to thirty-two with the hope that improved employee morale would bring on increased productivity. In many cases, this did not happen. In fact, labor costs rose and forced prices up. Higher labor costs might be the chief disadvantage of the shorter workweek.

One union has already signed a contract that comes close to a four-day week. Auto workers are often victims of cyclical/structural unemployment. Spending for autos drops off severely in a business recession, and auto workers face long lay-offs. In 1977 the United Auto Workers' contract provided for more than forty paid vacation days a year, a major step toward the four-day week.

In general, business firms resist such a change. To establish the four-day standard throughout the economy would require a new labor law, not likely in the near future.

---

force, new investment must provide the necessary tools and equipment.

Over the years, gross private domestic investment spending in the United States has been fairly stable at 16 to 17 percent of Gross National Product. The level of investment each year depends on business expectations of profit. Conditions of recent years have made many business firms more pessimistic with respect to future profits:

1. Frequent recessions have left firms with unsold goods and brought on business failures;

2. Inflated costs and wages and the persistent threat of government price controls have reduced profit projections;

3. Tax bills have risen faster than inflation and reduced funds for investment;

4. New environmental and health regulations might make new equipment unusable.

While profit expectations have been falling, the cost of borrowing investment funds has been rising. Lenders have increased interest charges to compensate for expected inflation. Government has been competing with business borrowers for a limited quantity of funds, driving interest rates up still farther. And finally, many holders of funds prefer to use their savings for safe, secure purchases like raw land, jewels, works of art, and gold. These purchases are not investments in the economic sense; that is, they are not capital resources capable of producing goods and services. Still, purchases like these reduce the savings available for true investment and keep interest rates on business loans high.

There is no single solution to the problem of insufficient growth of capital resources. An improved economic climate would probably improve business profit expectations. Greater confidence in government tax and regulatory policies would help, too. Without a substantial revival of private investment spending, the problem of unemployment becomes increasingly a government problem. And government may not have the answer!

EMPLOYMENT OPPORTUNITIES FOR THE FUTURE

Where are the greatest employment opportunities for young people entering the labor force during the 1980s? The demand for workers with particular skills or aptitudes will be high: professionals, technicians, managers, and clerical workers. Openings will grow more slowly in blue-collar fields.

Some service fields such as state and local government, trade, and financial services will also be expanding. Shortages will appear for health personnel, general salespeople, and accountants.

Listed in Table 11.2 are some job categories with expected annual job openings in 1990. The projections are taken from a survey by the U.S. Department of Labor.

Table 11.2 Projected Annual Job Openings, 1978–90.

Stenographers, secretaries	305,000
Retail trade, salespeople	226,000
Building custodians	180,000
Cashiers	119,000
Bookkeepers	96,000
Nurses' aides, orderlies	94,000
Cooks, chefs	86,000
Elementary-school teachers	86,000
Registered nurses	85,000
Assemblers	77,000
Waiters, waitresses	70,000
Supervisors	69,000
Accountants	61,000
Practical nurses	60,000
Typists	59,000
Carpenters	58,000
Industrial-machine repairmen	58,000
Construction workers	49,000
Bank clerks	45,000
Private household workers	45,000
Receptionists	41,000
Auto mechanics	37,000
Lawyers	37,000
Factory inspectors	35,000
Welders, arc cutters	35,000
Cosmetologists	28,000
Social workers	22,000
Long distance truck drivers	21,500
Machine-tool operators	19,600
Bank tellers	17,000
Personnel workers	17,000
File clerks	16,500
Police officers	16,500
Medical lab workers	14,800
Computer operators	12,500
College teachers	11,000
Drafters	11,000
Electrical engineers	10,500
Computer programmers	9200
Civil engineers	7800
Secondary-school teachers	7200
Chemists	6100
Airplane pilots	3800

SUMMARY

1. According to classical economists, in a smoothly functioning free-market system, unemployment would be only temporary. Wages would rise and fall with changes in the demand for labor, and all those willing to work at the equilibrium wage would be hired. Prices would fluctuate, too, so that real wages would not fall as much as money wages.

2. Organized groups of employers and workers interfere with the smooth adjustments under the market system. The result has been periods of unemployment with a substantial loss of goods and services that might have been produced. The loss has been called the GNP gap.

3. Frictional unemployment is a normal result of temporary idleness while changing jobs. Frictional unemployment may be relieved by policies to provide job information and to ease mobility into new types of employment.

4. Cyclical unemployment is associated with a decline in total spending. It is especially severe in industries producing durable goods whose purchase can be postponed. Cyclical unemployment is treated by expansionary monetary and fiscal policies to stimulate total spending.

5. Structural unemployment results from an imbalance between the skills of the labor force and the needs of modern industry. This type of unemployment may be relieved by job counseling and training.

6. In recent years the problem of unemployment has worsened and has often been accompanied by inflation. The usual inverse relationship between unemployment and inflation is shown by the Phillips curve. Changed conditions within the economy may have increased the levels of unemployment considered to be normal.

7. Unemployment rates differ among different groups of workers. In general, however, experienced workers during their peak years of productivity have about the same rate of unemployment. Young people and women may enter and leave the labor force more often and thus experience higher rates of unemployment. Blacks may suffer higher unemployment rates as a result of past discrimination.

8. Unemployment insurance helps workers maintain a moderate standard of living even while unemployed. Public-service employment provides jobs for the unemployed through the federal government. The nation's capital stock must grow to provide jobs for an expanding labor force.

TERMS TO REMEMBER

GNP gap: the difference between actual production of goods and services and that which would have been produced with the economy at full employment.

labor force: all people aged 16 and over who are currently employed or who are unemployed but actively seeking employment.

frictional unemployment: unemployment caused by the movement of labor from job to job or the movement of new workers into the labor force; considered a normal condition.

cyclical unemployment: unemployment caused by a decline in economic activity and a drop in total spending; treated with expansionary fiscal and monetary policy.

structural unemployment: unemployment caused by an imbalance between the structure or nature of the labor force and the requirements of modern industry; treated with job training and counseling.

Phillips curve: a graph showing the inverse relationship between price inflation and unemployment rates in years past.

TOPICS FOR DISCUSSION

1. Define the following terms and discuss how each is involved in the problem of unemployment:

> GNP gap
> Phillips curve
> ''natural rate'' of unemployment

2. Distinguish clearly among the three types of unemployment and describe the types of policies designed to remedy each.

3. Under the Comprehensive Employment and Training Act of 1974, the federal government began pumping many millions of dollars into state and local programs for public-service employment. Thousands of new jobs were created for unemployed workers, veterans, and welfare recipients. Jobs were in public schools, libraries, parks, hospitals, and fire and police departments. Workers were given on-the-job training in skills which would help them eventually move into employment in the private sector.

How does this program fit into our discussion of unemployment? What problems can you foresee with a program of this kind?

4. The recession of 1974–75 created a conflict within the labor force over seniority rules. Labor union contracts protected the jobs of experienced members by a "last hired, first fired" rule; this means that when lay-offs are necessary, the last workers hired will be the first fired.

In many firms the last workers hired are the minorities who have recently won job opportunities under the Equal Employment Opportunity Act. The result is that women and blacks are more subject to lay-offs and are less able to weather a long period of unemployment.

This dilemma has sharply divided the labor movement, producing problems for labor leaders. How would you resolve the problem?

5. During the 1980s, large numbers of workers will be added to the labor force as a result of the post-World War II "baby boom." A substantial number of new jobs must be created to absorb these workers and the many women and minority workers who will be competing for employment opportunities. Furthermore, many more college-trained workers will be competing for job openings requiring higher education. What are the social aspects of this problem? How might the new conditions change all our outlooks about what constitutes a successful life?

6. The classical economists believed that wage reductions would increase hiring. However, unions generally resist wage reductions. As a result, much of the government's employment policy in recent decades has brought on higher *prices* rather than more jobs. How has this policy affected *real* wages? How has it affected profits? How might it stimulate employment? If unions refuse to allow wage gains to lag behind price increases, what will be the result?

SUGGESTED READINGS

Collins, Lora S. "Straightening Out the Phillips Curve," *Across the Board,* March 1980, pp. 11–16.

Galbraith, James K., "Why We Have No Full Employment Policy," *Working Papers,* March/April 1978, p. 27.

General Accounting Office, "How to Dissuade Some People from Looking for Work," *Across the Board,* December 1979, pp. 19–24.

Guzzardi, Walter, Jr., "How to Deal with the 'New Unemployment,'" *Fortune,* October 1976, p. 132.

Kaufman, Roger, "Why the U.S. Unemployment Rate Is So High," *Challenge,* May/June 1978, pp. 40–49.

Miller, G. William, "The Not Impossible Goal: Full Employment and Price Stability," *Across the Board,* March 1978, p. 5.

Osterman, Paul, "Understanding Youth Unemployment," *Working Papers,* January/February 1978, p. 58.

Piore, Michael J., "Unemployment and Inflation: An Alternative View," *Challenge,* May/June 1978, pp. 24–31.

Stein, Herbert, "Thatcherism's Message for America," *Fortune,* June 2, 1980, p. 94.

Stein, Herbert, "A Way to Keep Economic Policy from Overshooting," *Fortune,* June 4, 1979.

Wachter, Michael L., "The Nature of the Unemployment Problem," *Challenge,* May/June 1978, pp. 32–39.

Welch, Finish, "The Trouble with the Minimum Wage," *Across the Board,* August 1979, pp. 36–49.

"Why Recovering Economies Don't Create Enough Jobs," *Business Week,* March 22, 1976, p. 114.

CHAPTER 12

Poverty and Income Distribution

or Poor Is
a Four-Letter Word

Tools for Study

Learning Objectives

After reading this chapter, you will be able to:

1. discuss the origins of our attitudes toward poverty.
2. describe the extent and composition of the problem.
3. list the three classifications of poverty.
4. discuss the advantages and disadvantages of a policy of direct payments to the poor.

Issues Covered

How is the scientific method applied to economic problems?
What has been accomplished in treating poverty?
What's ahead for social security?
What are the causes of urban poverty?

There is a story told of a little Spanish town whose only distinction was its annual poetry contest. Eager contestants came from miles around to compete for recognition. For the winners, three prizes were awarded: third prize was an artfully crafted silver rose; second prize, a dazzling golden rose; and first prize (can you guess it?) was a *real* rose.

Aside from its pleasing quaintness, the story allows us to compare value structures in different societies. In the first place, a literary contest would probably not be received with much enthusiasm in our materialistic society. And our citizens would certainly demand a different arrangement of awards!

We may conclude that standards of performance and reward differ sharply among people. The existence of poverty depends to a large extent on these standards. Whatever the value structure that emerges in a particular society, it virtually *ensures* a poor status for those at the bottom.

This means that definitions of poverty will differ from culture to culture. A family with a yearly income of $5000 may be quite well off in a nation such as India but below the poverty line in the United States. In primitive societies, one's wealth may be based on the number of pigs or cattle one owns. (High social status has at various times and places been based on quality of penmanship, length of ear lobes, skill in directing a javelin, and even the ability to detect a pea through numerous mattresses!)

THE SIZE AND SHAPE OF THE PROBLEM

In the United States, a definition of poverty is established by the federal government and based on the estimated cost of a nutritionally adequate diet. By the government's definition, a family is poor if its annual income is less than three times the amount necessary to purchase such a diet.

The poverty level is adjusted each year for price changes, and it differs according to family size, sex of family head, and type of residence (farm or nonfarm). The average poverty threshold in 1980 for a nonfarm family of four was $8410.

Table 12.1 gives a breakdown of persons below the government's low-income threshold in

selected years. As the table shows, only about 12 percent of all persons in the nation were classified as poor in 1976, compared with 22 percent in 1959. (Government in-kind benefits such as food stamps, public housing, and health care are not included as income in this classification.)

The decline in poverty in the United States is largely a result of economic growth. Labor skills and productivity have improved, and greater participation of wives in the labor market has increased family earnings. The greatest gains were for nonwhite families with a male head. Regrettably, a large percentage of female-headed families continue to be classified as poor, particularly among nonwhite families.

When all low-income families are considered together, female-headed families constitute 49 percent of all poor families, even though the percentage of female-headed families in the population as a whole is much smaller. This is probably because female heads of families often are not properly trained for employment or are prevented from seeking employment by the responsibility of caring for young children. Rural families and the aged

Table 12.1 Families Below the Low-Income Level.

	1959	1969	1972	1976
Percent of all white families with male head	14.7%	6.0%	5.6%	4.9%
Percent of all nonwhite families with male head	51.0%	19.8%	18.5%	13.9%
Percent of all white families with female head	40.2%	29.1%	27.4%	25.5%
Percent of all nonwhite families with female head	75.6%	57.8%	57.7%	50.0%
Total number of persons (in millions)	39.5	24.1	24.5	25.0
Percent of all persons in the nation	22.4%	12.1%	11.9%	11.8%

Sources: *Economic Report of the President,* February 1974, and *Statistical Abstract of the United States,* 1977.

also constitute a larger percentage of the poor than their percentage of the population as a whole.

More than one fourth of heads of poor families work, but their wages are not enough to move them above the poverty level.* Lack of education and skills limits their employment opportunities to the shrinking number of unskilled jobs. Most of the poor are children, old people, or women—only a small percent of the poor are able-bodied men.

CLASSIFICATIONS OF POVERTY

In addition to the statistical measures of poverty, the poor may be classified according to the sources of their poverty. Then, appropriate remedies can be suggested to aid the persons in the various classifications.

Business Cycle Poverty

Some families are temporarily poor because of fluctuations in the national economy. This **cyclical poverty** arises from a low level of total spending for goods and services. When spending drops, the demand for labor falls, throwing many unskilled and semiskilled laborers out of work. The Great Depression of the 1930s and the recession of 1974–75 pushed many families over the poverty line when the family wage-earner was laid off.

Cyclical poverty may be treated by fiscal and monetary policy designed to keep total spending high. Whenever private spending falls short of the full-employment level of aggregate demand, government action may be needed in the form of personal and corporate tax cuts, government spending for local or national projects, or expansion of the supply of money to encourage business investment.

Insular Poverty

Some families are trapped in islands of poverty when a particular industry or craft collapses, leaving workers with no other source of income. The most familiar examples of insular poverty are the decline of the coal-mining industry in Appalachia and the cutbacks in the space program in Florida.*

Insular poverty results from human immobilities—the difficulty of leaving familiar surroundings or abandoning a familiar trade to begin a new way of life. (For many families, five people to a room in a rural shack among family and friends is preferable to five people to a room in an urban slum, even if employment opportunities are somewhat greater in the city.)

Insular poverty is not easily treated. In particular, geographic pockets of poverty present a difficult dilemma. The question is whether to move new factories to the poverty areas or to move unemployed labor out to other industrialized areas. The first solution may be impractical from an economic standpoint. The second may run into human and social barriers.

One solution for workers whose jobs have been made technically obsolete is retraining for jobs in growing sectors of the economy. The cost of training may be looked upon as an investment in increased worker productivity. (However, this too may run into human barriers, with many workers being reluctant to take on new vocations.)

The Economic Development Act of 1965 and the Appalachian Regional Development Act of 1966 focused on area redevelopment in an effort to create new jobs. In 1974, the Comprehensive Employment and Training Act (CETA) began providing on-the-job training and work experience to Indians, migrants, and Job Corps participants. Efforts like these aim to correct insular poverty, but real gains have been slow. In 1981, the Reagan

---

* Working full-time at the minimum wage would yield annual income of $6968, below the poverty line for a non-farm family of four (1981).

* Insular poverty might also be associated with the baseball and air traffic controllers' strikes in 1981.

Viewpoint

ORIGINS OF OUR VIEWS ON POVERTY

In 1859, Charles Darwin's revolutionary work on evolution, *On the Origin of Species,* was published. Darwin's theory of evolution depended on the principle of "natural selection," or survival of the fittest. According to Darwin, nature would "select" those animals best suited for carrying on the stream of life. The weak and unadaptable of a species would perish; only the strongest would survive and reproduce.

A doctrine known as *Social Darwinism,* based on Darwin's theories, became popular in the latter nineteenth century. The doctrine seemed to justify opposition to government aid to weak or incompetent persons. To try to improve the living standards of persons who could not care for themselves, it was reasoned, would be to interfere with the laws of nature.

It was not difficult to find ways to reconcile such cold-bloodedness with religious and political principles as well. The Puritan ethic supported the idea of self-sufficiency, independence, and individualism. Religious sects like the Calvinists felt little responsibility for the well-being of others, and they rejected the idea of a paternalistic government. Personal wealth came to be seen as a sign that one was leading a life pleasing to God.

Democratic political theory supported the idea of individualism. In a free and democratic society, no individual would be locked into a particular economic or social class. All people would have unlimited opportunity to succeed (or fail) in line with society's evaluation of their particular energies and skills.

Therefore, with scientific and religious support, revolutions were fought to establish equality. Yet a disturbing dilemma arose: there seemed to be a contradiction between *equality of opportunity* and *equality of results*. In fact, *equality* of opportunity generally meant sharp *inequality* of results!

If all people were allowed absolute freedom in the pursuit of personal opportunity, their freedom would inevitably result in misery for the least competent. On the other hand, if all people were assured equal results in standards of living, a decline in motivation would diminish opportunity and thwart the drive for personal achievement.

The dilemma is still with us.

administration proposed to cut government jobs programs as a means of reducing federal expenditures and slowing inflation.

Categorical Poverty

Some people are locked into poverty because of personal inadequacies that prevent them from functioning within our economic system. These poor are classified according to *categories* and include the physically and mentally handicapped, the emotionally unstable, the chronically ill or aged, and children.

Victims of **categorical poverty** require regular, dependable support through public-assistance programs. Social workers are trained to locate poor people and inform them of the available aid and to administer special-purpose programs.

The categorical approach to public assistance originated with the Social Security Act of 1935. A major provision of the act is the Old Age, Survivors, Disability, and Health Insurance (OASDHI) program. Regular contributions from workers and employers finance benefits provided under this program. Benefits are paid on the basis of past contribution rather than need. Employers and employees each contribute 6.65 percent of earnings up to a certain level of income ($29,700 in 1981).

Social security legislation also provides non-insurance benefits or relief. Payments are given to the needy even if they have made no past contributions to the program. One noninsurance program which has grown to include two thirds of public assistance payments is Aid to Families with Dependent Children (AFDC). Other noninsurance aid is provided to the elderly, the blind, and the disabled under the Supplemental Security Income program (SSI).

In 1961, the federal food stamp program was started to provide further aid to needy families. Under this program, a family of four with no income is given about $150 in food stamps each month. Other poor families receive various amounts of food stamps, depending on their income during the month. Until 1977 recipients of food stamps paid a portion of their value. About 19 million people used food stamps in 1980 at a cost to the government of about $11 billion.

Total outlay of all these aid programs in 1980 was about $193 billion, a large part of which represents insured benefits under OASDHI.

A major objection to the categorical approach to aid is the vast and costly bureaucracy that it requires. Furthermore, there may be undesirable side effects for families receiving aid. The most serious side-effect is desertion, since AFDC aid is generally provided only to families without a father. Moreover, many poor people may not fit into any of the established categories. About half the nation's poor receive no public payments of any kind. On the other hand, many nonpoor may qualify for several categories and receive more than their fair share. Finally, the poor themselves object to categorical aid because they feel it is demeaning. The Reagan administration proposed to reduce federal welfare costs by cutting out waste and fraud in welfare programs.

AID PROPOSALS

Objections to current aid programs have come from business leaders, sociologists, and economists from both extremes of the ideological spectrum. Both Milton Friedman, a staunch defender of free markets, and Robert Theobald, an advocate of radical social reform, have argued in favor of direct aid to the poor. They would eliminate all aid categories and provide financial assistance solely on the basis of need.

Direct Grants

To raise the incomes of all poor families above the low-income threshold in 1980 would have required income transfers of about $37 billion. This is only about 1 percent of GNP and one third of the normal annual growth rate of GNP. (The $193 billion spent on income-support payments in 1980 could have been divided among the 9 million poor families for a direct income grant of more than $20,000, well above the poverty level.)

Direct grants could be administered without establishing a new bureaucracy, perhaps through the existing Internal Revenue Service. Grants would be made in cash so that recipients could pay for food, housing, and health and social services in the open market. For this reason, grants would provide economic incentives to business in the private sector. Direct grants would strengthen an individual's sense of responsibility to budget family income wisely. A disadvantage of grants would be the social stigma often attached to the "dole."

With the exception of the United States and Japan, all industrialized nations now pay a family allowance to all families based on number of family members. Payment of the grant is guaranteed to all families, regardless of income. Under a progressive tax structure, a portion of the total earned and unearned income is then returned to the government in income taxes. Thus, at very low levels of income, the family would keep the entire grant. At some level the grant would be just offset by income taxes. And at higher incomes, taxes would exceed the grant.

Negative Income Tax

A program based on the same principle as direct grants is the **negative income tax**, first proposed by Milton Friedman.* This plan is based on the fact that poor families have unused tax *credits*.

Our tax schedule allows tax credits in the form of exemptions of $1000 per person and a standard deduction from taxable income of roughly $1500 per family. But families whose income is too low to pay taxes do not receive the benefits of credits.

---

*The current Earned Income Tax Credit for poor families is a kind of negative income tax.

Under Friedman's proposal, families earning less than some established level of tax credits would pay no tax. Instead, they would receive an allowance or *negative* tax amounting to some percentage of the short-fall.

For instance, a family of four would be entitled to total deductions and exemptions of roughly $5500: $(4 \times \$1000) + \$1500 = \$5500$. Families with incomes of less than $5500 would receive some fraction of the difference between earned income and the $5500 tax credit. A typical family earning $4000 annually might pay no tax but receive a payment of, say, 50 percent of their unused tax credit: $.5(\$5500 - \$4000) = .5(\$1500) = \$750$. Total family income would be $4750. Family earnings could rise to $5500 before aid would be cut off.

Both direct grants and a negative income tax would eliminate the need for the welfare bureaucracies that administer categorical aid. Experiments with direct income grants have been conducted in communities in New Jersey, Iowa, and North Carolina. It is hoped that the results will help policymakers predict the possible effects nationwide.

Direct Payments and Economic Incentives

The major objection to public assistance is that it may destroy all incentives to make one's own way in life. This can be a real problem in view of the fact that we depend upon human labor for a large portion of production, particularly in the growing service sector. The disincentive effect is greatest, of course, under plans providing either direct grants or a negative income tax.

If government makes up the entire difference between earned income and some income floor, there is little incentive for an individual to increase earnings. And if government reduces aid dollar for dollar as earned income rises, it is, in effect, collecting a 100 percent tax on additional income. Again, there is little incentive to increase earnings.

The disincentive effect can be reduced by imposing a low tax rate on the earned portion of income. A low tax rate would allow a worker to earn additional income without losing an equal amount of government aid. Total income could rise above the guaranteed floor before grant payments would be cut off. A low tax rate would increase the costs of the program considerably, at least in the short run, but it might also strengthen economic incentives and help relieve critical shortages of low-skilled workers.

Another, less substantial, objection to direct grants is that simply awarding a poor family spending power does nothing to remove the basic causes of poverty. This criticism implies that we can identify and deal directly with the specific characteristics that predispose some people to poverty. Furthermore, it leads to the costly bureaucracy we now employ.

Direct Grants and Inflation

Direct grants may lead to a problem more difficult to handle than poverty—that of inflation. Whenever there is a net increase in incomes, there will be increased demand for goods and services. Unless production also increases, there will be inflationary pressures, as larger amounts of consumer spending compete for the same amount of goods and services.

The threat of inflation makes it important to build an incentive tax structure into a direct grant program so as to encourage increased productivity. Research and training grants and investment tax credits may also encourage increased productivity.

WHAT CAN WE CONCLUDE?

The limited state of knowledge about the causes of poverty leaves us with no real solutions to the problem. Without complete understanding we must fall back on a balanced approach: programs to improve health and nutrition, educational and vocational training, income maintenance, and emergency relief. To be successful, these programs should be carried on within a climate of increasing industrial production and equal opportunity.

A chief disadvantage of any program is its initial cost. Also, it is unlikely that there will be measurable results in any short period of time. One of the characteristics of the American approach to problems is excessive optimism at the start of a new program. Often, highly publicized promises fail to materialize immediately, and disillusionment sets in. As a result, many programs are abandoned prematurely, before a legitimate trial period has elapsed.

Viewpoint

DISCRIMINATION

A major cause of poverty is discrimination: discrimination in access to education or housing and discrimination in employment. Discrimination arises when people are treated differently on some basis other than their individual merit. Discrimination frequently affects blacks and women. The result is low status jobs of low productivity with low earnings and few opportunities for advancement.

Sometimes discrimination is the result of prejudice on the part of an employer, landlord, or school administrator. Although laws prohibit these forms of discrimination, laws are not fully enforced. Sometimes what appears to be discrimination in hiring is really only the result of discrimination in educational opportunities, which makes some workers more productive than others. Sometimes discrimination is actually self-imposed, when blacks or women unconsciously place limits on their own aspirations.

During the 1960s strong federal laws were passed forbidding discrimination on the basis of race, color, religion, sex, national origin, or age. As a result, many schools and business firms established "outreach" programs, seeking members of groups formerly subject to discrimination. In many cases, institutions have reevaluated their admission or hiring standards and eliminated any requirements that do not directly affect an individual's potential job performance.

In spite of these efforts, significant evidence of discrimination remains. Women and blacks are poorly represented in highly paid occupations like business management and production, and they are over-represented in low-paid occupations like clerical and service work. In every occupation the median income of women is only slighty more than half the median income of male workers in the same occupation. One result of low earnings is that one third of female-headed families and one fourth of black families have incomes below the poverty level. For black female-headed families the fraction is more than one-half. Women and blacks experience substantially higher unemployment than average—up to two or three times unemployment rates for other classes of workers.

Discrimination harms us all, whether or not we are ourselves a target of discrimination. When workers are unable to compete freely in the labor market, labor costs are kept artificially high. Higher labor costs raise the prices of many things we buy. When workers are deprived of educational or job opportunities, our economy fails to develop its productive capabilities. Total output is less than it might be. When workers' incomes are held artificially low, they cannot buy the goods and services our industries produce. Profits and economic growth are restrained as a result.

Can you cite specific examples of the harmful effects of discrimination?

Self-Check

1. **Poor people in the United States:**
   a. constitute about 25 percent of the population.
   b. consist mainly of able-bodied men.
   c. include only unemployed people.
   d. are concentrated in industrial areas.
   e. none of the above.

2. **Which of the following is treated primarily by categorical aid programs?**
   a. cyclical poverty
   b. insular poverty
   c. the aged poor
   d. all of the above
   e. none of the above

3. **Which of the following is a disadvantage of a program of direct grants?**
   a. Direct grants would reduce the need for a large bureaucracy.
   b. Direct grants would give the poor money to spend as they see fit.
   c. Taxes may take the entire grant away as earnings rise.
   d. Direct grants do not deal with the real causes of poverty.
   e. Direct grants would abolish categorical types of aid.

4. **Which of the following is not a danger of direct grants or the negative income tax?**
   a. There is a possibility of reducing incentives.
   b. Increased incomes may contribute to inflation.
   c. Some poor people would not receive aid.
   d. There may be a social stigma attached to aid.
   e. Many social workers may become unemployed.

5. **Which of the following terms is paired incorrectly?**
   a. insular poverty—Appalachian Redevelopment Act
   b. cyclical poverty—expansionary fiscal policy
   c. categorical poverty—Aid to Families with Dependent Children
   d. cyclical poverty—contractionary monetary policy
   e. categorical poverty—Social Security Act

Theory in Practice

APPLYING THE SCIENTIFIC METHOD TO ECONOMIC ISSUES

The scientific method of investigation requires that any problem be examined in systematic steps:

1. Clearly define the problem to be analyzed. One of the most baffling problems in economics is the problem of poverty.

2. Gather the data describing and measuring the problem.

3. Organize the data into an understandable arrangement that permits the drawing of an *hypothesis:* a theoretical explanation of the forces at work within the problem.

4. Test the hypothesis by varying the circumstances with the problem and noting the results.

5. Continue to alter the hypothesis until it appears to be a correct explanation of the problem. The

hypothesis is finally accepted if it can be used to predict the actual results of a change in the fundamental data. Then the hypothesis is stated as a law or principle which explains the problem under investigation.

In economic analysis, we would add another step to the scientific method. The *practical* goal of economic analysis is to design *policy* to correct the problem being examined.

Problems of Designing Policy

Economic analysis suffers from a disadvantage not encountered in scientific analysis. It is much more difficult to test hypotheses in a society than in a laboratory. For example, varying the kinds and amounts of government tax policy and aid programs (all the while holding other things constant) is not as easy as varying the temperature in a test tube. For this reason, many economic theories (or hypotheses) cannot be tested to produce definite conclusions and clear policy remedies.

This is especially true of the problem of poverty. There are no clear-cut laws to explain the problem. Consequently, there is no definite policy which is clearly acceptable as a cure.

Over the last several decades various approaches have been developed to deal with poverty. The objectives have been humanitarian as well as economic. Evaluating the results of these programs may be considered a form of hypothesis testing. A successful program may be assumed to be based on a correct assessment of the forces causing poverty. Lack of success would suggest an incorrect assessment of the roots of the problem.

But, again, it is difficult to evaluate results even when a program appears successful. Many forces other than the poverty program may be operating on the problem at one time. A decline in poverty may be a result of general economic growth or better education and health care. Thus, even if a program appears successful, it is impossible to prove whether success is the result of the program alone or of some outside influence.

Actual Experience

The Aid to Families with Dependent Children program (AFDC) illustrates the difficulty of designing a program when scientific analysis and control are not possible. The original purpose of the program was to assist children whose fathers were unable to support them because of death or disability. In 1930, about 75 percent of the fathers involved fit these classifications. The remainder were absent through divorce, separation, or desertion.

The availability of benefits under the program has had the unintended effect of encouraging fathers to desert their families. As a result, the number of families receiving aid is now five times the number receiving aid in 1950. The 3 million families now receiving aid under AFDC constitute almost 6 percent of the nation's population.

How can we deal with the problem of desertion and nonsupport by the fathers of these families? An effort has been made to keep fathers at home by extending benefits to families with an unemployed father. Twenty-two states now provide such aid.

Another program change was made to affect the work status of the mother. Originally, the program's intent was to enable mothers to care for their children without having to work outside the home. Benefits were reduced dollar for dollar for earned income, reducing the incentive to find a job. Work incentives were added to the program in 1967. A mother with earned income now loses less in AFDC benefits for each dollar earned. She is also eligible for job training and counseling and publicly supported child care under the Work Incentive Program. Still, only about one sixth of the mothers receiving AFDC are employed.

Without controlled experiments to test the effects of various aid programs, it is not possible to predict all the results. When results are unfavorable, new approaches should be tried. However, this is often costly. Also, new programs generally require new or expanded bureaucracies. All of this suggests that the problem of poverty may remain with us despite sincere efforts to solve it.

Table 12.2   Share of Aggregate Income Before Taxes Received by Each Fifth of Families, Ranked by Income.

	1947	1950	1960	1966	1972	1977
Lowest Fifth	5.1%	4.5%	4.8%	5.6%	5.4%	5.2%
Second Fifth	11.8	11.9	12.2	12.4	11.9	11.6
Third Fifth	16.7	17.4	17.8	17.8	17.5	17.5
Fourth Fifth	23.2	23.6	24.0	23.8	23.9	24.2
Highest Fifth	43.3	42.7	41.3	40.5	41.4	41.5
Top 5 Percent	17.5	17.3	15.9	15.6	15.9	15.7

Sources: *Economic Report of the President,* February 1974, *A Guide to Consumer Markets 1977/78,* and *Statistical Abstract of the U.S.,* 1979.

WHAT HAS BEEN ACCOMPLISHED?

Average levels of living in the Western world have improved regularly since the Industrial Revolution. For the last several centuries, *real* purchasing power per capita has doubled about every forty years.

Absolute and Relative Poverty

Such statistics show that *absolute* levels of poverty in the United States have declined over the last several decades. In fact, when an absolute income level is defined as poor (for example, under $8410), the percentage of U.S. families classified as poor has fallen by about half since 1959.

Nevertheless, there has been little change in *relative* poverty: proportional shares of income going to various income groups. This suggests that there has been no significant trend toward *equality* of incomes over at least the last thirty years.

When all U.S. families are ranked according to income and divided into fifths, we discover that the shares of total income going to each fifth have remained roughly the same in recent decades. Table 12.2 shows the shares of income before taxes for families in selected years since 1947.

The lowest fifth of families (or the lowest 20 percent) still receive about 5 percent of total income and the highest fifth, more than 40 percent. The share of the top 5 percent has fallen slightly.

Translated into dollar amounts, in 1977 this meant that the lowest fifth were those families with incomes of less than $7875; the second fifth had incomes of $7875 to $13,125; the third fifth, $13,125 to $18,310; the fourth fifth, $18,310 to $25,320; and the top fifth, more than $25,320. The top 5 percent had incomes of more than $39,212.*

The Lorenz Curve

A useful tool for illustrating relative shares of income is the **Lorenz curve.** The Lorenz curve is drawn in a square as in Figure 12.1. The horizontal axis measures percentage of families. The vertical axis measures percentage of income before taxes.

As you move from 0 to 100 percent along either axis, percentages are cumulative. That is, values are associated with the lowest 20 percent, the lowest 40 percent, the lowest 60 percent, and so forth.

The diagonal line across the square is a reference line. It associates equal percentages of the values along each axis and represents complete equality of income distribution. For example, point *A* on the diagonal line represents the condition where the lowest 20 percent of families receive 20 percent of income; point *B* represents the condition where the lowest 80 percent of families receive 80 percent of income; and so forth.

* The disparity of income is aggravated by the fact that the distribution of wealth is also uneven.

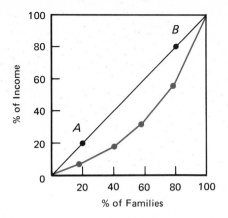

Figure 12.1   A Lorenz Curve Showing Distribution of Income.
Source: *Economic Report of the President,* February 1974.

If the *actual* graph of income shares corresponds to the diagonal, then income is distributed exactly equally. To the extent that the actual graph deviates from the diagonal, there is inequality in the distribution of income.

The Lorenz curve in Figure 12.1 tells us that the lowest 20 percent of families received about 5 percent of income. The lowest 80 percent of families received slightly more than 50 percent of income. This means that the top 20 percent of families received more than 40 percent of total income. Put another way, the top 20 percent of families received more than eight times as much income as the bottom 20 percent of families.

In fact, Figure 12.1 illustrates income distribution in the United States in 1947. Lorenz curves for the years 1950, 1960, 1970, and 1977 are shown in Figure 12.2 (page 242). As you can see, the curves have become somewhat flatter over the period, but there has been no significant change.

Conclusions

We may conclude that absolute levels of income (corrected for inflation) have indeed increased. Levels of living have improved with advancing technology and productivity. Nevertheless, there has been no major movement toward equality of income shares in recent years.

The greatest changes toward income equality probably took place in the early decades of this century. Antimonopoly laws, the growth of the labor movement, and greater opportunities for education and training in new expanding industries reduced the relative advantages of the upper fifth of families. The trend toward equality has slowed in recent decades, although antidiscrimination laws are now helping resume the trend.

WHAT'S AHEAD FOR SOCIAL SECURITY?

The Social Security program has been the mainstay of public-assistance programs in the United States since 1935. Social Security trust funds receive tax payments from workers and employers, and each month the agency sends checks to about 36 million retired persons, orphans, widows, and disabled persons.

In recent years, the Social Security Administration has had to dip into its emergency trust fund in order to meet its steadily rising obligations. There are several reasons for this. Retired persons are living longer and drawing more aid, and Congress has provided for increases in aid to allow for higher costs of living.

Probably the major reason for serious concern about Social Security is a change in the composition of the U.S. population. Families are having fewer children, so that in the future fewer new workers will enter the labor force each year relative to the numbers of nonworkers who will begin receiving income-support payments. The current ratio of fewer than 30 retired persons per 100 taxpaying workers is expected to rise to 45 per 100 by the year 2030.

If the Social Security Administration continues to run in the red, it may eventually run out of funds. How can this be avoided? One way would be to reduce the benefits paid. The trend recently,

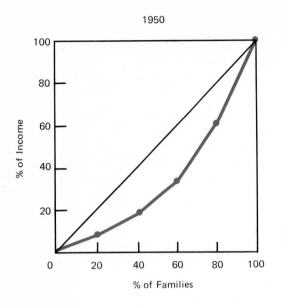

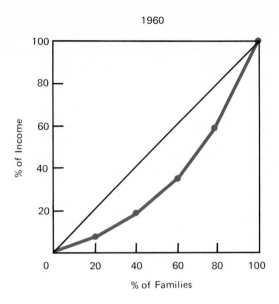

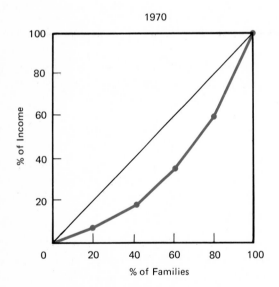

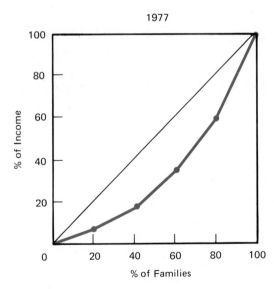

Figure 12.2   Relative Income Shares in the United States.

Source: *Economic Report of the President,* February 1974, and *A Guide to Consumer Markets 1977/78.*

however, has been to increase benefits in order to offset the effects of inflation, to add new beneficiaries, and to include health benefits in the program. Many recipients of Social Security are totally dependent on their monthly check. At present, the average monthly payment is less than $500 for a worker retiring at age sixty-five. It is difficult to imagine cutting these meager benefits.

Another way would be to increase taxes on employed workers. The current rate is 6.65 percent on earnings up to an income of $29,700 (as of 1981), for a maximum tax per worker of $3950 yearly. (Equal amounts are collected from employers and employees.) Current plans are to raise the tax rate and to raise the income level on which the tax is paid. (Social Security taxes are regressive, i.e., they take a higher portion of low incomes than high incomes. Therefore, many lawmakers oppose making the tax more regressive by raising the tax rate only.)

Some economists have proposed doing away with the Social Security tax altogether and paying benefits from federal income tax revenues. This would require an increase in income tax rates, but the change would be toward a more progressive tax structure. An alternative plan would be to move only the health provisions out of the Social Security program and into the general revenue portion of the federal budget. This would leave all Social Security funds for distribution in the form of dependent benefits.

There is another possibility. Raising the retirement age would enable many healthy workers to continue to pay into the trust fund and would reduce the benefit payments ultimately required. However, younger workers frequently urge their elders to retire and open up job opportunities to others.

More changes in the Social Security program will undoubtedly come soon. Social Security touches almost every one of us: either through taxes paid, benefits received, or benefits provided to our dependents. Thus, it is especially important that we develop the best solution to the current (and future) crisis.

LIVING POOR IN THE CITY

It used to be that poverty was mostly a rural problem. Tarpaper shacks dotted the rural landscape on farms hardly productive enough to supply minimum family needs. Today poverty is increasingly an urban problem. The evidence is aging and overcrowded tenement buildings, idle and bitter urban dwellers, crime and decay in urban neighborhoods.

No one could have predicted the change, although the trend began half a century ago. Probably the most significant cause of the growth of urban poverty is the advance of productivity in agriculture. New technology and scientific farming forced many small, inefficient farmers off the land. When farm workers were replaced by modern machinery, a steady flow of new job seekers into the cities began. Often these displaced farm workers are poorly educated and ill prepared for work in modern industry. Unable to find jobs, they have been unable to provide their children with the attitudes and skills needed for success. New generations of poor people are developing in a worsening spiral.

Other causes were also important. In the past, factories processed goods through the "gravity-flow method." Raw materials were first processed on the top floor of a compact building and then dropped through a chute for successive stages of processing on lower floors. In contrast, modern factories use the assembly-line method of production, requiring large continuous plant areas. Older factories could be built in cities, but urban land is too costly for the new assembly-line factories. Thus, manufacturing plants have moved to the outskirts of the cities, far from the masses of urban dwellers. The urban poor frequently lack the transportation facilities for traveling to jobs far from their homes.

The increasing population of dependent poor has imposed a drain on city tax revenues. Poor people need more police and fire protection, more emergency medical care, more specialized educational facilities—all costly to local governments.

To make matters worse, the inflow of poor people has been accompanied by an outflow of middle-income taxpayers in search of more pleasant and less costly living in the suburbs. The loss of its middle-income tax base has been a severe blow to many cities.

Some policies of the federal government have worsened the problem. Since the 1930s the government has provided subsidized mortgage loans for middle-income home buyers. It has subsidized the building of highways for low-cost commuting into the city. It has neglected some projects like mass transportation which would benefit the poor. Finally, a large part of federal revenue sharing funds is paid to state governments. Many state legislatures are strongly influenced by the voters in towns and suburbs; large city populations are under-represented. The result is a tendency to use federal money for projects that do not directly help the urban poor.

The problem is complex. Current poverty programs often focus on particular individuals but do little to improve the overall problem. Some new proposals have been advanced to deal with the problem of urban poverty in general. They include subsidized housing for the poor in suburban neighborhoods; compensatory education and skill development programs for urban youths; increased federal aid to city governments; and rigorous enforcement of antidiscrimination laws in hiring.

One analyst has concluded that American society is becoming two separate societies: the poor are increasingly set apart from the mainstream of American life. This result is destructive to the principles on which our society is based. It is also wasteful of the potential output the poor could be producing and consuming as full participants in our economy.

any society virtually ensures that those at the bottom will be poor.

2. Poverty is classified as cyclical, insular, or categorical. Cyclical poverty is best remedied by policies to stabilize cycles in total spending. Insular poverty is associated with isolated, depressed industries or regions. It may be treated by job training and relocating of workers. Categorical poverty requires public financial assistance to those who are unable to function in our economic system.

3. The Social Security Act of 1935 provides for insurance payments to the aged, dependent, disabled, and unemployed, and relief payments to the needy. Currently, two thirds of income-support payments go to Aid to Families with Dependent Children (AFDC).

4. Administration of aid is costly, involves undesirable side effects, and often fails to achieve its intended objectives. Some proposed alternatives to current programs include direct grants to all families and the negative income tax. However, the problem of reduced incentives among recipients plagues all programs.

5. It is difficult to apply the scientific method to economic problems. This means that we have no precise explanation for poverty and no clear policy remedies. Also, because many variables are involved, it is impossible to evaluate a program's success.

6. Although absolute levels of living have advanced continuously since the Industrial Revolution, there is still marked inequality of income in the United States. Relative shares of income have remained roughly the same since 1947.

7. Social Security legislation must be amended soon to deal with the problem of declining tax collections relative to benefits paid. Proposed plans include cutting benefits and increasing taxes.

8. The rise of urban poverty has strained the resources of local governments and calls for new policy approaches.

SUMMARY

1. A society's standards of performance and value will determine priorities of rewards in which some groups will have low status. The value structure of

TERMS TO REMEMBER

cyclical poverty: poverty that results from the lack of jobs during a business recession or depression.

insular poverty: poverty that results when islands of

depressed economic activity appear following the collapse of a particular craft or industry.

categorical poverty: poverty among particular groups who are unable to function in our economic system.

direct grants: flat payments to increase the incomes of families.

negative income tax: a payment to families whose earned income is less than the level of allowed income tax credits.

Lorenz curve: a graph showing a nation's income distribution.

TOPICS FOR DISCUSSION

1. Distinguish clearly between each of the following pairs of terms:

   > equality of opportunity and equality of results
   > categorical aid and direct grants
   > absolute poverty and relative poverty

2. Explain the basis of the three major classifications of poverty. What policy recommendations would you propose for dealing with each? Give specific instances of each kind of poverty and specific programs which have been used to remedy them.
3. What are the similarities and differences between scientific and economic analysis?
4. Minimum-wage legislation is usually defended as a means of relieving the plight of the poor. However, it may actually work against the poor. Explain.
5. Consider the dilemma of a low-skilled worker. If the legal minimum wage is kept low, he or she may find it more beneficial not to work and to draw welfare payments. If the legal minimum wage is raised, the worker may be unemployable because his or her skills do not justify paying the higher wage. Keeping welfare payments low increases the misery of the poor. But raising them reduces economic incentives and raises the burden to the taxpayer.

   Do you see any hope for resolving this problem in the future? Can you design a statistical study for evaluating the effects on incentives of various changes in welfare payments and the minimum wage?

SUGGESTED READINGS

Aaron, Henry, "Advisory Report on Social Security," *Challenge,* March/April 1980, pp. 12–16.

"The American Underclass," *Time,* August 19, 1977, p. 14.

Anderson, Martin, "Welfare Reform," in *The United States in the 1980s,* Peter Duignan and Alvin Rabushka, eds., Stanford University: Hoover Institution, 1980, p. 139.

Collins, Lora S., "Transfers," *Across the Board,* October 1979, pp. 42–47.

Danziger, Sheldon, Garfinkel, Irwin, and Haveman, Robert, "Poverty, Welfare, and Earnings: A New Approach," *Challenge,* September/October, 1979, pp. 28–34.

Feldstein, Martin S., "Seven Principles of Social Insurance," *Challenge,* November/December 1976, p. 6.

Jencks, Christopher, "The Minimum Wage Controversy," *Working Papers,* March/April 1978, p. 12.

Keeley, Michael, and Robins, Philip, "Work Incentives and the Negative Income Tax," *Challenge,* March/April, 1979, pp. 52–55.

"Propping Up Social Security," *Business Week,* July 19, 1976, p. 34.

Reynolds, Morgan, and Smolensky, Eugene, "The Fading Effect of Government on Inequality," *Challenge,* July/August 1978, pp. 32–37.

Schorr, Alvin L., "Welfare Reform and Social Insurance," *Challenge,* November/December 1977, p. 14.

"The $60 Billion Welfare Failure," *Business Week,* January 17, 1977, p. 48.

Teague, Burton W., "Social Insecurity," *Across the Board,* September 1977, p. 58.

Thurow, Lester, *The Zero-Sum Society,* New York: Basic Books, 1980, Chapter 7.

"249 Billions to Prop Incomes—Where Government Money Goes," *U.S. News and World Report,* November 28, 1977, p. 98.

"The World's Poor Flood the U.S.: The Economic Consequences of a New Wave," *Business Week,* June 23, 1980, p. 80.

CHAPTER 13

or Those Who Ride
the Tiger
Dare Not Dismount

Economic Growth

Tools for Study

Learning Objectives

After reading this chapter, you will be able to:

1. discuss the origins of our attitudes toward material growth.
2. describe trends in GNP.
3. explain how the process of growth takes place.
4. discuss the problems facing a mature economic society.
5. discuss some potential problems resulting from growth.
6. explain the sectoral and export-base theories of growth and how they affect policy alternatives.

Issues Covered

How can growth in production possibilities take place?

What are some disadvantages of growth?

What can be done about the world food shortage?

John Stuart Mill, a leading economist of the mid-nineteenth century, is said to have read Greek literature by the age of eight. I blush to admit that one of the most memorable cultural experiences of my own childhood was a literary jewel called ''Pigs Is Pigs.''

The story concerned a controversy between a clerk at the post office and the recipient of a package through the mail. The package contained a pair of guinea pigs; and the controversy centered on the amount of postage due, which the recipient refused to pay. During the course of the dispute, the family of pigs grew and grew—and GREW and GREW. And the postal worker was reduced to guardian of a flock ballooning out of control.

The story suggests the conflicting feelings with which we might view economic growth. Are we sure we want economic growth? Are we aware of its costs and benefits? What are the sources of growth and what are its results? Finally, can we *manage* growth so that we can enjoy its benefits and reduce its costs?

GROWTH AND GNP

The drive toward growth in this country has traditionally been strong and has been nurtured by seemingly limitless supplies of land and materials for our exploitation. Together these influences made our efforts toward growth a success. Seeking a simple and direct way to measure (or prove) our success, the United States developed the measure known as GNP. (We named the wild cards after we had seen our hand!)

Growth Trends

GNP provides a relatively simple way to measure economic growth. Over the period for which comparable statistics are available, both total and per capita GNP have risen fairly consistently. Since 1929, growth has averaged about 4 percent annually, slowing during periods of recession. (You may want to refer back to Table 6.1 for actual figures.)

GNP will tend naturally to grow as more and more production is carried on in the market. GNP grows as Grandpa's vegetable garden, the neighborhood sewing circle, and the live-in maiden aunt (whose value cannot be determined and, therefore, is not included in GNP) are replaced by the commercial farm, the clothing factory, and the nursery school.

In recent years, the decline of the traditional male-headed family has pushed many females into jobs outside the home. This has also had the effect of raising the level of GNP by the value of these new workers' production.

Some Limitations on the Use of GNP

In spite of the regular increases in the market value of GNP, it is not a perfect measure of how much better we live than in earlier times. GNP measures the quantity, but may not always reflect the quality, of our production. A popular journalist complained recently that the strawberries available at the supermarket (included in GNP) are not nearly as tasty as those his grandmother used to raise in her yard (not included in GNP). However, he showed no inclination to plow up *his* yard and spend hours bent over a superior strawberry crop. Apparently he was willing to give up a little home-grown flavor so that he could work at his chosen profession by day and enjoy professional sports in the evening (included in GNP, by the way).

GNP does leave out some significant goods— and some important "bads"—which our economic system produces. Adding all the goods and subtracting the "bads" would make the measure more correct. The "bads" include the changes in environmental quality (such as increasing levels of water pollution) which are not deducted from the value of goods produced but which certainly reduce our well-being. (The discussion of Net Economic Welfare in Chapter 6 treats this topic in more detail.)

Recent Experience and Projections

The National Bureau of Economic Research in New York City has studied recent growth trends in the United States and made some projections of future growth. After World War II, and especially in the 1960s, the United States experienced a tremendous growth in production. Growth was partially a result of the "baby boom" which increased labor resources about 2 percent annually. Technical advance added about 2 percent more to production, bringing on an increase in real output of almost 4 percent a year.

Since the 1950s, population growth has slowed, and may fall to 1 percent per year during the 1980s. In the 1980s we may notice a significant decline in the demand for such goods as autos, furniture, household appliances, and clothing. Along with the decline in consumer demand we may expect production growth to slow and unemployment to rise.

Viewpoint

WHY GROWTH?

Why has the drive toward higher and higher levels of growth been so strong in the United States? Why have we urged growth so enthusiastically?

Some say the drive for material wealth originated with the inferior status of our ancestors in the Old World. People who were denied social advancement because they were born into the lower classes often looked for other routes to advancement: first commerce, then industry and finance. The New World offered plentiful resources for new arrivals to use in overcoming the *challenges* of the environment, and it promised *rewards* in the form of rising social status.

Historian Arnold Toynbee has said that civilizations develop through challenge and reward. The correct balance between work and reward produces the incentives necessary for achievement. An individual is frustrated by repeated failure but is also weakened by excessive reward. The appropriate *challenge* will bring forth the most constructive response. In the United States, the balance between work and reward encouraged greater effort and helped us achieve rising levels of living.

Others say our growth psyche originated with Protestantism. The Catholic Church of the Middle Ages regarded greed as sinful, but the Protestants felt that idleness was a worse sin. Early Protestants emphasized hard work with little pleasure. The result was growth in the production of material goods. In Protestantism, personal wealth became associated with godliness.

Perhaps the best reason we have stressed economic growth has been our rapidly expanding population. Unless people are satisfied with smaller shares of food, clothing, and the comforts of life, production must grow at least as fast as population. Lately, growth has become important for the jobs it creates for our growing labor force.

HOW DOES GROWTH TAKE PLACE?

What determines the size of GNP? Any society, whether primitive or advanced, has potential GNP limited only by (1) the quantity and quality of its human and material resources; (2) its level of technical knowledge; and (3) the system through which it organizes its resources for production.

Saving and Investment

A South Pacific island with ten workers and the sea can produce a certain quantity of fish to feed their families. GNP growth will be slow. Production will grow as the population grows, but per capita GNP may not grow at all.

At some point production techiques may improve, and food for the islanders can be produced by fewer of the island's workers. Some workers might then agree to give up fishing for one day in order to build a boat for trips to richer fishing grounds. In effect, these workers would have **saved** one day's labor in order to **invest** in a capital resource. They have *saved* by not consuming the day's production. They have *invested* by building capital which will enable them to be more productive in the future.

It is important to note that *to save and invest requires sacrifice*. And sacrifice is possible only if necessary food for the people is easily obtained. It is possible only if the community is living somewhat beyond the bare, subsistence level.

Expansion

With capital equipment, the community can expand its output more rapidly. Now fewer workers are needed to catch the fish required to feed the population. The rest are free to develop other resources, and the community will experience economic growth as a result. New goods and services may be produced to enhance the quality of life. Ultimately, surplus labor may be diverted to less essential work such as the production of leisure goods and services.

Human and material resource supplies may continue to grow under these favorable conditions, and technical knowledge may continue to advance. Consequently, production of essential goods will continue to require fewer workers, releasing still more workers for other activities.

PROBLEMS OF THE MATURE ECONOMY

In his *Stages of Economic Growth,* economist Walt Whitman Rostow described how a primitive economy grows. First the society must develop the necessary *preconditions* for growth. Some necessary preconditions are basic health and education stan-

dards and a general disposition among workers to improve their status in life. With these preconditions the economy may experience a *take-off* into industrial development. Investment in transportation facilities and electric power make possible the growth of manufacturing. New manufacturing industries call for development of supplying industries, and higher incomes call for development of consumer goods industries. Healthy growth continues until finally the economy reaches maturity.

After having successfully reached this level, it would seem that an economy would be "home free." But, regrettably, more perplexing problems remain for the mature economy—in particular, the problem of maintaining the full employment of human resources.

In a mature economy, each family will own a fully stocked freezer, vehicles for all transportation or recreational needs, and comfortable surroundings in which to be soothed to sleep by various entertainment devices. In this contented state, what further production projects can the imaginative minds of humans devise?

Unless the mature economy needs new goods and services, there will be no new jobs for the growing labor force. Rostow warned that a society with a fully mature economy may have to choose one of three courses to employ its human and material resources:

1. The society may encourage population growth so that it will need more baby carriages, schools, housing, and so forth.
2. It may engage in aggression so that it will need military vehicles, food and supplies for military personnel, and explosives for destroying assets (which will then require replacement, taking care of unemployment problems far into the future).
3. Or it may use idle labor to produce *social* goods (as opposed to *private* goods): universities, parks, hospitals, cultural centers, and urban services.

Vance Packard, a popular critic of the American scene, has jokingly suggested a rather extreme plan for dealing with the problem of unemployment in a mature economy. He proposed that factories be designed so that the ends of assembly lines could be swung either to loading platforms in the front or to rear doors overhanging deep ravines. The output of assembly lines could then be either sold to consumers or pushed into the gorge! (Reckless waste already approaches this ideal in some manufacturing operations.)

Packard also suggested (as far back as 1960) that rockets might be constructed periodically and equipped with highly specialized equipment to be shot out into space. The announced objective might be to acquire scientific information about the back side of Neptune's moon. Vast quantities of many types of labor could be employed and there would be no need to sell the output to anyone!

Lacking sufficient high-employment/low-output projects of this type, American industry has turned to the curious task of persuading consumers to want more and more things. Through advertising, we are persuaded to change our fashion and habits of life often and in this way to keep the factory wheels turning.* Some goods are designed specifically to break down or go out of style, requiring replacement.

One unfortunate result is the decline of tasteful design. The only way to ensure that users will become dissatisfied with some item is to design it with built-in crudities of some kind. Eventually a new model will feature deformities of the opposite extreme, making the existing one obsolete.

AN END TO GROWTH?

An eighteenth-century economist, Thomas Malthus, earned for economics its nickname as the "dismal science." (It is a title some of us have been trying to live down ever since.) Malthus agreed with the other economists of his day that the economic system would be automatically self-regulating, but in a most pessimistic way. He predicted that growth must eventually come to an end.

Malthus predicted that if production were to be greater than that required for life, material standards of living will be high. Prosperity will encourage high rates of population growth. The larger population will then absorb the entire production until all people will be living barely above starvation. On the other hand, if production should become insufficient even for such misery, population growth will be checked by disease, famine, and war—until population is again adjusted to current production.

Pretty dismal, that Malthus!

The Limits to Growth

A recent report has revived interest in Malthus's predictions about the consequences of growth. The report, published in 1972 by the Club of Rome, is entitled *The Limits to Growth*. Club of Rome researchers used computer models to project the cause-and-effect results of growth on the world environment. Briefly, this is what they concluded:

1. High birth rates and falling death rates increase population growth.
2. Population growth increases food requirements and presses against supplies of farm land.
3. Dwindling food supplies require increased agricultural and industrial production which in turn affects environmental quality by polluting air and streams. Supplies of nonreplaceable resources are damaged or depleted.
4. Environmental decay and lack of productive resources eventually restricts population growth through disease and famine.

Feedbacks within and among these relationships were studied, and projections made of the effects of unrestrained growth. *All* of the tests predicted catastrophic population and resource problems within the lifetimes of many of us alive today. (The standard world model assumed no change in physical, economic, or social factors

---

* Not all advertising is limited to this objective, of course. Advertising is often necessary to inform consumers of the characteristics of available goods and services.

involved in growth. In the model, population growth is finally checked by a rise in the death rate due to declining supplies of food and health services—well before the year 2100!)

Exponential Changes

The frightening point made by the study was that environmental changes (such as levels of air and water pollution) are taking place exponentially (like the guinea pigs) rather than *linearly*.

Linear growth involves changes of the *same* amount every time period so that the line describing the change rises or falls in a straight line: 1, 2, 3, 4, 5. But **exponential growth** involves a percentage change in quantities so that the *amount* of the change rises or falls every time period: 1, 2, 4, 8, 16. The line describing the change curves upward or downward. (An example of exponential growth is world fuel consumption. The curve rises not only because larger numbers of people consume energy, but also because each person's energy consumption grows.)

Environmental Ceilings and Floors

This means that the curves describing environmental changes will reach their limits, whether ceilings or floors, very abruptly. We may bump into the global limits of supplies of air, water, and other resources only shortly after these limits are noticed. When the limits are reached, collapse follows. Linear and exponential growth and decline are shown graphically in Figure 13.1.

In the past, we in Western society have paid little attention to the side effects of our commitment to growth. If we are to avoid the catastrophic results prophesied by the Club of Rome study, however, we may have to concentrate on living within the limits of our environment. This may require a cut in population growth, a lower level of production, and more efficient investment, along with lower material standards of living.

The Other Side

Perhaps the reader will agree that the drive for growth can lead to some pretty frightening consequences. If so, then we should consider the other side of the argument.

Less fortunate nations and people living in poverty will certainly object to an end to growth: "Now that you have yours, you want to conserve," they might say, or "The party's over just before we arrive."

Modern communication and transportation have exposed the gap between living standards of

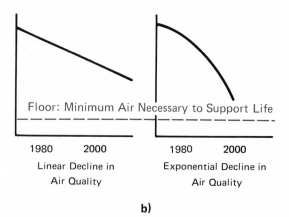

| | a) | | b) |

Figure 13.1 Environmental Ceilings and Floors.

the haves and the have-nots. This has produced a "revolution of rising expectations" among the have-nots in our nation and abroad. The have-nots are beginning to demand a better way of life for themselves. It may be that the only practical course is not stopping growth but *regulating* growth and distributing its fruits more evenly.

THEORIES OF GROWTH

Why do some nations enjoy strong growth trends and others continue to stagnate at primitive levels of production? What explains the difference in growth rates among regions within a single nation?

There are two major theories to explain how and why economic growth takes place. One theory emphasizes the internal circumstances within the region. It stresses how strategic sectors of the economy have evolved and is known as the *sectoral* theory of growth.

Another theory emphasizes the external relationships between the region and the rest of the world. It stresses the region's valuable export potential and is known as the *export-base* theory of growth.

Sectoral Theory of Growth

The **sectoral theory of growth** is based on studies of past growth in regions and nations. Studies show that the process of growth among sectors of the economy has followed similar patterns worldwide.

Typically, the first sector to experience growth is the *agricultural* sector. This is because agriculture provides basic necessities of life: food, clothing, medicine. Specialization in agriculture encourages the development of farm equipment and technology for increasing farm productivity. When agricultural productivity increases faster than the need for basic necessities, labor can be released for work in other sectors.

The second sector to experience growth is normally the *manufacturing* sector. After basic needs are satisfied, the population begins to demand other material goods. Consumer goods manufacturing grows, and support industries develop to supply materials and parts. An important support industry is transportation. Transportation facilities unite small communities into larger, interdependent markets. Larger markets permit greater specialization and division of labor and provide opportunities for large-scale, low-cost production. The effects of higher production and incomes spread throughout the economy as many different types of manufacturing mature and prosper.

The third sector to experience growth is the *service* sector. Once basic necessities and material goods are plentiful, consumers begin to demand services to improve the quality of life. There is growth in personal and homemaking services and in business services. In the first group are health and education, recreation and the arts, home decorating, and fashion. In the second group are financial and consulting services, communications, marketing, and economic forecasting.

Export-Base Theory of Growth

Under the **export-base theory of growth,** a region must produce exportable commodities which are in substantial demand elsewhere. Sales of the exported commodity bring income into the region. Income from sales is invested, first in facilities for producing the export commodity and eventually in industries that supply or support the export-base industry.

As rising incomes spread throughout the export and support industries, workers become more prosperous. They use their increased earnings to improve their living standards. Spending on consumer goods and services stimulates production in those industries, and development gradually extends throughout the entire spectrum of production.

MANAGING GROWTH

Understanding the sources of growth should lead to effective policies for managing growth. Designing proper policies is particularly important for poor nations, as well as for those regions within the United States where growth has stalled behind the rest of the nation. Ideally, we should be able to manage growth in such a way that we obtain its greatest benefits and avoid its more costly side effects.

Designing Policy

If we accept the *sectoral* theory of growth, we would recommend government programs to aid the agricultural sector. There would be research and development programs in agricultural techniques and investment in agricultural education for increasing productivity. There would be government-guaranteed loans to farmers for investment in agricultural equipment.

According to the sectoral theory, as agriculture becomes more productive, resources will move into other sectors of the economy. Development will then follow *automatically* in the manufacturing, and, finally, in the service sectors.

If we accept the *export-base* theory of growth, we would recommend government aid for the production of materials and goods for sale abroad. There might be programs for development of a mineral resource. Gold, diamonds, petroleum, and tin, for example, have been important export commodities for some countries. Or the export base for development might be an agricultural commodity such as cotton, coffee, rubber, sugar, cheese, or wine. In a more highly industrialized economy, the export base might be precision instruments, electronic equipment, or computers.

According to the export-base theory, as the export-base industry prospers, growth will spread to other industries. Rising incomes in the export-related industries will lead *automatically* to growth in production of consumer goods and services.

Policy Conflicts

These two alternative theories may produce opposite policy conclusions. The *sectoral* approach would dictate higher agricultural investment. Would this be practical in, say, the depressed regions of Appalachia in the United States or in the new nations of Africa? Why or why not?

The *export-base* approach would dictate higher investment in the production of export commodities. Would it be practical to invest in cotton production in the southern United States or in rubber plantations in Southeast Asia? Why or why not?

A single approach to development has certain disadvantages. If the favored sector or industry suffers a decline in demand, there may be major economic crises. If world food production outstrips demand, for example, the agricultural sector may collapse. Too great a dependence on one crop may also be disastrous. A bumper crop one year could mean falling prices and falling incomes for the exporting nation. Even worse, a technological change may make an export commodity worthless in world markets. Or an interruption in transportation during a war may bring on economic collapse.

In the past, substantial investment in agriculture or in an export industry has not always led to development in other sectors. Incomes earned in the favored sector may not be reinvested in less developed sectors. Savings may be sent to other regions or other countries where greater returns are expected. If this happens, profits from the first stages of development cannot be used to stimulate further stages of growth, and the region or nation may continue to stagnate at low levels of production and low material living standards.

The lack of a definitive theoretical explanation of growth makes policy decisions difficult. The result may be foiled expectations, wasted resources, and continued low standards of living for people in many areas of the world. Humanitarian concerns, as well as economic ones, compel a continued search for effective programs to manage growth.

Self-Check

1. **Which of the following illustrates the most likely sequence of growth?**
   a. saving, plentiful resources, capital equipment, investment
   b. plentiful resources, saving, investment, capital equipment
   c. investment, capital equipment, saving, plentiful resources
   d. plentiful resources, investment, capital equipment, saving
   e. saving, investment, capital equipment, plentiful resources

2. **When total resources reach high levels of productivity:**
   a. there is danger of unemployment.
   b. they may produce nonmaterial services to enrich the quality of life.
   c. production may focus on military equipment.
   d. there may be emphasis on wasteful production.
   e. all of the above.

3. **Which of the following is not a limit to growth?**
   a. pollution caused by increasing agricultural and industrial production
   b. rising birth rates relative to death rates
   c. limited supplies of farm land
   d. exponential trends in resource use
   e. All are limits to growth.

4. **The sectoral theory of growth:**
   a. is based on growing productivity in export industries.
   b. depends on inflows of spending from other nations.
   c. emphasizes the development of agriculture, manufacturing, and then services.
   d. would call for policy to increase agricultural investment in order to encourage growth.
   e. both (c) and (d).

5. **Under the export-base theory of growth:**
   a. a region must produce commodities which are in demand elsewhere.
   b. sales of an export good will cause outflows of spending from the producing region.
   c. growth would be encouraged by investment in the production of export commodities.
   d. all of the above.
   e. both (a) and (c).

Theory in Practice

GROWTH IN PRODUCTION POSSIBILITIES

Economic growth depends on increases in the quality and quantity of resources and improvements in technology. In the United States, labor resources have increased substantially. Our population grew from 5.3 million in 1800 to 223 million in 1981. The quality of labor has improved as well, through better health and education of the labor force and longer years of productive life. Improve-

ments in technology have come about through scientific and engineering advances and through better organizational and management techniques.

Growth in the stock of capital has also added to our production possibilities. Substantial investment has been made in transportation and communication facilities, power plants, and manufacturing plants and equipment.

Remember that investment in capital resources is possible only if individuals refrain from consuming a portion of their incomes. They must *save* and make their savings available to business for *investment* in productive facilities. Since 1929, Americans have saved an average of about 7 percent of their disposable personal income (income after taxes).

You will also recall that in order to save, a nation must own resources capable of producing more goods and services than the minimum necessary for life. Surplus production enables the society to shift resources from production of life's necessities into production of capital equipment. The American continent has fortunately provided our nation with plentiful resources. As a result, we have been able to increase our savings and investment fairly regularly throughout our history. In 1980, total investment expenditures amounted to almost $400 billion. Almost one third of this amount represented *net* additions to capital stock, i.e., additions over and above replacement of depreciated equipment.

Economic growth can be illustrated as a steady shift to the right of a nation's production possibilities curve. The production possibilities curves in Figure 13.2 illustrate the production capabilities of two countries, one rich in resources and one poor.

Suppose a minimum production of 10 units of goods and services is necessary to maintain the population in each nation. The rich nation can produce the necessary goods and services and also 20 units of capital. The poor nation is able to produce the necessary goods and services and only 5 units of capital. How will the ability to invest in capital affect future production possibilities for the rich nation? Pencil in the appropriate changes on the graph.

GROWTH AND THE ENVIRONMENT

We humans are the only animals on this earth who significantly change our environment. As our numbers have grown, our needs have grown, too. We have used our superior intelligence to produce a growing variety and quantity of goods. In the process of production, however, we have produced some unwanted materials that have changed our environment in unexpected ways.

Economists call these side effects of production *externalities*. Many externalities are useful and desirable, as when growth in manufacturing increases the skills of workers and enables them to produce a wider range of goods. Some other exam-

a) **Rich Nation**

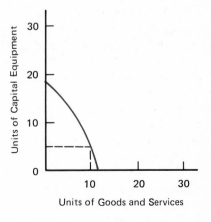

b) **Poor Nation**

Figure 13.2 Production Possibilities Curves for Two Nations.

ples of *positive externalities* are: improved technology of agriculture which enables more people to live healthy, productive lives and frees labor for other types of work; better homes which improve our landscape and help make our neighborhoods more stable; immunization against diseases, halting their spread and limiting exposure even for those who have not been immunized. These positive externalities are often called "social benefits" because the side effects of production extend broadly over the society.

Negative externalities are often called "social costs." The negative side effects of production also extend throughout the society, imposing costs on members of the community as a whole. Most of us are familiar with *negative externalities:* air pollution which worsens our health and dirties our homes and clothing; water pollution which destroys recreation areas and increases the cost of pure water; noise pollution which damages our hearing and rattles our nerves; discarded junk which breeds vermin and disease. No doubt, you can add more examples from your own personal experience.

The significant fact about externalities is that they are received by people who did not request them. Positive externalities extend to everyone within reach of the benefits; negative externalities become a burden to all within reach of the social costs . . . whether we want them or not!

This fact makes externalities different from goods and services traded in the market. The market is very careful to extend benefits only to those people who want them and are willing to pay the cost. We say the market is *efficient* because participants in the market evaluate the benefits they expect to receive from a purchase and pay only enough to compensate for those benefits; stated algebraically, $\dfrac{\text{Benefits}}{\text{Costs}} \geq 1$. In pure market transactions there is little danger that the costs paid might exceed the benefits received. Efficiency in many individual markets means efficiency for the economy as a whole. Through the market system, our scarce resources are used only to the extent that

the benefits received are at least as great as the costs paid.

This result is not necessarily true when there are externalities. When there are externalities, the costs of a production process are paid for by two groups: those who receive the benefits and pay for them, and those who receive no benefits but nevertheless suffer the social costs (or negative externalities).

There is another problem associated with externalities. The problem involves a principle called *equity,* a word that is difficult to define precisely, but involves fairness.*

By most definitions the market system is fair; that is, it gives people what they pay for. People who want the benefits pay the cost. Those who don't, don't.

The presence of externalities changes all this, and the result is definitely not fair.

How can understanding growth help our nation plan for growth? First, we must recognize that the market system does not account for externalities. Therefore, some decisions about production must be made outside the market, by communities as a whole through their elected representatives. Making decisions collectively enables us to evaluate new proposals' *total* benefits and costs in terms of its *total benefits* received by those who use the project directly *plus* the positive externalities enjoyed by the community as a whole; and *total costs* paid by private users and governments to construct and operate the project *plus* the negative externalities the community must suffer as a result. Stated algebraically:

$$\frac{\text{Total Benefits}}{\text{Total Costs}} =$$
$$\frac{\text{Private Benefits} + \text{Social Benefits}}{\text{Private Cost} + \text{Social Costs}} \geq 1.$$

Needless to say, the possible side effects of production are difficult to identify and impossible to measure precisely. But some effort must at least

---

* What is "fair" may mean different things to different people.

be made to make sure that scarce resources are used only for projects that provide total benefits greater than their total costs.

Once a project is determined to be efficient in the economic sense, it should be evaluated in terms of equity. Are the benefits and costs distributed fairly? Do those who enjoy the benefits also pay the costs? How much equity are we willing to sacrifice to build a project that is definitely efficient?

Test yourself: the economics of the environment can be summarized in three *E*'s: efficiency, externalities, and equity. Make sure you understand these terms and how they contribute to an understanding of economic choice. Then evaluate each of the following projects in terms of the three *E*'s.

1. A proposed highway would transport commuters quickly from the suburbs to their jobs in the city. But it would also disrupt an established inner-city neighborhood, cut off small local business firms from their regular customers, and remove much urban property from the city's tax base. Ninety percent of the cost of construction would be covered by the federal government, 10 percent by the state.

2. A proposed dam would provide electric power, flood control, and recreational facilities over a large area. It would stimulate industrial and commercial development and raise incomes for poor rural families. However, it would forever change the landscape, destroying valuable farm and timber land, eliminating white-water canoeing streams, and destroying the habitat of a unique species of fish.

3. A chemical process restructures the molecules of petroleum to produce a fiber for weaving into cloth. The cloth never wrinkles or needs ironing, enabling many homemakers to spend their time in other more creative ways. Although the miracle fiber increases the variety and durability of our clothing, production requires vast quantities of imported oil and natural gas and expels heat, chemicals, and nondegradable materials into our air and water.

ECONOMIC GROWTH AND THE FOOD CRISIS

Advances in technology have helped more of the world's population live better and longer—and that's part of our problem!

Better health standards have kept larger numbers of people alive. The world's population is now almost four billion and expected to double in twenty-five years. Growing population and slowly rising living standards have increased our need for food at the rate of 30 million tons per year. As a result, the world's stockpile of food is declining by about 10 million tons per year.

The Rise and Fall of the Green Revolution

From the early 1950s until 1972, world food production increased greatly. The "Green Revolution" extended scientific techniques to agriculture in the form of hybrid seed and livestock, chemical fertilizers and pesticides, and improved irrigation systems. Strains of corn, sorghum, soybeans, wheat, and rice were developed to flourish under particular climate and soil conditions around the world.

The Green Revolution has been especially successful in the United States. Corn production per acre has quadrupled since the early 1900s. Milk production has risen to 10,000 pounds per cow per year, compared with only 600 pounds per cow in India. Chickens have been bred to eat less, grow to maturity in a shorter time, and produce more eggs. As a result of such scientific advances, our twelve Midwestern states alone now feed one fourth of the world's people.

Worldwide crop disasters in 1972 brought an apparent end to the growth in agricultural production. Much of the increased yields had come from the use of chemical fertilizers, primarily petroleum-based and now in short supply. The drop in world supplies of petroleum-based fertilizers is expected to cause a drop in crop yields of ten tons for each one-ton decline in fertilizers applied.

Rising costs present a particular problem for developing nations that often lack the foreign exchange necessary for buying fertilizer. The problem is so severe that Philip Handler, former president of the National Academy of Sciences, has predicted one million child deaths per month in these nations by the year 2025.

Proposals and Problems

What can be done? At present we are cultivating only about half of the world's arable land. The most favorable lands are already in use, however, and the additional costs of clearing, transportation, and irrigation associated with developing new farmland would run in the billions of dollars. Adding only 10 percent to the amount of cultivated acreage cost as much as $1 trillion!

Land reform might increase productivity in some nations. New foods from the sea are also a possibility, but the potential gain is limited by pollution and by too intensive fishing in recent years. New varieties of seeds are still being developed, but the process is slow and costly. Fertilizer production may also be expanded, particularly in the less-developed countries.

Reduction of waste would also help relieve the food shortage. Decreased consumption in the developed nations could increase the quantities available to needy nations. The United States uses the equivalent of 7 pounds of grain in the production of 1 pound of meat; reducing meat consumption would free this grain for shipment abroad. It is estimated that the average person in poor countries consumes 400 pounds of grain per year, in contrast to the citizen of North America who consumes a ton (about 100 hundred pounds of which is in the form of beer or whiskey).

Lifeboat Ethics?

Policy on the problem of food production must eventually deal with the problem of population growth. Some analysts are beginning to recommend what is called "lifeboat" ethics. Their reasoning is as follows: in the ocean of life we are all adrift. We would like to bring all others aboard our boat, but that would exceed its capacity and we would sink. We must choose to help only those who are able and willing to make a tremendous effort to help themselves.

The decision to help only selected nations is similar to the principle of *triage* in classifying battlefield casualties. Victims are divided into three groups: those who will probably survive without aid, those who will probably survive with moderate aid, and those who will not survive without substantial aid. Limited medical resources are then concentrated on the second group. By implication, the third is left to perish, a morally difficult decision to make. We may not like it but, in the words of ecologist-biologist Garrett Hardin, it is like the law of gravity: "Once you know it's true, you don't sit down and cry about it. That's the way the world is."

In human terms, this conclusion may apply to the one third of the world's population who live in the hungry nations—nations unable to feed themselves or produce goods for export in sufficient quantities to pay for needed imports. These nations are centered in Asia and Africa below the Sahara; Bangladesh and Ethiopia are pitiful examples. It is estimated that one fourth of the population of these areas lives on a diet of less than 1000 calories per day.

We continue to hope for a more acceptable alternative than slow starvation for these people. Policy to relieve the crisis in food production will require the best efforts of scientists, sociologists, economists, and humanitarians for many years to come.

AN INTERNATIONAL PLAN FOR GROWTH

By now you are probably convinced that economic growth is:

(a) desirable   (b) undesirable
(c) possible   (d) impossible
(e) All of the above!

Of course, the question is much too complicated to summarize in a single answer. Even so, it is an important question, and in 1973 the United Nations established the United Nations Environment Program to study and plan for an International Development Strategy. Guiding the study was Wassily Leontief, a Russian-born economist who is now a professor of economics at New York University.

Professor Leontief is well qualified to conduct such a study. In the 1940s he was responsible for developing a major tool for planning economic growth in the United States. His economic model measures the necessary growth in inputs for producing larger outputs from many American industries. The result of his early work was an **Input-Output table** for the United States, showing all the various inputs required for producing all the outputs demanded by American consumers and business firms.

Measuring inputs and outputs is complicated because all inputs to one industry are actually outputs of another. Without the table it would be difficult to measure the necessary growth in inputs (which are also outputs) needed to produce more of any single good.

An example may be helpful. Consider the industry producing motor vehicles—automobiles, trucks, and moving equipment. On the average, to produce one dollar's worth of motor vehicles requires the following inputs:

textile products	1 cent
paint	1/2 cent
rubber and plastics	2 cents
glass	1 cent
metals	10 cents
metal products	7 cents
machinery and equipment	2 cents
electrical products	1 1/2 cents
motor vehicle products	33 cents
retail trade and services	3 cents

To double motor vehicle production would require that output in all these industries increase first. But to increase production of any one of these inputs requires additional production of many other inputs, including motor vehicles. *Motor vehicles are themselves necessary inputs in the industries producing inputs used in the motor vehicle industry.*

Interrelationships among industries create a kind of chain reaction, such that the necessary *total* change in output is greater than the amount required for a single increase in one industry. Making such complicated computations was not possible before Leontief developed his Input-Output table.

Leontief saw that his technique could be expanded to include all economies in the world. A global Input-Output table would enable planners to measure the necessary production of, say, chemical fertilizers in Venezuela for increasing rice production in Southeast Asia. The global Input-Output table is summarized in 2625 equations, each one describing the interrelationships between production and consumption of a particular good in a particular part of the world. Happily, computers are available for solving the equations!

Using his equations, Leontief was able to predict the necessary growth in all inputs for increasing living standards in any part of the world economy and for promoting more balanced growth worldwide. Where input supplies are scarce, Leontief's model can identify bottlenecks. Where new technology is applied, the model can predict the resulting increase in productivity. A flow of loans or grants from developed to less-developed nations shows up as increased investment for increasing global production possibilities. Even pollution is included in Leontief's model as the net result of new industrial emissions minus the effects of pollution-abatement equipment.

After comparing the expected growth in worldwide demand with potential growth in supply, Leontief came to these conclusions:

1. Under present growth projections, the gap in per capita income between developed and less-

developed nations will remain about 12 to 1 at least until the year 2000.

2. However, technological and institutional changes in the less-developed countries could double their food production.

3. A general scarcity of minerals is not yet a serious problem, but gains in production will become more and more costly in the future.

4. Less-developed nations must increase their investment to as much as 40 percent of their GNP. Increased investment will require cutbacks in personal consumption, increased taxes and government development programs, and more investment funds from developed nations.

If Leontief's technique is to become a basis for a global growth strategy, there must first be a new worldwide willingness to cooperate toward shared goals. Nations must agree to set aside purely national goals and fit their own growth plans into a world context. The prospects for such cooperation become better as more nations see the potential gains of cooperation relative to the costs of going it alone.

SUMMARY

1. Economic growth has been an accepted national goal. Abundant resources in the United States have helped us achieve rising standards of living.

2. GNP is a way of measuring production and growth. Growth in GNP requires saving so that investment can be made in capital equipment. However, a growing GNP depends on growing demand for goods and services.

3. The potential size of GNP depends on the quantity and quality of resources, the level of technology, and the system of organizing resources.

4. A fully mature society may suffer from unemployment as a result of declining demand for goods and services. In order to offset declining demand, a society may choose to use its resources to provide for a rising population, for military operations, or for social programs. Or it may choose to waste the output of its resources.

5. Some researchers predict that continued economic growth will eventually bring on environmental

crises. If so, it is necessary to plan for environmentally sound growth. More balanced growth will require more equal distribution of output with lower standards of living for some.

6. Growth may proceed through sectors of the economy or may depend on development of an export commodity. A correct analysis of growth should lead to correct policy to stimulate and manage growth.

7. The production possibilities curve is a useful tool for illustrating growth. A nation or region with large production possibilities is better able to save and invest for future growth.

8. Attempts are being made to improve agricultural techniques and increase productivity in order to deal with the food crisis. However, dealing with severe shortages in some nations may require difficult choices on the part of more fortunate nations.

TERMS TO REMEMBER

saving: refraining from consumption.

investment: using resources to construct capital equipment.

linear growth: growth of the same amount each time period.

exponential growth: growth of greater amounts each time period.

sectoral theory of growth: the theory that growth takes place systematically, first in agriculture, then in manufacturing, and finally in services.

export-base theory of growth: the theory that growth takes place through the development of a major export industry.

Input-Output table: a chart showing all resource inputs needed for producing various types of output.

TOPICS FOR DISCUSSION

1. Most of us have heard the old saying, "Necessity is the mother of invention." Recently a commentator on the American scene observed that today it would be more appropriate to say, "Invention is the mother of necessity." What do you think he meant by that? How is this related to our discussion of economic growth? Can you identify the advantages and disadvantages of this philosophy?

2. Nations differ with respect to the quantity of personal savings. *The Wall Street Journal* of August 20, 1974, reported that Swiss citizens were saving annually the equivalent of $4987 per capita, the highest in the world. The British were second with $4062, and Americans were third with $3247. Last on the list of twenty-nine countries was Ethiopia, with annual per capita savings of $4.36. What factors influence the different rates of savings? How do you think savings might be used in each of the countries mentioned?

3. Each year in the United States, labor resources increase at the rate of about 2 percent. Productivity per worker also increases. The potential growth in output is nearly 4 percent per year. If the new labor is to be employed and higher production to take place, there must be rising demand. And demand must be backed up by spending power. Someone must be willing and able to buy!

   What problems, if any, can you see in our rising productive potential? What solutions would you propose? Are there other long-range problems that might affect your answer?

4. Walt Rostow has suggested that a mature society may have trouble employing all its labor resources unless it encourages population growth, engages in military aggression, or invests in social goods and services. Vance Packard has pointed out that a mature society often wastes its resources or produces frivolous goods. Is this consistent with the problem of scarce resources and unlimited wants outlined in Chapter 1? Is it possible to have unlimited wants and unemployed resources at the same time? Why?

5. How do most Americans save and invest? Are you now saving and investing? How is your experience in school an example of the process of saving and investment?

SUGGESTED READINGS

Boretsky, Michael, "The Role of Innovation," *Challenge,* November/December 1980, pp. 9–15.

Bowen, William, "Better Prospects for Our Ailing Productivity," *Fortune,* December 3, 1979, p. 68.

Bowen, William, "The Decade Ahead: Not So Bad If We Do Things Right," *Fortune,* October 8, 1979, p. 82.

Bowen, William, "How to Regain Our Competitive Edge," *Fortune,* March 9, 1981, p. 74.

"Capital Crisis," *Business Week,* September 22, 1975, p. 42.

Collins, Lora S., "Grow We Must," *Across the Board,* March 1981, pp. 14–19.

Denison, Edward F., "The Puzzling Setback to Productivity Growth, *Challenge,* November/December 1980, pp. 3–8.

Fabricant, Solomon, "The Sky Isn't Falling Down," *Across the Board,* October 1977, p. 48.

"High Technology: Wave of the Future or a Market Flash in the Pan?" *Business Week,* November 10, 1980, p. 86.

"Increasing Investment, Supply and Productivity," *The Economic Report of the President,* Washington: Government Printing Office, January 1981, p. 68.

Jameson, Kenneth P., "Supply-Side Economics: Growth Versus Income Distribution," *Challenge,* November/December 1980, pp. 26–31.

Jorgenson, Dale W., "The Answer Is Energy," *Challenge,* November/December 1980, pp. 16–25.

Lewis, W. Arthur, "The Tropical Dilemma," Grow," *Across the Board,* April 1980, pp. 28–37.

Lipset, Seymour Martin, "To Grow or Not to Grow," *Across the Board,* April 1980, pp. 28–37.

Mason, Edward S., "Natural Resources and Environmental Restrictions to Growth," *Challenge,* January/February 1978, p. 14.

Mason, Edward S., "Natural Resources and Environmental Restrictions to Growth," *Challenge,* May/June 1978, pp. 14–20.

Maxey, Margaret N., "The Trouble with the Extreme Environmentalists," *Across the Board,* December 1977, p. 43.

Mayer, Lawrence A., "The World Economy: Climbing Back from Negative Growth," *Fortune,* August 1975, p. 150.

Meadows, Edward, "Favorable Omens for Capital Investment," *Fortune,* May 5, 1980, p. 194.

"The Reindustrialization of America," *Business Week,* June 30, 1980, entire issue.

Rostow, W.W., "Working Agenda for a Disheveled World Economy," *Challenge,* March/April 1981, p. 5.

Thurow, Lester C., "The Implications of Zero Economic Growth," *Challenge,* March/April 1977, p. 37.

Thurow, Lester, *The Zero-Sum Society,* New York: Basic Books, 1980, Chapters 4 and 5.

CHAPTER 14

International Trade and Finance

or How Everything
King Midas Touched Turned
to a Floating Exchange Rate

Tools for Study

Learning Objectives

After reading this chapter, you will be able to:

1. explain how free trade works.
2. distinguish between absolute advantage and comparative advantage.
3. explain how, through comparative advantage, each nation can benefit from trade with other nations.
4. explain how foreign exchange markets work.
5. explain the balance-of-payments account and identify inflows and outflows.
6. list the barriers to trade.

Issues Covered

How do tariffs interfere with free trade?
Where does gold fit into the international trade picture?
How can inflation and unemployment be exported?
What are the multinationals and how might they help or hurt the domestic economy?

One historian has identified the beginning of trade as a significant turning point in human progress. Trade began to flourish about 2000 B.C., when the Egyptians discovered how to make bronze by combining tin and copper. Bronze was a stronger and more useful metal than either tin or copper used separately. However, sufficient quantities of the two metals were found only in distant regions: tin in England and copper in India and parts of the Middle East. Trade was necessary to bring the metals together.

Trade opened many other opportunities for production within trading nations, and opportunities for other forms of communication as well. It helped bring together the cultural, intellectual, and technical accomplishments of many scattered peoples.

FREE TRADE

Throughout this text, we have associated economic progress with specialization and exchange. We have suggested that groups can increase their productivity if they specialize in a good or service which they can exchange for goods or services produced by others.

Why Specialization?

There are many reasons why specialization is desirable. Some regions are better suited geographically for certain types of production. Agricultural production is the most obvious example. Coffee beans grow well in tropical climates; wheat and corn do best in dry, sunny climates; livestock require grassy plains for grazing.

Other geographic features are favorable for other types of industries: a sheltered harbor provides protection for shipbuilding; rushing mountain streams provide power for operating machinery; mountainous terrain exposes layers of minerals for use in manufacturing.

Such geographical features are not easily mobile. They can be used to best advantage by local workers. Among local workers, special skills will develop. New processes and techniques will be designed, all of which will improve productivity and make more output available at lower costs.

It is likely that the region will produce more output than it needs. Surplus output can then be exchanged for the specialities of other regions. Trading regions will benefit from the large-scale, low-cost production of their neighbors.

Interdependence

There is one small (very small) fly in the ointment, however. Remember that specialization replaces self-sufficiency. Regions that specialize become dependent on other regions for the goods and services essential for a good life. Interdependent regions must be assured a free flow of goods and services. Otherwise, they will be reluctant to give up their self-sufficiency in production.

In the United States we have enjoyed the benefits of a large market area. We have many different regions with varied climates, resources, and geographical features. Also, we have one single national government, with laws prohibiting restrictions on the flow of goods and services. The ability to trade freely has enabled regions to specialize

and enjoy the benefits of specialization without the fears that would otherwise accompany interdependence.

In recent years, nine European nations have entered into trade agreements encouraging free trade. The nations of the European Economic Community—the Common Market—have agreed to allow goods, services, and productive resources to flow more freely over their national borders than was the case when each nation acted independently. The result for their populations has been rising productivity and lower costs, with increasing standards of living.

Communist nations of Eastern Europe and Latin American nations have also formed free trade blocs, known, respectively, as the Council for Mutual Economic Assistance (Comecon) and the Latin American Free Trade Association (LAFTA).

ABSOLUTE AND COMPARATIVE ADVANTAGE

To see how specialization and exchange develop, let us look at two imaginary nations, Kant and Troy. Each nation produces food and machinery for its home market. If they decide to specialize and trade, how will each nation determine its speciality?

Absolute Advantage

Each nation's production possibilities are as shown in Table 14.1. The table gives the number of units which can be produced in each nation per labor day.* Thus, Kant can produce either 5 units of food or 2 units of machinery per labor day. Troy can produce either 3 units of food or 4 units of machinery per labor day.

* A labor day is a unit of labor resources. It means the use of 1 laborer for 1 day. One hundred labor days may be the use of 100 laborers for 1 day, 1 laborer for 100 days, 10 laborers for 10 days, and so forth.

Table 14.1 Production Possibilities in Kant and Troy.

	Number of units which can be produced per labor day:		
	Food		Machinery
Kant	5	or	2
Troy	3	or	4

Apparently, Kant's resources are better adapted to food production and Troy's to machinery. We would say that Kant has absolute advantage in the production of *food*. It can provide more food per labor day than Troy. Troy has an absolute advantage in the production of *machinery*. It can produce more machinery per labor day than Kant. If each nation specializes in the production for which it has **absolute advantage**, both will be better off.

Can we prove this?

Independent Production
Suppose both countries have 100 labor days to use in production and no trade is taking place between them. Both decide to use 50 labor days to produce food and 50 labor days to produce machinery. What is the total combined output of food and machinery?

Kant can produce 5 units of food per labor day, or a total of 250 units. Troy can produce 3 units per labor day, or a total of 150 units. Total combined food production is 400 units. Thus,

$$\text{Food}$$

Kant	5 × 50	= 250
Troy	3 × 50	= 150
		400

Kant can produce 2 units of machinery per labor day, or a total of 100 units. Troy can produce 4 units per labor day, or 200 units. Total combined machinery production is 300 units. Thus,

$$\text{Machinery}$$

Kant	2 × 50	= 100
Troy	4 × 50	= 200
		300

Production with Specialization and Trade
What happens if both countries decide to specialize and trade? If Kant devotes all 100 labor days to food production, total output is (5 × 100) = 500 units. If Troy uses all 100 labor days to produce machinery, total production is (4 × 100) = 400 units. Thus,

	Food	Machinery
Kant	5 × 100	
Troy		4 × 100
	500	400

Specialization and trade have increased total production! Both food and machinery production have increased by 100 units.

Comparative Advantage

So far, so good. Now suppose that Troy discovers a new process which allows it to produce more food than before with each unit of labor resources. Its new production possibilities are shown in Table 14.2.

Table 14.2 Production Possibilities with Technological Advance.

	Number of units which can be produced per labor day:		
	Food		Machinery
Kant	5	or	2
Troy	5	or	4

Troy still has an absolute advantage in the production of machinery, but now its resources are equally as productive as Kant's in food. Will specialization and trade still produce benefits for both countries?

In order to determine this, we must compare the costs of production in Kant and Troy in terms of goods *not* produced. Note that Kant can produce either 2 units of machinery or 5 units of food per labor day. If Kant decides to produce food, it must give up 2 units of machinery for every 5 units of food it produces; if Kant decides to produce machinery, it must give up 5 units of food for every 2 units of machinery (our familiar opportunity cost).

To determine how much 1 unit of food costs in Kant, we divide units of machinery by units of food. (Can you explain why?*) Units of machinery/units of food = 2/5. This tells us that for every unit of food produced, Kant must give up 2/5 units of machinery. To find the cost of 1 unit of machinery in Kant, we divide units of food by units of machinery: 5/2, or 2 1/2. Kant must give up 2 1/2 units of food for every unit of machinery it produces.

Now look at the production possibilities for Troy. Troy must give up 4/5 units of machinery for 1 unit of food, and 5/4, or 1 1/4, units of food for 1 unit of machinery. Costs of production for both countries are shown in Table 14.3.

Table 14.3   Costs of Production.

	Cost of producing:	
	1 Unit of Food	1 Unit of Machinery
Kant	2/5 units of machinery	2 1/2 units of food
Troy	4/5 units of machinery	1 1/4 units of food

* The formula for computing comparative costs is a simple algebraic equation. For example, in Kant: 2m = 5f. To find the cost of 1f (food), we divide both sides of the equation by 5. To find the cost of 1m (machinery), we divide both sides of the equation by 2.

We can now compare cost ratios for the two countries, using Table 14.3 as a guide. One unit of machinery costs Troy 1 1/4 units of food and costs Kant 2 1/2 units of food. Kant must give up more food than Troy in order to produce machinery. Since Kant's opportunity costs are greater, it would certainly make sense for Troy to produce machinery. We can say that Troy has comparative advantage in the production of machinery: in terms of food *not* produced, the cost of 1 unit of machinery is less for Troy than for Kant.

What about the production of food? As we saw, neither country has absolute advantage in food production. Does this mean that trade will not be worthwhile?

Look again at Table 14.3. One unit of food costs Troy 4/5 units of machinery. However, a unit of food costs Kant only 2/5 units of machinery. Kant gives up less than Troy when it produces 1 unit of food. Thus, Kant has comparative advantage in the production of food. Since Kant's opportunity costs are lower, it would make sense for Kant rather than Troy to produce food.

If each nation produces the good for which it has **comparative advantage,** both nations can still benefit from specialization and trade.

Can we prove this?

Independent Production

Again, suppose both countries have 100 labor days to use in production and that no trade is taking place. Both decide to use 50 labor days to produce food and 50 labor days to produce machinery. What is the total combined output of food and machinery? (Use Table 14.2 to calculate total output.)

Without trade, Kant can produce 5 units of food per labor day, or a total of 250 units. Troy can also produce 5 units per labor day, or 250 in 50 labor days. Total combined food output is 500 units. Kant can produce a total of 100 units of machinery and Troy can produce 200 units. Total combined machinery output is 300 units. Thus,

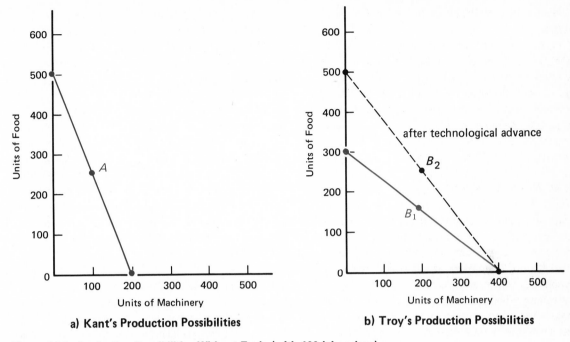

a) Kant's Production Possibilities

b) Troy's Production Possibilities

Figure 14.1   Production Possibilities Without Trade (with 100 labor days).

	Food	Machinery
Kant	5 × 50 = 250	2 × 50 = 100
Troy	5 × 50 = 250	4 × 50 = 200
	500	300

Production with Specialization and Trade

What happens if both countries decide to specialize and trade? If Kant devotes all 100 labor days to food production, total output is 500 units. If Troy uses all 100 labor days to produce machinery, total production is 400 units:

	Food	Machinery
Kant	5 × 100 = 500	
Troy		4 × 100 = 400

Again specialization and trade have increased total production! Output of machinery has increased by 100 units without sacrificing any quantity of food.

The advantages of trade may be illustrated through use of a production possibilities curve as shown in Figure 14.1. The curves in the figure are drawn as straight lines because we are assuming constant production costs. This means that each nation must give up constant (rather than increasing) amounts of one good in order to obtain additional units of the other good. Thus, cost ratios at any point on the line will be the same. (Test yourself: calculate the cost of producing 50 additional units of machinery in Kant at point A. Must the society give up 2 1/2 units of food for each unit of machinery?*)

Without trade, each nation can produce at some point on its own production possibilities curve: Kant may decide to produce at point A; Troy may have produced at B_1 before its technological

---

* With production of 150 units of machinery, Kant can produce only 125 units of food for a cost of 250 − 125 = 125 food units. Therefore, each unit of machinery costs 125/50 = 2 1/2 food units.

advance and may decide to produce at B_2 after the advance.

If Kant and Troy combine their economies into a large, free-trade area, their combined production possibilities will be as shown in Figure 14.2. Total production possibilities are greater with specialization and trade. (Test yourself: Compare total production at A and B_2 with total production at C.)

The Basis for Trade

Nations engage in international trade on the basis of comparative advantage. Each nation benefits from trade by producing and selling goods in which it has comparative advantage and buying goods in which other nations have comparative advantage. The society as a whole benefits because total production is greater with specialization than it would be if each nation were self-sufficient. Each nation is producing and exchanging goods at

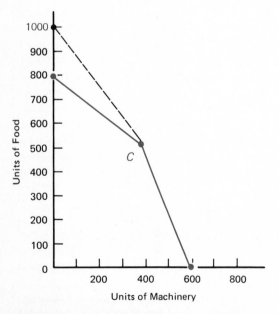

Figure 14.2   Combined Production Possibilities with Specialization and Trade.

the lowest possible cost. Of course, this is only true if nations are engaging in *free trade,* i.e., there are no barriers or restrictions to trade. As we will see later in this chapter, trade is not always free.

Who engages in international trade? When you purchase a German car or French wine, you are engaging in international trade just as the government is when it sells surplus military equipment to Saudi Arabia or grain to India. Business firms engage in international trade when they buy materials from foreign companies and sell American-made equipment. Many materials essential for U.S. manufacture are not found in this country, making international trade necessary.

BALANCE OF PAYMENTS

A nation, just like a business, must keep an account of all financial transactions that take place between it and other nations. It must keep a record of the value of inflows and outflows of spending. This record is known as a nation's **balance of payments.**

All inflows are added together to determine the flow of spending into a nation. All outflows are added together to determine the flow of spending from that nation to foreign nations. The difference between the two sums is the *net* flow of funds, or balance of payments.

A positive difference represents a *net inflow* of spending. It leaves a nation with unspent claims against the assets of other nations. A negative difference represents a *net outflow*. It means that foreign nations are holding unspent claims against the assets of that nation.

Accounts in the Balance of Payments

There are three kinds of transactions among nations, listed as three categories in the balance of payments: (1) the *current account* records the flows of spending for trade in goods and services;

Table 14.4   Inflows and Outflows in the U.S. Balance-of-Payments Account.

	Inflow or Outflow
Current Account (Trade)	
1. Exports:	
a. goods sold abroad (e.g., computers, aircraft, soybeans)	+
b. services sold abroad (e.g., financial services, insurance, tourism)	+
2. Imports:	
a. goods bought abroad (e.g., petroleum, bauxite, autos, bananas, perfume)	−
b. services bought abroad (e.g., shipping services, tourism)	−
3. Income:	
a. from U.S. investments abroad	+
b. to foreigners from their investments in the United States	−
4. U.S. Government Military Expenditures	−
Capital Account (Investments or Long-Term Loans)	
1. Long-Term Capital Investments:	
a. U.S. investment abroad (e.g., long-term bonds or stocks, factories, hotels, banks, mines)	−
b. foreign investment in the United States (e.g., long-term bonds or stocks, factories, mines)	+
2. U.S. Government Grants and Aid to Foreign Governments	−
Short-Term Capital Account (Short-Term Loans)	
1. U.S. Lending Abroad (e.g., short-term notes, bank accounts)	−
2. Foreign Lending in the United States (e.g., short-term notes, bank accounts)	+

(2) the *long-term capital account* records flows of spending for long-term investments; and (3) the *short-term capital account* records the flows of funds for short-term lending. Table 14.4 lists various types of transactions in the United States falling under each category and indicates whether these transactions are normally inflows (+) or outflows (−).

The U.S. Balance of Payments

The net flow of spending for goods and services is represented by the *balance on current account*. For most of the years until 1968, the United States sold many goods abroad, and this balance was positive; that is, inflows exceeded outflows. Since 1968, the balance has generally been negative, chiefly the result of the rising cost of petroleum imports into the United States, the rise in consumer goods production in other nations of the Western world, and certain barriers to U.S. exports in some nations.

The net flow of *long-term investment* and government spending is represented by the *balance on capital account*. Beginning with the Marshall Plan following World War II, more long-term investment and U.S. government spending has flowed abroad than foreigners have invested in this country. Dollars from private investors and from the U.S. government helped provide materials and equipment for rebuilding Europe after the war. As a result, the balance on capital account has been negative in recent decades. However, the outflow of investment funds represents growing U.S. ownership of productive facilities in other countries, with a potential inflow of investment income.

The outflow of *short-term* investment from the United States has also been substantial. In all but a few years since World War II, we have loaned more short-term funds abroad than foreigners have loaned in the United States. The result has been a negative *balance on short-term capital account*. In 1980, the net outflow of short-term lending was almost $34 billion.

When the balance on current account, balance on long-term capital account, and balance on short-term capital account are added together, the result is the net flow of funds between the U.S. and other nations. Values of each account and the net flow of funds for selected recent years are shown in Table 14.5.

As the table shows, the net flow of funds was negative for most of the period. A negative flow

means that we were experiencing a *deficit* in our balance of payments. We were spending more money abroad than we were bringing into the country. A negative balance of payments means that there remains an excess of U.S. dollars in the hands of foreigners. Foreigners have claims against the United States which they may spend in any of the three ways corresponding to the balance of payment accounts, as explained in the following sections.

Short-Term Capital Account

Foreigners can lend money on short-term to American individuals, banks, and other businesses, or to the U.S. Treasury. They do this by buying certificates of deposit or other securities, or by simply depositing their dollars in banks. Foreigners will

Table 14.5   U.S. Balance of Payments (in millions of dollars).*

	1960	1964	1969	1974	1977
Current Account					
Exports:					
Goods	+ 19,650	+ 25,501	+ 36,414	+ 94,696	+ 120,472
Services	+ 632	+ 1088	+ 2034	+ 3837	+ 2460 (net)
Imports:					
Goods	− 14,758	− 18,700	− 35,807	− 100,379	− 151,713
Services and Transfers	− 964	− 1149	− 1763	− 2355	− 2008
Income (net):					
difference between income from U.S. investments abroad and foreign investments in the United States	+ 2287	+ 3935	+ 3811	+ 9516	+ 11,935
U.S. Government Transactions	− 2753	− 2133	− 3344	− 2150	− 1355
Capital Account					
Long Term:					
U.S. Government	− 884	− 1353	− 1933	− 2571	+ 31,237
Private	− 2100	− 4511	− 70	− 3287	− 6384
Short-Term Capital Account					
Net Short-Term Capital Flows	− 1405	− 1643	− 640	− 14,751	− 4564
Net Flow of Funds	− 3677	− 2696	− 6081	− 15,655	+ 80

Source: *Economic Report of the President,* February 1975, and *Federal Reserve Bulletin,* May 1978.
*Values may not total because of minor omissions.

choose short-term lending if the interest earnings on short-term loans in the United States are at least as great as they could earn elsewhere.

Long-Term Capital Account

Foreigners may make long-term capital investments in American businesses. They do this by buying stocks or bonds or by investing directly in productive facilities in the United States. Foreigners will choose long-term investment if the expected earnings on U.S. investments are at least as great as they could earn elsewhere.

Some Problems

Both short-term and long-term capital inflows present some problems. Short-term capital seeks the highest interest return possible. If interest rates in the United States should fall, savers will quickly move their funds out of the United States into other more profitable nations of the world.

The risk of losing short-term capital means that the Federal Reserve will have less freedom to use expansionary monetary policy and that, if expansionary monetary policy is used, it may have little effect.

Why is this so?

The goal of expansionary monetary policy is to reduce interest rates in the United States in order to stimulate spending and speed recovery from a recession. But lower interest rates will cause more dollars to flow abroad to nations where interest rates are higher on short-term loans. If these dollars flow abroad, they will not be available for spending here and cannot stimulate domestic investment.

(Test yourself: how can short-term capital flows interfere with *contractionary* monetary policy?*)

* Efforts to reduce the money supply and increase interest rates may fail if higher interest rates encourage holders of dollars to move them back to the U.S.

Long-term capital investment has additional disadvantages in that it implies a degree of foreign control of American enterprises. Foreigners already own about .5 percent of the nation's total of almost $10 trillion in assets, including an increasing share of U.S. government securities, and foreign investment grew at the rate of almost 10 percent per year during the 1970s. There is always the lurking fear that foreign owners of U.S. productive capital might someday use their financial power to influence American policies.

Current Account

From the U.S. viewpoint, the best use of dollars by foreigners would be the purchase of American-made goods. This would add enough spending inflows to the current account to offset spending outflows in the other accounts. It would also stimulate production in American factories and provide jobs for American workers. Finally, it would raise incomes in the United States and permit Americans to buy more from other nations. If foreigners are to be persuaded to spend their dollars for American goods and services, however, they must be convinced of their quality and low price. A goal of American industry must be to make our products more attractive to foreign buyers.

THE FOREIGN EXCHANGE MARKET

Some foreign holders of U.S. dollars may decide not to spend their claims for goods and services, for long-term investment, or for short-term lending. Instead, they may want to exchange their dollars for other currencies. For this purpose, they must use the foreign exchange market.

International trade requires the use of many national currencies: francs, marks, dollars, yen, and so forth. The foreign exchange market provides a means for trading national currencies, and, like other markets, operates according to the laws of supply and demand. The price of a currency is called its **exchange rate.**

Fixed and Floating Exchange Rates

When currency exchange rates are **fixed,** the price of a currency remains an established amount; the market cannot adjust to changes in supply and demand. For most of the years since World War II, the price of a German mark was fixed at about $.25; the price of a British pound was fixed at $2.80. Currency values were agreed on by the financial ministers of major nations and were maintained by their Central Banks. A currency's price was maintained by Central Bank purchases or sales of currencies, adding to the supply or demand of private consumers or business firms and influencing the equilibrium price.

In 1971, Western nations decided to stop fixing their exchange rates and allow their currencies to **float.** When exchange rates are allowed to float, they will rise and fall according to supply and demand among private consumers and business firms only. An increase in private demand for marks, for example, would cause their price to rise. An increase in the supply of dollars, on the other hand, would cause their price to fall. Floating exchange rates were expected to influence trade and help correct balance-of-payments deficits.

Exchange Rates and Balance-of-Payments Deficits

When dollars pile up in the hands of foreign banks, business firms, and individuals as a result of balance-of-payments deficits, the dollar's price in terms of foreign currency will tend to fall. This is because the market value of anything falls if its supply increases faster than its demand. A fall in the price of a currency as a result of market forces is called **depreciation.** *Depreciation* is distin-

guished from **devaluation,** which results from an act of government.*

We have said that the value of the dollar depreciates as it accumulates in foreign hands. How will the depreciation of the dollar affect sales of American goods?

Suppose dollars have been exchanging for German marks at an exchange rate of 1 mark = $0.25 or $1.00 = 4 marks. If the supply of dollars held by foreigners increases faster than demand, the dollar's exchange rate (price) will tend to fall relative to the mark. Under floating exchange rates, the new exchange rate may be 1 mark = $0.50 or $1.00 = 2 marks.

At the lower dollar exchange rate, a German citizen must give up only 2 (rather than 4) marks for every dollar. He or she can buy the same quantity of American goods with fewer marks. Thus, depreciation of the dollar makes American goods cheaper for foreign buyers. The German citizen is likely to want to acquire more dollars for spending in the United States, and our dollars will flow back, all of which tends to reduce accumulated holdings of dollars abroad.

At the same time, a U.S. citizen will receive only 2 marks for each dollar rather than 4; purchasing German goods will require twice as many dollars as before. The U.S. citizen is less likely to exchange dollars for marks to buy the more expensive German goods, and more of our dollars will stay at home. In both cases, the result is to correct the uneven distribution of currencies that results from balance-of-payments deficits.

(Test yourself: can you think of any possible disadvantages of depreciation of the dollar?**)

---

* A government devalues a currency when it sets a lower value on it in terms of its worth in gold and in terms of other currencies evaluated in gold.

** The dollar price of some *necessary* imports will rise also, increasing production costs in the U.S. and aggravating inflation.

BARRIERS TO TRADE

In the past, nations have often tried to correct balance-of-payment deficits by setting up barriers to trade. The most common trade barrier is a **tariff,** a tax on imports which makes foreign goods more expensive than goods produced at home. A tariff discourages imports and thus reduces the outflow of domestic currency.

Imposing a tariff means sacrificing specialization and the benefits of free trade. It means that consumers cannot buy from the lowest-cost producer. Moreover, when one nation imposes a tariff to keep its currency at home, other nations will often impose tariffs in retaliation. International trade will decline as a result, and producers and consumers in many nations will have to accept lower standards of living.

During the years preceding the Great Depression, many nations sought to protect their local manufacturers by imposing high tariffs on imports. In the United States, the Hawley-Smoot Tariff of 1930 imposed duties of 60 percent on the value of many imports. Tariffs reduced international sales of goods and services, causing production and incomes to fall around the world. Lower incomes meant still fewer purchases. Thus the decline in international trade aggravated the problem of low production and high unemployment during the 1930s.

In 1934, President Franklin Roosevelt embarked on a program of Reciprocal Trade Agreements with other nations to reduce tariff barriers. Cooperating nations agreed to reduce certain tariffs together so that trade could flow more freely. After World War ii, the General Agreement on Tariffs and Trade (GATT), enacted in 1948, continued to improve trading relations. Under this act, the United States and the nations of Western Europe agreed to meet regularly in negotiations to reduce tariffs and other barriers to trade.

Trade agreements in recent years have often granted "most favored nation" status to particular nations. This means that any tariff reduction given to a favored nation will immediately be extended to all other nations who are parties to the agreement. Other negotiations have aimed at reducing *nontariff* barriers to free trade: (1) import quotas, limiting quantities of particular imports; (2) product standards, prohibiting certain imports; and (3) export subsidies, enabling producers to sell abroad at lower prices than at home.

Self-Check

Use the following table to answer questions 1–3:

	Number of units which can be produced per labor day:		
	Watches		Cameras
Albia	2	or	3
Verda	3	or	4

1. Which of the following statements is incorrect?
   a. Verda has absolute advantage in the production of both watches and cameras.
   b. Verda has comparative advantage in the production of watches.
   c. Verda must give up 4 cameras in order to produce 3 watches, or 1 1/3 cameras for each watch.
   d. Albia must give up 3 cameras to produce 2 watches, or 1 1/2 cameras for each watch.
   e. All answers are correct.

2. Assume each nation has 50 labor days to use in production. If each specializes in the product in which it has a comparative advantage, total output will be:
   a. 100 watches and 200 cameras.
   b. 150 watches and 150 cameras.
   c. 100 watches and 150 cameras.
   d. 150 watches and 200 cameras.
   e. none of the above.

3. In Verda, the cost of producing each camera is:
   a. 3/4 watches.
   b. 2 2/3 watches.
   c. 3 watches.
   d. 1 1/3 watches.
   e. 4 watches.

4. Which of the following may cause an outflow in the balance of payments?
   a. General Motors sells a Cadillac to an Arabian sheik.
   b. A U.S. technician trains Brazilian computer programmers.
   c. An Italian tourist takes his family to Disney World.
   d. A Mexican subsidiary of a U.S. firm increases its income from sales.
   e. IBM builds a plant in Belgium.

5. Our balance of trade has generally been:
   a. positive, because we export more than we import.
   b. positive, because foreign nations have imposed barriers on American-made goods.
   c. negative, because we have invested heavily abroad.
   d. negative, because of heavy demand for American grain.
   e. positive, because foreigners have bought stock in American firms.

6. The value of the dollar declines in relation to other currencies:
   a. when foreigners buy gold from the U.S. Treasury.
   b. when foreigners demand more dollars for spending in the United States.
   c. when the supply of dollars increases in foreign hands.
   d. when exchange rates are fixed.
   e. when foreign banks buy dollars.

7. Which of the following does not belong with the others?
   a. General Agreement on Tariffs and Trade
   b. Hawley-Smoot Tariff
   c. European Common Market
   d. LAFTA
   e. Reciprocal Trade Agreements

Theory in Practice

FREE TRADE IN CONSUMER MARKETS

The benefits of free trade can be illustrated by microeconomic models before and after trade. Figure 14.3a shows a hypothetical demand curve for compact cars in the United States. Figure 14.3b shows a similar demand curve for cars produced in West Germany. The supply curves show that Germany's costs of production are lower than production costs in the United States. According to the figure, any quantity of autos in Germany can be produced at a lower average unit cost than that quantity can be produced in the United States. Without trade, the equilibrium price for cars is lower in Germany than in the United States.

With free trade, more American car buyers will want to purchase German-made autos, shifting demand for imports to the right and raising the price of German autos. Demand for American cars

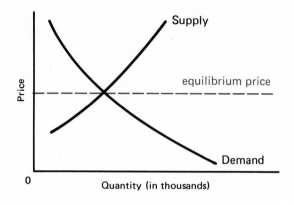

a) Market for U.S.-Made Cars

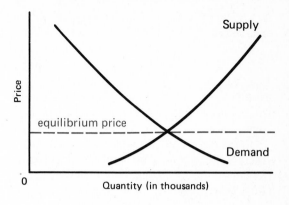

b) Market for German Cars

Figure 14.3   Markets for Compact Cars.

will shift to the left, reducing U.S. car prices. Demand curves will continue to shift until there is no longer a price advantage in either market. Finally, all buyers will be satisfied at a price somewhere between the two extremes. (Test yourself: pencil in possible shifts in demand and determine the final equilibrium price.)

Free trade will cause Germany to move toward greater specialization in the production in which it enjoys comparative advantage. Likewise, free trade will cause the United States to move away from specialization in compact car production. Auto workers will move into other types of

jobs. Often the transition to new jobs is slow and painful, but eventually U.S. workers will find employment in production for which the United States has (or can develop) comparative advantage—perhaps electronic calculators, agricultural equipment, or technical services.

A tariff interferes with this free-trade adjustment process. A tariff may be imposed to protect U.S. auto firms from foreign competition. Its effect is to raise the selling price of foreign autos. This is because the tariff is added to Germany's costs of production, shifting Germany's supply curve upward and to the left. Figure 14.4 shows

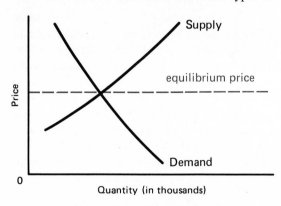

a) Market for U.S.-Made Cars

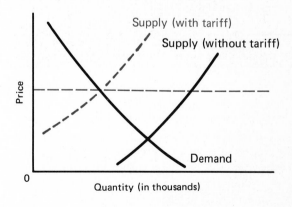

b) Market for German Cars

Figure 14.4   Effects of a Tariff.
A tariff artificially increases selling price. U.S. customers cannot take advantage of low-cost foreign goods.

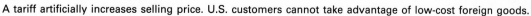

the addition of a tariff to the selling price of German autos.

Now any quantity of German autos can be sold in the United States only at a higher price. American buyers will be unable to shop freely in the least-cost market, and American workers will not be encouraged to move into other employments.

When tariffs are imposed, nations will fail to specialize according to the principle of comparative advantage. As a result, total world output will be lower and unit costs of production higher than under free trade.

TRADING WITH THE "THIRD WORLD"

World trade relations have changed greatly since 1973 when the Organization of Petroleum Exporting Countries (OPEC) raised the price of oil. OPEC is an international cartel with monopoly control over the output and price of a commodity vitally needed for industrial development and growth. The effect of the oil cartel has been to shift the power of trade away from developed nations to nations of the "Third World"—newly developing nations not aligned with either the United States or the Soviet Union.

Actually, the new power has gone only to certain members of the Third World—those with ample oil resources. Developing nations that lack oil may be even worse off now than before. Sale of high-priced oil brings wealth to some nations, wealth for investment in productive facilities, community development, education, and research. For other nations that need oil to begin the long process of economic development, high oil prices may close off their last chance for growth.

Some nonoil nations have tried to establish similar cartels in other commodities that they produce. The aim is to increase the price of their own export commodity and increase export earnings. Minerals like bauxite and agricultural products like coffee, cocoa, and sugar are already sold under international agreements. Producing nations agree to limit exports to a specified amount so as to hold prices within some acceptable range.

Commodity agreements may work rather well when world demand is rising and prices are high. The disadvantage comes when demand falls and exporters face a substantial drop in earnings. Moreover, when prices rise, users of these commodities may seek out substitute supplies or develop techniques for using other cheaper materials.

Substitution is most likely to occur when demand is highly elastic with respect to price. High elasticity of demand characterizes materials that are widely produced around the world or are easily stored as a hedge against shortages. These characteristics are true of copper, cobalt, tin, and possibly even bauxite. On the other hand, chromium and manganese are characterized by low price elasticity of demand, at least in the short-run. Large deposits are found only in Africa and the Soviet Union, and these minerals are essential for producing high-grade stainless steel. Even so, given time buyers could eventually find substitutes and avoid paying cartel prices.

Many nonoil developing countries have little hope for solving the problem of rising import bills and falling export earnings. Direct assistance from developed nations may be the only way to acquire funds for economic development. Development programs should focus on low-technology, labor-intensive industries so as to use the resources developing nations have in abundance. Then the developed nations should eliminate the tariffs and quotas that restrict imports from these countries. The final result might be a loss of jobs in some industries in the developed nations and a shift of resources into other, high-technology industries.

Can you cite industries which are experiencing a painful loss of jobs as a result of this process?

GOLD IN INTERNATIONAL FINANCE

Several hundred years ago when industry and trade began to flourish, exchange was carried on through the use of gold. Eventually gold came to be used as "backing" for paper money used in trade.

With free trade, gold served as an automatic regulator of a nation's balance of payments. Manufactured goods would be exchanged according to relative costs of production in trading nations. Temporary price differences would be corrected by gold flows. Thus, a low-priced region would accumulate gold as it was able to sell more goods abroad. It would enjoy a balance-of-payments surplus. High-priced regions would lose gold as they purchased more goods from foreign nations than they were able to sell abroad. They would have a balance-of-payments deficit.

The flow of gold into the low-priced nation would increase its money supply. Prices would tend to rise, removing its price advantage. Sales abroad would fall and gold inflows would drop. At the same time, the high-priced nations would experience gold outflows and falling prices. Their sales abroad would rise and gold would begin to flow back. These flows of gold would work to stabilize prices throughout the trade area.

The Gold Standard

A system that balances international payments through gold flows is called a gold standard. Under the gold standard, a nation with a payments deficit would have to redeem its outstanding currency in gold. A nation with a payments surplus would exchange its holdings of foreign currencies for gold. A nation's money supply would then depend on its holdings of gold.

Modern democratic governments became reluctant to base their domestic money supply on inflows and outflows of gold. A high level of imports and a corresponding outflow of gold from a nation would call for a decrease in that nation's money supply. This would mean falling prices, lower production, and fewer jobs. A substantial inflow of gold, on the other hand, would increase the money supply and aggravate tendencies toward inflation.

A society such as the United States found it difficult to tolerate such swings in the money sup-

ply. Frequently, the Federal Reserve would act to offset the flows of gold. In particular, if gold should flow out and employment and production fall, the Federal Reserve would create additional money in order to offset the loss of gold and permit a high level of domestic spending to continue. Prices would tend to rise further, deficits would increase, and still more gold would flow out of the country.

Steady outflows of gold from the United States eventually led to a monetary crisis. By 1971, foreign holdings of dollars had grown to almost $40 billion and our gold stock was only $10 billion!

Finally, in August 1971, President Nixon announced that the United States was abandoning the gold standard; our currency was no longer redeemable in gold. We would determine our money supply on the basis of domestic economic needs rather than on the basis of our gold stock. (The United States and other nations still hold gold as a reserve asset, along with other national currencies.)

Nevertheless, the steady outflow of dollars remains a problem. Negotiations are under way with other nations to reduce their tariff barriers, exchange controls, import quotas, and export subsidies. These actions will allow foreigners to buy more from American manufacturers and help reduce our persistent payments deficit.

Gold and Paper Gold

Only about eighty thousand tons of gold have been mined in the history of the world. The entire world supply could be stored in one large oil tanker. The Union of South Africa and the USSR are the major sources of gold, mining about 700 metric tons, respectively, annually.

The world's stock of gold is held in Central Banks as a reserve asset and by individuals as assets or decorative objects. The United States holds the largest stock of gold, followed by West Germany, France, and the USSR.

In the past, paper money convertible to gold

was used in international trade. As world trade mushroomed, larger quantities of paper money were needed to finance trade. But the limited supply of gold eventually made it impossible to redeem all currencies in gold. Many nations dealt with the problem by devaluing their currencies in relation to gold.

In 1934, President Franklin Roosevelt devalued the dollar, from $1 = 1/20.67 ounce of gold to $1 = 1/35 ounce of gold. This meant that foreign holders of dollars would need $35, rather than $20.67, to buy each ounce of gold—an unhappy circumstance for large holders of dollars. (U.S. citizens could not buy gold.) It also meant that major producers of gold—South Africa and the USSR—would receive $35, rather than $20.67, for each ounce of new gold produced.

Following the 1930s, the U.S. government tried to maintain confidence in the dollar by avoiding further devaluations. However, large outflows of dollars in the early 1970s led President Nixon to announce two devaluations, fourteen months apart. The first, in December 1971, reduced the value of a dollar to 1/38 ounce of gold. The second, in February 1973, reduced the value to 1/42.22 ounce of gold. Gold owned by the U.S. Treasury is now valued at $42.22 an ounce.

Although our currency is no longer convertible to gold, the devaluation does mean that U.S. currency is "cheaper" in relation to other currencies. A cheaper dollar should encourage foreigners to buy goods from us, increasing our exports, and discourage Americans from buying foreign goods, decreasing our imports. The net result should be a more favorable balance of payments for the United States.

EXPORTING INFLATION

Near the end of World War II, the finance ministers of Western nations met in Bretton Woods, New Hampshire, to establish conditions for the orderly revival of trade after the war. They agreed to establish fixed exchange rates for their currencies. Central Banks would buy and sell currencies as needed so as to maintain the established price. This meant that currency values could not float in response to supply and demand.

For example, suppose German manufacturers sold more automobiles to Americans than Americans sold goods and services abroad. The supply of dollars in Germany would increase relative to their demand. A large supply would tend to force down the price of dollars in terms of marks (and to raise the price of marks in terms of dollars).

To avoid this, the Central Banks agreed to continue to exchange marks for dollars at the old rate. Banks would accumulate dollars and issue marks in exchange. Central Bank purchases of dollars would keep their value from falling in terms of other currencies.

Fixed Exchange Rates and Inflation

For a number of years, the system worked reasonably well. The United States sent many dollars abroad in foreign aid and in private investments. Other nations welcomed the dollars, which they used to buy consumer goods and capital equipment from the United States.

The supply of money in the United States continued to grow, spending and incomes grew, and our purchases of foreign goods grew. But as European nations recovered from the war, they needed fewer of our dollars. They began to buy fewer goods from us and more from other, low-cost nations. Dollars piled up in foreign Central Banks as they accumulated dollars in exchange for other currencies at the agreed-upon exchange rates.

The Vietnam War added to our problems. Heavy military spending worsened inflation in this country and caused more dollars to flow abroad, both as military spending and as payment for lower-priced foreign goods. Foreign banks continued to absorb dollars, as agreed, at the old rate. But each time a dollar was bought by the banks, local currency was issued in exchange, raising the domestic money supply and fueling inflation in the foreign countries.

Many European nations resented having to absorb dollars of less real purchasing power at the old price and complained about the inflationary effect on their own economies. They felt that they were, in a sense, helping pay for the U.S. war in Southeast Asia.

Floating Exchange Rates

Finally, foreign banks could no longer abide by the agreement to support the value of the U.S. dollar. Western finance ministers met again and, in 1971, decided to let currency values float according to supply and demand. Now when the supply of a currency increases in relation to its demand, its value will fall.

Under fixed exchange rates, the dollar was worth about four marks. In 1981, under floating exchange rates, it was worth about two marks. This means that it takes more dollars to buy German goods, but that American goods are cheaper for German citizens.

The effect of floating exchange rates was a decline in the value of the dollar in relation to other currencies. As with the devaluation of our currency, the U.S. balance of payments benefited from the cheaper dollar. However, the favorable results were offset to some extent by our continuing imports of crude oil even at much higher prices. (What does this tell you about the elasticity of demand for oil?) Too, greater exports of food came at a time of domestic crop failure and reduced supply. The effect of both has been much higher prices in the United States with rising costs of production and inflation, accompanied by rising unemployment.

EXPORTING UNEMPLOYMENT

When a nation's economic health is in danger, it may try to improve its own position at the expense of other nations. Such actions are called "beggar my neighbor" policies and are often associated with efforts to deal with unemployment.

Tariffs and Unemployment

Following World War I, many nations had war debts to be paid. They tried to earn foreign currencies by selling more goods abroad. At the same time, they tried to keep their own currency from flowing out by imposing tariffs limiting their own imports from foreign producers.

Obviously, all countries cannot be successful in this objective. All countries cannot sell more to other nations and at the same time buy less from all of them. As a result of the attempt, however, trade declined, production was cut, and unemployment increased.

Many governments tried to "export" their unemployment by imposing still higher tariffs. In the United States, the Hawley-Smoot Tariff of 1930 collected an average of 60 percent of the value of many imports. The intent of the law was to avoid the loss of local jobs, but the result was to spread unemployment more widely among other nations.

Pros and Cons of Tariffs

Tariffs *can* export unemployment. But because of the disruption in trade that results, a policy of high tariffs may backfire. The Great Depression of the 1930s was partly a result of the rise in tariff barriers among industrialized nations of the Western world.

Labor unions generally support a protective tariff to prevent competition from foreign producers. Support for protection is widespread in the textile and steel industries. Without a tariff or import quota, a lower-cost foreign producer would be able to undersell American producers. According to the principle of comparative advantage, however, this is as it should be. The nation whose resources and technology are best adapted to textile or steel production should specialize in that kind of manufacture. U.S. workers should move into production for which the United States has comparative advantage.

When a particular industry is just beginning, it may need a protective tariff until it becomes well established. Otherwise, established producers abroad may be able to undersell it and drive it out of business. The "infant industry" tariff should be only temporary, however. As the industry comes of age, it should compete with foreign producers by operating at low costs and improving production techniques.

Other reasons are often advanced for tariffs (although the fundamental reason is generally to protect domestic jobs). One reason is to encourage domestic production and avoid dependence on a foreign supply for a *strategic* commodity: food, energy, and uranium, for instance. A "strategic industry" tariff may protect other kinds of production, too, since it is difficult to draw the line between essential and nonessential commodities. Before deciding to protect domestic suppliers, a nation should calculate the opportunity cost involved: the sacrifice of goods and services that could have been produced if high-cost production of the strategic commodity had not been protected.

THE MULTINATIONALS

The United States experienced a long period of surpluses in its balance of trade. Our agricultural products and manufactured goods were in great demand abroad. Many American firms experienced inflows of currencies from foreign sales. They used their export earnings to build foreign branch plants or to acquire productive facilities abroad. A firm that carries on productive operations in more than one country is called a *multinational* firm.

There are advantages to operating in several countries. First, goods manufactured in a foreign nation are not subject to that nation's tariffs or quotas. They can be sold more cheaply in a foreign market. Second, earnings in foreign operations are not subject to U.S. income taxes until profits are brought back to the United States. Third, multinational firms can arrange their operations to take advantage of differences in costs in many nations. They will use more labor in low-wage countries and borrow funds in low-interest countries. They will shift profits into low-tax countries by reducing the prices of component parts made in one country and selling them to a branch plant in the low-tax country for final assembly.

The result of these advantages has been rising financial power and influence for multinational firms. In 1981, the foreign holdings of U.S. firms alone were more than $400 billion.

Occasionally, multinational firms have been accused of attempting to influence a nation's political affairs. Accusations that the International Telephone and Telegraph Company used corporate funds to influence elections in Chile provide a recent example.

Some nations are now taking steps to reduce some of the advantages enjoyed by multinational firms. The U.S. Congress has voted to reduce tax advantages on foreign income. Other nations are investigating earnings to ensure that profits cannot be shifted to other low-tax countries. Also, the rise in wage rates in many countries has reduced the advantage of low-cost labor.

Recently, our balance-of-trade deficits have permitted foreign firms to use their excess dollars to acquire firms in the U.S. Multinationalism is no longer an exclusively American idea!

Although American firms still own about 60 percent of total international direct investment, the foreign share is growing rapidly. Some important multinationals with home bases in European countries are Shell, Unilever, Olivetti, Bayer, Volkswagen, and Nestle. Japanese firms are also entering the international arena. Mitsubishi, Matsushita, Mitsui, Sony, and others have plants in the United States.

Multinationalism has increased the interdependency of nations. It has encouraged production in low-cost areas according to the principle of comparative advantage. Furthermore, the income from foreign investment appears as an inflow in the U.S. balance of payments. The inflow of earnings from branch plants has helped offset outflows of spending for imports. To the extent that multinationals enhance the efficiency of the global economy, they should be encouraged. But they should be subject to the same rules and regulations—tax and antitrust laws—which affect domestic firms.

SUMMARY

1. The beginnings of trade brought economic progress through specialization and division of labor. Trade helped spread cultural, intellectual, and technical achievements.
2. Specialization replaces self-sufficiency. Specializing nations must be assured a free flow of trade if they are to realize maximum benefits from specialization.
3. Nations (or regions) specialize according to the principles of absolute advantage and comparative advantage. Specialization increases total output. The exchange rate for goods depends on relative costs of production.
4. A nation's balance of payments records international transactions. The trade portion of the U.S. balance of payments has recently turned negative. The long-term capital portion has been negative for decades, chiefly because of U.S. investments abroad. The short-term capital portion shifts from negative to positive depending on interest rates in the United States and abroad.
5. U.S. dollars can come back to the United States through trade or through long- or short-term investment. Trade produces the most favorable results for the U.S. economy.
6. A falling exchange rate for dollars as a result of market forces is called depreciation. Dollar depre-

ciation can encourage greater exports and improve a U.S. balance-of-payments deficit.
7. Tariffs reduce international trade and slow down economic activity. Tariffs have been used in attempts to export unemployment. Recent agreements have aimed at reducing tariffs and other barriers to trade: import quotas, product standards, and export subsidies.
8. Multinational firms are becoming an important part of international trade. Multinationalism enables firms to take advantage of low-cost resources and increases the interdependency of nations.

TERMS TO REMEMBER

absolute advantage: the ability to produce a good more cheaply than it can be produced in some other region.

comparative advantage: the ability to produce a good more cheaply in terms of other goods.

balance of payments: an account of the net value of transactions between a nation and other nations (inflows and outflows of spending).

exchange rate: the price of one currency in terms of another.

fixed exchange rate: the situation when currency prices are set at an established amount and do not vary.

floating exchange rate: the situation when currency prices are allowed to rise and fall according to supply and demand.

depreciation: a fall in the price of a currency in relation to other currencies as a result of market forces.

devaluation: a reduction in the price of a currency that results from an act of government.

tariff: a tax on imports whose intent is to make foreign goods more expensive than domestic goods.

TOPICS FOR DISCUSSION

1. The term "petrodollars" refers to recent outflows of U.S. dollars for high-priced Arab petroleum. In what three ways can Arab holders use their dollars? Explain the advantages and disadvantages of each use. Cite current examples of flows of petrodollars back to the United States.

2. Explain how gold flows under the gold standard helped adjust trade and correct deficits and surpluses in the balance of payments.

3. Paradox: the dollar is said to be "weak" when foreigners hold a large supply in relation to their demand. However, a weak currency may be an advantage to the American economy. Explain.

4. Explain how opportunity cost is involved in international trade.

5. List the advantages and disadvantages of tariffs, import quotas, and other barriers to free trade. On the basis of your list, what groups do you think are likely to support or oppose tariffs? Why?

6. Look up the exchange rates for foreign currencies in the financial pages of your local newspaper. Using these rates, calculate the cost to a Mexican tourist of a night in a U.S. motel. About how many pesos would you pay for a night in a Mexican hotel? Calculate in marks an approximate price for a steak dinner in Berlin. How many marks would the German citizen need for a steak dinner in New York?

SUGGESTED READINGS

"Arab Banks Grow: A Tool to Control the World's Capital," *Business Week,* October 6, 1980, p. 70.

Ball, Robert, "Europe's U.S. Shopping Spree," *Fortune,* December 1, 1980, p. 82.

Balogh, Thomas, "Monetarism and the Threat of a World Financial Crisis," *Challenge,* May/June 1977, p. 40.

Bowen, William, "Closing the Trade Gap Could Take Ten Years," *Fortune,* July 14, 1980, p. 128.

Bryant, Ralph C., and Krause, Lawrence B., "World Economic Interdependence," in *Setting National Priorities: Agenda for the 1980s,* Joseph A. Pechman, ed., Washington: The Brookings Institution, 1980, p. 71.

"Challenges to the International Financial System" and "Challenges to International Trade Relations," *The Economic Report of the President.* Washington: Government Printing Office, January 1981, pp. 201 and 203.

Davenport, John A., "The New Allure of the Gold Standard," *Fortune,* April 7, 1980, p. 86.

"Floating Exchange Rates: The Calm Before an Economic Storm," *Business Week,* October 3, 1977, p. 68.

Givens, William L., and Rapp, William V., "What It Takes to Meet the Japanese Challenge," *Fortune,* June 13, 1979, p. 104.

Hein, John, "Paging Adam Smith," *Across the Board,* January 1981, p. 44.

"Japanese Multinationals: Covering the World with Investment," *Business Week,* June 16, 1980, p. 92.

Main, Jeremy, "The Battle for Quality Begins," *Fortune,* December 29, 1980, p. 28.

Mayer, Martin, "Our Butter-and-Egg Men Are Winning Big Abroad," *Fortune,* May 19, 1980, p. 146.

Menzies, Hugh D., "It Pays to Brave the New World," *Fortune,* July 30, 1979, p. 86.

Meyer, Herbert E., "How U.S. Textiles Got to Be Winners in the Export Game," *Fortune,* May 5, 1980, p. 260.

"Mounting Clamor for Trade Barriers," *U.S. News and World Report,* February 6, 1978, p. 57.

"The New Export Policy Works Like the Old—Badly," *Business Week,* July 21, 1980, p. 88.

Nickel, Herman, "The Right Road for OPEC's Billions," *Fortune,* November 17, 1980, p. 38.

Nulty, Peter, "Why the 'Tokyo Round' Was a U.S. Victory," *Fortune,* May 21, 1979, p. 130.

Plaut, Steven E., "Why Dumping Is Good For Us," *Fortune,* May 5, 1980, p. 212.

Rose, Sanford, "Coping with a Tumbling Dollar," *Fortune,* October 1977, p. 272.

Rose, Sanford, "How to Think About the Dollar," *Fortune,* August 1975, p. 117.

Triffin, Robert, "The American Response to the European Monetary System," *Challenge,* March/April 1980, pp. 17–25.

"U.S. Food Power: Ultimate Weapon in World Politics?" *Business Week,* December 15, 1975, p. 54.

Volcker, Paul L., "The Recycling Problem Revisited," *Challenge,* July/August 1980, pp. 3–14.

Wallich, Henry C., "Evolution of the International Monetary System," *Challenge,* January/February 1979, pp. 13–17.

Whalen, Richard, "International Business," in *The United States in the 1980s,* Peter Duignan and Alvin Rabushka, eds., Stanford University: Hoover Institution, 1980, p. 639.

Answers to Self-Check

CHAPTER 1

1. The basis for the economic problem is choosing how to use society's scarce resources (d). The other answers reflect problems which grow out of the problem of scarcity.
2. Scarcity imposes the problem of choice, so (a) is correct. Careful choices may result in full employment, which would be desirable in view of scarcity.
3. All are limited (e). We are becoming more aware of scarcities of the things we used to consider free goods: fresh air, water, and even sunshine!
4. It is important to think of capital as a produced means of production. Money may be used to *buy* capital, but money itself is not capital. Your answer should be (b).
5. The market economy is a kind of economic democracy; it responds to "dollar" votes (d). A command economy is described in (b); a traditional economy in (c) and (e). All economies must make sacrifices, so (a) is never correct.
6. Opportunity costs may be measured in many units other than dollars: accomplishments, satisfactions, rewards. Your answer should be (d).

CHAPTER 2

1. The correct answer is (c). Perfect competition can exist only if all firms in an industry produce identical products. This is to ensure that no firm can charge a premium price based on product differences. (Of course, we don't have many examples of identical products in American industries. The best example is probably agricultural products.)

2. The correct answer is (d). Changing *one word* in each of the other answers would make that answer correct. Can you find the word in each?
3. Consumer A's demand will not change much if price changes (d). Apparently A regards pizza as a necessity—no substitutes!
4. Only (c) describes a change in quantity demanded. Identify the source of the shift in *demand* associated with each of the remaining choices.
5. Only (c) has no clear substitute—and is not substitutable for other goods. Consumers either must buy (c) whatever the price, or will *not* buy (c) whatever the price.
6. Answer (b) includes substitutes—for most palates! The other answers are complements.

CHAPTER 3

1. Answers (a), (b), (c), and (d) are necessary payments to owners of productive land, labor, capital, or entrepreneurial ability. Answer (e) is not an economic cost but is described as economic profit.
2. Only (d) is correct. Can you change each of the other choices to make it correct?
3. Answer (d) is correct. Cite recent examples of each of the other changes.
4. The pizza parlor must be able to expand (or contract) quantities fairly easily in response to price changes. All answers are correct (e).
5. Equilibrium is defined as the level of output at which there is no incentive to change plans. Buyers and producers are satisfied with price and quantity. The correct answer is (b).
6. Answer (d) is correct. Illustrate graphically as many examples as you can of market changes which affect price and quantity.

CHAPTER 4

1. All answers describe the benefits of production under conditions of perfect competition (e).
2. The correct answer is (a). Answers (b), (d), and (e) would help reduce monopoly. (Can you explain why?) Answer (a) is more likely to cause firms to operate as monopolies.
3. Oligopoly occurs because high capital requirements prevent the entry of new firms. The established firms have similar cost and pricing policies. The correct answer is (d).
4. An important characteristic of monopolistic competition is the slight differences among products. Designs are changed often (d).
5. All of the practices mentioned favored large, established firms. They were a means of preventing new competition from getting a share of the market. All are forbidden by current laws when the effect would be to reduce competition (e).
6. Answer (d) is correct. A monopoly firm may lose revenue if it reduces prices. This is because it may not gain enough new customers to make up for the lower price.

CHAPTER 5

1. All answers are correct (d). Specialization, division of labor, and exchange will generally produce larger output on either a regional or a national level.
2. The employment level of a variable resource is based on its price and the market value of its output. Both (a) and (b) are correct, so your choice should be (d).
3. The correct Marxian prediction is (b). Why is each of the other answers incorrect?
4. The law most harmful to labor was the Taft-Hartley Act (c), which restricted certain union activities such as closed shop and secondary boycott. The Wagner Act established certain union rights, e.g., the right to organize and bargain collectively. The Clayton Act removed labor from prosecution under the antimonopoly

laws. The Landrum-Griffin Act ensured democratic union elections and proper reporting of union finances.
5. Union membership in the United States is only about one fifth of the labor force, down from one-third in 1950. The correct answer is (c).

CHAPTER 6

1. Only (a), an appendicitis operation, is included in GNP. Refer to the definition of GNP and explain why each of the other answers is incorrect.
2. The correct answer is (b).
3. The correct answer is (c). How could you change the question to make each of the other answers correct?
4. Only (e) would cause an increase in GNP. The others would cause GNP to fall. Which part of total spending (C, I, or G) is affected by each of the other answers?
5. Both (a) and (c) are correct, so your choice should be (e). The circular flow will stabilize only if total spending flows are high enough to purchase the entire output supplied by business firms.
6. The correct answer is (c). Show how each of the other answers can be changed to make it correct.

CHAPTER 7

1. *Marginal propensity to consume* is defined as the fraction of *additional* income that will be spent. Your answer should be (d). Can you explain how each of the other conditions would change your *MPC?*
2. All answers are correct (e). The economy will stabilize at the level of GNP at which total spending is equal to the value of output. However, this may not be a healthy equilibrium in terms of the wise and efficient use of our scarce resources.
3. You are respending a government expenditure. This is an example of the multiplier effect (c).

4. The hamburger chain is increasing its capacity in order to fill a higher demand. This is an example of an increase in investment (d).
5. The Queen is cutting spending to reduce aggregate demand and eliminate the inflationary gap. The correct answer is (b).
6. Congress wants consumers to spend more, shifting the C component of aggregate demand upward. Congress must believe there is a deflationary gap (c).

CHAPTER 8

1. The correct answer is (c). Highway construction, health, education, and welfare are large outlays of state governments.
2. When the federal *net* tax structure is considered, the only correct answer is (e). Each of the other answers is associated with other taxes. Can you identify each? Answer (c) would apply to the tax structure as a whole, including federal, state, and local taxes.
3. The correct answer is (a). Answers (b) and (c) would worsen the situations that fiscal policy is meant to correct.
4. Answer (c) is correct. Some of the other answers describe the disadvantage of discretionary fiscal policy.
5. The best answer is (d). Spending power is redistributed as taxes are used to pay interest to bondholders only if all bondholders are paid at once.
6. The correct answer is (e). Give examples of (a) and (d).
7. Only (e) would be correct. All other choices would increase spending and add to the problem of inflation.

CHAPTER 9

1. The use of money *removed* the need for barter. Your answer should be (d).

2. Gold has many advantages as money, but ease of transporting and storing is not one of them! It is costly and risky to transport and store, so (c) is the correct answer.
3. The Federal Reserve does not deal with the public, but acts as banker for member banks and the U.S. Treasury. The correct answer is (a).
4. All answers are correct (d).
5. A major problem with monetary policy is the problem of persuading business to borrow during recession and discouraging them from borrowing during inflation. The correct answer is (c). Answers (a), (b), and (e) would be correct if one word were changed. Can you spot the word?
6. The best answer is (b). Trace the effects of each of the other policy actions.

CHAPTER 10

1. The correct answer is (d). Can you explain how each of the other answers would interfere with the free adjustment process between money and goods?
2. Those on fixed incomes suffer from inflation as their *real* income falls (c). Borrowers and speculators may make substantial gains in spending power. Escalator clauses protect workers from inflation. And the government gains in tax revenues when prices and incomes rise.
3. Demand-pull inflation results from a high level of total spending (d). Explain how each of the other answers would affect the general price level.
4. The monetarists believe that a steady increase in the supply of money in line with the average growth in production will keep prices stable. The correct answer is (b).
5. Incomes should rise only as much as the average growth in productivity (a). This would keep prices from rising.
6. All answers describe structural inflation which may result from the power of large firms (e). Many economists have attributed our recent inflation to these structural changes in industry.

CHAPTER 11

1. All of the conditions stated would be true under the classical assumption of perfect competition in the markets for labor and for goods and services (e).
2. During periods of unemployment, workers tend to lose their skills through idleness. The correct answer is (a).
3. Structural unemployment (c) is not easily corrected by government programs. Can you explain why?
4. The chief disadvantage of public-service employment is that it may interfere with hiring for private production. The correct answer is (c).
5. The only incorrect answer is (a). Your answer should be (e). Employers generally react to an expectation of wage increases by raising their prices, but they do not necessarily hire more labor.
6. Only (d) is correct.

CHAPTER 12

1. None of the answers is correct (e). Can you change each incorrect answer to make it correct?
2. Categorical aid programs are aimed at particular categories, or groups, of poor people. One of these groups includes the aged; others are the blind, the disabled, and dependent children. Cyclical poverty includes a broader range of persons unable to find work because of a downturn in economic activity. Insular poverty is confined to particular geographic or industrial areas. The correct answer is (c).
3. Most of the answers given are considered advantages of direct grants. Answer (d) might be considered a disadvantage if one assumes that the real causes of poverty can be determined and dealt with directly. However, the best answer is (c). Direct grants may have a disincentive effect, particularly if the government reduces aid dollar for dollar as income rises.
4. Direct grants and negative income tax payments would apply to the entire population. This

would ensure aid to all poor people. Answer (c) is correct. These programs may, however, result in the problems listed in the other answers.
5. Answer (d) would be the incorrect approach to cyclical poverty. Can you change the answer to make it correct?

CHAPTER 13

1. The best sequence is shown in answer (b). Plentiful resources are necessary before an economy can produce enough to save. Saving permits investment in capital equipment, ensuring greater production in the future.
2. All answers are possible (e). The mature economy may select some combination of these possibilities.
3. All are limits to growth (e). The interaction among population, agricultural and industrial production, pollution, and resource depletion presents real problems for the global economy.
4. The correct answer is (e). If the sectoral theory is the best explanation of growth, policy should encourage investment in the primary sectors of the economy.
5. The answer is (e); both (a) and (c) are correct. Sales of export goods will cause an *inflow* of dollars into the producing region, so (b) is incorrect.

CHAPTER 14

1. All answers are correct (e). Can you explain why? (Look back at the definitions of absolute and comparative advantage and the explanation of computing comparative costs.)
2. After specialization, Verda will be producing 150 (3×50) watches and Albia will be producing 150 (3×50) cameras. The correct answer is (b).
3. The cost of producing any good is the other types of goods which must be given up. In Verda, the cost of producing 4 cameras is 3 watches, or 3/4 watches for each camera (a).

4. With the exception of (e), every transaction would bring currency into the United States. When an American firm makes direct investment abroad, as in (e), dollars flow out. This is a form of long-term capital.

5. The correct answer is (a). See if you can find the errors in each of the other answers.

6. In a free market for foreign exchange, the value of currency fluctuates according to supply and demand. The value of a currency will decline when its supply increases (relative to demand) or when demand falls. The only correct answer is (c).

7. In order to answer this question you must know the provisions of each act and each policy. With the exception of (b), all actions were an attempt to increase free trade by removing tariff barriers.

Index